Survival Communications in Maine

John E. Parnell, KK4HWK

ISBN 978-1-62512-040-3

Cover design by:
Lynda Colón
FREELANCE GRAPHIC DESIGN &
MARKETING COMMUNICATIONS
www.hirelynda.webs.com

Titles available in this series:

Survival Communications in Alabama
Survival Communications in Alaska
Survival Communications in Arizona
Survival Communications in Arkansas
Survival Communications in California
Survival Communications in Colorado
Survival Communications in Connecticut
Survival Communications in Delaware
Survival Communications in Florida
Survival Communications in Georgia
Survival Communications in Hawaii
Survival Communications in Idaho
Survival Communications in Illinois
Survival Communications in Indiana
Survival Communications in Iowa
Survival Communications in Kansas
Survival Communications in Kentucky
Survival Communications in Louisiana
Survival Communications in Maine
Survival Communications in Maryland
Survival Communications in Massachusetts
Survival Communications in Michigan
Survival Communications in Minnesota
Survival Communications in Mississippi
Survival Communications in Missouri

Survival Communications in Montana
Survival Communications in Nebraska
Survival Communications in Nevada
Survival Communications in New Hampshire
Survival Communications in New Jersey
Survival Communications in New Mexico
Survival Communications in New York
Survival Communications in North Carolina
Survival Communications in North Dakota
Survival Communications in Ohio
Survival Communications in Oklahoma
Survival Communications in Oregon
Survival Communications in Pennsylvania
Survival Communications in Rhode Island
Survival Communications in South Carolina
Survival Communications in South Dakota
Survival Communications in Tennessee
Survival Communications in Texas
Survival Communications in Utah
Survival Communications in Vermont
Survival Communications in Virginia
Survival Communications in Washington
Survival Communications in West Virginia
Survival Communications in Wisconsin
Survival Communications in Wyoming

The above titles are available from your favorite online or brick-and-mortar bookstore or directly from the publisher at Tutor Turtle Press LLC, 1027 S. Pendleton St. – Suite B-10, Easley, SC 29642.

TABLE OF CONTENTS

Appendix A – Maine Ham Radio Clubs

ARRL Affiliated Amateur and Ham Radio Clubs – By City

Appendix B – Maine Ham Licensees by City

Survival Communications in Maine

Perhaps you have prepared for WTSHTF or TEOTWAWKI with respect to food, water, self-defense and shelter. But what about communication?

Whenever there is a disaster (hurricane, earthquake, economic collapse, nuclear war, EMF, solar eruption, etc.), the normal means of communication that we're all reliant upon (cell phone, land line phone, the Internet, etc.) will probably be, at best, sporadic and at worst, non-existent.

As this author sees it, short of smoke signals and mirrors, there are three options for two-way communication in "trying times": (1) GMRS or FRS radios; (2) CB radios; and (3) ham or amateur radio. Let's consider each of these options to come up with the most acceptable one.

GMRS (General Mobile Radio Service) / FRS (Family Radio Service)

GMRS (General Mobile Radio Service) / FRS (Family Radio Service) radios work optimally over short distances where there is minimal interference. Originally designed to be used as pagers, particularly inside a building or other such confined area, these radios are low-cost and convenient to carry. Unfortunately their small size and light weight comes with a trade-off – short range and short battery life. These radios are supposed to be able to communicate for up to 25-30 miles. Right. That's on level terrain, without buildings or trees getting in the way. While battery life technology is constantly improving, you will need spare batteries to keep communicating or someway of recharging the ones in the radio. In this author's opinion, GMRS/FRS radios are not first choice when concerned with medium or long range communication.

CB (Citizens Band)

CB (Citizens Band) radios operate in a frequency range originally reserved for ham or amateur radio operation. Because of the overwhelming number of people wishing quick, low-cost, regulation-free communication, the FCC (Federal Communication Commission) split off a portion of the frequency spectrum and allowed anyone to purchase a CB radio and start communicating. No test. No license. Just personal/business communication. Today, CB radios are readily available in such outlets as eBay and Craigslist. This author has seen them at yard/garage/tag sales and at flea markets.

CB radios come in a variety of "flavors." Fixed units, sometimes referred to as base units are intended for home use. For the most part, they derive their power from the utility company. In the event of loss of electricity, most base units can also be connected to a 12-volt battery, like that in your car/truck. If you choose to obtain a fixed unit, make sure you know how to connect the unit to the battery – ahead of time. Trying to figure this out when you're under extra stress is not a good situation.

A second type of CB radio is designed to be mobile, that is, installed in your car/truck. It gets its power from the vehicle's battery. You can either attach an antenna permanently to the vehicle or have a removable, magnetic type antenna.

The third type of CB radio is designed for handheld use. They are small and light. Most weigh less than a pound and operate on batteries. Yes, using batteries in a CB poses the same limitations as those by the GMRS/FRS radios, but have the added advantage that most handheld units come with a cigarette lighter adapter. Comes in handy when you are on the move and wish to be able to communicate both from a vehicle and also when you have to abandon it.

While they have a greater range than GMRS/FRS radios, CB radios are, legally, limited to operate on 40 channels, with a power rating of four (4) watts or less. Yes, it is possible to alter CB radios to get around these limitations, but not legally,

Ham/Amateur Radio

Ham/Amateur radio is very appealing. With a ham radio, you are not limited to less than 50 miles, but can communicate with anyone in the world (who also has access to a ham radio, of course).

Standardized Amateur Radio Prepper Communications Plan

In the event of a nationwide catastrophic disaster, the nationwide network of Amateur Radio licensed preppers will need a set of standardized meeting frequencies to share information and coordinate activities between various prepper groups. This Standardized Amateur Radio Communications Plan establishes a set of frequencies on the 80 meter, 40 meter, 20 meter, and 2 meter Amateur Radio bands for use during these types of catastrophic disasters.

Routine nets will not be held on all of these frequencies, but preppers are encouraged to use them when coordinating with other preppers on a routine basis. Routine nets may be conducted by The American Preparedness Radio Net (TAPRN) on these or other frequencies as they see fit. However, TAPRN will promote the use of these standardized frequencies by all Amateur Radio licensed preppers during times of catastrophic disaster. The promotion of this Standardized Amateur Radio Communications Plan is encouraged by all means within the prepper community, including via Amateur Radio, Twitter, Facebook, and various blogs.

Standardized Frequencies and Modes
80 Meters – 3.818 MHz LSB (TAPRN Net: Sundays at 9 PM ET) 40 Meters – 7.242 MHz LSB 40 Meters Morse Code / Digital – 7.073 MHz USB (TAPRN: Sundays at 7:30 PM ET on   CONTESTIA 4/250) 20 Meters – 14.242 MHz USB 2 Meters – 146.420 MHz FM

Nets and Network Etiquette

In times of nationwide catastrophic disaster, the ability of any one prepper to initiate and sustain themselves as a net control may be limited by the availability of power and other resource shortages. However, all licensed preppers are encouraged to maintain a listening watch on these frequencies as often as possible during a catastrophic disaster. Preppers may routinely announce themselves in the following manner:

• This is [Your Callsign Phonetically] in [Your State], maintaining a listening watch on [Standard Frequency] for any preppers on frequency seeking information or looking to provide information. Please call [Your Callsign Phonetically]. Preppers exchanging information that may require follow up should agree upon a designated time to return to the frequency and provide further information. If other stations are utilizing the frequency at the designated time you return, maintain watch and proceed with your communications when those stations are finished. If your communications are urgent and the stations on frequency are not passing information of a critical nature, interrupt with the word "Break" and request use of the frequency.

For More Information

Catastrophe Network: http://www.catastrophenetwork.org or @CatastropheNet on Twitter The American Preparedness Radio Network: http://www.taprn.com or @TAPRN on Twitter

In order to use a ham radio, legally, one must be licensed to do so by the FCC (other countries have analogous governmental bodies to regulate ham radio). To obtain a license is quite easy – take a test and pay your license fee. There are currently three classes of license – Technician, General, and Amateur Extra. With each of these licenses come specific abilities.

Technician class is the beginning level. The exam consists of 35 multiple choice questions randomly drawn from a pool of 395 questions. The question pool is readily available online for free downloading (http://www.ncvec.org/downloads/Revised%20Element%202.Pdf) or in such publications at *Ham Radio License Manual Revised 2nd Edition* (ISBN 978-0-87259-097-7). The current Technician pool of questions is to be used from July 1, 2010 to June 30, 2014. Be sure the question pool you are studying from is current. You will need to score at least 26 correct to pass. (Do not worry, Morse Code is no longer on the test, although many ham operators use it anyway.) You do not need to take a formal class in order to qualify to take the exam. You can learn the material on your own. Most people spend 10-15 hours studying and then successfully take the exam. The cost of taking the exam is under $20. The exam is given in MANY locations throughout the US. Usually the exam is given by area ham clubs. You do not have to belong to the club to take the exam. Check Appendix A for a listing of clubs in Maine.

Topics for the Technician License in Amateur Radio

The Technician license exam covers such topics as basic regulations, operating practices, and electronic theory, with a focus on VHF and UHF applications. Below is the syllabus for the Technician Class.

Subelement T1 – FCC Rules, descriptions and definitions for the amateur radio service, operator and station license responsibilities

[6 Exam Questions – 6 Groups]

T1A – Amateur Radio services; purpose of the amateur service, amateur-satellite service, operator/primary station license grant, where FCC rules are codified, basis and purpose of FCC rules, meanings of basic terms used in FCC rules

T1B – Authorized frequencies; frequency allocations, ITU regions, emission type, restricted sub-bands, spectrum sharing, transmissions near band edges

T1C – Operator classes and station call signs; operator classes, sequential, special event, and vanity call sign systems, international communications, reciprocal operation, station license licensee, places where the amateur service is regulated by the FCC, name and address on ULS, license term, renewal, grace period

T1D – Authorized and prohibited transmissions

T1E – Control operator and control types; control operator required, eligibility, designation of control operator, privileges and duties, control point, local, automatic and remote control, location of control operator

T1F – Station identification and operation standards; special operations for repeaters and auxiliary stations, third party communications, club stations, station security, FCC inspection

---

Subelement T2 – Operating Procedures

[3 Exam Questions – 3 Groups]

T2A – Station operation; choosing an operating frequency, calling another station, test transmissions, use of minimum power, frequency use, band plans

T2B – VHF/UHF operating practices; SSB phone, FM repeater, simplex, frequency offsets, splits and shifts, CTCSS, DTMF, tone squelch, carrier squelch, phonetics

T2C – Public service; emergency and non-emergency operations, message traffic handling

---

Subelement T3 – Radio wave characteristics, radio and electromagnetic properties, propagation modes

[3 Exam Questions – 3 Groups]

T3A – Radio wave characteristics; how a radio signal travels; distinctions of HF, VHF and UHF; fading, multipath; wavelength vs. penetration; antenna orientation

T3B – Radio and electromagnetic wave properties; the electromagnetic spectrum, wavelength vs. frequency, velocity of electromagnetic waves

T3C – Propagation modes; line of sight, sporadic E, meteor, aurora scatter, tropospheric ducting, F layer skip, radio horizon

Subelement T4 - Amateur radio practices and station setup

[2 Exam Questions – 2 Groups]

T4A – Station setup; microphone, speaker, headphones, filters, power source, connecting a computer, RF grounding

T4B – Operating controls; tuning, use of filters, squelch, AGC, repeater offset, memory channels

Subelement T5 – Electrical principles, math for electronics, electronic principles, Ohm's Law

[4 Exam Questions – 4 Groups]

T5A – Electrical principles; current and voltage, conductors and insulators, alternating and direct current

T5B – Math for electronics; decibels, electronic units and the metric system

T5C – Electronic principles; capacitance, inductance, current flow in circuits, alternating current, definition of RF, power calculations

T5D – Ohm's Law

Subelement T6 – Electrical components, semiconductors, circuit diagrams, component functions

[4 Exam Groups – 4 Questions]

T6A – Electrical components; fixed and variable resistors, capacitors, and inductors; fuses, switches, batteries

T6B – Semiconductors; basic principles of diodes and transistors

T6C – Circuit diagrams; schematic symbols

T6D – Component functions

Subelement T7 – Station equipment, common transmitter and receiver problems, antenna measurements and troubleshooting, basic repair and testing

[4 Exam Questions – 4 Groups]

T7A – Station radios; receivers, transmitters, transceivers

T7B – Common transmitter and receiver problems; symptoms of overload and overdrive, distortion, interference, over and under modulation, RF feedback, off frequency signals; fading and noise; problems with digital communications interfaces

T7C – Antenna measurements and troubleshooting; measuring SWR, dummy loads, feedline failure modes

T7D – Basic repair and testing; soldering, use of a voltmeter, ammeter, and ohmmeter

Subelement T8 – Modulation modes, amateur satellite operation, operating activities, non-voice communications

[4 Exam Questions – 4 Groups]

T8A – Modulation modes; bandwidth of various signals

T8B – Amateur satellite operation; Doppler shift, basic orbits, operating protocols

T8C – Operating activities; radio direction finding, radio control, contests, special event stations, basic linking over Internet

T8D – Non-voice communications; image data, digital modes, CW, packet, PSK31

Subelement T9 – Antennas, feedlines

[2 Exam Groups – 2 Questions]

T9A – Antennas; vertical and horizontal, concept of gain, common portable and mobile antennas, relationships between antenna length and frequency

T9B – Feedlines; types, losses vs. frequency, SWR concepts, matching, weather protection, connectors

Subelement T0 – AC power circuits, antenna installation, RF hazards

[3 Exam Questions – 3 Groups]

T0A – AC power circuits; hazardous voltages, fuses and circuit breakers, grounding, lightning protection, battery safety, electrical code compliance

T0B – Antenna installation; tower safety, overhead power lines

T0C – RF hazards; radiation exposure, proximity to antennas, recognized safe power levels, exposure to others

Once your name and call sign are available in the FCC database, you have the privilege of operating on all VHF (2 m) and UHF (70 cm) frequencies above 30 megahertz (MHz) and HF frequencies 80, 40, and 15 meter, and on the 10 meter band using Morse code (CW), voice, and digital mode. For a Technician license in Maine, your call sign will consist of a two-letter prefix beginning with K or W, the number one (1), and a three-letter suffix. The single digit number in the call sign is determined according to which area of the US you obtain your first license. Even though you may move to another state, you keep this number in your call sign. This is also true should you upgrade to a higher license and get a new call sign. The numeral portion of your call sign stays the same.

Call Sign Numbers

Below is a chart showing the various numbers and the state(s) in which you would obtain the number.

Call Sign Number	State(s)
0	CO, IA, KS, MN, MO, NE, ND, SD
1	CT, ME, MA, NH, RI, VT
2	NJ, NY
3	DE, DC, MD, PA
4	AL, FL, GA, KY, NC, SC, TN, VA
5	AR, LA, MS, NM, OK, TX
6	CA
7	AZ, ID, MT, NV, OR, WA, UT, WY
8	MI, OH, WV
9	IL, IN, WI

Residents of Alaska may have any of the following call sign prefixes assigned to them: AL0-7, KL0-7, NL0-7, or WL0-7. Likewise, residents of Hawaii may have the prefix AH6-7, KH6-7, NH6-7, or WH6-7 assigned.

Once you obtain your Technician license, do not stop there. Go and get your General license.

General is the second of three ham license classes. Like the Technician license, to get a General license, you merely have to take a 35-question multiple choice exam and pay your license fee. Passing is still at least 26 correct answers and the fee is the same (less than $20). Again the question pool is available for free online (http://www.ncvec.org/page.php?id=358). It is also available in such print publications as *The ARRL General Class License Manual 7th Edition* (ISBN 978-0-87259-811-9). The current General pool of questions is to be used from July 1, 2011 to June 30, 2015. Be sure the question pool you are using is current. Being a bit more comprehensive than the Technician license, the General license usually requires 15-20 hours of study to learn the material. Check Appendix A for a listing of clubs in Maine where you might take your exam. Once your name and NEW call sign is listed in the FCC database, you're good to go. For a General license in Maine, your call sign will consist of a one-letter prefix beginning with K, N or W, the number one (1), and a three-letter suffix.

Topics for the General License in Amateur Radio

The General license exam covers regulations, operating practices and electronic theory. Below is the syllabus for the General Class.

Subelement G1 – Commission's Rules

(5 Exam Questions – 5 Groups)
G1A – General Class control operator frequency privileges; primary and secondary allocations
G1B – Antenna structure limitations; good engineering and good amateur practice, beacon operation; restricted operation; retransmitting radio signals
G1C – Transmitter power regulations; data emission standards
G1D – Volunteer Examiners and Volunteer Examiner Coordinators; temporary identification
G1E – Control categories; repeater regulations; harmful interference; third party rules; ITU regions

---

Subelement G2 – Operating procedures

(5 Exam Questions – 5 Groups)
G2A – Phone operating procedures; USB/LSB utilization conventions; procedural signals; breaking into a OSO in progress; VOX operation
G2B – Operating courtesy; band plans, emergencies, including drills and emergency communications
G2C – CW operating procedures and procedural signals; Q signals and common abbreviations; full break in
G2D – Amateur Auxiliary; minimizing interference; HF operations

G2E – Digital operating; procedures, procedural signals and common abbreviations

Subelement G3 – Radio wave propagation

(3 Exam Questions – 3 Groups)

G3A – Sunspots and solar radiation; ionospheric disturbances; propagation forecasting and indices

G3B – Maximum Usable Frequency; Lowest Usable Frequency; propagation

G3C – Ionospheric layers; critical angle and frequency; HF scatter; Near Vertical Incidence Sky waves

Subelement G4 – Amateur radio practices

(5 Exam Questions – 5 Groups)

G4A – Station Operation and setup

G4B – Test and monitoring equipment; two-tone test

G4C – Interference with consumer electronics; grounding; DSP

G4D – Speech processors; S meters; sideband operation near band edges

G4E – HF mobile radio installations; emergency and battery powered operation

Subelement G5 – Electrical principles

(3 Exam Questions – 3 Groups)

G5A – Reactance; inductance; capacitance; impedance; impedance matching

G5B – The Decibel; current and voltage dividers; electrical power calculations; sine wave root-mean-square (RMS) values; PEP calculations

G5C – Resistors; capacitors and inductors in series and parallel; transformers

Subelement G6 – Circuit components

(3 Exam Questions – 3 Groups)

G6A – Resistors; capacitors; inductors

G6B – Rectifiers; solid state diodes and transistors; vacuum tubes; batteries

G6C – Analog and digital integrated circuits (ICs); microprocessors; memory; I/O devices; microwave ICs (MMICs); display devices

Subelement G7 – Practical circuits

(3 Exam Questions – 3 Groups)

G7A – Power supplies; schematic symbols

G7B – Digital circuits; amplifiers and oscillators

G7C – Receivers and transmitters; filters, oscillators

Subelement G8 – Signals and emissions

(2 Exam Questions – 2 Groups)

G8A – Carriers and modulation; AM; FM; single and double sideband; modulation envelope; overmodulation

G8B – Frequency mixing; multiplication; HF data communications; bandwidths of various modes; deviation

Subelement G9 – Antennas and feed lines

(4 Exam Questions – 4 Groups)

G9A – Antenna feed lines; characteristic impedance and attenuation; SWR calculation, measurement and effects; matching networks

G9B – Basic antennas

G9C – Directional antennas

G9D – Specialized antennas

Subelement G0 – Electrical and RF safety

(2 Exam Questions – 2 Groups)

G0A – RF safety principles, rules and guidelines; routine station elevation

G0B – Safety in the ham shack; electrical shock and treatment, safety grounding, fusing, interlocks, wiring, antenna and tower safety

With a General license, you can use all VHF and UHF frequencies and most of the HF frequencies. You would have access to the 160, 30, 17, 12, and 10 meter bands and access to major parts of the 80, 40, 20, and 15 meter bands. Of course, this is in addition to all bands available to Technician license holders.

Amateur Extra is the third of three ham license classes. Like the Technician and General classes, you merely have to pass a test and pay your fee to get your Amateur Extra license. This class of license is more comprehensive than the lower license classes. The exam is longer – 50 questions – and the minimum passing score is higher – 37. However, once you get your Amateur Extra license, all ham frequencies, VHF, UHF and HF are available for your enjoyment. The Extra exam covers regulations, specialized operating practices, advanced electronics theory, and radio equipment design.

Like for the other license classes, the question pool for the Amateur Extra license is available online for downloading (http://www.ncvec.org/downloads/REVISED%202012-2016%20Extra%20Class%20Pool.doc). It is also available in print form in such publications as *The ARRL Extra Class License Manual Revised 9th Edition* (ISBN 978-0-87259-887-4). If you are downloading the question pool from the above web address, the address is for the pool valid from July 1, 20012 until June 30, 2016.

Topics for the Extra License in Amateur Radio (July 1, 2012 to June 30, 2016)

Below is the syllabus for the Amateur Extra Class for July 1, 2012 to June 30, 2016. (If you are going to take the Amateur Extra exam prior to July 1, 2012, use the above syllabus.)

Subelement E1 – Commission's Rules

[6 Exam Questions – 6 Groups]

E1A – Operating Standards: frequency privileges; emission standards; automatic message forwarding; frequency sharing; stations aboard ships or aircraft

E1B – Station restrictions and special operations: restrictions on station location; general operating restrictions, spurious emissions, control operator reimbursement; antenna structure restrictions; RACES operations

E1C – Station control: definitions and restrictions pertaining to local, automatic and remote control operation; control operator responsibilities for remote and automatically controlled stations

E1D – Amateur Satellite service: definitions and purpose; license requirements for space stations; available frequencies and bands; telecommand and telemetry operations; restrictions, and special provisions; notification requirements

E1E – Volunteer examiner program: definitions, qualifications, preparation and administration of exams; accreditation; question pools; documentation requirements

E1F – Miscellaneous rules: external RF power amplifiers; national quiet zone; business communications; compensated communications; spread spectrum; auxiliary stations; reciprocal operating privileges; IARP and CEPT licenses; third party communications with foreign countries; special temporary authority

---

Subelement E2 – Operating procedures

[5 Exam Questions – 5 Groups]

E2A – Amateur radio in space: amateur satellites; orbital mechanics; frequencies and modes; satellite hardware; satellite operations

E2B – Television practices: fast scan television standards and techniques; slow scan television standards and techniques

E2C – Operating methods: contest and DX operating; spread-spectrum transmissions; selecting an operating frequency

E2D – Operating methods: VHF and UHF digital modes; APRS

E2E – Operating methods: operating HF digital modes; error correction

---

Subelement E3 – Radio wave propagation

[3 Exam Questions – 3 Groups]

E3A – Propagation and technique, Earth-Moon-Earth communications; meteor scatter

E3B – Propagation and technique, trans-equatorial; long path; gray-line; multi-path propagation

E3C – Propagation and technique, Aurora propagation; selective fading; radio-path horizon; take-off angle over flat or sloping terrain; effects of ground on propagation; less common propagation modes

Subelement E4 – Amateur practices

[5 Exam Questions – 5 Groups]

E4A – Test equipment: analog and digital instruments; spectrum and network analyzers, antenna analyzers; oscilloscopes; testing transistors; RF measurements

E4B – Measurement technique and limitations: instrument accuracy and performance limitations; probes; techniques to minimize errors; measurement of "Q"; instrument calibration

E4C – Receiver performance characteristics, phase noise, capture effect, noise floor, image rejection, MDS, signal-to-noise-ratio; selectivity

E4D – Receiver performance characteristics, blocking dynamic range, intermodulation and cross-modulation interference; 3rd order intercept; desensitization; preselection

E4E – Noise suppression: system noise; electrical appliance noise; line noise; locating noise sources; DSP noise reduction; noise blankers

Subelement E5 – Electrical principles

[4 Exam Questions – 4 Groups]

E5A – Resonance and Q: characteristics of resonant circuits: series and parallel resonance; Q; half-power bandwidth; phase relationships in reactive circuits

E5B – Time constants and phase relationships: RLC time constants: definition; time constants in RL and RC circuits; phase angle between voltage and current; phase angles of series and parallel circuits

E5C – Impedance plots and coordinate systems: plotting impedances in polar coordinates; rectangular coordinates

E5D – AC and RF energy in real circuits: skin effect; electrostatic and electromagnetic fields; reactive power; power factor; coordinate systems

Subelement E6 – Circuit components

[6 Exam Questions – 6 Groups]

E6A – Semiconductor materials and devices: semiconductor materials germanium, silicon, P-type, N-type; transistor types: NPN, PNP, junction, field-effect transistors: enhancement mode; depletion mode; MOS; CMOS; N-channel; P-channel

E6B – Semiconductor diodes

E6C – Integrated circuits: TTL digital integrated circuits; CMOS digital integrated circuits; gates

E6D – Optical devices and toroids: cathode-ray tube devices; charge-coupled devices (CCDs); liquid crystal displays (LCDs); toroids: permeability, core material, selecting, winding

E6E – Piezoelectric crystals and MMICs: quartz crystals; crystal oscillators and filters; monolithic amplifiers

E6F – Optical components and power systems: photoconductive principles and effects, photovoltaic systems, optical couplers, optical sensors, and optoisolators

Subelement E7 – Practical circuits

[8 Exam Questions – 8 Groups]

E7A – Digital circuits: digital circuit principles and logic circuits: classes of logic elements; positive and negative logic; frequency dividers; truth tables

E7B – Amplifiers: Class of operation; vacuum tube and solid-state circuits; distortion and intermodulation; spurious and parasitic suppression; microwave amplifiers

E7C – Filters and matching networks: filters and impedance matching networks: types of networks; types of filters; filter applications; filter characteristics; impedance matching; DSP filtering

E7D – Power supplies and voltage regulators

E7E – Modulation and demodulation: reactance, phase and balanced modulators; detectors; mixer stages; DSP modulation and demodulation; software defined radio systems

E7F – Frequency markers and counters: frequency divider circuits; frequency marker generators; frequency counters

E7G – Active filters and op-amps: active audio filters; characteristics; basic circuit design; operational amplifiers

E7H – Oscillators and signal sources: types of oscillators; synthesizers and phase-locked loops; direct digital synthesizers

Subelement E8 – Signals and emissions

[4 Exam Questions – 4 Groups]

E8A – AC waveforms: sine, square, sawtooth and irregular waveforms; AC measurements; average and PEP of RF signals; pulse and digital signal waveforms

E8B – Modulation and demodulation: modulation methods; modulation index and deviation ratio; pulse modulation; frequency and time division multiplexing

E8C – Digital signals: digital communications modes; CW; information rate vs. bandwidth; spread-spectrum communications; modulation methods

E8D – Waves, measurements, and RF grounding: peak-to-peak values, polarization; RF grounding

Subelement E9 – Antennas and transmission lines

[8 Exam Questions – 8 Groups]

E9A – Isotropic and gain antennas: definition; used as a standard for comparison; radiation pattern; basic antenna parameters: radiation resistance and reactance, gain, beamwidth, efficiency

E9B – Antenna patterns: E and H plane patterns; gain as a function of pattern; antenna design; Yagi antennas

E9C – Wire and phased vertical antennas: beverage antennas; terminated and resonant rhombic antennas; elevation above real ground; ground effects as related to polarization; take-off angles

E9D – Directional antennas: gain; satellite antennas; antenna beamwidth; losses; SWR bandwidth; antenna efficiency; shortened and mobile antennas; grounding

E9E – Matching: matching antennas to feed lines; power dividers

E9F – Transmission lines: characteristics of open and shorted feed lines: 1/8 wavelength; 1/4 wavelength; 1/2 wavelength; feed lines: coax versus open-wire; velocity factor;

electrical length; transformation characteristics of line terminated in impedance not equal to characteristic impedance
E9G – The Smith chart
E9H – Effective radiated power; system gains and losses; radio direction finding antennas

Subelement E0 – Safety

[1 exam question – 1 group]
E0A – Safety: amateur radio safety practices; RF radiation hazards; hazardous materials

Once your new call sign is listed in the FCC database, you are good to go. For an Amateur Extra license in Maine, your call sign will consist of a prefix of K, N or W, the number one (1), and a two-letter suffix, or a two-letter prefix beginning with A, N, K or W, the number one (1), and a one-letter suffix, or a two-letter prefix beginning with A, the number one (1), and a two-letter suffix.

Ham radio equipment can be expensive or you can do it "on the cheap." The cost will run from a couple hundred dollars to well in the thousands, depending on what you have available. eBay, and Craigslist are good places to start looking. Most ham clubs do some sort of hamfest annually wherein club members or others are willing to part with older equipment. See Appendix A for a list of clubs in Maine.

Another excellent source of equipment, as well as advice on setting the equipment up and how to use it properly, is current ham operators. In Appendix B, the author has listed all the FCC licensed ham operators in Maine, listed by city, and then sorted by street and house number on the street. Who knows, maybe someone who lives close to you is a ham operator. Be a good neighbor, stop by and have a chat with him/her.

Like CB radios, ham radios come in three formats – base, mobile, and handheld. They can use the electric company for power, or operate off a car battery. In the opinion of this author, in spite of the slightly higher cost of the equipment and having to take a test to legally use the equipment, ham radio is the way to go when concerned about communication during times of crisis.

Canadian Call Sign Prefixes

Because of our proximity to Canada, many times ham contact is made with our northern neighbors. Below is a chart showing the origin of Canadian call sign prefixes.

Call Sign Prefix	Provence or Territory
CY0	Sable Island
CY9	St. Paul Island
VA1, VE1	New Brunswick, Nova Scotia
VA2, VE2	Quebec
VA3, VE3	Ontario
VA4, VE4	Manitoba
VA5, VE5	Saskatchewan

VA6, VE6	Alberta
VA7, VE7	British Columbia
VE8	North West Territories
VE9	New Brunswick
VO1	Newfoundland
VO2	Labrador
VY0	Nunavut
VY1	Yukon
VY2	Prince Edward Island

Common Radio Bands in the United States

Certain radio bands are more popular with ham radio enthusiasts than others. Below is a chart showing these bands and when they are most popular.

	Band (meter)	Frequency (MHz)	Use
HF	160	1.8 – 2.0	Night
	80	3.5 – 4.0	Night and Local Day
	40	7.0 – 7.3	Night and Local Day
	30	10.1 – 10.15	CW and Digital
	20	14.0 – 14.350	World Wide Day and Night
	17	18.068 – 18.168	World Wide Day and Night
	15	21.0 – 21.450	Primarily Daytime
	12	24.890 – 24.990	Primarily Daytime
	10	28.0 – 29.70	Daytime during Sunspot highs
VHF	6	50 – 54	Local to World Wide
	2	144 – 148	Local to Medium Distance
UHF	70 cm	430 – 440	Local

Common Amateur Radio Bands in Canada

160 Meter Band - Maximum bandwidth 6 kHz
1.800 - 1.820 MHz - CW
1.820 - 1.830 MHz - Digital Modes
1 830 - 1.840 MHz - DX Window
1.840 - 2.000 MHz - SSB and other wide band modes

80 Meter Band - Maximum bandwidth 6 kHz
3.500 - 3.580 MHz - CW
3.580 - 3.620 MHz - Digital Modes
3.620 - 3.635 MHz - Packet/Digital Secondary
3.635 - 3.725 MHz - CW
3.725 - 3.790 MHz - SSB and other side band modes*
3.790 - 3.800 MHz - SSB DX Window
3.800 - 4.000 MHz - SSB and other wide band modes

40 Meter Band - Maximum bandwidth 6 kHz
7.000 - 7.035 MHz - CW
7.035 - 7.050 MHz - Digital Modes
7.040 - 7.050 MHz - International packet
7.050 - 7.100 MHz - SSB
7.100 - 7.120 MHz - Packet within Region 2
7.120 - 7.150 MHz - CW
7.150 - 7.300 MHz - SSB and other wide band modes

30 Meter Band - Maximum bandwidth 1 kHz
10.100 - 10.130 MHz - CW only
10.130 - 10.140 MHz - Digital Modes
10.140 - 10.150 MHz - Packet

20 Meter Band - Maximum bandwidth 6 kHz
14.000 - 14.070 MHz - CW only
14.070 - 14.095 MHz - Digital Mode
14.095 - 14.099 MHz - Packet
14.100 MHz - Beacons
14.101 - 14.112 MHz - CW, SSB, packet shared
14.112 - 14.350 MHz - SSB
14.225 - 14.235 MHz - SSTV

17 Meter Band - Maximum bandwidth 6 kHz
18.068 - 18.100 MHz - CW
18.100 - 18.105 MHz - Digital Modes
18.105 - 18.110 MHz - Packet
18.110 - 18.168 MHz - SSB and other wide band modes

15 Meter Band - maximum bandwidth 6 kHz
21.000 - 21.070 MHz - CW
21.070 - 21.090 MHz - Digital Modes
21.090 - 21.125 MHz - Packet
21.100 - 21.150 MHz - CW and SSB
21.150 - 21.335 MHz - SSB and other wide band modes
21.335 - 21.345 MHz - SSTV
21.345 - 21.450 MHz - SSB and other wide band modes

12 Meter Band - Maximum bandwidth 6 kHz
24.890 - 24.930 MHz - CW
24.920 - 24.925 MHz - Digital Modes
24.925 - 24.930 MHz - Packet
24.930 - 24.990 MHz - SSB and other wide band modes

10 Meter Band - Maximum band width 20 kHz

28.000 - 28.200 MHz - CW
28.070 - 28.120 MHz - Digital Modes
28.120 - 28.190 MHz - Packet
28.190 - 28.200 MHz - Beacons
28.200 - 29.300 MHz - SSB and other wide band modes
29.300 - 29.510 MHz - Satellite
29.510 - 29.700 MHz - SSB, FM and repeaters

160 Meters (1.8-2.0 MHz)

1.800 - 2.000 CW
1.800 - 1.810 Digital Modes
1.810 CW QRP
1.843-2.000 SSB, SSTV and other wideband modes
1.910 SSB QRP
1.995 - 2.000 Experimental
1.999 - 2.000 Beacons

80 Meters (3.5-4.0 MHz)

3.590 RTTY/Data DX
3.570-3.600 RTTY/Data
3.790-3.800 DX window
3.845 SSTV
3.885 AM calling frequency

40 Meters (7.0-7.3 MHz)

7.040 RTTY/Data DX
7.080-7.125 RTTY/Data
7.171 SSTV
7.290 AM calling frequency

30 Meters (10.1-10.15 MHz)

10.130-10.140 RTTY
10.140-10.150 Packet

20 Meters (14.0-14.35 MHz)

14.070-14.095 RTTY
14.095-14.0995 Packet
14.100 NCDXF Beacons
14.1005-14.112 Packet
14.230 SSTV
14.286 AM calling frequency

17 Meters (18.068-18.168 MHz)

18.100-18.105 RTTY

18.105-18.110 Packet

15 Meters (21.0-21.45 MHz)
21.070-21.110 RTTY/Data
21.340 SSTV

12 Meters (24.89-24.99 MHz)
24.920-24.925 RTTY
24.925-24.930 Packet

10 Meters (28-29.7 MHz)
28.000-28.070 CW
28.070-28.150 RTTY
28.150-28.190 CW
28.200-28.300 Beacons
28.300-29.300 Phone
28.680 SSTV
29.000-29.200 AM
29.300-29.510 Satellite Downlinks
29.520-29.590 Repeater Inputs
29.600 FM Simplex
29.610-29.700 Repeater Outputs

6 Meters (50-54 MHz)
50.0-50.1 CW, beacons
50.060-50.080 beacon subband
50.1-50.3 SSB, CW
50.10-50.125 DX window
50.125 SSB calling
50.3-50.6 All modes
50.6-50.8 Nonvoice communications
50.62 Digital (packet) calling
50.8-51.0 Radio remote control (20-kHz channels)
51.0-51.1 Pacific DX window
51.12-51.48 Repeater inputs (19 channels)
51.12-51.18 Digital repeater inputs
51.5-51.6 Simplex (six channels)
51.62-51.98 Repeater outputs (19 channels)
51.62-51.68 Digital repeater outputs
52.0-52.48 Repeater inputs (except as noted; 23 channels)
52.02, 52.04 FM simplex
52.2 TEST PAIR (input)
52.5-52.98 Repeater output (except as noted; 23 channels)
52.525 Primary FM simplex
52.54 Secondary FM simplex
52.7 TEST PAIR (output)

53.0-53.48 Repeater inputs (except as noted; 19 channels)
53.0 Remote base FM simplex
53.02 Simplex
53.1, 53.2, 53.3, 53.4 Radio remote control
53.5-53.98 Repeater outputs (except as noted; 19 channels)
53.5, 53.6, 53.7, 53.8 Radio remote control
53.52, 53.9 Simplex

2 Meters (144-148 MHz)

144.00-144.05 EME (CW)
144.05-144.10 General CW and weak signals
144.10-144.20 EME and weak-signal SSB
144.200 National calling frequency
144.200-144.275 General SSB operation
144.275-144.300 Propagation beacons
144.30-144.50 New OSCAR subband
144.50-144.60 Linear translator inputs
144.60-144.90 FM repeater inputs
144.90-145.10 Weak signal and FM simplex (145.01,03,05,07,09 are widely used for packet)
145.10-145.20 Linear translator outputs
145.20-145.50 FM repeater outputs
145.50-145.80 Miscellaneous and experimental modes
145.80-146.00 OSCAR subband
146.01-146.37 Repeater inputs
146.40-146.58 Simplex
146.52 National Simplex Calling Frequency
146.61-146.97 Repeater outputs
147.00-147.39 Repeater outputs
147.42-147.57 Simplex
147.60-147.99 Repeater inputs

1.25 Meters (222-225 MHz)

222.0-222.150 Weak-signal modes
222.0-222.025 EME
222.05-222.06 Propagation beacons
222.1 SSB & CW calling frequency
222.10-222.15 Weak-signal CW & SSB
222.15-222.25 Local coordinator's option; weak signal, ACSB, repeater inputs, control
222.25-223.38 FM repeater inputs only
223.40-223.52 FM simplex
223.52-223.64 Digital, packet
223.64-223.70 Links, control
223.71-223.85 Local coordinator's option; FM simplex, packet, repeater outputs
223.85-224.98 Repeater outputs only

70 Centimeters (420-450 MHz)

420.00-426.00 ATV repeater or simplex with 421.25 MHz video carrier control links and experimental

426.00-432.00 ATV simplex with 427.250-MHz video carrier frequency

432.00-432.07 EME (Earth-Moon-Earth)

432.07-432.10 Weak-signal CW

432.10 70-cm calling frequency

432.10-432.30 Mixed-mode and weak-signal work

432.30-432.40 Propagation beacons

432.40-433.00 Mixed-mode and weak-signal work

433.00-435.00 Auxiliary/repeater links

435.00-438.00 Satellite only (internationally)

438.00-444.00 ATV repeater input with 439.250-MHz video carrier frequency and repeater links

442.00-445.00 Repeater inputs and outputs (local option)

445.00-447.00 Shared by auxiliary and control links, repeaters and simplex (local option)

446.00 National simplex frequency

447.00-450.00 Repeater inputs and outputs (local option)

33 Centimeters (902-928 MHz)

902.0-903.0 Narrow-bandwidth, weak-signal communications

902.0-902.8 SSTV, FAX, ACSSB, experimental

902.1 Weak-signal calling frequency

902.8-903.0 Reserved for EME, CW expansion

903.1 Alternate calling frequency

903.0-906.0 Digital communications

906-909 FM repeater inputs

909-915 ATV

915-918 Digital communications

918-921 FM repeater outputs

921-927 ATV

927-928 FM simplex and links

23 Centimeters (1240-1300 MHz)

1240-1246 ATV #1

1246-1248 Narrow-bandwidth FM point-to-point links and digital, duplex with 1258-1260.

1248-1258 Digital Communications

1252-1258 ATV #2

1258-1260 Narrow-bandwidth FM point-to-point links digital, duplexed with 1246-1252

1260-1270 Satellite uplinks, reference WARC '79

1260-1270 Wide-bandwidth experimental, simplex ATV

1270-1276 Repeater inputs, FM and linear, paired with 1282-1288, 239 pairs every 25 kHz, e.g. 1270.025, .050, etc.

1271-1283 Non-coordinated test pair

1276-1282 ATV #3

1282-1288 Repeater outputs, paired with 1270-1276

1288-1294 Wide-bandwidth experimental, simplex ATV
1294-1295 Narrow-bandwidth FM simplex services, 25-kHz channels
1294.5 National FM simplex calling frequency
1295-1297 Narrow bandwidth weak-signal communications (no FM)
1295.0-1295.8 SSTV, FAX, ACSSB, experimental
1295.8-1296.0 Reserved for EME, CW expansion
1296.00-1296.05 EME-exclusive
1296.07-1296.08 CW beacons
1296.1 CW, SSB calling frequency
1296.4-1296.6 Crossband linear translator input
1296.6-1296.8 Crossband linear translator output
1296.8-1297.0 Experimental beacons (exclusive)
1297-1300 Digital Communications

2300-2310 and 2390-2450 MHz

2300.0-2303.0 High-rate data
2303.0-2303.5 Packet
2303.5-2303.8 TTY packet
2303.9-2303.9 Packet, TTY, CW, EME
2303.9-2304.1 CW, EME
2304.1 Calling frequency
2304.1-2304.2 CW, EME, SSB
2304.2-2304.3 SSB, SSTV, FAX, Packet AM, Amtor
2304.30-2304.32 Propagation beacon network
2304.32-2304.40 General propagation beacons
2304.4-2304.5 SSB, SSTV, ACSSB, FAX, Packet AM, Amtor experimental
2304.5-2304.7 Crossband linear translator input
2304.7-2304.9 Crossband linear translator output
2304.9-2305.0 Experimental beacons
2305.0-2305.2 FM simplex (25 kHz spacing)
2305.20 FM simplex calling frequency
2305.2-2306.0 FM simplex (25 kHz spacing)
2306.0-2309.0 FM Repeaters (25 kHz) input
2309.0-2310.0 Control and auxiliary links
2390.0-2396.0 Fast-scan TV
2396.0-2399.0 High-rate data
2399.0-2399.5 Packet
2399.5-2400.0 Control and auxiliary links
2400.0-2403.0 Satellite
2403.0-2408.0 Satellite high-rate data
2408.0-2410.0 Satellite
2410.0-2413.0 FM repeaters (25 kHz) output
2413.0-2418.0 High-rate data
2418.0-2430.0 Fast-scan TV
2430.0-2433.0 Satellite
2433.0-2438.0 Satellite high-rate data

2438.0-2450.0 WB FM, FSTV, FMTV, SS experimental

3300-3500 MHz
3456.3-3456.4 Propagation beacons

5650-5925 MHz
5760.3-5760.4 Propagation beacons

10.00-10.50 GHz
10.368 Narrow band calling frequency 10.3683-10.3684 Propagation beacons
10.3640 Calling frequency

Now that you have your license (you do, don't you?), and your equipment, you are ready to go live. Below is a suggested start.

1) Assuming you have the HT set up to the appropriate frequency, and offset, press the mic button on the HT and say, "KK4HWX listening." Replace the KK4HWX with your own call sign, the one assigned to you by the FCC (it's the law). If no one responds to your call, you may wish to try again. Hopefully someone will respond to your call.

2) Once you get a response, it will be in the form of something like, "KK4HWX this is ??1??? in Eastport returning. My name is Florence. Back to you. ??1???" then a tone. Let us examine the response more closely. She first acknowledged your call sign (KK4HWX), then identified hers (??1???). From the 1 in her call sign, you know that she first got her license in Region 1, meaning she got it while a resident of CT, ME, MA, NH, RI, or VT. She then told you where she's transmitting from (Eastport). The term "returning" means that she is returning your call. Her name is Florence. The phrase, "Back to you" indicates that she is turning over the conversation to you. She then repeats her call sign. The tone indicates to you that it is okay to proceed with your response. BTW if she had used the term "Over" instead of "Back to you," it would mean the same thing, just fewer words.

3) At this point, press the mic button and continue with the conversation. You should restate your call sign often during the conversation (perhaps every 10 minutes or less and whenever you begin transmitting). Don't forget to say, "Over" or "Back to you" whenever you are giving Florence control of the conversation again.

4) When you are ready to stop the conversation, you should say goodbye or use the phrase "73", meaning "best wishes." Your conversation would end something like, "??1??? 73, this is KK4HWX clear and monitoring." The "clear and monitoring" indicates that you are going to continue to monitor the frequency. If you are not going to continue monitoring, you may wish to end the conversation with Florence with, "clear and QRT" instead. The QRT means that you are stopping transmissions.

Call Sign Phonics

Because of different accents of various people, sometimes it is difficult to understand call sign letters when spoken. For this reason, most ham operators verbalize their call sign using phonics. Below is a table listing the accepted phonics for letters and numbers.

A = ALFA	S = SIERRA
B = BRAVO	T = TANGO
C = CHARLIE	U = UNIFORM
D = DELTA	V = VICTOR
E = ECHO	W = WHISKEY
F = FOXTROT	X = X-RAY
G = GOLF	Y = YANKEE
H = HOTEL	Z = ZULU (ZED)
I = INDIA	1 = ONE
J = JULIETT	2 = TWO
K = KILO	3 = THREE (TREE)
L = LIMA	4 = FOUR
M = MIKE	5 = FIVE (FIFE)
N = NOVEMBER	6 = SIX
O = OSCAR	7 = SEVEN
P = PAPA (PA-PA')	8 = EIGHT
Q = QUEBEC (KAY-BEK')	9 = NINE (NINER)
R = ROMEO	0 = ZERO

The words in parentheses are the pronunciation or the alternate pronunciations for the words or numbers, but you will hear both used. With the letter Z, (ZED) is by far the most commonly used. With the number 9, NINER is the most common and easiest to understand ON THE AIR.

If you wish to use Morse code (CW) instead of voice communication, the "conversation" would follow the same steps, with a few modifications. To type out each word would require a lot of typing and translating. If you are like this author, more means more, i.e., more typing means more typos are likely. To help with this situation, CW enthusiasts have developed a language all their own – they use abbreviations for common phrases. Below is a chart showing some of these abbreviations.

Abbreviation	Use
AR	Over
de	From or "this is"
ES	And
GM	Good Morning
K	Go
KN	Go only
NM	Name

QTH	Location
RPT	Report
R	Roger
SK	Clear
tnx	Thanks
UR	Your, you are
73	Best Wishes

Morse Code and Amateur Radio

If you wish to use CW, but are concerned about accuracy, you might consider purchasing a Morse code translator. This is an electronic device that you place in front of your speakers. It takes the CW sounds and translates them into English and displays the transmission on an LCD display. For the reverse, you can pick up a CW keyboard. With the keyboard, you type in your message and it converts the text to Morse code. The translator does not need to be attached to your ham equipment, whereas the keyboard would.

For your convenience, below is a table showing the Morse code signals and their meaning.

Character	Code
A	· —
B	— · · ·
C	— · — ·
D	— · ·
E	·
F	· · — ·
G	— — ·
H	· · · ·
I	· ·
J	· — — —
K	— · —
L	· — · ·
M	— —
N	— ·
O	— — —
P	· — — ·
Q	— — · —
R	· — ·
S	· · ·
T	—
U	· · —
V	· · · —
W	· — —

X	— · · —
Y	— · — —
Z	— — · ·
0	— — — — —
1	· — — — —
2	· · — — —
3	· · · — —
4	· · · · —
5	· · · · ·
6	— · · · ·
7	— — · · ·
8	— — — · ·
9	— — — — ·
Ampersand [&], Wait	· — · · ·
Apostrophe [']	· — — — — ·
At sign [@]	· — — · — ·
Colon [:]	— — — · · ·
Comma [,]	— — · · — —
Dollar sign [$]	· · · — · · —
Double dash [=]	— · · · —
Exclamation mark [!]	— · — · — —
Hyphen, Minus [-]	— · · · · —
Parenthesis closed [)]	— · — — · —
Parenthesis open [(]	— · — — ·
Period [.]	· — · — · —
Plus [+]	· — · — ·
Question mark [?]	· · — — · ·
Quotation mark ["]	· — · · — ·
Semicolon [;]	— · — · — ·
Slash [/], Fraction bar	— · · — ·
Underscore [_]	· · — — · —

An advantage of using Morse Code is that when broadcasting CW, you are using reduced power, thereby saving your battery. Your battery is used only while actually transmitting or receiving.

International Call Sign Prefixes

As was stated earlier, all ham radio call signs begin with letters (or numbers) taken from blocks assigned to each country of the world by the *ITU - International Telecommunications Union,* a body controlled by the United Nations. The following chart indicates which call sign series are allocated to which countries.

Call Sign Series	Allocated to
AAA-ALZ	United States of America

AMA-AOZ	Spain
APA-ASZ	Pakistan (Islamic Republic of)
ATA-AWZ	India (Republic of)
AXA-AXZ	Australia
AYA-AZZ	Argentine Republic
A2A-A2Z	Botswana (Republic of)
A3A-A3Z	Tonga (Kingdom of)
A4A-A4Z	Oman (Sultanate of)
A5A-A5Z	Bhutan (Kingdom of)
A6A-A6Z	United Arab Emirates
A7A-A7Z	Qatar (State of)
A8A-A8Z	Liberia (Republic of)
A9A-A9Z	Bahrain (State of)
BAA-BZZ	China (People's Republic of)
CAA-CEZ	Chile
CFA-CKZ	Canada
CLA-CMZ	Cuba
CNA-CNZ	Morocco (Kingdom of)
COA-COZ	Cuba
CPA-CPZ	Bolivia (Republic of)
CQA-CUZ	Portugal
CVA-CXZ	Uruguay (Eastern Republic of)
CYA-CZZ	Canada
C2A-C2Z	Nauru (Republic of)
C3A-C3Z	Andorra (Principality of)
C4A-C4Z	Cyprus (Republic of)
C5A-C5Z	Gambia (Republic of the)
C6A-C6Z	Bahamas (Commonwealth of the)
C7A-C7Z	World Meteorological Organization
C8A-C9Z	Mozambique (Republic of)
DAA-DRZ	Germany (Federal Republic of)
DSA-DTZ	Korea (Republic of)
DUA-DZZ	Philippines (Republic of the)
D2A-D3Z	Angola (Republic of)
D4A-D4Z	Cape Verde (Republic of)
D5A-D5Z	Liberia (Republic of)
D6A-D6Z	Comoros (Islamic Federal Republic of the)
D7A-D9Z	Korea (Republic of)
EAA-EHZ	Spain
EIA-EJZ	Ireland
EKA-EKZ	Armenia (Republic of)
ELA-ELZ	Liberia (Republic of)
EMA-EOZ	Ukraine
EPA-EQZ	Iran (Islamic Republic of)
ERA-ERZ	Moldova (Republic of)

ESA-ESZ	Estonia (Republic of)
ETA-ETZ	Ethiopia (Federal Democratic Republic of)
EUA-EWZ	Belarus (Republic of)
EXA-EXZ	Kyrgyz Republic
EYA-EYZ	Tajikistan (Republic of)
EZA-EZZ	Turkmenistan
E2A-E2Z	Thailand
E3A-E3Z	Eritrea
E4A-E4Z	Palestinian Authority
E5A-E5Z	New Zealand - Cook Islands (WRC-07)
E7A-E7Z	Bosnia and Herzegovina (Republic of) (WRC-07)
FAA-FZZ	France
GAA-GZZ	United Kingdom of Great Britain and Northern Ireland
HAA-HAZ	Hungary (Republic of)
HBA-HBZ	Switzerland (Confederation of)
HCA-HDZ	Ecuador
HEA-HEZ	Switzerland (Confederation of)
HFA-HFZ	Poland (Republic of)
HGA-HGZ	Hungary (Republic of)
HHA-HHZ	Haiti (Republic of)
HIA-HIZ	Dominican Republic
HJA-HKZ	Colombia (Republic of)
HLA-HLZ	Korea (Republic of)
HMA-HMZ	Democratic People's Republic of Korea
HNA-HNZ	Iraq (Republic of)
HOA-HPZ	Panama (Republic of)
HQA-HRZ	Honduras (Republic of)
HSA-HSZ	Thailand
HTA-HTZ	Nicaragua
HUA-HUZ	El Salvador (Republic of)
HVA-HVZ	Vatican City State
HWA-HYZ	France
HZA-HZZ	Saudi Arabia (Kingdom of)
H2A-H2Z	Cyprus (Republic of)
H3A-H3Z	Panama (Republic of)
H4A-H4Z	Solomon Islands
H6A-H7Z	Nicaragua
H8A-H9Z	Panama (Republic of)
IAA-IZZ	Italy
JAA-JSZ	Japan
JTA-JVZ	Mongolia
JWA-JXZ	Norway
JYA-JYZ	Jordan (Hashemite Kingdom of)
JZA-JZZ	Indonesia (Republic of)
J2A-J2Z	Djibouti (Republic of)

J3A-J3Z	Grenada
J4A-J4Z	Greece
J5A-J5Z	Guinea-Bissau (Republic of)
J6A-J6Z	Saint Lucia
J7A-J7Z	Dominica (Commonwealth of)
J8A-J8Z	Saint Vincent and the Grenadines
KAA-KZZ	**United States of America**
LAA-LNZ	Norway
LOA-LWZ	Argentine Republic
LXA-LXZ	Luxembourg
LYA-LYZ	Lithuania (Republic of)
LZA-LZZ	Bulgaria (Republic of)
L2A-L9Z	Argentine Republic
MAA-MZZ	United Kingdom of Great Britain and Northern Ireland
NAA-NZZ	**United States of America**
OAA-OCZ	Peru
ODA-ODZ	Lebanon
OEA-OEZ	Austria
OFA-OJZ	Finland
OKA-OLZ	Czech Republic
OMA-OMZ	Slovak Republic
ONA-OTZ	Belgium
OUA-OZZ	Denmark
PAA-PIZ	Netherlands (Kingdom of the)
PJA-PJZ	Netherlands (Kingdom of the) - Netherlands Antilles
PKA-POZ	Indonesia (Republic of)
PPA-PYZ	Brazil (Federative Republic of)
PZA-PZZ	Suriname (Republic of)
P2A-P2Z	Papua New Guinea
P3A-P3Z	Cyprus (Republic of)
P4A-P4Z	Netherlands (Kingdom of the) - Aruba
P5A-P9Z	Democratic People's Republic of Korea
RAA-RZZ	Russian Federation
SAA-SMZ	Sweden
SNA-SRZ	Poland (Republic of)
SSA-SSM	Egypt (Arab Republic of)
SSN-STZ	Sudan (Republic of the)
SUA-SUZ	Egypt (Arab Republic of)
SVA-SZZ	Greece
S2A-S3Z	Bangladesh (People's Republic of)
S5A-S5Z	Slovenia (Republic of)
S6A-S6Z	Singapore (Republic of)
S7A-S7Z	Seychelles (Republic of)
S8A-S8Z	South Africa (Republic of)
S9A-S9Z	Sao Tome and Principe (Democratic Republic of)

TAA-TCZ	Turkey
TDA-TDZ	Guatemala (Republic of)
TEA-TEZ	Costa Rica
TFA-TFZ	Iceland
TGA-TGZ	Guatemala (Republic of)
THA-THZ	France
TIA-TIZ	Costa Rica
TJA-TJZ	Cameroon (Republic of)
TKA-TKZ	France
TLA-TLZ	Central African Republic
TMA-TMZ	France
TNA-TNZ	Congo (Republic of the)
TOA-TQZ	France
TRA-TRZ	Gabonese Republic
TSA-TSZ	Tunisia
TTA-TTZ	Chad (Republic of)
TUA-TUZ	Côte d'Ivoire (Republic of)
TVA-TXZ	France
TYA-TYZ	Benin (Republic of)
TZA-TZZ	Mali (Republic of)
T2A-T2Z	Tuvalu
T3A-T3Z	Kiribati (Republic of)
T4A-T4Z	Cuba
T5A-T5Z	Somali Democratic Republic
T6A-T6Z	Afghanistan (Islamic State of)
T7A-T7Z	San Marino (Republic of)
T8A-T8Z	Palau (Republic of)
UAA-UIZ	Russian Federation
UJA-UMZ	Uzbekistan (Republic of)
UNA-UQZ	Kazakhstan (Republic of)
URA-UZZ	Ukraine
VAA-VGZ	Canada
VHA-VNZ	Australia
VOA-VOZ	Canada
VPA-VQZ	United Kingdom of Great Britain and Northern Ireland
VRA-VRZ	China (People's Republic of) - Hong Kong
VSA-VSZ	United Kingdom of Great Britain and Northern Ireland
VTA-VWZ	India (Republic of)
VXA-VYZ	Canada
VZA-VZZ	Australia
V2A-V2Z	Antigua and Barbuda
V3A-V3Z	Belize
V4A-V4Z	Saint Kitts and Nevis
V5A-V5Z	Namibia (Republic of)
V6A-V6Z	Micronesia (Federated States of)

V7A-V7Z	Marshall Islands (Republic of the)
V8A-V8Z	Brunei Darussalam
WAA-WZZ	**United States of America**
XAA-XIZ	Mexico
XJA-XOZ	Canada
XPA-XPZ	Denmark
XQA-XRZ	Chile
XSA-XSZ	China (People's Republic of)
XTA-XTZ	Burkina Faso
XUA-XUZ	Cambodia (Kingdom of)
XVA-XVZ	Viet Nam (Socialist Republic of)
XWA-XWZ	Lao People's Democratic Republic
XXA-XXZ	China (People's Republic of) - Macao (WRC-07)
XYA-XZZ	Myanmar (Union of)
YAA-YAZ	Afghanistan (Islamic State of)
YBA-YHZ	Indonesia (Republic of)
YIA-YIZ	Iraq (Republic of)
YJA-YJZ	Vanuatu (Republic of)
YKA-YKZ	Syrian Arab Republic
YLA-YLZ	Latvia (Republic of)
YMA-YMZ	Turkey
YNA-YNZ	Nicaragua
YOA-YRZ	Romania
YSA-YSZ	El Salvador (Republic of)
YTA-YUZ	Serbia (Republic of) (WRC-07)
YVA-YYZ	Venezuela (Republic of)
Y2A-Y9Z	Germany (Federal Republic of)
ZAA-ZAZ	Albania (Republic of)
ZBA-ZJZ	United Kingdom of Great Britain and Northern Ireland
ZKA-ZMZ	New Zealand
ZNA-ZOZ	United Kingdom of Great Britain and Northern Ireland
ZPA-ZPZ	Paraguay (Republic of)
ZQA-ZQZ	United Kingdom of Great Britain and Northern Ireland
ZRA-ZUZ	South Africa (Republic of)
ZVA-ZZZ	Brazil (Federative Republic of)
Z2A-Z2Z	Zimbabwe (Republic of)
Z3A-Z3Z	The Former Yugoslav Republic of Macedonia
2AA-2ZZ	United Kingdom of Great Britain and Northern Ireland
3AA-3AZ	Monaco (Principality of)
3BA-3BZ	Mauritius (Republic of)
3CA-3CZ	Equatorial Guinea (Republic of)
3DA-3DM	Swaziland (Kingdom of)
3DN-3DZ	Fiji (Republic of)
3EA-3FZ	Panama (Republic of)
3GA-3GZ	Chile

3HA-3UZ	China (People's Republic of)
3VA-3VZ	Tunisia
3WA-3WZ	Viet Nam (Socialist Republic of)
3XA-3XZ	Guinea (Republic of)
3YA-3YZ	Norway
3ZA-3ZZ	Poland (Republic of)
4AA-4CZ	Mexico
4DA-4IZ	Philippines (Republic of the)
4JA-4KZ	Azerbaijani Republic
4LA-4LZ	Georgia (Republic of)
4MA-4MZ	Venezuela (Republic of)
4OA-4OZ	Montenegro (Republic of) (WRC-07)
4PA-4SZ	Sri Lanka (Democratic Socialist Republic of)
4TA-4TZ	Peru
4UA-4UZ	United Nations
4VA-4VZ	Haiti (Republic of)
4WA-4WZ	Democratic Republic of Timor-Leste (WRC-03)
4XA-4XZ	Israel (State of)
4YA-4YZ	International Civil Aviation Organization
4ZA-4ZZ	Israel (State of)
5AA-5AZ	Libya (Socialist People's Libyan Arab Jamahiriya)
5BA-5BZ	Cyprus (Republic of)
5CA-5GZ	Morocco (Kingdom of)
5HA-5IZ	Tanzania (United Republic of)
5JA-5KZ	Colombia (Republic of)
5LA-5MZ	Liberia (Republic of)
5NA-5OZ	Nigeria (Federal Republic of)
5PA-5QZ	Denmark
5RA-5SZ	Madagascar (Republic of)
5TA-5TZ	Mauritania (Islamic Republic of)
5UA-5UZ	Niger (Republic of the)
5VA-5VZ	Togolese Republic
5WA-5WZ	Samoa (Independent State of)
5XA-5XZ	Uganda (Republic of)
5YA-5ZZ	Kenya (Republic of)
6AA-6BZ	Egypt (Arab Republic of)
6CA-6CZ	Syrian Arab Republic
6DA-6JZ	Mexico
6KA-6NZ	Korea (Republic of)
6OA-6OZ	Somali Democratic Republic
6PA-6SZ	Pakistan (Islamic Republic of)
6TA-6UZ	Sudan (Republic of the)
6VA-6WZ	Senegal (Republic of)
6XA-6XZ	Madagascar (Republic of)
6YA-6YZ	Jamaica

6ZA-6ZZ	Liberia (Republic of)
7AA-7IZ	Indonesia (Republic of)
7JA-7NZ	Japan
7OA-7OZ	Yemen (Republic of)
7PA-7PZ	Lesotho (Kingdom of)
7QA-7QZ	Malawi
7RA-7RZ	Algeria (People's Democratic Republic of)
7SA-7SZ	Sweden
7TA-7YZ	Algeria (People's Democratic Republic of)
7ZA-7ZZ	Saudi Arabia (Kingdom of)
8AA-8IZ	Indonesia (Republic of)
8JA-8NZ	Japan
8OA-8OZ	Botswana (Republic of)
8PA-8PZ	Barbados
8QA-8QZ	Maldives (Republic of)
8RA-8RZ	Guyana
8SA-8SZ	Sweden
8TA-8YZ	India (Republic of)
8ZA-8ZZ	Saudi Arabia (Kingdom of)
9AA-9AZ	Croatia (Republic of)
9BA-9DZ	Iran (Islamic Republic of)
9EA-9FZ	Ethiopia (Federal Democratic Republic of)
9GA-9GZ	Ghana
9HA-9HZ	Malta
9IA-9JZ	Zambia (Republic of)
9KA-9KZ	Kuwait (State of)
9LA-9LZ	Sierra Leone
9MA-9MZ	Malaysia
9NA-9NZ	Nepal
9OA-9TZ	Democratic Republic of the Congo
9UA-9UZ	Burundi (Republic of)
9VA-9VZ	Singapore (Republic of)
9WA-9WZ	Malaysia
9XA-9XZ	Rwandese Republic
9YA-9ZZ	Trinidad and Tobago

Third-Party Communications and Amateur Radio

If all of this information about ham radios is somewhat intimidating, do not despair. "You" can still use ham radios for communications without being a licensed operator. Yes, you do have to have a ham license in order to legally transmit by ham equipment (or be under the direct supervision of someone else who is licensed), but there is an alternative – third-party communication.

31

Third-party communications occur when a licensed operator sends either written or verbal messages on behalf of unlicensed persons or organizations. There are two "controls" on third-party communication.

First, the communication must be noncommercial and of a personal nature. Asking a ham operator to contact another ham operator located in an area just hit by tornados and, because of being without power, phones do not work in Grandma Sally's city so you can check up on her, is okay. Asking a ham to send a message out that you have an old Chevy for sale would not be okay.

Second, the message must be going to a permitted area. Transmitting from a US location to another US location is okay, but transmitting from the US to another country may not. Because third-party communications bypass a country's normal telephone and postal systems, many foreign governments forbid such communications. In order to transmit from one country to another, the other country must have signed a third-party agreement with the US. What follows is a list of those countries that do have third-party a communications agreement with the US.

V2	Antigua / Barbuda
LU	Argentina
VK	Australia
V3	Belize
CP	Bolivia
T9	Bosnia-Herzegovina
PY	Brazil
VE	Canada
CE	Chile
HK	Colombia
D6	Comoros (Federal Islamic Republic of)
TI	Costa Rica
CO	Cuba
HI	Dominican Republic
J7	Dominica
HC	Ecuador
YS	El Salvador
C5	Gambia, The
9G	Ghana
J3	Grenada
TG	Guatemala
8R	Guyana
HH	Haiti
HR	Honduras
4X	Israel
6Y	Jamaica
JY	Jordan

EL	Liberia
V7	Marshall Islands
XE	Mexico
V6	Micronesia, Federated States of
YN	Nicaragua
HP	Panama
ZP	Paraguay
OA	Peru
DU	Philippines
VR6	Pitcairn Island
V4	St. Christopher / Nevis
J6	St. Lucia
J8	St. Vincent and the Grenadines
9L	Sierra Leone
ZS	South Africa
3DA	Swaziland
9Y	Trinidad / Tobago
TA	Turkey
GB	United Kingdom
CX	Uruguay
YV	Venezuela
4U1ITUITU	Geneva
4U1VICVIC	Vienna

Remember, before TSHTF, keep your pantry well stocked, your powder dry, and your batteries fully charged. 73

APPENDIX A

American Radio Relay League

Affiliated Amateur Radio Clubs in

Maine

ARRL Affiliated Club	**Wide Area Amateur Radio Network**
City	Acton, ME
Call Sign	WA1ARN
Section	ME
Links	www.wa1arn.net

ARRL Affiliated Club	**Androscoggin Amateur Radio Club**
City	Auburn, ME
Call Sign	W1NPP
Section	ME
Links	www.w1npp.org/

ARRL Affiliated Club	**Yankee Amateur Radio Club Inc.**
City	Augusta, ME
Call Sign	KB1IDI
Section	ME
Links	www.yarcme.org

ARRL Affiliated Club	**Ellsworth Amateur Wireless Association**
City	Bar Harbor, ME
Call Sign	W1TU
Section	ME
Links	www.w1tu.org or www.eawa.org

ARRL Affiliated Club	**Saint Croix Valley Amateur Radio Club**
City	Calais, ME
Call Sign	WW1IE
Section	ME
Links	www.stcroixvalleyamateurradioclub.org

ARRL Affiliated Club	**Blackstrap Repeater Association**
City	Cape Elizabeth, ME
Call Sign	K1GAX
Section	ME

ARRL Affiliated Club	**Augusta Amateur Radio Association**
City	Farmingdale, ME
Call Sign	W1TLC
Section	ME

ARRL Affiliated Club	**St. John Valley Amateur Radio Association**
City	Fort Kent, ME
Section	ME
Links	www.sjvara.org

ARRL Affiliated Club	**Pine State Amateur Radio Club**
City	Holden, ME
Call Sign	N1ME
Section	ME
Links	www.n1me.com/

ARRL Affiliated Club	**Kennebec Amateur Radio Society**
City	Kents Hill, ME
Call Sign	W1PIG
Section	ME
Links	k1pig.homestead.com/repeaters.html

ARRL Affiliated Club	**Merrymeeting Amateur Radio Association**
City	Phippsburg, ME
Call Sign	KS1R
Section	ME
Links	www.ks1r.net

ARRL Affiliated Club	**Portland Amateur Wireless Association**
City	Portland, ME
Call Sign	W1KVI
Section	ME
Links	www.pawa-maine.org

ARRL Affiliated Club	**Pen Bay Amateur Radio Club, Inc.**
City	Washington, ME
Call Sign	W1PBR
Section	ME
Links	penbayarc.org

ARRL Affiliated Club	**Wireless Society of Southern Maine**
City	Westbrook, ME
Call Sign	WS1SM
Section	ME
Links	www.qsl.net/ws1sm

ARRL Affiliated Club	**Yarmouth Radio Club Inc.**
City	Yarmouth, ME
Call Sign	W1YAR
Section	ME
Links	www.YarmouthRadioClub.org

APPENDIX B

Amateur Radio License Holders

in

Maine
(by City)

FCC Amateur Radio Licenses in Abbot

Call Sign: N1XMW
Lesley Weymouth
Abbot ME 04406

Call Sign: KB1WPX
Ian A Maines
58 River Rd
Abbot ME 04406

FCC Amateur Radio Licenses in Abbot Village

Call Sign: N1NPM
Wanda J Chadwick
Rr 2 Box 149b
Abbot Village ME 04406

Call Sign: K1VAV
Alice K Weymouth
27 West Rd
Abbot Village ME 04406

Call Sign: WB1BWJ
Pamela R Weymouth
West Rd
Abbot Village ME 04406

Call Sign: N1GPI
Donna J Gesner
Abbot Village ME 04406

Call Sign: N1GPJ
Charles L Gesner Jr
Abbot Village ME 04406

Call Sign: WA1SBI
Howard C Weymouth
Abbot Village ME 04406

FCC Amateur Radio Licenses in Acton

Call Sign: WA1WOQ
Lawrence A Valliere
659 13th St
Acton ME 04001

Call Sign: KA1YPQ
Steven J Casey
2005 Acton Ridge Rd
Acton ME 04001

Call Sign: KB1DKS
Deborah J Casey
2005 Acton Ridge Rd
Acton ME 04001

Call Sign: KA1SEY
Deborah J Casey
2005 Acton Ridge Rd
Acton ME 04001

Call Sign: KB1NZM
Joshua S Gore
23 Birchwood Lane
Acton ME 04001

Call Sign: KB1TCB
Daniel L Worcester
174 Buzzell Rd
Acton ME 04001

Call Sign: KB1NZO
William E Catanesye Jr
127 Heath Brook Dr
Acton ME 04001

Call Sign: KB1CAT
William E Catanesye Jr
127 Heath Brook Dr
Acton ME 04001

Call Sign: KB1QGS
James P Mckinley
47 Hopper Rd
Acton ME 040015803

Call Sign: KA1YAX
William J Bearse
Acton ME 04001

Call Sign: N1GDT
Larry F Emery
Acton ME 040010542

Call Sign: KB1NZL
Jennifer L Sayre
Acton ME 04001

Call Sign: KB1NZN
Benjamin C Gore
Acton ME 04001

Call Sign: KB1NZP
Peter R Holtby
Acton ME 04001

Call Sign: KB1OOL
Wide Area Amateur Radio
Network
Acton ME 04001

Call Sign: W0RMI
Jennifer L Sayre
Acton ME 04001

Call Sign: WA1ARN
Wide Area Amateur Radio
Network
Acton ME 04001

Call Sign: KB1RKB
Jane Runnels
Acton ME 04001

FCC Amateur Radio Licenses in Addison

Call Sign: KR4ZY
Thomas Davis Jr
283 Cape Split Rd
Addison ME 04606

Call Sign: N1QLL
Gerald A Metz
61 Cape Split Road
Addison ME 046063600

Call Sign: WA1KCW
Charles Zatrepalek
Riverbend 9
Addison ME 04606

Call Sign: KA1MSP
Paul C Meyer
Addison ME 04606

**FCC Amateur Radio
Licenses in Albany**

Call Sign: KB1NJJ
Dana A Dyke
1153 Hunts Corner Rd
Albany ME 04217

**FCC Amateur Radio
Licenses in Albany
Township**

Call Sign: KA1HAU
Gary M Inman
829 Flat Rd
Albany Twp ME 04217

**FCC Amateur Radio
Licenses in Albion**

Call Sign: KB1MOG
John F Rolfson
301 Barnes Rd
Albion ME 04910

Call Sign: N1QAP
Brent C Barstow
241 Belfast Rd
Albion ME 04910

Call Sign: KA1AWB
Karen A Noyes Moody
Dutton Pond Rd Box 1945
Albion ME 04910

Call Sign: KB1BJH
Lynnda H Sawtelle
246 Hussey Rd
Albion ME 04910

Call Sign: KB1BJU
Deanna L Sawtelle
246 Hussey Rd
Albion ME 04910

Call Sign: KT1W
Timothy D Sawtelle
246 Hussey Rd
Albion ME 04910

Call Sign: N1XTD
Keith H Friedrich
Box 4780 Knights Rd
Albion ME 04910

Call Sign: KB1SLC
Michael J Clark
126 Winslow Rd
Albion ME 04910

Call Sign: KM1O
Michael J Clark
126 Winslow Rd
Albion ME 04910

Call Sign: WA2UMO
Arthur F Schwab
Albion ME 04910

Call Sign: KB1KRL
David E Rundlett
Albion ME 04910

Call Sign: KB1NPX
Nancy A Wolff

Albion ME 04910

**FCC Amateur Radio
Licenses in Alexander**

Call Sign: KB1HXC
Kenneth J Colson Jr
35 Berry Rd
Alexander ME 04694

Call Sign: WA1GKL
William C Holst
Rfd 1 Box 1449
Alexander ME 04694

Call Sign: KB1SAG
Weibley J Dean Ii
35 Cedar Lane
Alexander ME 04694

Call Sign: W1LH
Roger W Holst
70 Cooper Rd
Alexander ME 04694

Call Sign: KA1OBD
Mavis E Snyder
511 Cooper Rd
Alexander ME 04694

Call Sign: N1VNY
Marilyn D Dwelley
543 Cooper Rd
Alexander ME 046946326

Call Sign: W1DEY
Lloyd T Dwelley
543 Cooper Rd
Alexander ME 046946326

Call Sign: W1UH
Dennis L Snyder
784 Cooper Rd
Alexander ME 04694

Call Sign: K1QA
Iamoka Railroad Wireless
Association
240 Davis Rd
Alexander ME 04694

Call Sign: W0AQ
Charles E Dix
240 Davis Road
Alexander ME 04694

Call Sign: KB1KII
Alex W Henry Jr
24 Pine Tree Shore
Alexander ME 04694

Call Sign: WA4KEO
Pedro I Ceijas
203 S Princeton Rd
Alexander ME 04694

Call Sign: KB1IZG
Saint Croix Valley Amateur
Radio Club
203 S Princeton Rd
Alexander ME 04694

Call Sign: WW1IE
Saint Croix Valley Amateur
Radio Club
203 S Princeton Rd
Alexander ME 04694

Call Sign: KB1KYI
Saint Croix Valley Amateur
Radio Club
203 S Princeton Rd
Alexander ME 04694

Call Sign: W1SCV
Saint Croix Valley Amateur
Radio Club
203 S Princeton Rd
Alexander ME 04694

**FCC Amateur Radio
Licenses in Alfred**

Call Sign: KB1TZB
Jean Paul Ferland
75 Alewive Rd
Alfred ME 04002

Call Sign: KB1SFN
Arin J Auger
360 Back Rd
Alfred ME 04002

Call Sign: W1JTS
Douglas J Spencer
Rfd 2 Box 105
Alfred ME 04002

Call Sign: N1CMU
William R Croninger
Rfd 1 Box 267
Alfred ME 04002

Call Sign: KB5GZ
Jack M Cox
Rr 1 Box 35c
Alfred ME 04002

Call Sign: WD5ILI
Elizabeth D Cox
Rr 1 Box 35c
Alfred ME 04002

Call Sign: N1CCJ
Dan M Ihle
Rfd 2 Box 67
Alfred ME 04002

Call Sign: KB1VUI
Mitchell C Cyr
52 Cyr Dr
Alfred ME 04002

Call Sign: KB1QOH
David S Migneault

411 Mouse Ln
Alfred ME 04002

Call Sign: WB9KVD
Jack W Ham
13 Windsor Dr
Alfred ME 04002

Call Sign: N9PMF
Catherine J Ham
13 Windsor Drive
Alfred ME 04002

Call Sign: KA1ZRU
Philip R Genest
Alfred ME 04002

Call Sign: KF6VFH
Eric S Burgett
Alfred ME 04002

Call Sign: KF6VFI
Lori A Bennett Tetrick
Alfred ME 040020011

Call Sign: KL7GF
Albert J Heinrich
Alfred ME 040020159

Call Sign: WC1AAP
County Courthouse York
County Civil Emergency
Preparedness
Alfred ME 04002

Call Sign: KB1ONE
John L Josserand Jr
Alfred ME 04002

Call Sign: KB1PRF
David R Vanasse
Alfred ME 04002

Call Sign: KB1VUH
Kenneth F Hoose

Alfred ME 04002

FCC Amateur Radio Licenses in Alna

Call Sign: N1XQB
Larry D Cilley
188 Dock Road
Alna ME 04535

Call Sign: N1YII
Linda S Morris
841 West Alna Road
Alna ME 04535

FCC Amateur Radio Licenses in Amherst

Call Sign: W1PRM
Paul R Macomber
11 Ridge Lane
Amherst ME 04605

FCC Amateur Radio Licenses in Amity

Call Sign: KB1EAN
Patricia A Miller
1131 Estabrook Rd
Amity ME 04471

Call Sign: N1PAM
Patricia A Miller
1131 Estabrook Rd
Amity ME 04471

Call Sign: KC0TTY
Kevin A Lundy
784 Us Route One
Amity ME 04471

FCC Amateur Radio Licenses in Andover

Call Sign: KB1VUZ
Scott L Owings
Andover ME 04216

FCC Amateur Radio Licenses in Anson

Call Sign: WB1CXV
Ronald H Gallant
1 Beane St
Anson ME 04911

Call Sign: WB1CVL
Blanchard G Hupper
Rfd 1 Box 2030
Anson ME 04911

Call Sign: N1GJA
Richard P Plourd
Rr 1 Box 2560
Anson ME 04911

Call Sign: N1URU
Lloyd E Hardy
Rr 01 Box 860
Anson ME 04911

Call Sign: KC1NA
Robert E Demchak
790 Horseback Rd
Anson ME 04911

Call Sign: KE6IOY
Margaret A Demchak
790 Horseback Rd
Anson ME 04911

Call Sign: N1YUI
William J O Sullivan
Anson ME 04911

Call Sign: KB1OCW
William E St Peter
Anson ME 04911

FCC Amateur Radio Licenses in Appleton

Call Sign: KB1KPX
Bruce A Madara
Appleton Ridge Rd
Appleton ME 04862

Call Sign: N1UHK
Patricia A Kennedy
2509 Appleton Ridge Road
Appleton ME 04862

Call Sign: N1UBU
Edward R Kennedy
2509 Applrton Ridge Road
Appleton ME 04862

Call Sign: KA1UKY
Timothy J Pulsifer
Rr 1 Box 1730
Appleton ME 04862

Call Sign: KA1ZFT
Lloyd E Leigher
442 Guinea Ridge Rd
Appleton ME 04862

Call Sign: KA1QNQ
Charles A Woodman
1426 Searsmont Rd
Appleton ME 04862

Call Sign: KB1NDM
Chris K Conner
1761 Senebel Rd
Appleton ME 04862

Call Sign: AA1JU
Robert H Tiews
405 Town Hill Road
Appleton ME 04862

Call Sign: AA1JV
Thalia Hearne

405 Town Hill Road
Appleton ME 04862

FCC Amateur Radio Licenses in Argyle

Call Sign: N1YAQ
Willard C Corliss Jr
1376 Southgate Rd
Argyle ME 04468

FCC Amateur Radio Licenses in Argyle Township

Call Sign: KB1GAR
Joseph C Levesque
2901 Edinburg Rd
Argyle Twp ME 04468

Call Sign: N1ZMT
Brent F White
1036 Southgate Rd
Argyle Twp ME 04468

Call Sign: KB2LXP
Bruce D Herbert
357 Argyle Rd.
Argyle Twp. ME 04468

FCC Amateur Radio Licenses in Arrowsic

Call Sign: KB1OWC
John L White Sr
46 Arrowsic Rd
Arrowsic ME 04530

Call Sign: KB1SYT
Kip Stone
461 Bald Head Rd
Arrowsic ME 04530

Call Sign: W1FPZ
John F Rollins

21 Bald Head Road
Arrowsic ME 04530

Call Sign: N1PL
Paul Kalkstein
42 Doubling Point Rd
Arrowsic ME 04530

Call Sign: KB1SCV
Heather K Baker
12 Sirois Rd
Arrowsic ME 04530

FCC Amateur Radio Licenses in Arundel

Call Sign: W1HZY
Paul F Mc Carron
58 Arundel Rd
Arundel ME 04046

Call Sign: W1IY
Paul F Mc Carron
58 Arundel Rd
Arundel ME 04046

Call Sign: KA1GOO
Joseph P Bouchard
8 Arundel Woods Dr
Arundel ME 04046

Call Sign: N1MZR
Kelly J Demers
372 Curtis Rd
Arundel ME 04005

Call Sign: N1LKZ
James L Mc Kenzie Jr
13 Foxcroft Lane
Arundel ME 04046

Call Sign: WB9EIU
Gerald J Williamson
6 Katie Lane
Arundel ME 04046

Call Sign: W1AWZ
Gerald J Williamson
6 Katie Lane
Arundel ME 04046

Call Sign: KB1IMX
Daren W Keller
42 Kayla Dr
Arundel ME 04046

Call Sign: N1WFH
Daniel L Dubois
86 Liberty Acres Dr
Arundel ME 04046

Call Sign: KB1VUX
Ryan P Connary
83 New Rd
Arundel ME 04046

Call Sign: KA1VMK
Bernard P Valliere
219 New Rd
Arundel ME 04046

Call Sign: N5YXK
Michael J Sherwood
48 Riverwynde Dr
Arundel ME 04046

Call Sign: W1BCX
David E Campbell
19 Sinnott Rd.
Arundel ME 04046

Call Sign: KB1VPE
Michelle A Sherwood
18 Windward Lane
Arundel ME 04046

FCC Amateur Radio Licenses in Ashland

Call Sign: KB1EJS

David H Gordon
45 Garfield Rd
Ashland ME 04732

Call Sign: K1WJK
Ernest H Weaver
57 Main Street
Ashland ME 047320196

Call Sign: KF6FLX
Harold L Sutherland
Ashland ME 04732

Call Sign: N1UYC
Artemas O Coffin
Ashland ME 04732

Call Sign: N1UYH
Rosemary M Coffin
Ashland ME 047320042

FCC Amateur Radio Licenses in Athens

Call Sign: K1III
Joseph C Chandler
Box 4074d
Athens ME 04912

Call Sign: K1DDC
Robert S Turnbull
34 Main Street
Athens ME 04912

Call Sign: W1REZ
Raymond F Bohmer
242 Stickney Hill Rd
Athens ME 049124114

Call Sign: KB1OBP
Bernadette C Breault
26 Valley Rd
Athens ME 04912

Call Sign: KB1OCX

Joseph G Breault
26 Valley Rd
Athens ME 04912

Call Sign: KB1OBM
Nathaniel B Foss
Athens ME 04912

Call Sign: KB1OBN
Eric A Foss
Athens ME 04912

FCC Amateur Radio Licenses in Atkinson

Call Sign: WA2CIQ
Richard A Gallison
136 Dyer Rd
Atkinson ME 04426

Call Sign: NC1Y
Daniel W Juska
204 Maple Rd
Atkinson ME 044266016

Call Sign: KA1EFL
Mark L Kinney
106 Merrill Rd
Atkinson ME 04426

FCC Amateur Radio Licenses in Auburn

Call Sign: N1YIV
Gregory K Sawyer
83 Amberley Way
Auburn ME 04210

Call Sign: N0BAR
Bryce A Royal
710 Beech Hill Road
Auburn ME 04210

Call Sign: N1WBJ
George E Tarbox

26 Bolster St
Auburn ME 04210

Call Sign: W1EZR
Bernard R Langley
Rfd 4 Box 208
Auburn ME 04210

Call Sign: KA1RQG
David L Nadeau
Rt 4 Box 297a
Auburn ME 04210

Call Sign: KA1NXC
Ralph R Perkins Jr
208 Broad St
Auburn ME 04210

Call Sign: N1NSH
Maurice A Raymond
231 Broad St
Auburn ME 04210

Call Sign: KB1OSA
Brian J Pelletier
253 Broad St
Auburn ME 04210

Call Sign: K1GHP
Brian J Pelletier
253 Broad St
Auburn ME 04210

Call Sign: N1TGS
Jodd P Bowles
60 Broadview Ave
Auburn ME 04210

Call Sign: K1PEH
Jonathan F Whitmore
45 Candleberry Dr
Auburn ME 04210

Call Sign: KE4TIZ
Timothy E Burdick

20 Cherry Vale Circle
Auburn ME 04210

Call Sign: N1YTK
Gerard J Cyr
14 Chestnut St
Auburn ME 042105487

Call Sign: N1KLJ
Brian D Snow
35 Clover Ln
Auburn ME 04210

Call Sign: KB1TPH
James A Bois
2 Colonial Way
Auburn ME 04210

Call Sign: W1OKS
Edward M Fahey Jr
24 Colonial Way
Auburn ME 04210

Call Sign: N1NIM
Harold E Hersey
374 Court St
Auburn ME 04210

Call Sign: K1ACR
Anthony C Redes
271 Court St Apt 6
Auburn ME 04210

Call Sign: N1CSW
Claire G White
108 Cove Rd
Auburn ME 04210

Call Sign: KQ1D
Wallace H White
Cove Rd
Auburn ME 04210

Call Sign: KB1IEC
James K Gahagan

93 Crest Ave
Auburn ME 04210

Call Sign: KB1WIA
Savannah F Larsen
42 Damy Dr Apt 120
Auburn ME 04210

Call Sign: N1MBW
Otis H Nelson
45 Damy Dr Apt 65
Auburn ME 04210

Call Sign: KB1VKA
Cameron S Mcgary
511 Danville Corner Road
Auburn ME 04210

Call Sign: KA1NTV
Michael P Nicolaides
14 Dexter Ave
Auburn ME 04210

Call Sign: WB1CTR
Michael A Poto
29 Dexter Ave
Auburn ME 04210

Call Sign: N1AKQ
Arthur G Laird
43 Elmwood Rd
Auburn ME 04210

Call Sign: KA1RSR
James M Smith
18 Enfield St
Auburn ME 04210

Call Sign: N1OSZ
Robert G Cavanagh
127 Field Ave.
Auburn ME 04210

Call Sign: WB1DUV
Arthur J Vanier Jr

178 Gamage Ave
Auburn ME 04210

Call Sign: KA1JXV
Milton G Farris Jr
1100 Garfield Rd
Auburn ME 04210

Call Sign: KB1VPH
Joseph R Fournier
68 Gill Street Apt 2
Auburn ME 04210

Call Sign: KB1EJJ
Ronald C Hopping
39 Gillander Ave
Auburn ME 042104507

Call Sign: WW1HOP
Ronald C Hopping
39 Gillander Avenue
Auburn ME 042104507

Call Sign: W1HOP
Ronald C Hopping
39 Gillander Avenue
Auburn ME 042104507

Call Sign: N1AKA
Russell P Freve
137 Harvard St
Auburn ME 04210

Call Sign: N1MRZ
Timothy J Henry
12 Hazel St Apt 1
Auburn ME 04210

Call Sign: KB1NJP
David G Lowe
68 High St Apt 2
Auburn ME 04210

Call Sign: WE1U
David G Lowe

68 High St Apt 2
Auburn ME 04210

Call Sign: KB1QEO
Luke L Vigneault
15 High St Apt 6
Auburn ME 04210

Call Sign: N2TFV
David G Lowe
68 High Street Apartment 2
Auburn ME 042105852

Call Sign: KB1JTC
Michael Staffenski
51 Hillsdale St
Auburn ME 04210

Call Sign: K1MST
Michael Staffenski
51 Hillsdale St
Auburn ME 04210

Call Sign: KB1LCC
Herbert Staffenski
51 Hillsdale St
Auburn ME 04210

Call Sign: N1WFN
Robert J L Italien Jr
19 Holly St.
Auburn ME 04210

Call Sign: N1TXB
George J St Hilaire
2424 Hotel Rd
Auburn ME 04210

Call Sign: N1LJO
Michael J Breton
1841 Hotel Road
Auburn ME 042108818

Call Sign: KA1NXB
Donald R Dean Jr

133 Howe
Auburn ME 04210

Call Sign: KB1FIA
Michael T Potvin
1280 Jordan School Road
Auburn ME 04210

Call Sign: KB1WRD
Raymond J Grady Iii
241 Lake St
Auburn ME 04210

Call Sign: KB1OJY
Shane J Campbell - Henning
425 Lake St
Auburn ME 04210

Call Sign: N1SYT
Marion S Sampson
115 Lake St.
Auburn ME 04210

Call Sign: KA5AWW
Larry R Gilbert
16 Lamplighter Circle
Auburn ME 04210

Call Sign: K1CXX
Richard C Huntress
27 Linden St
Auburn ME 04210

Call Sign: KB5SUD
Robert A Sessums
68 Madison St
Auburn ME 04210

Call Sign: N1KAT
William A Woodhead
68 Madison St
Auburn ME 04210

Call Sign: W1MFJ

Quarter Century Wireless
Association
68 Madison St
Auburn ME 04210

Call Sign: KB1KAC
Dominique L Pomerleau
256 Manley Rd
Auburn ME 04210

Call Sign: KB1KAD
Neil C Pomerleau
256 Manley Rd
Auburn ME 04210

Call Sign: WA1MED
Richard C Maxwell
11 Maple Point St
Auburn ME 04210

Call Sign: N1GLR
Charles E Kerr Jr
29 Marshall Ave
Auburn ME 04210

Call Sign: N1QHW
Joseph G Y Pelletier
1360 Minot Ave
Auburn ME 04210

Call Sign: KB1ALF
Thomas J Englehart Sr
1371 Minot Ave
Auburn ME 04210

Call Sign: W1QUI
George M Harris
59 Musket Drive
Auburn ME 04210

Call Sign: KB1HBD
Stephen J Lagueux
51 Northern Avenue
Heights Apt. 21
Auburn ME 04210

Call Sign: KB1OVU
Wayne L Frankhauser
53 Partridge Ln
Auburn ME 04210

Call Sign: KA1ROV
Davis B Carter
33 Pinewood Dr
Auburn ME 04210

Call Sign: KB1FOP
Steven E Cornett
162 Pleasant St
Auburn ME 04210

Call Sign: N4FPN
Raymond O Anderson
18 Plummer St 137
Auburn ME 04210

Call Sign: N1OWV
Randall P Dehetre
145 Poland Rd
Auburn ME 04210

Call Sign: KB1SUU
Andrew S Cluff
74 Poliquin Ave
Auburn ME 04210

Call Sign: N1HWT
Michael A Martel
1234 Pownal Rd
Auburn ME 04210

Call Sign: KB1HYV
Eric L Moore
191 Riverside Dr
Auburn ME 04210

Call Sign: KB1VFR
Matthew B Brodeur
83 Sixth St
Auburn ME 04210

Call Sign: KB1CIJ
Donald J Young
15 Sterling Rd
Auburn ME 042103729

Call Sign: W1KDZ
Clark H Dunlap
22 Sterling Rd
Auburn ME 04210

Call Sign: AD1RV
Robert V Damon
151 Stetson Rd
Auburn ME 04210

Call Sign: KA1JOL
Alvin H Kopp
200 Stetson Rd Apt 515
Auburn ME 04210

Call Sign: KB1NHC
Gerald R Lamontagne
10 Stevens Mill Park Rd
Auburn ME 04210

Call Sign: KB1BMM
Robert D Bruce
9 Summit St Apt B
Auburn ME 04210

Call Sign: N1KAY
Richard M Lewis
52 Taft Ave
Auburn ME 04210

Call Sign: N1TCL
David P Gahris
30 Tailwind Ct. Apt. 63c
Auburn ME 04210

Call Sign: N1AVJ
Paul F Jones
196 Trapp Rd
Auburn ME 04210

Call Sign: N1HUD
Richard J Pare Jr
193 Washington St
Auburn ME 04210

Call Sign: KB1QDP
Ronald M Watson
905 Washington St N
Auburn ME 04210

Call Sign: W1LPF
Ronald M Watson
905 Washington St N
Auburn ME 04210

Call Sign: KB1VBC
Aaron T Johnson
16 West Bates St
Auburn ME 04210

Call Sign: K1ATJ
Aaron T Johnson
16 West Bates St
Auburn ME 04210

Call Sign: N1BKD
Howard Feldman
33 Western Ave
Auburn ME 04210

Call Sign: W1HOW
Howard Feldman
33 Western Ave
Auburn ME 04210

Call Sign: N1MDL
Brian W Foss
155 Winter St
Auburn ME 04210

Call Sign: KA1HUE
Sarkis L Ahlijian
Auburn ME 04212

Call Sign: N8NDU
Jeffrey E Dettori
Auburn ME 042120742

Call Sign: W1NPP
Androscoggin Amateur
Radio Club Inc
Auburn ME 042120001

Call Sign: W1TT
Arnold W Chick
Auburn ME 042120385

Call Sign: KB1IJD
Kendall M Knowles
Auburn ME 042111191

Call Sign: KB1JBG
S Christina Thornton
Auburn ME 04212

Call Sign: K1PN
R Rex Thornton
Auburn ME 04212

FCC Amateur Radio Licenses in Augusta

Call Sign: KB1OWS
Emily Cyr
600 A Riverside Dr
Augusta ME 04330

Call Sign: W1RAH
Richard A Hyatt
47 Allenwood Park Road
Augusta ME 04330

Call Sign: KG0IZ
Walter W Gowen
53 B State St
Augusta ME 04330

Call Sign: AA1VJ
Walter W Gowen

53 B State St
Augusta ME 04330

Call Sign: KA1ULT
Justin M Hughes
7 Blaine Ave
Augusta ME 04330

Call Sign: W1KMN
Hugo B Eckman
9 Blaine Ave
Augusta ME 04330

Call Sign: KB1VJU
Pamela A Seltsam
7 Blaine Avenue
Augusta ME 04330

Call Sign: KC4STS
Timothy J Brady
Rr12 Box 1160
Augusta ME 04331

Call Sign: KA1DLX
Horace A Coskery
Rfd 10 Box 1307
Augusta ME 04330

Call Sign: KA1WLZ
Jeffrey L Bourque
Rr 7 Box 1407
Augusta ME 04330

Call Sign: WA1OQE
Howard S Gilley
Rfd 10 Box 145
Augusta ME 04330

Call Sign: KA1ZWZ
Benjamen R Tompkins
Rfd 4 Box 2900
Augusta ME 04330

Call Sign: KA1YNG
Michael S Kinney

Rfd 4 Box 3415
Augusta ME 04330

Call Sign: KA1ZVE
John F Hite
Rfd 3 Box 398
Augusta ME 04330

Call Sign: KA1JBD
Oakley E Woodward
Rfd 4 Box 625
Augusta ME 04330

Call Sign: N1WPX
Alexander D Smith
Rr 1 Box 7130
Augusta ME 04331

Call Sign: KA1LPV
Lloyd S Smith
Rfd 2 Box 76
Augusta ME 04330

Call Sign: W1DNI
Vincent E Volowski
Rr 7 Box 901
Augusta ME 04331

Call Sign: KB1EOD
Dale J Sanford
311 Burns Rd
Augusta ME 04330

Call Sign: N1BFH
Melicent B Versteeg
81 Church Hill Rd
Augusta ME 043309750

Call Sign: N1OYB
John C Versteeg
81 Church Hill Rd
Augusta ME 04330

Call Sign: N1ZXC
Janice M Turner

494 Church Hill Rd
Augusta ME 04330

Call Sign: N1TZR
Donald G Trask Jr
689 Church Hill Rd
Augusta ME 04330

Call Sign: N1XVF
Michelle M Trask
689 Church Hill Rd
Augusta ME 04330

Call Sign: KB1CZG
Rahvi Barnum
Box 1050 Churchill Rd
Augusta ME 04330

Call Sign: KB1PWJ
Roy T Jones
45 Commerce Dr
Augusta ME 04330

Call Sign: WA1LMA
Lawrence A Roy
16 Congress St
Augusta ME 04330

Call Sign: KB1IDI
Yankee Radio Club Inc
198 Cony St
Augusta ME 04330

Call Sign: KB1HPA
Steven F Ochmanski
197 Cony St Ext
Augusta ME 04330

Call Sign: KB1HPB
Jennifer J Ochmanski
197 Cony St Ext
Augusta ME 04330

Call Sign: N1JLZ
Paul D Gilley

182 Cony St Ext Apt 3
Augusta ME 04330

Call Sign: KQ1L
David A Hawke
198 Cony Street
Augusta ME 043305309

Call Sign: N1CMZ
Ronald L Dishman
312 Cross Hill Rd
Augusta ME 04330

Call Sign: KB1FHW
David P Smith
37 Davenport St
Augusta ME 043305812

Call Sign: WB1ALY
George E Davis Jr
28 Eastern Ave
Augusta ME 04330

Call Sign: KB1OWR
Nancy E Medeiros
60 Eastern Ave
Augusta ME 04330

Call Sign: N1VIB
Daniel S Collins
667 Eastern Ave
Augusta ME 04330

Call Sign: KB1ULB
Daniel S Durgin Sr
22 Eight Rod Rd
Augusta ME 04330

Call Sign: KB1NVE
Brandon W Keene
17 Fowler St
Augusta ME 04330

Call Sign: K1ADM
Alan D Mc Gary

102 Ganneston Drive
Augusta ME 04330

Call Sign: KA1NWV
Herbert F Mann Jr
42 Green St Apt 3
Augusta ME 043307435

Call Sign: N1NYU
Gautrey J Musk
14 Greenwood St
Augusta ME 04330

Call Sign: N1KMS
Michael J Doucette
26 Grove St
Augusta ME 04330

Call Sign: KB1CNG
Philip H Corbett
33 Hillcrest St
Augusta ME 04330

Call Sign: W1SIN
Carleton E Miller
49 Hutchinson Dr
Augusta ME 04330

Call Sign: N1KHT
Richard A Hook
55 Hutchinson Dr
Augusta ME 043306622

Call Sign: AB1JI
Richard A Hook
55 Hutchinson Dr
Augusta ME 043306622

Call Sign: KG1ZR
Richard A Hook
55 Hutchinson Dr
Augusta ME 043306622

Call Sign: KB1IEL
Michael A Harrington

2 James St
Augusta ME 04330

2059 N Belfast Ave
Augusta ME 043304366

646 Riverside Dr
Augusta ME 04330

Call Sign: W1BCA
Raymond C Knight
28 Knight Rd
Augusta ME 04330

Call Sign: KA1AWG
Robert R Ouellette
57 Newland Ave
Augusta ME 04330

Call Sign: KC9AIC
Joel A Epley
160 Riverside Drive
Augusta ME 04330

Call Sign: N1UMF
D Loren Fields
52 Lafayette St
Augusta ME 04330

Call Sign: KA1HMA
Joan M Ouellette
57 Newland Ave
Augusta ME 04330

Call Sign: KA1YGR
Michael W Fortin
61 S Grove St
Augusta ME 09330

Call Sign: KA1PMJ
Barbara A Scott
36 Linwood Ave
Augusta ME 04330

Call Sign: KB1LNM
Aaron W Selwood
17 Noth St
Augusta ME 04330

Call Sign: N1PNV
Marcel J Fortin Jr
61 S Grove St
Augusta ME 04330

Call Sign: W1JTH
Philip M Young
47 Longwood Ave
Augusta ME 04330

Call Sign: N1VYP
James A Trainor
43 Patterson
Augusta ME 04330

Call Sign: KB1ING
William J Mckenna
145 Sewall St
Augusta ME 04330

Call Sign: W1TGY
Dorothy I Young
47 Longwood Ave
Augusta ME 043304130

Call Sign: N1ITR
Frank R Naiman
121 Purinton Ave
Augusta ME 04330

Call Sign: KA1PJN
Michael W Scott
179 Spring Road
Augusta ME 04330

Call Sign: K1HCH
Merle I Auclair
3 Lyon Lane
Augusta ME 04330

Call Sign: N1LVR
Carolyn R Naiman
121 Purinton Ave
Augusta ME 04330

Call Sign: WA1ABB
William B Merrill Sr
11 Spring St
Augusta ME 04330

Call Sign: N1UJW
Catherine M Foster
3 Mayfair Cir
Augusta ME 04330

Call Sign: KA1YZW
Sarah A Viles
Rfd 3
Augusta ME 04330

Call Sign: KB1NXP
John E Baldacci
192 State St
Augusta ME 04330

Call Sign: KA1NEP
John W Sadler
54 N Belfast Ave
Augusta ME 04330

Call Sign: KZ1P
Richard W Horner
576 Riverside Dr Apt 18b
Augusta ME

Call Sign: KA1FBL
Philip G Tracy
9 Sunrise Cir
Augusta ME 04330

Call Sign: WB1AGP
Harland C Leighton Jr

Call Sign: N1VKQ
Joshua A Blanche

Call Sign: KB1NAT
Herbert T Bunker

5 Sunrise Circle
Augusta ME 04330

Call Sign: W1JB
Joseph G Jolda
1079 Tasker Road
Augusta ME 04330

Call Sign: W1SXY
Eugene B Dostie
56 Townsend Rd
Augusta ME 04330

Call Sign: KB1ITI
William A Goodwin Ii
12 Vaughn St
Augusta ME 04330

Call Sign: KA1VLC
Paul J Lerley
5 W Sewall St
Augusta ME 04330

Call Sign: KA1ZGP
Michael D Lerley
5 W Sewall St
Augusta ME 04330

Call Sign: KD1XM
Andre D Chabot
56 Washington St
Augusta ME 04330

Call Sign: KC1AC
Duane E Tracy
999 West River Rd
Augusta ME 04330

Call Sign: K1LOB
Gilfred J Parent
126 Western Ave #179
Augusta ME 04330

Call Sign: KB1HZW
Gilfred J Parent

126 Western Ave 179
Augusta ME 04330

Call Sign: W1RVV
Nelson Bigelow Jr
21 Western Ave Apt 1
Augusta ME 04331

Call Sign: N1UXQ
Donald L Kopyc
126 Western Ave.#163
Augusta ME 04330

Call Sign: AA1RT
Lawrence A Oches
5 Westwood Rd
Augusta ME 04330

Call Sign: N1ZSS
Matthew L Oches
5 Westwood Rd
Agusta ME 04330

Call Sign: KB1CRV
Brian A Oches
5 Westwood Rd
Augusta ME 04330

Call Sign: KB1DAZ
Mary M Oches
5 Westwood Rd
Augusta ME 04330

Call Sign: N5UYH
Phillip G Laird
30 Windy Street
Augusta ME 04330

Call Sign: KD6TAR
Margaret S Forsyth
99 Winthrop St
Augusta ME 04330

Call Sign: KA1MSB
Elaine R Badershall

17 Worcester St
Augusta ME 04330

Call Sign: KA1MSD
Roger C Badershall
17 Worcester St
Augusta ME 04330

Call Sign: K1IV
R E Myra Jr
Augusta ME 04332

Call Sign: KA1AWI
Richard B Theberge
Augusta ME 043325115

Call Sign: KB1CGL
Francis H Jodrey
Augusta ME 04338

Call Sign: KD1LG
Edward I Heath
Augusta ME 04332

Call Sign: N1CBA
John A Peterson Jr
Augusta ME 04330

Call Sign: N1JZZ
John J O Dea Iii
Augusta ME 04332

Call Sign: KB1LZW
George S White Ii
Augusta ME 04330

Call Sign: KB1ORM
Dennis J Young
Augusta ME 04332

Call Sign: W2NV
R E Myra Jr
Augusta ME 04332

Call Sign: K1JOD

John J O Dea Iii
Augusta ME 04332

FCC Amateur Radio Licenses in Bailey Island

Call Sign: KB1KPV
Carl J Cecil
1950 Harpswell Islands Rd
Bailey Island ME 04003

Call Sign: KA1JTO
Elizabeth J Jones
Ocean St
Bailey Island ME
040030160

Call Sign: KA1XY
Henry J Godbois
Bailey Island ME 04003

Call Sign: W1DYP
John Y Scruton
Bailey Island ME 04003

Call Sign: W2OLV
Lionel H Lawrie
Bailey Island ME 04003

Call Sign: WB2KSN
Lionel H Lawrie Iii
Bailey Island ME 04003

FCC Amateur Radio Licenses in Baileyville

Call Sign: KB1LMF
Robert A Harriman
5 2nd Ave
Baileyville ME 04694

Call Sign: KB1PMF
Robert A Harriman
5 2nd Ave
Baileyville ME 04694

Call Sign: KB1SZP
Carl V Mckain
179 Cooper Rd
Baileyville ME 04694

Call Sign: KA1WXN
Keith E Hanson
57 Maple St
Baileyville ME 04694

Call Sign: KD5LS
Kathleen M Payne
2296 S. Princeton Rd.
Baileyville ME 04694

Call Sign: W1QWW
Arnold E Fountain
21 Washington St
Baileyville ME 046940937

Call Sign: N1GXW
Frank A Gagner Sr
Baileyville ME 04694

Call Sign: N1OYA
Gary R Santerre
Baileyville ME 04694

Call Sign: N1UBT
Dale E Lingley
Baileyville ME 04694

Call Sign: WA1FZX
Michael C James
Baileyville ME 04694

Call Sign: KB1GEO
Michael C Sanford
Baileyville ME 046940165

Call Sign: KB1IHJ
Tammy L Sanford
Baileyville ME 04694

Call Sign: KB1LSK
Morris E Chase
Baileyville ME 04694

Call Sign: KB1QFD
John A Mcphee
Baileyville ME 04694

Call Sign: W1LGX
Dale E Lingley
Baileyville ME 04694

FCC Amateur Radio Licenses in Bangor

Call Sign: K1HXB
James E Downes
146 13th St
Bangor ME 04401

Call Sign: K1ONY
Alfred L Cormier
6h Birch Hill Estates
Bangor ME 04401

Call Sign: N1WAH
Edward W Treat
6 A St
Bangor ME 04401

Call Sign: N1FGQ
Kenneth H Myers
12 Adams St
Bangor ME 04401

Call Sign: N1CO
John W Mc Neely
16 Airedale Pl
Bangor ME 044012400

Call Sign: KB1OLN
Martha E Mcneely
16 Airedale Pl
Bangor ME 04401

Call Sign: N1RDO
Martha E Mcneely
16 Airedale Pl
Bangor ME 04401

Call Sign: KB1RET
Mihali A Bonatakis
205 Bolling Dr
Bangor ME 04401

Call Sign: N1IPB
Michael W Beal
Rr#3 Box 242
Bangor ME 04401

Call Sign: N1UCU
Wendy M Warren
92a Allen St.
Bangor ME 04401

Call Sign: KB1UEQ
Manoli A Bonatakis
205 Bolling Dr
Bangor ME 04401

Call Sign: KB1EIY
Cheryl L Bailey
Rr2 Box 4372
Bangor ME 04402

Call Sign: N1OQS
Jimmy D Mathews
16 Apple Ln
Bangor ME 04401

Call Sign: KB1KIR
Penobscot County Ares
14 Bomarc
Bangor ME 04401

Call Sign: N1MKT
Angie A Turner
Rr 02 Box 7370
Bangor ME 04401

Call Sign: KB1IZS
Dale A Horne
24 B St
Bangor ME 04401

Call Sign: WA1RES
Penobscot County Ares
14 Bomarc
Bangor ME 04401

Call Sign: K1DUI
William J Bendery
21 Boyd St - Apt 1311
Bangor ME 04401

Call Sign: KA1ZHV
Gigi Ho
72 Baldwin Dr
Bangor ME 04401

Call Sign: KB1JQK
Kevin D Spain
67 Boutelle Rd
Bangor ME 04401

Call Sign: W1RJR
John G Ryan
1850 Broadway
Bangor ME 04401

Call Sign: KB1KJH
Andrew C Spruce
80 Balsam Rd
Bangor ME 04401

Call Sign: K1KDS
Kevin D Spain
67 Boutelle Rd
Bangor ME 04401

Call Sign: KB1JHL
Jason E Dembowski
2381 Broadway
Bangor ME 04401

Call Sign: WB1GED
Earl R Kingsbury
G6 Birch Hill Estates
Bangor ME 04401

Call Sign: N1NEK
John A Rowe
Rfd 3 Box 1470
Bangor ME 04401

Call Sign: K7ABA
Andrew J Gray
686 Broadway Apt 5
Bangor ME 04402

Call Sign: KB1VZS
Brian A Hodgins
113 Birch St
Bangor ME 04401

Call Sign: N1QAV
Phyllis M Rowe
Rt 3 Box 1470
Bangor ME 04401

Call Sign: WD6GCD
Patrick L Grover
499 Broadway Pmb 221
Bangor ME 04401

Call Sign: N1JNS
Richard B Bendure Jr
300 Birch Street
Bangor ME 04401

Call Sign: W1OEN
Darwin E Turner
Rr 2 Box 2290
Bangor ME 04401

Call Sign: KA1GHJ
Alton F Wilcox
201 Buck
Bangor ME 04401

Call Sign: N1DE
Dennis A Mills
217 Burleigh Rd
Bangor ME 04401

Call Sign: KB1RHF
Joseph C Kellner
64 Catell St 3
Bangor ME 04401

Call Sign: KB1CNI
Stanley J Stewart
156 Cedar Street Apt 3
Bangor ME 04401

Call Sign: N1QPL
Donald M Frye Jr
330 Center
Bangor ME 04401

Call Sign: KA1BWH
Harvey E Byther
201-1 Center St
Bangor ME 044014839

Call Sign: KB1VEU
Sean D Heath
101 Center St Apt 4
Bangor ME 04401

Call Sign: WB1CXJ
Robert N Rosen
120 Clark Ave
Bangor ME 04401

Call Sign: KB1IQA
Eric N Wages
72 Cottage St
Bangor ME 04401

Call Sign: K1WRX
Eric N Wages
72 Cottage St
Bangor ME 04401

Call Sign: KB1JHK
Margaret C Michaels
72 Cottage St
Bangor ME 04401

Call Sign: K1IVJ
Nicholas J Brountas
73 Court St
Bangor ME 04401

Call Sign: KA1KDO
Willard J Foss
117 Court St Apt 405
Bangor ME 04461

Call Sign: KA1LYH
Philip H Smith
90 Crestmont Rd
Bangor ME 04401

Call Sign: KB1JAO
Joshua H Griffin
101 Crestmont Rd
Bangor ME 044015877

Call Sign: KB1EGP
Diane C Haslett
134 Cumberland St
Bangor ME 04401

Call Sign: W1JWH
Jared W Haslett
134 Cumberland St
Bangor ME 044015235

Call Sign: K1DCH
Diane C Haslett
134 Cumberland St
Bangor ME 04401

Call Sign: KB1OGZ
Peter A Bither
41 Davis Rd
Bangor ME 04401

Call Sign: AI1O
Peter A Bither
41 Davis Rd
Bangor ME 04401

Call Sign: N1EVN
Simon J Hassis
9 Dean St
Bangor ME 04401

Call Sign: N1GRN
Randall H Loring
90 Drew Ln
Bangor ME 04401

Call Sign: KB1SEM
Jared R Crane
40 Earle Ave
Bangor ME 04401

Call Sign: WA1UCV
Richard S Chatfield
31a Earle Ave
Bangor ME 04401

Call Sign: K1AHD
Clifford O Royal
46 East Summer
Bangor ME 04401

Call Sign: KB1UAR
Kevin S Olmstead
202 Essex St Rm 2
Bangor ME 04401

Call Sign: W1KEV
Kevin S Olmstead
202 Essex St Rm 2
Bangor ME 04401

Call Sign: KA8KGI
Anita L Mc Cormick
58 Everett St Apt 2
Bangor ME 04401

Call Sign: WB1GKL
Oma E Ingerson
66 Falvey St
Bangor ME 04401

Call Sign: KB1TOA
James E Frye
38 Fawn Ct
Bangor ME 04401

Call Sign: W1ZMO
Robert C White
8 Fenton Way
Bangor ME 044012536

Call Sign: W1IDN
Andrew W Marshall
17 Fenton Way
Bangor ME 044012537

Call Sign: KB2YDH
Richard W Mellerup
213 Fern St
Bangor ME 04401

Call Sign: N1QPN
Jennifer Lambert
75 Fifth St
Bangor ME 04401

Call Sign: WA1ERJ
Thomas W Lambert
75 Fifth St
Bangor ME 04401

Call Sign: KC8VRC
Robert J Lal
438 Finson Lot 5
Bangor ME 04401

Call Sign: N1NUY
Jean C Bellemer
666 Finson Rd Lot 282
Bangor ME 04401

Call Sign: KB1VES
Robert M Mcquoid
192 Forest Ave
Bangor ME 04401

Call Sign: N1YIL
John B Blalack
260 Forest Ave
Bangor ME 04401

Call Sign: KB1JDU
Allison W B Tunick
267 Forest Ave
Bangor ME 04401

Call Sign: N1TSH
Glenn S Harriman
11 Fort Knox Ave
Bangor ME 04401

Call Sign: N1UBW
Terry L Harriman
11 Fort Knox Ave
Bangor ME 04401

Call Sign: W1AGL
Barry L Darling
159 Fountain St
Bangor ME 04401

Call Sign: WB5WMY
Milledge B Lewis
112 Franklin St B9
Bangor ME 044014927

Call Sign: KB1WLS
Erick C Chambers
206 Fruit St
Bangor ME 04401

Call Sign: KA1BWK
Avon O Severance
24 G St
Bangor ME 04401

Call Sign: KC1YA
Dennis F Stubbs
194 Griffin Rd Apt 103
Bangor ME 04401

Call Sign: N1JRL
Phillip J Hurley
303 Hammond St Apt 25
Bangor ME 04402

Call Sign: N1JFR
Anthony R Randazzo
200 Hancock St Apt 402
Bangor ME 04401

Call Sign: WA1ZMQ
Robert B Palmer
315 Harlow Street #403
Bangor ME 04401

Call Sign: N1VTO
Michael C Belcher
10 Hersey Ave
Bangor ME 04401

Call Sign: KB1BOS
Eastern Maine Community
College Arc
354 Hogan Rd
Bangor ME 04401

Call Sign: KA1ESN
Neil F Comins
159 Howard St.
Bangor ME 04401

Call Sign: N1UYF
Brian A Charette
150 Husson Ave Apt 41
Bangor ME 04401

Call Sign: N1MNP
Catherine B Hunter
1 J St
Bangor ME 04401

Call Sign: N1XMT
John C Springer
120 Jackson St
Bangor ME 04401

Call Sign: N1UHB
Kurt M Anderson
23 James St
Bangor ME 04401

Call Sign: N1NQV
Casey O Henderson
45 Jefferson Street
Bangor ME 04401

Call Sign: KA1TYY
Steven F Scott
19 Joulett St
Bangor ME 04401

Call Sign: NG1D
Roger A Bloom
1000 Kenduskeag
Bangor ME 04401

Call Sign: KB1VFQ
David R Mcnulty
70 Kenduskeag Ave
Bangor ME 04401

Call Sign: KB1MOO
Daniel E Cassidy
151 Kenduskeag Ave
Bangor ME 04401

Call Sign: KB1MYF
Dina S Cassidy
151 Kenduskeag Ave
Bangor ME 04401

Call Sign: KB1AYI
Garrett D Speirs Iii
188 Kenduskeag Ave
Bangor ME 04401

Call Sign: N1ATO
James A Larner
619 Kenduskeag Ave
Bangor ME 04401

Call Sign: KA1NKZ
Lewis J Nutter
986 Kenduskeag Ave
Bangor ME 04401

Call Sign: KB1OGX
David E Cassidy
151 Kenduskeay Ave
Bangor ME 04401

Call Sign: W1LFZ
Richard L Nutter
19 Kossuth St
Bangor ME 04401

Call Sign: N1KGU
Earl R Johnson
24 Kossuth St
Bangor ME 04401

Call Sign: K1XVM
Drew N Baxter
21 Labarca Ln
Bangor ME 044012645

Call Sign: KB1IKM
Drew N Baxter
21 Laburca Ln
Bangor ME 044012645

Call Sign: KB1FSO
Kevin D Murch
97 Langley St
Bangor ME 04401

Call Sign: N1DAG
Kevin D Murch
97 Langley Street
Bangor ME 04401

Call Sign: N1AHE
Janice P Budden
60 Larkin
Bangor ME 04401

Call Sign: WB1DKO
Ronald B Budden
60 Larkin St
Bangor ME 04401

Call Sign: N1OJH
Thomas L Lambert
71 Larkin St
Bangor ME 04401

Call Sign: WE1J
Robert D Tomlinson
38 Leighton St
Bangor ME 04401

Call Sign: WB1GKH
Eleanor M Ducharme
99 Lincoln St
Bangor ME 04401

Call Sign: W1PCD
Danville S Webber
100 Linden St
Bangor ME 04401

Call Sign: N1DPA
C Peter Marini
7 M St
Bangor ME 04401

Call Sign: KB1SCA
Joshua E Perry
711 Main St Apt 5
Bangor ME 04401

Call Sign: KA1IJZ
George H Barr
55 Manners Ave
Bangor ME 044014554

Call Sign: WA1WZW
James A Hetley
42 Maple St
Bangor ME 04401

Call Sign: N1YGS
Bethany L Thompson
200 Maple St
Bangor ME 04401

Call Sign: W1VII
Edward B Fisk
204 Maple St
Bangor ME 04401

Call Sign: KB1NRI
Jeffrey P Collins
294 Maple St
Bangor ME 04401

Call Sign: W1JFF
Jeffrey P Collins
294 Maple St
Bangor ME 04401

Call Sign: KB1UAQ
Laurence G Hayward
9 March St Apt 7
Bangor ME 04401

Call Sign: W1LGH
Laurence G Hayward
9 March St Apt 7
Bangor ME 04401

Call Sign: N1KNH
Jeffrey L Allen
28 Molly Lane
Bangor ME 04401

Call Sign: KB1TXJ
James W Turner
29 Montgomery St
Bangor ME 04401

Call Sign: N1QPK
Alison R Carter
130 Moosehead Blvd
Bangor ME 04401

Call Sign: AA1IH
Charles E Hershey Jr
871 N Main St Lot 34
Bangor ME 044011223

Call Sign: KB1LDA
Richard P Ozog
202 Norfolk St
Bangor ME 04401

Call Sign: N1QDS
Paul C Salkaln
51 Norway Rd
Bangor ME 04401

Call Sign: KE9VJ
John E Koskie
235 Norway Rd
Bangor ME 04401

Call Sign: N1PVC
Jeffry W Fitch
846 Ohio St
Bangor ME 04401

Call Sign: WA2OUU
John C Schneck
2078 Ohio St
Bangor ME 044012019

Call Sign: KB1FEL
Kevin M Carman
178 Ohio St Apt 1
Bangor ME 044014740

Call Sign: W1DRJ
Keith E Hamilton
1030 Ohio St Apt 16
Bangor ME 04402

Call Sign: N5KGK
Lewis C Sams Iii
1343 Ohio St Lot 17
Bangor ME 04401

Call Sign: KA1PF
Walter J Harris
922 Ohio Street Apt. 126
Bangor ME 04401

Call Sign: N1CLP
Carl E Libby Sr
92 Packard Dr
Bangor ME 04401

Call Sign: K1AG
William J Sullivan
37 Packard Drive
Bangor ME 04401

Call Sign: W1MCM
Joseph H Striar
35 Parkview Ave
Bangor ME 04401

Call Sign: N0UKM
Kevin E Badger
135 Parkview Avenue Apt
C
Bangor ME 04401

Call Sign: N3LMX
John P Eckert Iii
46 Patten Street Apt. #2
Bangor ME 044017500

Call Sign: N1JRN
William E Kelly
291 Pearl St
Bangor ME 044014115

Call Sign: KB1UPV
Randall J Canarr
4 Pine Grove Ave

Bangor ME 04401

Call Sign: WA2GFF
Clarence G Jewell
35 Pleasant View Ave
Bangor ME 04401

Call Sign: N1STJ
James E Morgan
Rainbow Mobile Home
Court Box 56
Bangor ME 04401

Call Sign: W1LIC
Wesley L Linscott
97 Randolph Dr
Bangor ME 044012829

Call Sign: KA1GYF
Daniel L Watt
113 Randolph Dr
Bangor ME 04401

Call Sign: KB1EST
Christopher J Ricci
196 Randolph Dr
Bangor ME 04401

Call Sign: N1CJR
Christopher J Ricci
196 Randolph Dr
Bangor ME 04401

Call Sign: W6IMU
William H Shaw
20 Roger St
Bangor ME 04401

Call Sign: KB1PTO
Michael J Mower
48 Saratoga Ave
Bangor ME 04401

Call Sign: K1JK
John G Krass

78 Saratoga Ave
Bangor ME 04401

Call Sign: N1DYM
Jonathan P Canfield
33 Sidney St
Bangor ME 044012104

Call Sign: KA1DAI
Cornelius H Murphy
302 Silver Rd
Bangor ME 04401

Call Sign: WA1YSB
Harold R Veits
316 State St
Bangor ME 04401

Call Sign: N1TOH
Thomas N Thompson
489 State St
Bangor ME 04401

Call Sign: KC0GSG
Jonathan V Williams
38 Stillwater Ave
Bangor ME 04401

Call Sign: KD1KK
Alton F Sabin Jr
161 Stillwater Ave
Bangor ME 04401

Call Sign: N1AZN
Raymond H Knowlton Jr
Park East Apt 12-321
Stillwater Ave
Bangor ME 04401

Call Sign: N1VLQ
Bruce A Worcester
239 Third St
Bangor ME 04401

Call Sign: WA1LSG

Lawrence S Greenfield
23 Thornton Rd
Bangor ME 04401

Call Sign: N1PQZ
Gregory D Bailey
385 Union
Bangor ME 04401

Call Sign: KB1PAC
Scott A Woodward
849 Union St
Bangor ME 04401

Call Sign: KB1PAE
Cecil A Woodward
849 Union St
Bangor ME 04401

Call Sign: KB1IHH
John F Cassidy Iv
1576 Union St
Bangor ME 04401

Call Sign: N1FCW
David L Bishop Mr.
3143 Union St.
Bangor ME 04401

Call Sign: KB3CRW
Jonnathan M Busko
152 Webster Ave
Bangor ME 04401

Call Sign: KA1NGX
Richard A Condon
17 Winter St
Bangor ME 04401

Call Sign: K1JCQ
Robert J Sawyer
20 Woodbury St
Bangor ME 04401

Call Sign: K1CZ

Howard L Soule
Bangor ME 04402

Call Sign: KD1OM
Stephen G Jordan
Bangor ME 044028028

Call Sign: N1JAF
Matthew S Thomas
Bangor ME 04402

Call Sign: N1NOI
Robert E Jordan
Bangor ME 044028028

Call Sign: WA1CHE
Frank M Mroz
Bangor ME 044028059

Call Sign: KB1GUR
Maine Aprs Working Group
Bangor ME 044022372

Call Sign: KG1R
Donald A Seavey
Bangor ME 04402

Call Sign: KB1ION
Gary S Jordan
Bangor ME 04402

Call Sign: W1DT
Lance C Lobo
Bangor ME 04402

Call Sign: AE1DT
Lance C Lobo
Bangor ME 04402

Call Sign: KB1TDJ
Sonya D Jordan
Bangor ME 044028028

Call Sign: N1KKQ
Sonya D Jordan

Bangor ME 044028028

FCC Amateur Radio Licenses in Bar Harbor

Call Sign: KB1VKN
Benjamin E Smith
19 1st South St
Bar Harbor ME 04609

Call Sign: W1DZI
Joseph E Biron
Rfd 1 Box 1705
Bar Harbor ME 04609

Call Sign: KB1GRE
Keith C Pearson
Rr 1 Box 1993
Bar Harbor ME 04609

Call Sign: N1GCM
Craig W Greene
Rfd 1 Box 910
Bar Harbor ME 04609

Call Sign: WA1PXD
John G Cox Sr
28 Bridge St
Bar Harbor ME 04609

Call Sign: KF6CKF
Gina Silverman
61 Cottage St 104
Bar Harbor ME 04609

Call Sign: KB1NWM
James A Robinson
126 Cromwell Harbor Rd
Bar Harbor ME 04609

Call Sign: KB1HQD
Andrew J Keblinsky
848 Eagle Lake Road
Bar Harbor ME 04609

Call Sign: WA1KDW
Andrew J Keblinsky
848 Eagle Lake Road
Bar Harbor ME 04609

Call Sign: N1WMR
Andrew Peterson
105 Eden St
Bar Harbor ME 04609

Call Sign: W1MRH
Matthew R Horton
8 Federal Street
Bar Harbor ME 04609

Call Sign: KB1WLR
Lawrence A Nuesslein Iii
28 Glen Mary Rd
Bar Harbor ME 04609

Call Sign: KA1BRA
Evelyn E Sargent
28 Knox Rd
Bar Harbor ME 04609

Call Sign: KB1WKN
John F Kollman
22 Ledgelawn Avenue
Bar Harbor ME 04609

Call Sign: KB1MOM
Kam H Lam
195 Main St
Bar Harbor ME 04609

Call Sign: WB1BQK
William Fenton
354 Main St
Bar Harbor ME 04609

Call Sign: KA1JZI
James T Lambert
17 Meadow Drive
Bar Harbor ME 04609

Call Sign: K1CQE
Roger W Hodgkins
80 Mt Desert St Apt 24
Bar Harbor ME 04609

Call Sign: K1WJY
Donald M Frost
9 Myrtle Ave
Bar Harbor ME 04609

Call Sign: W3HBM
George W Kidder Iii
509 Norway Drive
Bar Harbor ME 04609

Call Sign: KA1DBE
Jeffrey D Hanscom
286 Oak Hill Rd
Bar Harbor ME 04609

Call Sign: W1TPO
John L Dorey
47 Rodick St
Bar Harbor ME 04609

Call Sign: WB1GDZ
Robert P Noonan
28 Russell Farm Rd
Bar Harbor ME 04609

Call Sign: WB1GFX
Judith R Noonan
28 Russell Farm Rd
Bar Harbor ME 04609

Call Sign: W1WCT
William C Townsend
12 Spring St
Bar Harbor ME 04609

Call Sign: KB1JWN
Dallas P Hodgkins
1012 St Hwy 3
Bar Harbor ME 04609

Call Sign: KB1LIH
James G Merritt
46 W Street Ext Unit 9
Bar Harbor ME 04610

Call Sign: KA1ZXT
Allan R Wentworth Jr
23 Wentworth Way
Bar Harbor ME 04509

Call Sign: K1PDM
Ralph J Mc Farland
90 West St
Bar Harbor ME 04609

Call Sign: KA1ZXU
Thomas G Karnofsky
Bar Harbor ME 04609

FCC Amateur Radio Licenses in Bar Mills

Call Sign: N1HTV
Debra A Bartlett
Towle St
Bar Mills ME 04004

Call Sign: KB1PWK
Jacob W Moorman
Bar Mills ME 04004

FCC Amateur Radio Licenses in Bass Harbor

Call Sign: N1NYT
Kathe P Simons
24 Ledges Rd
Bass Harbor ME 04653

Call Sign: N3XVG
Marc L Fink
Bass Harbor ME 04653

Call Sign: AA1ZS
John T Dunn

Bass Harbor ME 04653

Call Sign: KB1KBS
Linda M Hill
Bass Harbor ME 046530052

FCC Amateur Radio Licenses in Bath

Call Sign: K1BRI
William A Kimball
Hc 33 61t
Bath ME 04530

Call Sign: N1OGJ
Michael D Mc Glinchey
49 Bath St
Bath ME 04530

Call Sign: K1QYO
Joseph R Melrose Jr
22 Bedford St
Bath ME 04530

Call Sign: W1JBZ
Robert W Ramsay
Rfd 1 Box 23
Bath ME 04530

Call Sign: N1MFZ
Robert F Searle
Star Route 3 Box 241
Bath ME 04530

Call Sign: WB1GYI
Frederick M Haggett
Hc 31 Box 400
Bath ME 04530

Call Sign: KA1DGI
John E Lowe
Box 566
Bath ME 04530

Call Sign: K1VOL

Stanley D Henderson
Rr 02 Box 60
Bath ME 04530

Call Sign: N1WLU
Allison L Nicholson
Hc 33 Box 61n
Bath ME 04830

Call Sign: KB1PLB
Rick Rodriguez
67 Chestnut St
Bath ME 045302448

Call Sign: KA1DFY
Philip E Whitmore
125 Congress Ave
Bath ME 04530

Call Sign: KB1HOC
Carolee A Tribou
38 Court St 3
Bath ME 04530

Call Sign: N1HOC
Carolee A Tribou
38 Court St 3
Bath ME 04530

Call Sign: KB1EQC
Brian D Mccue
8 Crawford Drive
Bath ME 04530

Call Sign: KB1PMA
Brian D Mccue
8 Crawford Drive
Bath ME 04530

Call Sign: WA1NMC
Raymond C Bower
20 Dikes Landing Rd
Bath ME 04530

Call Sign: N1WUV

Donald P Fischer
11 Elsinore Ave
Bath ME 04530

Call Sign: K1IMA
Paul A Breton
15 Floral St
Bath ME 04530

Call Sign: N1ZLH
William D Cutlip
1492 High St
Bath ME 04530

Call Sign: KD1JS
Steven L Alexander
14 Huse St
Bath ME 04530

Call Sign: KB1LJW
Theodore E Wolfe
59 Lemont St
Bath ME 04530

Call Sign: W1LNO
Theodore E Wolfe
59 Lemont St
Bath ME 04530

Call Sign: N1BLX
Robert S Oxton
13 Marshall Ave
Bath ME 04530

Call Sign: WA1VZF
Phippsburg School Amateur
Radio Club
60 Oak St
Bath ME 04530

Call Sign: N1JMP
Haluk A Karamanoglu
435 Robinhood Rd
Bath ME 04530

Call Sign: KB1WRV
John E Knowles
78 Rockweed Rd
Bath ME 04530

Call Sign: N1VVK
James F Thelen
118 Sabino Road
Bath ME 04530

Call Sign: N1JOW
David J Wetherbee
11 Seekins Drive
Bath ME 04530

Call Sign: KA1FKE
George W Alexander Jr
1 Sheridan Rd
Bath ME 04530

Call Sign: KB1CV
Dana L Mc Curdy
3 Sheridan Rd
Bath ME 04530

Call Sign: W1AXJ
Leonard Thombs
58 Union St
Bath ME 045302536

Call Sign: W1LHD
Loren H Dudley
14 Valley Rd
Bath ME 045302811

Call Sign: AA1UK
Michael J Knudsen
940 Washington St
Bath ME 045302623

Call Sign: WB1DUD
Elmer W Kilcauley
1369 Washington St
Bath ME 04530

Call Sign: KA1NAX
Daniel L Lord Jr
1483 Washington St
Bath ME 04530

Call Sign: WA1UAY
Robert N Westlake Sr
1484 Washington St
Bath ME 04530

Call Sign: KA1TOI
Barbara E Esmond
16 Willow St
Bath ME 04530

Call Sign: KA1NBG
David J Ritchie
Bath ME 04530

Call Sign: N1KSZ
Brian V Ryder
Bath ME 04530

Call Sign: N1RLF
Roland T Robbins
Bath ME 04530

Call Sign: KB1RSC
William B Temple
Bath ME 04530

Call Sign: KA1KGR
William B Temple
Bath ME 04530

FCC Amateur Radio
Licenses in Beaver Cove

Call Sign: W3VNE
Scott D Higgins
795 Lily Bay Rd. Unit 708
Beaver Cove ME 0

FCC Amateur Radio
Licenses in Belfast

Call Sign: KB1AMG
Daniel C Mc Carthy
15 Anderson Street
Belfast ME 04915

Call Sign: KB1TNS
Douglas E Nelson
15 Back Belmont Rd
Belfast ME 04915

Call Sign: N1DEN
Douglas E Nelson
15 Back Belmont Rd
Belfast ME 04915

Call Sign: N1MSQ
Kevin P Kratka
99 Back Searsport Rd.
Belfast ME 04915

Call Sign: KB1NDJ
Justin L Vertefeville
256 Belmont Ave
Belfast ME 04915

Call Sign: W1FKH
Leonard W Gilmore
20 Birch St
Belfast ME 04915

Call Sign: KB1FDH
Sarah L Baldwin
Rr 4 Box 2650
Belfast ME 04915

Call Sign: KA1ZMV
Judith A Ryder
Rfd 2 Box 290
Belfast ME 04915

Call Sign: N1WZJ
Michael H Ryder
Rfd 2 Box 290
Belfast ME 04915

Call Sign: K1QAX
2 Swan Lake Dx
Association
Dx Drive Rr 2 Box 3480
Belfast ME 04915

Call Sign: K1CP
Clifton Power
6 Charles Street Ext
Belfast ME 04915

Call Sign: WB1GXP
Karl R Thompson
27 Church St
Belfast ME 04915

Call Sign: KB1HZV
Avery B Stone
156 Church St
Belfast ME 049156502

Call Sign: KB1ROT
John C Butler
4 Cobb Rd
Belfast ME 04915

Call Sign: KA1ZCP
Robert C Fowler
15 Congress St
Belfast ME 04915

Call Sign: K1RCF
Robert C Fowler
15 Congress St
Belfast ME 04915

Call Sign: KB1ENM
Samuel A Mehorter
84 Congress St
Belfast ME 04915

Call Sign: W8SAM
Samuel A Mehorter
84 Congress St

Belfast ME 04915

Call Sign: NK1A
Esther R Grossman
10 Dockside La
Belfast ME 04915

Call Sign: NJ1Z
Henry L Grossman
10 Dockside La.
Belfast ME 04915

Call Sign: KA1ZMB
Evelyn L Carroll
2 Dx Dr
Belfast ME 04916

Call Sign: KB1LDW
Francis J Mccarrier
10 Elm St
Belfast ME 04915

Call Sign: K3FP
Robin J Staebler
144 Head Of The Tide Rd
Belfast ME 04915

Call Sign: W1SLB
Sarah L Baldwin
144 Head Of The Tide Rd
Belfast ME 04915

Call Sign: KB1GZI
Medical Amateur Radio
Council
144 Head Of The Tide Rd
Belfast ME 04915

Call Sign: WE1MD
Robin J Staebler
144 Head Of The Tide Rd
Belfast ME 04915

Call Sign: WE4MD

Medical Amateur Radio
Council
144 Head Of The Tide Rd
Belfast ME 04915

Call Sign: N1VD
Medical Amateur Radio
Council
144 Head Of The Tide Rd
Belfast ME 04915

Call Sign: WF1R
Robin J Staebler
144 Head Of The Tide Rd
Belfast ME 04915

Call Sign: KB1EWK
Waldo County Ares Group
2650 Head Of The Tide Rd
Belfast ME 04915

Call Sign: W1GYS
Almonde F Harding
147 High St
Belfast ME 04915

Call Sign: K1AES
Robert U Bishop
225 High St
Belfast ME 04915

Call Sign: KB1GES
Anirut Limtrakool
149a High Street Apt 5
Belfast ME 04915

Call Sign: KB1LDX
Thomas D Crandall
82 Hunt Rd
Belfast ME 04915

Call Sign: K1EBG
John R Stover
29 Huntress Av
Belfast ME 049156050

Call Sign: WD4ENN
John R Stover
29 Huntress Ave.
Belfast ME 049156050

Call Sign: N1LFG
Nikki G Terry
67 Kaler Road
Belfast ME 04915

Call Sign: KB1NGM
Eric W Levangie
255 Lincolnville Ave
Belfast ME 04915

Call Sign: KA1HEH
James B Davis
48 Mayo St
Belfast ME 04915

Call Sign: WA1ATX
Alfred J Staples
72 Miller St
Belfast ME 04915

Call Sign: N1SO
John D Carr
83 Miller St
Belfast ME 04915

Call Sign: W1JDC
John D Carr
83 Miller St
Belfast ME 04915

Call Sign: WJ1C
John D Carr
83 Miller St
Belfast ME 04915

Call Sign: AE4UL
Ronald W Bjelland
55 Northport Avenue
Belfast ME 04915

Call Sign: KA1AII
Robert A Ackley
84 Oak Hill Rd
Belfast ME 04915

Call Sign: K1FZ
Bruce A Clark
65 Patterson Hill Road
Belfast ME 049159608

Call Sign: N7MAK
Stephen A Makrecky
27 Pitcher Road
Belfast ME 04915

Call Sign: N1SO
Stephen A Makrecky
27 Pitcher Road
Belfast ME 04915

Call Sign: N1YKM
Robert J Struba
34 Race St
Belfast ME 04915

Call Sign: N1YPL
Roberta A Goff
34 Race Street
Belfast ME 04915

Call Sign: AA1VK
Robert J Struba
34 Race Street
Belfast ME 04915

Call Sign: W2QF
Henry D Wyatt
231 Searsport Ave
Belfast ME 04915

Call Sign: KB1NGL
Robert D Stover Sr
7 Stover Lane
Belfast ME 04915

Call Sign: W1OUM
Norman W Pearson
Rr 1 Swan Lake Ave Lot 59
Belfast ME 04915

Call Sign: K1YXY
Harry W Balmforth
2 Tozier St
Belfast ME 04915

Call Sign: KB1VSK
Daniel E Bennett
11 Union St
Belfast ME 04915

Call Sign: KB1KPH
Richard A Farris
54 Waldo Ave
Belfast ME 04915

Call Sign: WO1EMA
Richard A Farris
54 Waldo Ave
Belfast ME 04915

Call Sign: KB1LDV
John D Gage
78 Waldo Ave
Belfast ME 04915

Call Sign: KB1PBZ
Margaret E Avener
99 Woods Rd
Belfast ME 04915

Call Sign: N1CQZ
David J Davenport
Belfast ME 04915

Call Sign: N1OJC
Bruce A Simmons
Belfast ME 04915

Call Sign: N1ZDF

Michael E Mc Gray
Belfast ME 04915

Call Sign: KC2KZH
Kenneth A Ihnken
Belfast ME 04915

FCC Amateur Radio Licenses in Belgrade

Call Sign: KB1EWX
Sherry I Keene
10 Keene Dr
Belgrade ME 04917

Call Sign: KB1FAL
David A Keene
10 Keene Dr.
Belgrade ME 04917

Call Sign: N1DAV
David A Keene
10 Keene Dr.
Belgrade ME 04917

Call Sign: W1GHK
Carl L Mason
25 Lenfesty Lane
Belgrade ME 04917

Call Sign: KB1EHN
Arlene J Hutchinson
477 Manchester Rd
Belgrade ME 04917

Call Sign: K1AOK
Roger A Emmons
18 Merryweather Rd
Belgrade ME 04917

Call Sign: KB1GOV
Roger J Veilleux
203 Oakland Rd
Belgrade ME 04917

Call Sign: KB1WRG
Carroll G Weymouth
701 Oakland Rd
Belgrade ME 04917

Call Sign: N2FRH
Stewart E Brittner
37 Rock Garden Estates
Belgrade ME 04917

Call Sign: KB8DIR
Gregory B Odell
325 Smithfield Road
Belgrade ME 04917

Call Sign: KB1OWQ
Michael P Benecke Sr
187 West Rd
Belgrade ME 04917

Call Sign: KB1WEB
Michael P Benecke Sr
187 West Rd
Belgrade ME 04917

Call Sign: KA1LAY
John P Dyer
67 West Road
Belgrade ME 049179723

Call Sign: KB1EHM
Marie R Doucette
810 Wings Mills Rd
Belgrade ME 04917

Call Sign: KB1AD
Martin J Baker
Belgrade ME 04917

Call Sign: K1MJB
Martin J Baker
Belgrade ME 04917

FCC Amateur Radio Licenses in Belgrade Lakes

Call Sign: N1WBU
Arthur E De Angelis
Rt 27 Box 136
Belgrade Lakes ME 04918

Call Sign: WA1EKJ
John V Haag Sr
Rr 1 Box 630
Belgrade Lakes ME 04919

Call Sign: K1MAN
Glenn A Baxter
Rr 1 Box 776
Belgrade Lakes ME 04918

Call Sign: N1MRC
Robert Bruce
1 Long Point Rd
Belgrade Lakes ME 04918

Call Sign: AE1Q
Donald R Smith
Belgrade Lakes ME 04918

Call Sign: K2MG
Richard C Bourne
Belgrade Lakes ME 04918

Call Sign: W1CRA
Central Area Repeater
Association
Belgrade Lakes ME 04918

Call Sign: WA1CDM
Childrens Discovery
Museum
Belgrade Lakes ME 04918

Call Sign: WA1WA
Waterville Area Wireless
Assn

Belgrade Lakes ME
049180571

FCC Amateur Radio Licenses in Belmont

Call Sign: K1XXX
Dan D Grass
681 Augusta Road
Belmont ME 049523023

Call Sign: KB1FTH
Maurice L Breau
92 Bicknell Rd
Belmont ME 04952

Call Sign: KB1QKO
Charles W Gradie
16 Maple Road
Belmont ME 04952

FCC Amateur Radio Licenses in Benton

Call Sign: KA1AKF
David L Mitchell
2 Crummett St
Benton ME 04901

Call Sign: N1OSY
Daniel R Richardson
291 East Benton Rd
Benton ME 04901

Call Sign: N1WPY
Robert W Arno
71 Gogan Rd
Benton ME 04901

Call Sign: KB1TV
Frederick A Simmons
61 School Drive
Benton ME 04901

Call Sign: N1VOG

Alan D Sanborn
36 Spencer Rd
Benton ME 04901

Call Sign: WA1LUH
Gerald A Walls
Bernard ME 046120203

Call Sign: KB1KBE
Karen M Akin
28 Bell St
Berwick ME 03901

Call Sign: AA1BQ
Thomas E Whitten
31 Blackberry Hill Rd
Berwick ME 03901

Call Sign: WA1TJX
Barbara A Whitten
31 Blackberry Hill Rd
Berwick ME 03901

Call Sign: KB1SED
Gary P Branyen
20 Cincotta Lane
Berwick ME 03901

Call Sign: K1DRV
Dennis R Vincent
182 Cranberry Meadow Rd
Berwick ME 03901

Call Sign: N1UCC
Jeffrey W Burnham
4 Heritage Drive
Berwick ME 03901

Call Sign: KB1PRU

Joseph J Lebel
23 Jordan St Apt - 1
Berwick ME 039011226

Call Sign: KA1IXK
Joseph J Lebel
23 Jordan St Apt - 1
Berwick ME 039011226

Call Sign: N1LBJ
Robert A Poor
27 Keay Rd
Berwick ME 03901

Call Sign: KB1GZY
Eleanor R Butler
88 Keay Rd
Berwick ME 03901

Call Sign: KB1CQY
Brian J Mayo
88 Keay Road
Berwick ME 03901

Call Sign: W1QHG
Scott A Richardson
29 Knox Lane
Berwick ME 03901

Call Sign: N1AIA
Scott A Richardson
29 Knox Lane
Berwick ME 03901

Call Sign: W1EMW
Quentin E Martin
Knox Ln Box 45
Berwick ME 03901

Call Sign: KA1WHI
Keith D Mortensen
57 Little River Rd
Berwick ME 03901

Call Sign: N1MMJ

David A Coelho
215 Little River Rd
Berwick ME 03901

Call Sign: WA1YRT
Fred F Chellis
245 Little River Rd
Berwick ME 03901

Call Sign: KB1LPV
Donald O Chembars
338 Little River Rd
Berwick ME 03901

Call Sign: W1BIU
Donald E Cheney
9 Morse St
Berwick ME 03901

Call Sign: KB1WMW
Cyrus I Morgan
41 Old Pine Hill Rd South
Berwick ME 03901

Call Sign: W1PLN
Walter M Amazeen
10 Old Sanford Rd
Berwick ME 03901

Call Sign: N1WFK
Jeffrey A Brooks
124 Old Sanford Road
Berwick ME 03901

Call Sign: N1GEO
Harold J Oulton Sr
255 Pine Hill Rd
Berwick ME 03901

Call Sign: N1NOF
Lawrence J Wescott Iii
81 Pine Hill Road
Berwick ME 03901

Call Sign: K1CXW

Lawrence J Wescott Iii
81 Pine Hill Road
Berwick ME 03901

Call Sign: N1VJB
Scott A Waldrom
19 Pine Hill Ter
Berwick ME 039010746

Call Sign: N1ZVY
Benjamin J Higgins
343 Pinehill Rd
Berwick ME 039012426

Call Sign: W1RUW
Leslie F Mills
534 Route 9
Berwick ME 03901

Call Sign: KA1MCI
David K Horne
124 School St
Berwick ME 03901

Call Sign: N1XYG
Grace C Horne
124 School St
Berwick ME 03901

Call Sign: KA1UEH
Kathy L Mills
536 School St
Berwick ME 03901

Call Sign: WA1WPR
Frederick L Mills
536 School St
Berwick ME 03901

Call Sign: N1MIR
Mark W Smith
1 Second Street
Berwick ME 03901

Call Sign: KA1KUD

Rosanna Sheldon
72 Sullivan St
Berwick ME 03901

Call Sign: WA1TCQ
Richard D Hawley
36 Sunrise Hill Estates
Berwick ME 03901

Call Sign: N1PZZ
Louis P Le Veille
60 Tall Timbers Dr
Berwick ME 039012536

Call Sign: KB1PFY
Marcus P Despres
5 Thompson Hill Rd
Berwick ME 03901

Call Sign: KE1CL
Tylor V Wentworth
100 Wentworth Rd
Berwick ME 03901

Call Sign: N1UJK
Julie A Wentworth
100 Wentworth Rd
Berwick ME 03901

Call Sign: KB1FUM
Eric F Chellis
17 Worster Rd
Berwick ME 03901

Call Sign: KB1HUS
George H Perreault Sr
Berwick ME 03901

FCC Amateur Radio
Licenses in Bethel

Call Sign: AB1OP
Ralph L Mills
Rr 1 Box 540
Bethel ME 04217

Call Sign: WA1JWJ
Jack A Chapman
11 Eden Ln
Bethel ME 04217

Call Sign: N1UUB
Randy D Autrey
139 Intervale Rd
Bethel ME 04217

Call Sign: KB1NVS
Scott T Kennagh
206 Intervale Rd
Bethel ME 04217

Call Sign: AA1MY
Seabury A Lyon
99 Sparrow Hawk Mountain
Rd
Bethel ME 04217

Call Sign: KA1IS
Thomas K Zicarelli
Bethel ME 04218

Call Sign: KA1SG
Norman G Clanton
Bethel ME 04219

Call Sign: KA9KFR
Eric A Hoke
Bethel ME 04220

Call Sign: KA9KXA
Sylvia D Clanton
Bethel ME 04221

Call Sign: N1AUM
Robert E Ferreira
Bethel ME 04222

Call Sign: N1ITY
James A Stoner
Bethel ME 04223

Call Sign: N1TGQ
Charles P Taylor
Bethel ME 04224

Call Sign: N1XYL
Danny C Wheeler
Bethel ME 04218

Call Sign: W3FSA
John K Shorb
Bethel ME 04219

Call Sign: AA1US
Michael J Grenier
Bethel ME 04217

Call Sign: KB1RFO
Robert L Dion
Bethel ME 04217

Call Sign: KB1RIU
Paul K Moniz
Bethel ME 04217

Call Sign: KB1URI
Joseph D Zicarelli
Bethel ME 04217

FCC Amateur Radio Licenses in Biddeford

Call Sign: KB1NZQ
Karl R Reed
47 Adams St Apt 5
Biddeford ME 04005

Call Sign: KB1VUK
Neil B Tolman
6 Alexander Dr
Biddeford ME 04005

Call Sign: N1OYD
Eugene A Giesler
Rr 4 Box 537

Biddeford ME 04006

Call Sign: WB1EAD
David R La Pierre
4 Burleigh Ln
Biddeford ME 04005

Call Sign: WA1ZYB
Richard P Ouellette
4 Calixte Ln
Biddeford ME 04005

Call Sign: K1JDP
William J Beliveau
331 Elm St
Biddeford ME 04005

Call Sign: N1UKA
Edward A Berry
80 Graham St
Biddeford ME 04005

Call Sign: N1RXE
Paul N Michaud
158 Graham St
Biddeford ME 04005

Call Sign: KB1FTO
Paul D Ouellette
40 Grayson Street
Biddeford ME 04005

Call Sign: W1PDO
Paul D Ouellette
40 Grayson Street
Biddeford ME 04005

Call Sign: KA1QBY
Norman M Giguere
83 Guinea Rd
Biddeford ME 04005

Call Sign: KB1MKE
Steven R Quinn
312 Guinea Rd

Biddeford ME 04005

Call Sign: WA1GTT
Grady L Sexton Jr
158 Guinea Road
Biddeford ME 04072

Call Sign: WA1ODM
Suzanne Y Sexton
158 Gunea Road
Biddeford ME 04005

Call Sign: KA1JWM
David R Paquette
35 Highland St
Biddeford ME 04005

Call Sign: N1HZR
Deborah J Paquette
35 Highland St
Biddeford ME 04005

Call Sign: N1JTF
Richard K Marshall Jr
32 Hill St Apt 201
Biddeford ME 04005

Call Sign: KB1HOY
Henry L Ferland Iii
203 Hill Street
Biddeford ME 04005

Call Sign: KB1AOQ
Edward L Eisenstadt
200 Hills Beach Rd
Biddeford ME 04005

Call Sign: N1UKB
Gary R Desmarais
4 John Street
Biddeford ME 04005

Call Sign: KB1GEL
Shawn R Linscott
23 Lambert St Apt 101 A

Biddeford ME 04006　　　　Biddeford ME 04005　　　　Biddeford ME 04005

Call Sign: KB1DKB　　　　Call Sign: KA1VHS　　　　Call Sign: N1QHV
Andrew Cartier Iii　　　　Robert G Bissell　　　　Stephen J Dow
16 Laurier St.　　　　111 Old Pool Rd　　　　5 Vine Street Apt 8
Biddeford ME 04005　　　　Biddeford ME 04005　　　　Biddeford ME 04005

Call Sign: KN1WNC　　　　Call Sign: N1RNZ　　　　Call Sign: KB1QKD
Barry J Daniels　　　　Paul C Gendron　　　　Malcolm C Lund
365 Main Street 103　　　　96 Prospect St　　　　11 Waco Drive
Biddeford ME 04005　　　　Biddeford ME 04005　　　　Biddeford ME 04005

Call Sign: KA1VOQ　　　　Call Sign: N1NDD　　　　Call Sign: K1GDN
Roland A Menard　　　　Albert V Pelletier　　　　Malcolm C Lund
25 Mason St　　　　28 Raymond St　　　　11 Waco Drive
Biddeford ME 04005　　　　Biddeford ME 04005　　　　Biddeford ME 04005

Call Sign: KB1VUJ　　　　Call Sign: KB1LBZ　　　　Call Sign: KE1Q
Vermal G Dailey　　　　Christine Pelletier　　　　Malcolm C Lund
7 Mason St Apt 2　　　　28 Raymond St　　　　11 Waco Drive
Biddeford ME 04005　　　　Biddeford ME 04005　　　　Biddeford ME 04005

Call Sign: KB1VSE　　　　Call Sign: K1EJA　　　　Call Sign: KD1WB
Ethan T Nadeau　　　　Raymond N Beliveau　　　　Raymond R Boucher
6 Middle St. #101　　　　7 Rockwood Drive　　　　266 West St
Biddeford ME 04005　　　　Biddeford ME 04005　　　　Biddeford ME 04005

Call Sign: KA1SIY　　　　Call Sign: W1ED　　　　Call Sign: K1HOI
Alexander S Montgomery Ii　　　　Ervin S Davis　　　　Emilien J Bellerose
61 Newtown Rd　　　　8 Shore Road　　　　305 West St
Biddeford ME 04005　　　　Biddeford ME 04005　　　　Biddeford ME 04005

Call Sign: KA1ARE　　　　Call Sign: N1DOW　　　　Call Sign: K1ZLO
Paul R Adams　　　　Stephen J Dow　　　　Jean P Lamontagne
9 Oak St　　　　68 South Street #2　　　　154 West St Lot 28
Biddeford ME 04005　　　　Biddeford ME 04005　　　　Biddeford ME 04005

Call Sign: N6SEC　　　　Call Sign: N1EFV　　　　Call Sign: KB1MQL
Brian E Hatton　　　　Donald R Binette　　　　Michael D Clukey
3 Old Kings Hwy　　　　11 Taylor St　　　　88 West Street
Biddeford ME 04005　　　　Biddeford ME 04005　　　　Biddeford ME 04005

Call Sign: N6SED　　　　Call Sign: KA1RPI　　　　Call Sign: KB1PCP
Maureen Hatton　　　　Robert E Reidy　　　　Bryce H Young
3 Old Kings Hwy　　　　9 Thorndike Ave　　　　205 West Street

Biddeford ME 04005

Call Sign: KB1HPP
Peter M Carpenter
45 Western Ave Apt 104
Biddeford ME 04005

Call Sign: N1MZS
Michael J Quigley
16 Westwood Dr
Biddeford ME 04005

Call Sign: N3ZNC
Richard A Brown
20 Wilson Street
Biddeford ME 04005

Call Sign: KA1DYA
Roland F Bergeron
Biddeford ME 04005

Call Sign: N1MZQ
Michael R Demers
Biddeford ME 04005

Call Sign: N1TJE
Dickie L Chadbourne
Biddeford ME 04005

Call Sign: N1UVI
Scott V Knox
Biddeford ME 04005

Call Sign: W6BZ
John V Di Liddo
Biddeford ME 04005

Call Sign: W1GU
Edward A Berry
Biddeford ME 04005

FCC Amateur Radio Licenses in Bingham

Call Sign: N1UBY

Tess L Laweryson
Meadow St
Bingham ME 049200197

Call Sign: N1RPR
Barry E Laweryson
Bingham ME 04920

Call Sign: N1UBS
Joseph W Kiernan
Bingham ME 04920

Call Sign: N1ZJD
Michael G Schrader
Bingham ME 04920

FCC Amateur Radio Licenses in Birch Harbor

Call Sign: N1VVQ
George R Strohmeyer
Birch Harbor ME 04613

Call Sign: KB1OTL
William H Bell
Birch Harbor ME 04613

FCC Amateur Radio Licenses in Blaine

Call Sign: KB1CCL
Walter A Mosher Iii
Blaine ME 047340202

Call Sign: N1TNQ
George T Belford
Blaine ME 04734

Call Sign: N1YQT
Janice L Mosher
Blaine ME 047340202

Call Sign: WA1UQA
Janet L Clayton
Blaine ME 04734

FCC Amateur Radio Licenses in Blue Hill

Call Sign: KB1VJ
Donald P Eley
49 Beech Hill Rd.
Blue Hill ME 04614

Call Sign: N1GVN
Judy M Garvey
Rr 1 Box 105
Blue Hill ME 04614

Call Sign: KA1UEE
James F Bergin
Rr1 Box 3215
Blue Hill ME 04614

Call Sign: KB1IMS
Bruce Gordon
Box 474
Blue Hill ME 04614

Call Sign: KB1DHF
Sherry C Degroff
Hc 64 Box 505
Blue Hill ME 04614

Call Sign: KC1MQ
Rachel Miller
Hc 63 Box 63
Blue Hill ME 04614

Call Sign: K1YVV
Jerry L Durnbaugh
Box O
Blue Hill ME 04614

Call Sign: N1GTG
Randy L Rhodes
Hcr 64 Box 130
Bluehill ME 04614

Call Sign: W1TJS

Groves E Herrick
33 Falls Bridge Road
Blue Hill ME 046146503

Call Sign: KB1ONP
Susan M Grindle
324 Grindleville Rd
Blue Hill ME 04614

Call Sign: KB1ONQ
Scott J Grindle
324 Grindleville Rd
Blue Hill ME 07784604

Call Sign: KB1LDY
Gregory C Carroll
329 Parker Point Rd
Blue Hill ME 04614

Call Sign: W1ZBQ
Edward S Liscombe
Box 568 Parker Point Rd
Blue Hill ME 04614

Call Sign: N1MZT
Newell Garfield
Parker Point Rd
Blue Hill ME 04614

Call Sign: KB1BXR
Paul H Cummings
1463 Pleasant St
Blue Hill ME 04614

Call Sign: W1KKW
Paul H Cummings
1463 Pleasant St
Blue Hill ME 04614

Call Sign: W1MOZ
Robert K Slaven
Stone House Box 567
Blue Hill ME 04614

Call Sign: K2EII

Donald W Shanks
Blue Hill ME 046141269

Call Sign: KA1RPN
Michael A Bain
Blue Hill ME 04614

Call Sign: KA1YPG
Richard Raeburn
Blue Hill ME 04614

Call Sign: KB1CJM
Kevin J Piper
Blue Hill ME 04614

Call Sign: KC1XN
Jane W Garfield
Blue Hill ME 04614

Call Sign: KF6RTU
Catharine L Leonard
Blue Hill ME 046141152

Call Sign: N1OYZ
Royce Dixon
Blue Hill ME 046141211

Call Sign: N1STP
Geoffrey A Anthony
Blue Hill ME 04614

Call Sign: W1KA
Almon A Gray
Blue Hill ME 04614

Call Sign: WH6AYI
John S Sisson Iii
Blue Hill ME 04614

Call Sign: KB1IMP
Ian R Riley
Blue Hill ME 04614

Call Sign: KB1IMR
John F Riley

Blue Hill ME 04614

Call Sign: KB1TGK
Gordon J Gianninoto
Blue Hill ME 04614

Call Sign: KB1TLC
Christopher C Eccles
Blue Hill ME 04614

Call Sign: KB1VSJ
Robert E Steele
Blue Hill ME 04614

FCC Amateur Radio Licenses in Blue Hill Falls

Call Sign: KA1KIW
William A Stevens
Cannery Row
Blue Hill Falls ME 04615

Call Sign: WA1IZY
Richard W Britt
Route 175
Blue Hill Falls ME 04615

FCC Amateur Radio Licenses in Boothbay

Call Sign: N1NYP
Robert J Abernathy
53 Annable Road
Boothbay ME 04537

Call Sign: KB1SCZ
Grady E Jones
908 Back River Rd
Boothbay ME 04537

Call Sign: KB1SZB
Kathleen M Jones
908 Back River Rd
Boothbay ME 04537

Call Sign: KB1TBD
Kathleen M Jones
908 Back River Rd
Boothbay ME 04537

Call Sign: W9XK
Grady E Jones
908 Back River Rd
Boothbay ME 04537

Call Sign: W9XKK
Kathleen M Jones
908 Back River Rd
Boothbay ME 04537

Call Sign: KB1UTF
William C Jones
908 Back River Rd
Boothbay ME 04537

Call Sign: N1MQU
John C Dickinson
Box 173
Boothbay ME 04537

Call Sign: KB1IJB
Alan J Barker
8 Burning Bush Dr
Boothbay ME 04537

Call Sign: AA1GH
Eric H Traphagen
93 Isle Of Spring Road
Boothbay ME 04537

Call Sign: W1NV
Carl E Watson
Lakeside Dr
Boothbay ME 04537

Call Sign: KB1MMX
Jonathan W South
78 Tavenner Road
Boothbay ME 04537

Call Sign: KB1MMK
Janice Newell Long
35a Union Street
Boothbay ME 04538

Call Sign: WS1E
John L Gaffey
922 Wiscasset Road
Boothbay ME 04537

Call Sign: KB7IFQ
Matthew A Mc Nutt
999 Wiscasset Road
Boothbay ME 04537

Call Sign: N1RLN
John D Mc Nutt
1001 Wiscasset Road
Boothbay ME 04537

Call Sign: KB1EQF
Susan C Boisvert
Boothbay ME 04537

Call Sign: KB1UXE
John G Kelley
Boothbay ME 04537

**FCC Amateur Radio
Licenses in Boothbay
Harbor**

Call Sign: N1NAE
Fred R Reed
37 Bay St
Boothbay Harbor ME 04538

Call Sign: N1MIQ
Rexford E Bell
23 Campbell St
Booth Bay Harbor ME
04538

Call Sign: N1UXZ
William M Stephenson

33 Kenney Field Dr
Booth Bay Harbor ME
04538

Call Sign: N1YPC
Charles E Gillespie
99 Emery Lane
Boothbay Harbor ME 04538

Call Sign: WA1MOU
Richard C Smith
99 Lakeside Dr
Boothbay Harbor ME
045381705

Call Sign: N1VVH
Robert M Mc Fetridge
155 Middle Road
Boothbay Harbor ME 04538

Call Sign: K9QYF
Joseph H Rohrer
9 Signal Point
Boothbay Harbor ME 04538

Call Sign: KB1PYJ
Brent E Giles
66 Townsend Ave Apt A
Boothbay Harbor ME 04538

Call Sign: N1MGR
Walter S Reed Iii
25 Western Ave
Boothbay Harbor ME 04538

Call Sign: KA1UHJ
John J Papineau
Boothbay Harbor ME 04538

Call Sign: N1LLA
James I Norman
Boothbay Harbor ME 04538

Call Sign: W1HOW
William H Bowers

Boothbay Harbor ME 04538

Call Sign: WH6CSW
Kelly L Mc Manus
Boothbay Harbor ME 04538

Call Sign: KB1HGB
Robert W Karns
Boothbay Harbor ME 04538

Call Sign: KB1IEM
Robert W Karns
Boothbay Harbor ME 04538

Call Sign: AB1AU
Robert W Karns
Boothbay Harbor ME 04538

Call Sign: KB1MML
Raymond C Christy
Boothbay Harbor ME 04538

FCC Amateur Radio Licenses in Bowdoin

Call Sign: N1YAG
Ronnie P Kupfer
2298 Augusta Rd.
Bowdoin ME 04287

Call Sign: N1QDR
Dale A Woerter
1715 Augusta Road
Bowdoin ME 04287

Call Sign: KB1MQM
Kevin R Chute
22 Beechnut Hill
Bowdin ME 04287

Call Sign: N1ZMU
Jason M Gasper
18 Birch Ridge Lane
Bowdoin ME 04287

Call Sign: W1LVW
Henry H Eckman
15 Forest Pass
Bowdoin ME 04287

Call Sign: N1ERY
Gary R Burk
200 John Tarr Rd
Bowdoin ME 04287

Call Sign: KB1TNT
George S Byras Ii
176 Litchfield Rd
Bowdoin ME 04287

Call Sign: KB1MED
Brian C Flynn Jr
330 Litchfield Rd
Bowdoin ME 04287

Call Sign: KB1PHE
Earl M Glasscock
1174 Litchfield Rd
Bowdoin ME 04287

Call Sign: W1RXH
Ernest L Parsons
397 Litchfield Road
Bowdoin ME 04287

Call Sign: WA1OJB
Robert C Glassbrook Jr
1163 Meadow Rd
Bowdoin ME 04287

Call Sign: N2NQM
Paul R Gillett
421 West Burrough Rd
Bowdoin ME 04287

FCC Amateur Radio Licenses in Bowdoinham

Call Sign: N1RXB
Scott D Flouher

Rr 2 Box 3623-2
Bowdoinham ME 04008

Call Sign: KA1CYV
Eric W Rollins
349 Millay Rd
Bowdoinham ME 04008

Call Sign: KB1UFE
Arthur F Frizzle
508 Post Rd
Bowdoinham ME 04008

Call Sign: KA1ORQ
Bill J Gray Jr
Ridge Rd
Bowdoinham ME 04008

Call Sign: N1JIM
Mark A Rideout
892 Ridge Road
Bowdoinham ME 04008

Call Sign: N1KIE
Patricia A Mc Queeney
892 Ridge Road
Bowdoinham ME 04008

Call Sign: N1OMS
Brad L Gebhardt
214 River Road
Bowdoinham ME 04008

Call Sign: N1YTN
Glenn B Billings
777 River Road
Bowdoinham ME 04008

Call Sign: N1CGJ
John C Walchli
948 River Road
Bowdoinham ME
040085610

Call Sign: KB1UFD

Richard T Ellis
127 Wildes Rd
Bowdoinham ME 04008

Call Sign: KA1IQA
Robert L Rowland
Bowdoinham ME
040080115

Call Sign: KB1GR
Arthur G Drew
Bowdoinham ME 04008

Call Sign: N1QMR
Leo D Davis
Bowdoinham ME 04008

Call Sign: KB1OJW
David C Mention
Bowdoinham ME 04008

FCC Amateur Radio Licenses in Bowerbank

Call Sign: N1ZXU
Dorothy L Gustafson
586 Bowerbank Rd.
Bowerbank ME 04426

Call Sign: N1ZXT
James B Gustafson
586 Bowerbank Road
Bowerbank ME 04426

Call Sign: KB1QU
Henry A Swett
36 Grapevine Brook Rd
Bowerbank ME 04426

FCC Amateur Radio Licenses in Bradford

Call Sign: KB1DRU
Brandon Z Tarbet
144 Atkinson Rd

Bradford ME 04410

Call Sign: KD1XU
Don D Tarbet
144 Atkinson Rd
Bradford ME 04410

Call Sign: KB1LUL
Jason A Tarbet
144 Atkinson Rd
Bradford ME 04410

Call Sign: KB1JXZ
Carol A Rickards
94 Reeves Rd
Bradford ME 044103422

Call Sign: KB1UJS
Kenneth A Worster
185 Wilder Davis Rd
Bradford ME 04410

Call Sign: KB1VTD
Jenny M Worster
185 Wilder Davis Rd
Bradford ME 04410

Call Sign: KB1NLB
Krisy L Tear
Bradford ME 04410

FCC Amateur Radio Licenses in Bradley

Call Sign: WA3PZJ
John E Penney
28 Highland Ave
Bradley ME 04411

Call Sign: KB1PDP
Allan F Smallwood
352 Main St
Bradley ME 04411

Call Sign: KB1MF

Kenneth Salisbury
21 Main St Box 272
Bradley ME 044110272

Call Sign: W1SKS
Harold E Knight
Bradley ME 04411

FCC Amateur Radio Licenses in Bremen

Call Sign: KW1D
Richard R Corson
696 Biscay Rd
Bremen ME 04551

Call Sign: WB3HEP
George B Apgar
1031 Biscay Road
Bremen ME 04551

Call Sign: KE1MM
George B Apgar
1031 Biscay Road
Bremen ME 04551

Call Sign: N1ADV
Horace U Ransom
387 Heath Rd
Bremen ME 045513217

FCC Amateur Radio Licenses in Brewer

Call Sign: N1ZFK
Joseph E Hayes
11 Allen Rd
Brewer ME 04412

Call Sign: KB1NKI
Walter P Hilenski
36 Allen Rd Apt 2
Brewer ME 04412

Call Sign: KB1UUT

Ben Fuchs
13 Black Bear Rd
Brewer ME 04412

Call Sign: N1NAD
Randal C Hunt
21 Blake St Apt 1a
Brewer ME 04413

Call Sign: KA1VEX
Donald F Goodness Sr
R2 Box 1103
Brewer ME 04412

Call Sign: KA1DMP
Laurence V Wade
Rr 2 Box 685
Brewer ME 04412

Call Sign: N1XJR
Nancy O Brown
Rfd 2 Box 85
Brewer ME 04412

Call Sign: N1QAQ
Timothy L Jordan
50 Brimmer Street
Brewer ME 044122131

Call Sign: N1YAP
Brian A Berry
32 Century St
Brewer ME 04412

Call Sign: N1JYA
Harold E De Grasse
249 Chamberlain
Brewer ME 04412

Call Sign: KB1JHM
Richard C Young
145 Chamberlain St
Brewer ME 04412

Call Sign: KB1DHE

Thomas H Flanagan
54 Clover Ln
Brewer ME 044121302

Call Sign: N1BXL
David E Beers
15 Country Way
Brewer ME 04412

Call Sign: WA1BWS
Roger L Burnham
8 Craig Dr
Brewer ME 04412

Call Sign: N1RXC
KRISTY L Willett
191 Day Rd. Lot 17
Brewer ME 04412

Call Sign: N1KVJ
Orville C Leighton
14 Eastern Ave
Brewer ME 04412

Call Sign: N1ROU
Ella M Leighton
14 Eastern Ave
Brewer ME 04412

Call Sign: KB1BNH
Heather J Pawson
191 Eastern Ave
Brewer ME 04412

Call Sign: W1YTQ
Fred W Bean Sr
380 Eastern Ave
Brewer ME 04412

Call Sign: N1WMP
Keith C Brown
75 Grove St
Brewer ME 04412

Call Sign: KA1SVU

Harold F Beaulieu
103 Grove St
Brewer ME 04412

Call Sign: KA1WLU
Randolph R Tomasik
52 Holyoke St
Brewer ME 04412

Call Sign: N1MKP
Roderick P Houston
2 Houston Ln
Brewer ME 04412

Call Sign: N1AAQ
Darryl R Rowles
72 Nottingham Way
Brewer ME 04412

Call Sign: WB1GKK
Robert N Lord
145 Parker St
Brewer ME 04412

Call Sign: N1FKM
Noel L Mccann
110 Parker St Apt 2
Brewer ME 04413

Call Sign: W1BSU
Randolph G Whitten
221 Parkway South
Brewer ME 04412

Call Sign: NC1S
Donald R Golding
52 Shadow Ln
Brewer ME 04412

Call Sign: KB1SUY
Scott A Arbo
18 Sky View Ave
Brewer ME 04412

Call Sign: WA1ZRG

Gary A Locke
49 Sunset Strip
Brewer ME 04412

Call Sign: KA1FHG
Mario J Sirabella
11 Washington St
Brewer ME 04412

Call Sign: KA1RJL
Harland E Blanchard
195 Washington St
Brewer ME 04412

Call Sign: NW1O
Louis R Bligh
231 Wiswell Road
Brewer ME 04412

Call Sign: KB1CSN
Rita S Poirier
Brewer ME 04412

Call Sign: KC1WQ
Stephen A Doherty
Brewer ME 044123793

Call Sign: KE1IS
Michael J Colson
Brewer ME 04412

Call Sign: WA2HIP
John R Petrocelli
Brewer ME 04412

Call Sign: KB1IMT
Thomas J Sockolosky
Brewer ME 04412

FCC Amateur Radio
Licenses in Bridgewater

Call Sign: N1YIT
Ira L Scherr
Rr 1 Box 27

Bridgewater ME 04735

FCC Amateur Radio
Licenses in Bridgton

Call Sign: N1IZA
Kenneth A Wright
17 Beechwood Ln
Bridgton ME 04009

Call Sign: KB1KDZ
Jason M Lavoie
2 Bennett St
Bridgton ME 04009

Call Sign: KA1ZZA
Teresa L Ross
Rr 1 Box 1028b
Bridgton ME 04009

Call Sign: KA1ZYZ
Glynn J Ross Sr
Rr 1 Box 1028b Snowy
Acres
Bridgton ME 04009

Call Sign: KB1GT
John P Davison
Rr 1 Box 109
Bridgton ME 04009

Call Sign: KB1ADU
Warren S Noble
Rr 1 Box 1461
Bridgton ME 04010

Call Sign: KB1KRV
Donald W Wright
Rr 2 Box 296a Pond Rd
Bridgton ME 040099515

Call Sign: KB1KRW
Patricia A Wright
Rr 2 Box 296a Pond Rd
Bridgton ME 040099515

Call Sign: WB1AJY
Robert Gelles
Rr1 Box 500
Bridgton ME 040099730

Call Sign: AC1I
Robert Gelles
Rr1 Box 500
Bridgton ME 040099730

Call Sign: N1SHD
Robert W Liscoe
Rr2 Box 574
Bridgton ME 04009

Call Sign: N1BLY
Mark G Allen
Rr 2 Box 625
Bridgton ME 04009

Call Sign: N1BMF
Phyllis Allen
Rr2 Box 625
Bridgton ME 04009

Call Sign: KB1KND
Robert W Pierce
Rfd 2 Box 671
Bridgton ME 04009

Call Sign: KB1COI
Lewis M Pierce
Rr 2 Box 671
Bridgton ME 04009

Call Sign: K4ZTT
James L Gilbert
15 Burnham Rd
Bridgton ME 04009

Call Sign: N4WHU
Myra S Gilbert
15 Burnham Rd
Bridgton ME 04009

Call Sign: N1BJD
Clyde A Gerry
218c Burnham Rd
Bridgton ME 04009

Call Sign: KA1SFT
Debbie A Howard
4 Church St
Bridgton ME 04009

Call Sign: WA3GCZ
Ethan B May
8 Church St
Bridgton ME 04009

Call Sign: KB1IT
Peter J Howard
181 Dugway Road
Bridgton ME 04009

Call Sign: KA1ZIJ
Charles E Warner
2 Fern St
Bridgton ME 04009

Call Sign: N1YBD
Fred E Whiting Jr
3 Fowler St
Bridgton ME 04009

Call Sign: W1PAR
Philip A Reynard
34 Green St
Bridgton ME 04009

Call Sign: WA1GWU
Kenneth C Jackson
516 Harrison Road
Bridgton ME 04009

Call Sign: K1SDC
James D Medcalf
514 Hio Ridge Road
Bridgton ME 04009

Call Sign: KA1ZYD
Lega S Medcalf
514 Hio Ridge Road
Bridgton ME 04009

Call Sign: KA1ZID
Thomas J Stuart
149 Main St
Bridgton ME 04009

Call Sign: KB1LOP
John E Sims
16 Maple
Bridgton ME 04009

Call Sign: W1GAF
John E Sims
16 Maple
Bridgton ME 04009

Call Sign: N1GDS
Duane E Prugh
Moose Pond Dr
Bridgton ME 04009

Call Sign: AC1I
Robert Gelles
16 North Bay Road
Bridgton ME 040099730

Call Sign: N1LEM
Brett H Bishop
17 Nulty St
Bridgton ME 04009

Call Sign: KB1AQE
George T Drisko Jr
5 Pine St
Bridgton ME 040091321

Call Sign: KB1OV
Norman W Nielson
95 Pond Rd
Bridgton ME 04009

Call Sign: KA1LG
Stevens H Barker
21 Smith Ave
Bridgton ME 04009

Call Sign: KB1YI
Neal P Edwards
256 Sweden Road
Bridgton ME 04009

Call Sign: N1EBN
Jo Anne M Edwards
256 Sweden Road
Bridgton ME 04009

Call Sign: AD5VB
Martyn Gregory
30 Tanner Way
Bridgton ME 04009

Call Sign: WA6DBE
Albert J Sweney
1245 Ward Acres
Bridgton ME 04009

Call Sign: K1EOX
Harold S Fellman
14 Wayside Ave
Bridgton ME 04009

Call Sign: KA1ZYW
Daniel E Ross I
1497 Winn Rd
Bridgton ME 04009

Call Sign: KA1ZYX
Pamela S Noble
Box 1461 Winn Rd
Bridgton ME 04009

Call Sign: KA1ZYY
Vickie H Ross
Box 1497 Winn Rd
Bridgton ME 04009

Call Sign: N1QPQ
Alfred W Maxwell Iii
143 Winn Road
Bridgton ME 04009

Call Sign: KA1ZIH
Eric J H Bell
Bridgton ME 04009

Call Sign: KB1KAE
Sheila M Sullivan
Bridgton ME 04009

Call Sign: KB1KAF
Peter P Sullivan
Bridgton ME 04009

Call Sign: KB1PYI
Richard E Carpenter
Bridgton ME 04009

Call Sign: N1ATF
Richard E Carpenter
Bridgton ME 04009

Call Sign: KB1SSH
Beth A Lyon
Bridgton ME 04009

**FCC Amateur Radio
Licenses in Bristol**

Call Sign: N1MHB
Craig E Elliott Sr
1714 Bristol Rd
Bristol ME 045393510

Call Sign: K1CEE
Craig E Elliott Sr
1714 Bristol Rd
Bristol ME 045393510

Call Sign: KA1MMY
Douglas E Clark

644 Bristol Rd.
Bristol ME 045393040

Call Sign: K1YCS
Norman L Chase
Fogler Rd
Bristol ME 04539

Call Sign: KB1TXW
Ralph Hassenpflug
138 Lower Round Pond Rd
Bristol ME 04539

Call Sign: KB1BXX
Melvin C Fountain
282 Lower Round Pond Rd
Bristol ME 04539

Call Sign: N1VNO
Michael C Sykes
Bristol ME 04539

Call Sign: W1HZC
George E Bergey
Bristol ME 045390031

Call Sign: W7KLU
Dana D Dyer
Bristol ME 045390186

Call Sign: KB1HTK
Allyson L Dyer
Bristol ME 04539

Call Sign: KB1IJF
Lynn Dyer
Bristol ME 04539

Call Sign: KB1KOF
Robert B Larkin
Bristol ME 04539

**FCC Amateur Radio
Licenses in Bristol Mills**

Call Sign: KA1DAX
William A Clark Iii
Bristol Mills ME 04539

**FCC Amateur Radio
Licenses in Brooklin**

Call Sign: KA1LBG
Newell F Varney
Hcr 64 Box 900
Brooklin ME 04616

Call Sign: N4UBJ
Philip Wick
110 Naskeag Rd
Brooklin ME 04616

Call Sign: KB1PTR
Kevin J Duddy
768 Reach Rd
Brooklin ME 04616

Call Sign: W1IU
John E Frake
Brooklin ME 04616

**FCC Amateur Radio
Licenses in Brooks**

Call Sign: W1LEM
Arthur M Vuilleumier
Grant Rd
Brooks ME 04921

Call Sign: KB1LRC
Roger L Pariseau
922 Kenney Rd
Brooks ME 04921

Call Sign: N1ITK
Arthur E Hildebrandt
54 Moosehead Trail
Highway
Brooks ME 04921

Call Sign: KB1DVM
Eric M Watkins
96 Payson Rd
Brooks ME 04921

Call Sign: KB1WOV
Matthew H Hall
219 Valley Rd
Brooks ME 04921

Call Sign: N1ROV
Matthew H Hall
219 Valley Rd
Brooks ME 04921

Call Sign: N1BRD
Arthur M Vuilleumier Jr
Brooks ME 04921

**FCC Amateur Radio
Licenses in Brooksville**

Call Sign: KA1UQT
Blaine L Lymburner
Box 111
Brooksville ME 04617

Call Sign: N1NJQ
Robert K Cassatt
44 Cassatt Rd
Brooksville ME 04617

Call Sign: N1NJR
Carol D Cassatt
44 Cassatt Rd
Brooksville ME 04617

Call Sign: W1DMP
Samuel C Goldman
93 Herrick Road
Brooksville ME 04617

Call Sign: KB1IOM
Jeremy R Chapman
455 Varnumvill Rd

Brooksville ME 04617

Call Sign: AA1TU
Christopher D Bailey
434 Varnumville Rd
Brooksville ME 04617

Call Sign: KA1RXX
Steven D Bailey
434 Varnumville Rd
Brooksville ME 04617

Call Sign: N1THB
Alison S Bramham
434 Varnumville Rd
Brooksville ME 04617

Call Sign: KB1JQN
Kamilla A Bramham
434 Varnumville Rd
Brooksville ME 04617

Call Sign: KB1KHU
Kalle A Bailey
434 Varnumville Rd
Brooksville ME 04617

Call Sign: KD1ZN
Karl S Webster
Brooksville ME 04617

Call Sign: W1BU
Franklin W Eaton
Brooksville ME 04617

Call Sign: N1RJU
Earle E Bubar
125 Main St
Brookton ME 04413

**FCC Amateur Radio
Licenses in Brownfield**

Call Sign: N3LYT
Theodor W Mommers Jr

24 Bog Rd
Brownfield ME 04010

Call Sign: N1LCU
Richard J F King Sr
Rr 1 Box 381
Brownfield ME 04010

Call Sign: WB0OPR
Albert G Mc Kinney Jr
375 Main Street
Brownfield ME 04010

Call Sign: K1FZU
William A Haworth
352 Riverbend Rd
Brownfield ME 040100201

Call Sign: KB1WKT
Michael F Hatch
712 Spring St
Brownfield ME 04010

Call Sign: N1SPR
John Sherman
Brownfield ME 04010

Call Sign: W1TNV
Charles W Harmon
Brownfield ME 04010

**FCC Amateur Radio
Licenses in Brownville**

Call Sign: KB1WPZ
Robert E Campbell
25 Big Pine Dr
Brownville ME 04414

Call Sign: N1UFU
Herve F Jalette Jr
259 Church St
Brownville ME 04414

Call Sign: KB1HCP

Richard E Whitten
362 Davis St
Brownville ME 04414

Call Sign: N1RCU
Terrance R Knowles
106 Front Street
Brownville ME 04414

Call Sign: N1UCN
Margaret A Williams
106 Front Street
Brownville ME 04414

Call Sign: AA1QT
Harry A Hilton Jr
37 Henderson Street
Brownville ME 04414

Call Sign: KB1KBR
Beatrice Hilton
37 Henderson Street
Brownville ME 04414

Call Sign: WA1JMM
George R Dean
39 Railroad Ave
Brownville ME 04414

Call Sign: KB1WRY
Debra A Kaczowski
40 Rips Rd
Brownville ME 04414

Call Sign: KB1WRZ
David J Ramsey
40 Rips Rd
Brownville ME 04414

Call Sign: KB1WWH
George B Peterle
351 Williamsburg Rd.
Brownville ME 04414

Call Sign: N1MCK

Patricia A Getchell
Brownville ME 04414

Call Sign: KB1LVA
Christopher B Mitchell
Brownville ME 044140308

Call Sign: KB1VTC
Daniel E Thomas
Brownville ME 04414

Call Sign: KB1VZU
Patrick S Thomas
Brownville ME 04414

FCC Amateur Radio Licenses in Brownville Junction

Call Sign: WA1LFW
Thomas E Belvin
Box 306 Henderson St
Brownville Junction ME 04415

Call Sign: N3YDR
Malcolm M Blue
Muelendyke Ave
Brownville Junction ME 04415

Call Sign: N1MCA
Robert E Campbell Iii
1 School St
Brownville Junction ME 04415

FCC Amateur Radio Licenses in Brunswick

Call Sign: N1WZV
Christopher L Williams
16 Antietam D
Brunswick ME 04011

Call Sign: KB1UHW
Gerald L Brace
12 Bailey Ln
Brunswick ME 04011

Call Sign: K4HGY
James E Knight
24 Baribeau Dr
Brunswick ME 04011

Call Sign: WA1ZHX
Daniel L Regan
27 Barrows St
Brunswick ME 04011

Call Sign: KC1UZ
Kenneth N Matteson Sr
22 Bay Bridge Rd
Brunswick ME 04011

Call Sign: N1TUV
Gerald A Giggey
15 Baybridge Road
Brunswick ME 04011

Call Sign: W1CEX
Frederick M Beck
40 Beech Drive
Brunswick ME 04011

Call Sign: N1CHN
Harold B Bubar
25 Beverly Drive
Brunswick ME 04011

Call Sign: KB1DBM
William J Congdon
56 Boody St
Brunswick ME 04011

Call Sign: N2AHZ
Roland T Girard
10 Bowdoin St
Brunswick ME 04011

Call Sign: WA1GZZ
Murray M Bolton Jr
Rr 2 Box 2178h
Brunswick ME 040119612

Call Sign: N1DCK
Kenneth A Ault
Rt 5 Box 2353
Brunswick ME 04012

Call Sign: W1BHR
Arthur W Lee
Rr3 Box3184
Brunswick ME 04012

Call Sign: AA4AK
Stephen W Kercel
2 Brian Drive
Brunswick ME 04011

Call Sign: KA1NBF
Gerry S Hayes
124 Bunganuc Rd
Brunswick ME 04011

Call Sign: N1NAC
Cara J Hayes
124 Bunganuc Rd
Brunswick ME 04011

Call Sign: N1OGN
H M Ballard
239 Casco Rd
Brunswick ME 04011

Call Sign: N1ZIS
Wallace S Smith
22 Cluf Bay Rd
Brunswick ME 04011

Call Sign: N1DPX
Darrell R Cox
7 Coach Ln
Brunswick ME 04011

Call Sign: WH6BQR
Richard A Lay
28 College St
Brunswick ME 040112539

Call Sign: KB1KAT
Barbara J Schroeder
164 Coombs Rd
Brunswick ME 04011

Call Sign: KB1KTN
Linda C Hebert
182 Coombs Rd
Brunswick ME 04011

Call Sign: KC2GE
Douglas A Fisher
17 Damarin Lane
Brunswick ME 04011

Call Sign: KB1IPZ
Angela J Bryant
326 Durham Rd
Brunswick ME 04011

Call Sign: N1DSV
Zeke W Holland
86 Echo Rd
Brunswick ME 04011

Call Sign: KA1SKO
Jonathan C Shepherd
13 Federal St
Brunswick ME 04011

Call Sign: N1KGJ
Kenneth B Reidy
Box 2207 Great Is
Brunswick ME 04011

Call Sign: N1PGI
Jamie S Makepeace
7 Guadalcanal St
Brunswick ME 04011

Call Sign: K1PLT
Patricia L Tauro Mrs
175 Hacker Rd
Brunswick ME 04011

Call Sign: KI1TT
Anthony R Tauro
175 Hacker Rd.
Brunswick ME 04011

Call Sign: KA1TT
Anthony R Tauro
175 Hacker Rd.
Brunswick ME 04011

Call Sign: N6DRL
Richard F Michael
11 Heath Street
Brunswick ME 04011

Call Sign: KB1HPQ
Allen W Michaels
44 Hemlock Rd
Brunswick ME 04011

Call Sign: KB1HPR
Glenn A Michaels
44 Hemlock Rd
Brunswick ME 04011

Call Sign: N1TZU
Robert L Robinson Jr
19 Hennessey Ave
Brunswick ME 04011

Call Sign: KB1KJY
Harry Mcnelley
281 Hillside Rd
Brunswick ME 04011

Call Sign: N1TTT
Harry Mcnelley
281 Hillside Rd
Brunswick ME 04011

Call Sign: N1VEW
Clifford B Day
39 James St
Brunswick ME 04011

Call Sign: KA1TMP
Alban G Hannigan
4 Jeff St
Brunswick ME 04011

Call Sign: KC2VWP
Anthony C Redes
113a Jordan Ave
Brunswick ME 04011

Call Sign: KA1SKM
David L Cockburn
10 Katherine St
Brunswick ME 04011

Call Sign: N1HOA
Karen E Frey
9 Krampf Cir
Brunswick ME 04011

Call Sign: KB1EXC
Brian L Dorval
28 Lamb Farm Rd
Brunswick ME 04011

Call Sign: AA1WI
Brian L Dorval
28 Lamb Farm Rd
Brunswick ME 04011

Call Sign: KB1HNU
Annette L Dorval
28 Lamb Farm Rd
Brunswick ME 04011

Call Sign: KB1LJX
Shane B Dorval
28 Lamb Farm Rd
Brunswick ME 04011

Call Sign: KA1KV
Will R Havey
18 Larry Ln
Brunswick ME 04011

Call Sign: K1SYZ
Conrad E Parker
19 Larry Ln
Brunswick ME 04011

Call Sign: N1LHO
Walter F Barker
16 Locust Ln
Brunswick ME 04011

Call Sign: W1JJK
John J Kaiser
17 Long St
Brunswick ME 040119471

Call Sign: N1IZG
Michael L Gerardi
43 Longfellow Ave
Brunswick ME 04011

Call Sign: KE1JX
Clarence W Davis
117 Lunt Rd
Brunswick ME 04011

Call Sign: W1BQB
Clarence W Davis
117 Lunt Rd
Brunswick ME 04011

Call Sign: N1XBN
Evelyn G Mc Queeney
39 Mac Millan Dr
Brunswick ME 04011

Call Sign: N1VVF
Robert D Mc Queeney
39 Macmillan Dr
Brunswick ME 04011

Call Sign: W1KJU
Murray H Litchfield
3 Magean St
Brunswick ME 04011

Call Sign: KA1LVM
David E Hunt
284 Maine St
Brunswick ME 04011

Call Sign: N1CQG
Maxwell A Fletcher
96 Maine St Pmb 175
Brunswick ME 04011

Call Sign: N1KSJ
Bradley Galuza
58b Maquoit Rd
Brunswick ME 04011

Call Sign: KA1SKP
Jennifer B Mc Intyre
19 Mc Keen St
Brunswick ME 04011

Call Sign: KB1LNR
Karen L Manley
152 Mc Keen St 16-D
Brunswick ME 04011

Call Sign: W3HHU
George L Rosol
8 Mclellan St
Brunswick ME 04011

Call Sign: KA1SKQ
Peter J Fife
34 Melden Dr
Brunswick ME 04011

Call Sign: KB1SYN
Gordon E Field
124 Mere Point Rd
Brunswick ME 04011

Call Sign: K1CAH
Alden J Bonang
135 Mere Point Rd
Brunswick ME 04011

Call Sign: W1MZA
Roger W Doran
236 Mere Point Rd
Brunswick ME 04011

Call Sign: W1RME
Roger W Doran
236 Mere Point Rd
Brunswick ME 04011

Call Sign: NJ1I
Gregory L Gimbel
1147 Mere Point Rd
Brunswick ME 04011

Call Sign: KB1FYP
Dana Baer
556 Mere Point Road
Brunswick ME 04011

Call Sign: KB1FYQ
Andrew J Baer
5856 Mere Pt Rd
Brunswick ME 04011

Call Sign: N5AGG
Daniel P Lindsley
12 Meredith Dr
Brunswick ME 040117416

Call Sign: N1OIG
John T Munton Jr
57 Merrymeeting Rd
Brunswick ME 04011

Call Sign: N1HGN
Michael J Hughes
14 Minat Ave
Brunswick ME 04011

Call Sign: K1MJH
Michael J Hughes
14 Minat Ave
Brunswick ME 04011

Call Sign: N1DLP
Robert C Tucker
19 Minat Ave
Brunswick ME 040111626

Call Sign: W1QII
Joseph M Chirnitch
6 Mountain Ash Ave
Brunswick ME 04011

Call Sign: N1VVL
Nancy S Chesley
3 Nancy Dr
Brunswick ME 04011

Call Sign: N1SYX
Harvey B Lesh Jr
2617 Oakledge Rd
Brunswick ME 04011

Call Sign: N1TKA
Richard J Stein
24 Oakwood Terr
Brunswick ME 04011

Call Sign: K1NF
Nelson H Frost Jr
208 Old Bath Rd
Brunswick ME 04011

Call Sign: N1KLO
Neal H Frost
208 Old Bath Rd
Brunswick ME 04011

Call Sign: KB1OGR
Dorothy L Burgess
110 Old Pennellville Rd
Brunswick ME 04011

Call Sign: KB1KTO
Donna M Dawson
179a Peterson Ln
Brunswick ME 04011

Call Sign: W1VY
Albert Hansen Jr
90 Pleasant Hill Rd
Brunswick ME 040117426

Call Sign: KA1YLQ
Phyllis M Harlow
11 Pleasant St Apt 4
Brunswick ME 04012

Call Sign: KB1MRZ
Marjorie A Turner
19 Potter St
Brunswick ME 04011

Call Sign: KX1I
Marjorie A Turner
19 Potter St
Brunswick ME 04011

Call Sign: KB1PHP
Samuel G Turner
19 Potter St
Brunswick ME 04011

Call Sign: KB1PHQ
Isaac J Turner
19 Potter St
Brunswick ME 04011

Call Sign: KB1JOV
Matthew T Baldwin
40 Primrose Lane
Brunswick ME 04011

Call Sign: KB1ACS
James F Oikle
322 Princes Point Rd
Brunswick ME 04011

Call Sign: KA1KXR
Edward M Mc Guigan
28 R School St
Brunswick ME 04011

Call Sign: N1ROF
Shawn J Thompson Sr
Box 2262 Rfd 5
Brunswick ME 09011

Call Sign: N1XHC
Christopher W Thing
129 River Rd
Brunswick ME 04011

Call Sign: AD1K
Geoffrey P Bates
22 Rocky Hill Dr
Brunswick ME 04011

Call Sign: N1HYV
Louis D Fucini
10 Shea Street
Brunswick ME 04011

Call Sign: N1NFK
Robin J Walls
6 Short St
Brunswick ME 04011

Call Sign: N1NUO
Robin D Walls
6 Short St
Brunswick ME 04011

Call Sign: W1NDC
Robert L Ward
1 Short Street
Brunswick ME 04011

Call Sign: WA1GPH
Carroll A Groves
12 Stone St Apt C01
Brunswick ME 040111545

Call Sign: KE7WMV
Nicholas C Rathbone
4 Sunset Way
Brunswick ME 04011

Call Sign: KA1UVT
Robert H Morris
29 Thompson St
Brunswick ME 04011

Call Sign: KA1SKN
Joshua R Weems
44 Thompson St
Brunswick ME 04011

Call Sign: KB1HNX
Richard F Dutting
25 Thornton Way Apt 309
Brunswick ME 04011

Call Sign: K1MNW
William F Messier
40 Tower Lane
Brunswick ME 04011

Call Sign: N1EIJ
David R Carpenter
50 Varney Lane
Brunswick ME 04011

Call Sign: N1SYY
Robert F Barr
5 Ward Cir
Brunswick ME 04011

Call Sign: N7CHG
George T Garcia
38 Ward Cir
Brunswick ME 040119340

Call Sign: N1GWE
Robert D Watson
30 Water Street Apt. 506
Brunswick ME 04011

Call Sign: N1CHA
John W Dresser
57 Willow Grove Rd
Brunswick ME 040112970

Call Sign: KB1IEI
William P Fisher
3 Windward Walk
Brunswick ME 04011

Call Sign: WZ1J
Stephen A Hanks
61 Woodside Rd
Brunswick ME 04011

Call Sign: W1GR
Growstown Repeater Users
61 Woodside Road
Brunswick ME 04011

Call Sign: AI1B
Jeffrey B Herbster
189 Woodside Road
Brunswick ME 04011

Call Sign: K1QDL
Calvin E Morgan
21 Woodward Pt Rd
Brunswick ME 040113826

Call Sign: K1TDI
William H Tims
139 Woodward Pt Rd
Brunswick ME 04011

Call Sign: K1IU
Timothy A Sweeney
Brunswick ME 040110464

Call Sign: KA1RWS
Barbara K Sweeney
Brunswick ME 040110464

Call Sign: KB1CLV

Family Christian Fellowship
Amateur Radio Clb
Brunswick ME 04011

Call Sign: N1XDK
Charles T Haskell
Brunswich ME 04011

Call Sign: N1CYK
William J May
Brunswick ME 04011

Call Sign: K1BR
Timothy A Sweeney
Brunswick ME 040110314

Call Sign: KB1VLD
Ann G Beal
Brunswick ME 04011

FCC Amateur Radio Licenses in Bryant Pond

Call Sign: KB1KPW
Ronald A Dorman
95 Bird Hill Rd
Bryant Pond ME 04219

Call Sign: KA1ABL
Richard W Berry
Box 123 Church St
Bryant Pond ME 04219

Call Sign: N1YIX
Ellen A Brochu
361 Koskela Rd
Bryant Pond ME 04219

Call Sign: N1ZEL
Brian L Brochu
361 Koskela Rd
Bryant Pond ME 04219

Call Sign: N1JTJ
Don E Parker

8 South Main Street
Bryant Pond ME 04219

Call Sign: NJ1Y
Don E Parker
8 South Main Street
Bryant Pond ME 04219

Call Sign: N1NHN
Harold F Clufey
Bryant Pond ME 04219

FCC Amateur Radio Licenses in Buckfield

Call Sign: N1YKW
Cynthia P Tucker
16 Benson Road
Buckfield ME 04220

Call Sign: N1TGR
Lance O Mc Innis
Rr 1 Box 2910
Buckfield ME 04420

Call Sign: N1JTI
Claude W Gagnon
Rfd 2 Box 2980
Buckfield ME 04220

Call Sign: KB1CNJ
James H Tucker
343 Darnit Rd
Buckfield ME 04220

Call Sign: K1GAL
S Ginger Gallin
270 Decoster Rd
Buckfield ME 04220

Call Sign: KB0OYB
August J Schau
224 Gammon Road
Buckfield ME 042204028

Call Sign: N1TOF
Frank G Monica
117 Hebron Rd
Buckfield ME 04220

Call Sign: N1VHJ
Virginia K Monica
117 Hebron Rd.
Buckfield ME 04220

Call Sign: KA1ZET
Thomas L Narhuminti
327 No Buckfield Rd
Buckfield ME 04220

Call Sign: N1PBH
David M Tribou
259 North Hill Road
Buckfield ME 04220

Call Sign: N1KID
Edward Mc Kenzie Jr
282 North Hill Road
Buckfield ME 04220

Call Sign: N1OMO
David A Goodrow
315 Old Sumner Road
Buckfield ME 04220

Call Sign: KB1URN
Mark Burton
200 Purkis Road
Buckfield ME 04220

Call Sign: KB1QYE
Jamie L Fowler
18 Shed Hollow Rd
Buckfield ME 04220

Call Sign: KA1VLD
Donald L White
97 Shedd Hollow Road
Buckfield ME 04220

Call Sign: KB1IHY
Cortney Hladik
71 Sumner Rd
Buckfield ME 04220

Call Sign: KB1IIB
Kyle A Hladik
71 Sumner Rd
Buckfield ME 04220

Call Sign: N1ASL
Michael D Newton
195 Turner St
Buckfield ME 04220

Call Sign: W1BFA
Michael D Newton
195 Turner St
Buckfield ME 04220

Call Sign: KA1JSP
Anton Topole
463 Turner St
Buckfield ME 04220

Call Sign: N1QAX
Janet M Topole
463 Turner St
Buckfield ME 04220

Call Sign: N1YIS
Wayne N Strout Jr
Buckfield ME 04220

Call Sign: KB1IEK
Gerald N Mathieu
Buckfield ME 04220

**FCC Amateur Radio
Licenses in Bucksport**

Call Sign: NY1S
Joseph P Zdrojowy
Rr 1 Box 517
Bucksport ME 04416

Call Sign: KB2RDA
Dirk J W Van Offel
Hcr 78 Box 56
Bucksport ME 04416

Call Sign: N1UYX
Austin G O Donnell
State Route 46 Box 695
Bucksport ME 04416

Call Sign: N1YIM
Suzette L O Donnell
State Route 46 Box 699
Bucksport ME 04416

Call Sign: N1BWI
C Robert Johnson
16 Conners Rd.
Bucksport ME 04416

Call Sign: N1IT
James F Beach
52 Cross Road
Bucksport ME 04416

Call Sign: KB1ALE
Morris C R Ford
321 Duck Cove Rd
Bucksport ME 04416

Call Sign: N1DAG
Gerald T Ledwith
15 First St
Bucksport ME 04416

Call Sign: KB6SU
William M Phillips
1 Forsythe Avenue
Bucksport ME 04417

Call Sign: WA1YRU
Raymond W Davis Ii
32 Moosehorn Drive
Bucksport ME 04416

Call Sign: K1RQG
Joseph M Demaso
79 Orcutt Mountain Road
Bucksport ME 04416

Call Sign: N1QAK
John S Knight
1353 River Road
Bucksport ME 04416

Call Sign: N5WPG
Ralph M Bohm
Bohm Palace River Road
Bucksport ME 04416

Call Sign: KB1FDP
Bruce A Clement Sr
198 Russell Hill Rd
Bucksport ME 04416

Call Sign: KB1FDQ
Bruce A Clement Jr
100 Russell Hill Road
Bucksport ME 04416

Call Sign: KA1TKN
Martin E Mann
75 School St
Bucksport ME 04416

Call Sign: KA1ZGT
Lorraine Mc Callister
8 Second St
Bucksport ME 04416

Call Sign: N1NIZ
Kenneth M Bouchard
Bucksport ME 04416

Call Sign: W1VEH
Benjamin B Blodget
Bucksport ME 04416

Call Sign: WA1ZCE

Blake E Gray
Bucksport ME 04416

FCC Amateur Radio Licenses in Burlington

Call Sign: KB1NKJ
Joan L Gauthier
Burlington ME 04417

FCC Amateur Radio Licenses in Burnham

Call Sign: N1PGZ
Roland D Bussey
Rr 1 Box 2792
Burnham ME 04923

Call Sign: K1TWJ
Edward M Solheim
110 Garcelon Rd
Burnham ME 04922

Call Sign: KB1OLL
James A Bergdoll
135 Lasselle Rd
Burnham ME 04922

Call Sign: N1PRA
Ronald E Trafton
Box 2310 Morgan Rd
Burnham ME 04922

Call Sign: N1WBP
Britt D Knowles
126 South Main St
Burnham ME 04922

Call Sign: KB1HTI
Darrell V Foss
Burnham ME 04922

Call Sign: W1DVF
Darrell V Foss
Burnham ME 04922

Call Sign: KB1LJC
Joy Lynne Foss
Burnham ME 04922

Call Sign: K1SEW
Joy Lynne Foss
Burnham ME 04922

FCC Amateur Radio Licenses in Buxton

Call Sign: KN1M
Thornton L Stokes
8 Carll Rd
Buxton ME 04093

Call Sign: AA1FM
Roy O Gorman
200 Chicopee Rd
Buxton ME 04093

Call Sign: KB1UFS
Adam W Mains
37 Denali Trail
Buxton ME 04093

Call Sign: N3AWM
Adam W Mains
37 Denali Trail
Buxton ME 04093

Call Sign: KB1NQW
Gregory A Pooler
173 Depot St
Buxton ME 04093

Call Sign: KD1M
Gregory A Pooler
173 Depot St
Buxton ME 04093

Call Sign: KA1PRD
Lewis D Waye
193 Dunnel Rd

Buxton ME 04093

Call Sign: N1LW
Lewis D Waye
193 Dunnel Rd
Buxton ME 04093

Call Sign: KB1VVA
Clarence A Tweedie
78 Eaton Dr
Buxton ME 04039

Call Sign: N1SDE
Brian J Dyer
39 Emery Cir
Buxton ME 04093

Call Sign: N1ZQA
Shelbie J Dyer
39 Emery Cir
Buxton ME 04093

Call Sign: KB1HHE
James D Presby
51 Emery Circle
Buxton ME 04093

Call Sign: KB1BGU
John W Small
45 Fogg Road
Buxton ME 040930522

Call Sign: N1JWS
John W Small
45 Fogg Road
Buxton ME 040930522

Call Sign: N1SH
Stephen A Houser
93 Fogg Road
Buxton ME 04093

Call Sign: KB1KSD
Ross Anderson
140a Haines Meadow Rd

Buxton ME 04093

Call Sign: W1TNT
Ross Anderson
140a Haines Meadow Rd
Buxton ME 04093

Call Sign: KB1NDC
Dennis T Palmer
128 Joy Valley Rd
Buxton ME 040936239

Call Sign: KB1ILE
Walden Charette Jr
66 Line Rd
Buxton ME 04093

Call Sign: AA1CZ
Albert W Noble Jr
14 Mertie Dr
Buxton ME 04093

Call Sign: WE1T
Harland B Gower
1197 Narragansett Trail
Buxton ME 04093

Call Sign: W1POR
Harland B Gower
1197 Narragansett Trail
Buxton ME 04093

Call Sign: KE1KH
Richard M Harrison
267 Old Orchard Rd
Buxton ME 04093

Call Sign: K1YH
Richard M Harrison
267 Old Orchard Rd
Buxton ME 04093

Call Sign: N1ZPD
Richard L Munson
44 Old Thompson Rd

Buxton ME 04093

Call Sign: KB1NQX
Robert L Connary
53 Overlook Dr
Buxton ME 04093

Call Sign: K1RLC
Robert L Connary
53 Overlook Dr
Buxton ME 04093

Call Sign: KC4ZZG
Burdette B Amen
19 Proprietors Rd
Buxton ME 04093

Call Sign: AA1YC
Burdette B Amen
19 Proprietors Rd
Buxton ME 04093

Call Sign: W1GFD
Sean P Binette
1135 River Rd
Buxton ME 040936123

Call Sign: W1WLC
David S Hubley
10 Sanctuary Drive
Buxton ME 04093

Call Sign: K5IC
Audie Kaufman
64 Seavey Drive
Buxton ME 04093

Call Sign: KB1GEM
Jerome D Williams
Union Falls Farm - 283
Simpson Road
Buxton ME 04093

Call Sign: AA1XX
Jerome D Williams

Union Falls Farm - 283
Simpson Road
Buxton ME 04093

Call Sign: KB1OJV
Gerhard O Gross
32 Twin Brook Dr
Buxton ME 04093

Call Sign: K1CAP
Thomas E Filieo
Buxton ME 04093

Call Sign: KB1JIH
Daniel R Weston
Buxton ME 04093

Call Sign: KB1WRU
Wesley J Wiese
Buxton ME 04093

**FCC Amateur Radio
Licenses in Buxton Saco**

Call Sign: K1VRQ
Amy Lyn Harrison
149 Old Orchard Rd
Buxton Saco ME 04072

**FCC Amateur Radio
Licenses in Calais**

Call Sign: KB1UER
Harold E Lee Jr
37 Barker St Apt 2
Calais ME 04619

Call Sign: KC0MVG
Kent A Shafer
36 Bayview Lane
Calais ME 04619

Call Sign: N1ZCI
Alan K Ames
Rr 1 Box 22

Calais ME 04619

Calais ME 04619

Calais ME 046191364

Call Sign: KB1FKG
Merrill R Parker
Rr 1 Box 66
Calais ME 04619

Call Sign: WB1DRO
Edward F Harvey
319 Main St
Calais ME 04619

Call Sign: NA1BC
John L Thompson Sr
67 St. Croix Dr
Calais ME 04619

Call Sign: KA1MZ
Billy A Monteer
37 Church St
Calais ME 04619

Call Sign: W1HAR
Edward F Harvey
777 Main St
Calais ME 04619

Call Sign: KB1DHD
Karyn L Demmons
58 Swan St
Calais ME 04619

Call Sign: N1BIA
Shirley M Monteer
37 Church St
Calais ME 04619

Call Sign: KB1UEY
Richard L Macmillan
C/O C E Feeds 486 North St
Calais ME 04619

Call Sign: WB1DUQ
Thomas M Brigham
Calais ME 04619

Call Sign: W1FJP
John C Reynolds Sr
22 Elm St
Calais ME 04619

Call Sign: W1MTB
Richard L Macmillan
C/O C E Feeds 486 North St
Calais ME 04619

**FCC Amateur Radio
Licenses in Cambridge**

Call Sign: KA1WYG
Peter R Guhl
20 Franklin St
Calais ME 04619

Call Sign: WA1QVQ
Percy G Haddon
128d Palmer St
Calais ME 04619

Call Sign: WB1FXN
Michael W Luellen
144 Bailey Rd
Cambridge ME 04923

Call Sign: WA1LFQ
Wallace M Haycock
19 Germain
Calais ME 04619

Call Sign: KB1UEU
Mary L Reiss
280 River Rd
Calais ME 04619

Call Sign: N1TEF
Lloyd R Haggert
Rfd 1 Box 1553
Cambridge ME 04923

Call Sign: N1JXP
Michael F Breckinridge
32 Harrison St
Calais ME 046191106

Call Sign: N1MJ
James M Jacobs
600 River Rd.
Calais ME 04619

Call Sign: N1MDS
Glen G Larson
Rfd 1
Cambridge ME 04923

Call Sign: KB1LDD
Rebecca L Colson
40 King St
Calais ME 04619

Call Sign: N1XBY
Alan C Smith
255 River Road
Calais ME 04619

Call Sign: WA1ROI
Frederick A Larson Sr
138 Ripley Rd
Cambridge ME 04923

Call Sign: KA1URR
Ruth F Brogan
233 Main St

Call Sign: KB1IEV
Derek Czerwinski
7 Spruce Street

Call Sign: K1FAL
Frederick A Larson Sr
138 Ripley Rd
Cambridge ME 04923

Call Sign: KB1IAT

Cambridge Maine Radio
Club
138 Ripley Road
Cambridge ME 04923

Call Sign: K1NAN
Cambridge Maine Radio
Club
138 Ripley Road
Cambridge ME 04923

Call Sign: KB1PSY
Cambridge Maine Military
Retirees Radio Club
138 Ripley Road
Cambridge ME 04923

Call Sign: WA1ROI
Cambridge Maine Military
Retirees Radio Club
138 Ripley Road
Cambridge ME 04923

**FCC Amateur Radio
Licenses in Camden**

Call Sign: KB1HSM
Peter J Theriault
58 Bayview St
Camden ME 04843

Call Sign: KF1R
Peter A Mc Bride
11 Belmont Ave
Camden ME 04843

Call Sign: KU4UO
Nancy D Plunkett
7 Blake Street
Camden ME 04843

Call Sign: KA1PPJ
Joseph J Gunther
Rr 1 Box 4444
Camden ME 048439719

Call Sign: WB1CXH
Edward W Emerson
Rr 1 Box 4876
Camden ME 04843

Call Sign: KA1CKF
Robert H Grobe
25 Curtis Ave
Camden ME 04843

Call Sign: KA1QJK
George G Barnard Ii
16 Eaton Ave.
Camden ME 04843

Call Sign: WA1WFB
June A Sears
108 Elm St
Camden ME 04843

Call Sign: K1LJJ
Gregory B Currier
6 Good Wind Ln
Camden ME 04843

Call Sign: KA1QNN
Alan J Mc Clelland
24 Gould St
Camden ME 04843

Call Sign: N1PGP
Martin L Zeigler Jr
8 Grove St
Camden ME 04843

Call Sign: KA1QEX
Robert R Smith
Highland Park Dr Apt 41
Camden ME 04843

Call Sign: KB1PPH
Michael S White
17 Hoffses Dr
Camden ME 04843

Call Sign: KA1DAZ
Sidney G Lindsley
2 Lantern Ln
Camden ME 04843

Call Sign: WA1VCY
Priscilla B Lindsley
2 Lantern Ln
Camden ME 04843

Call Sign: KB1SJA
Scott S Entwistle
25 Limerock St
Camden ME 04843

Call Sign: KB1LHZ
William H Welte
33 Megunticook St
Camden ME 04843

Call Sign: KB1LIA
William J Welte
33 Megunticook St
Camden ME 04843

Call Sign: KB1LGO
Duncan Matlack
49 Megunticook St
Camden ME 04843

Call Sign: N1DVD
William L Houle
104 Molyneaux Rd
Camden ME 048434424

Call Sign: WB2QQV
Steve A Masone
8 Mountain St
Camden ME 04843

Call Sign: KA1APH
Jerome W Young
84 Pearl St
Camden ME 04843

Call Sign: KC1FI
Jory I Squibb
13 Pleasant Ridge
Camden ME 04843

Call Sign: AA1OM
Charles E Seal
9 Pleasant Ridge Dr
Camden ME 04843

Call Sign: KD1WR
James C Titus
13 Pleasant Ridge Dr
Camden ME 048431041

Call Sign: KB1JHP
David R Getchell Jr
17 Rawson Ave
Camden ME 04843

Call Sign: W1JRW
Gary Domestico
40 Union St
Camden ME 04843

Call Sign: KA1YXY
Barry P King
Camden ME 04843

Call Sign: W1MHH
Roy E Watkins
Camden ME 04843

Call Sign: KB1IYL
Andy Boutin
Camden ME 04843

Call Sign: K1BRO
Andy Boutin
Camden ME 04843

Call Sign: KB1LRB
Robert Burns
Camden ME 04843

FCC Amateur Radio Licenses in Canaan

Call Sign: N1ZAX
Gary L Greenaway
984 Hartland Road
Canaan ME 04924

Call Sign: N5HIL
Kelly J Legault
46 Overlook Drive
Canaan ME 04924

Call Sign: KB1NGA
Kelly J Legault
46 Overlook Drive
Canaan ME 04924

Call Sign: KB1LZY
Thomas Novak
12 Browns Corner Rd
Cannaan ME 04924

FCC Amateur Radio Licenses in Canton

Call Sign: K1SJO
Michael A Timberlake
4 Brittany Lane
Canton ME 04221

Call Sign: N1UFW
Michelle L Timberlake
4 Brittany Lane
Canton ME 04221

Call Sign: N1VHF
Theodore E Therrien
120 Laplant Rd
Canton ME 04221

Call Sign: KA1YYJ
Norman A Vashaw
Canton ME 04221

Call Sign: WD8RZT
Allen R Ward
20 Farrand Hill Rd.
Canton, ME 042213011

FCC Amateur Radio Licenses in Cape Elizabeth

Call Sign: K1TYS
Charles W Vickerson
27 Angell Ter
Cape Elizabeth ME 04107

Call Sign: AB1QI
Alan S Putnam
32 Beach Bluff Terrace
Cape Elizabeth ME 04107

Call Sign: KB1BFT
John T Devlin
48 Broad Cove Rd
Cape Elizabeth ME 04107

Call Sign: KB1JBF
Stephen R Edmondson
10 Canterbury Way
Cape Elizabeth ME 04107

Call Sign: N1CGY
Maynard H Rosenberg
31 Concord Pl
Cape Elizabeth ME 04107

Call Sign: K1GUK
Glenda L Lentz
19 Cross Hill Rd
Cape Elizabeth ME
041075108

Call Sign: W1VBY
Philip C Lentz
19 Cross Hill Rd
Cape Elizabeth ME
041075108

Call Sign: KB1VFU
Robert L Benoit
26 Cross Hill Rd
Cape Elizabeth ME 04107

Call Sign: KA1NMH
Dodge D Morgan
18 Delano Park
Cape Elizabeth ME 04107

Call Sign: N2HWB
Carle D Porter
78 Dyer Road
Cape Elizabeth ME 04107

Call Sign: KB1ISR
Laura K Wilcox
59 Edgewood Road
Cape Elizabeth ME 04107

Call Sign: KB1SNC
L Mark Stone
18 Fieldstone Road
Cape Elizabeth ME 04107

Call Sign: KB1NPW
Warren D Alpern
6 Granite Ridge Rd
Cape Elizabeth ME 04107

Call Sign: N7FE
Reginald O Tremblay Jr
16 Hillcrest Drive
Cape Elizabeth ME 04107

Call Sign: KB1VDI
John Wise
10 Hunts Point Rd
Cape Elizabeth ME 04107

Call Sign: KB1KRY
Richard A Grotton
7 Ivie Rd
Cape Elizabeth ME 04107

Call Sign: N1LWD
Susan R Bergeron
2 Jewett Rd
Cape Elizabeth ME 04107

Call Sign: WA1YKI
James H Rand Sr
10 Jewett Rd
Cape Elizabeth ME
041072429

Call Sign: KB1VYX
Heidi Tait
10 Longfellow Dr
Cape Elizabeth ME 04107

Call Sign: KB1JGU
Jacqueline R Clark
57 Longfellow Drive
Cape Elizabeth ME 04107

Call Sign: KB1JGX
Robert L Clark
57 Longfellow Drive
Cape Elizabeth ME 04107

Call Sign: W1BTR
Albert E Craig Sr
19 Meadow Way
Cape Elizabeth ME 04107

Call Sign: KA1WFT
Adam C Weiss
27 Merrimac Place
Cape Elizabeth ME 04107

Call Sign: N1HQQ
David C Weiss
27 Merrimac Place
Cape Elizabeth ME 04107

Call Sign: WA1EPL
Lawrence J Frazier
345 Mitchell Rd

Cape Elizabeth ME 04107

Call Sign: W2XR
John O Seaver
15 Oakview Dr
Cape Elizabeth ME
041071131

Call Sign: N1JPJ
Christopher A Bond
207 Ocean House Rd
Cape Elizabeth ME 04107

Call Sign: W1ROU
Herbert L Cobb
495 Ocean House Rd
Cape Elizabeth ME 04107

Call Sign: KB1HIT
Southern Maine Ares/Races
75 Ocean House Road
Cape Elizabeth ME
041071111

Call Sign: KB1EZW
Michael D Powers
25 Orchard Rd
Cape Elizabeth ME 04107

Call Sign: KB1EAL
Joseph O Shevenell
2 Pine St
Cape Elizabeth ME 04107

Call Sign: WA1YOS
Robert E Armitage
18 Reef Rd
Cape Elizabeth ME 04107

Call Sign: K2VJE
Anthony R Bogosian
13 Salt Spray Ln
Cape Elizabeth ME 04107

Call Sign: KA1UGR

Husen Tu
1050 Sawyer Rd
Cape Elizabeth ME 04107

Call Sign: KB1LBQ
Leighton B Sargent
1080 Shore Rd
Cape Elizabeth ME 04107

Call Sign: W1LBS
Leighton B Sargent
1080 Shore Rd
Cape Elizabeth ME 04107

Call Sign: K1OSJ
John R Sutherland
1199 Shore Road
Cape Elizabeth ME 04107

Call Sign: W1ITU
Donovan A Robertson
16 Stonybrook Rd
Cape Elizabeth ME 04107

Call Sign: KB1UOX
Lawrence R Clough
57 Stonybrook Rd
Cape Elizabeth ME 04107

Call Sign: W1DEO
Herbert F Strout
14 Strout Road
Cape Elizabeth ME 04107

Call Sign: N1MZI
Bruce W Gasque
7 Winslow Place
Cape Elizabeth ME 04107

Call Sign: N1TLQ
William T Blake
15 Winslow Place
Cape Elizabeth ME 04107

Call Sign: N1AKP

Peter S Eastman
24 Woodland Rd
Cape Elizabeth ME
041071304

Call Sign: KC8HOA
Andrew M Millecchia
93 Zeb Cove Rd
Cape Elizabeth ME 04107

Call Sign: W1MGX
William R Landry Jr
7 Longfellow Dr
Cape Elizibeth ME 04107

FCC Amateur Radio Licenses in Cape Neddick

Call Sign: N1SVM
Joseph S Fox
26 Algonquin Dr
Cape Neddick ME 03902

Call Sign: N1TJW
Thomas S Fox
26 Algonquin Dr
Cape Neddick ME 03902

Call Sign: KB1SXP
David A Weare
291 Pine Hill Rd
Cape Neddick ME 03902

Call Sign: KB1KVR
Robert M Kelly
Cape Neddick ME 03902

Call Sign: KB1LPZ
Cindy L Kelly
Cape Neddick ME 03902

FCC Amateur Radio Licenses in Cape Porpoise

Call Sign: K1WJE

Maurice B Hutchins
Cape Porpoise ME 04014

Call Sign: KB1VHL
Stephen G Lapalme
Cape Porpoise ME 04014

FCC Amateur Radio Licenses in Caratunk

Call Sign: KA4YWB
Douglas D Brackett
180 Main Street
Caratunk ME 04925

Call Sign: WB4KYW
Jon J Sherlock
Caratunk ME 04925

Call Sign: KB1UGD
Edward A Hanscom
Caratunk ME 04925

FCC Amateur Radio Licenses in Caribou

Call Sign: KB1WGP
John P Thornton
104 Beckstrom Rd
Caribou ME 04736

Call Sign: KA1SO
Paul N Duffy
Rfd 2 Box 3000
Caribou ME 04736

Call Sign: N1CUQ
Carol C Duffy
Rfd 2 Box 3000
Caribou ME 04736

Call Sign: WA1URS
Dennis L Bosley Sr
95 Collins St.
Caribou ME 047362450

Call Sign: KB1JJJ
Edgar L Lower Jr
3 Corbin St
Caribou ME 04736

Call Sign: KB1WGN
Roy E Woods
19 Elmwood Ave
Caribou ME 04736

Call Sign: N1RTX
Dana G Jones
11 Elmwood Ave,
Caribou ME 04736

Call Sign: W1YXC
Elizabeth J Lamb
50 Harvest Rd
Caribou ME 04736

Call Sign: KA3YJJ
Angela A Abbott
137 High St
Caribou ME 04736

Call Sign: KA1SOT
Luke R Dyer
4 Hillside Ave
Caribou ME 04736

Call Sign: KB1WGO
Hermel A Turcotte
1 Lafayette St
Caribou ME 04736

Call Sign: KA1ORT
Christopher C York
628 Main St
Caribou ME 04736

Call Sign: WX1CAR
National Weather Service -
Skywarn
810 Main St

Caribou ME 04736

Call Sign: KF4JVB
Patrick S Morgan
35 Page Ave
Caribou ME 04736

Call Sign: KB1QIC
Penni A Morgan
35 Page Ave
Caribou ME 04736

Call Sign: WA1PCT
Reginald P Hanson
32 Paris Snow Dr
Caribou ME 04736

Call Sign: KE1JQ
Freeman F Dow
32 Powers Rd
Caribou ME 04736

Call Sign: WA1YOC
David W Wilcox
55 Russ St
Caribou ME 04736

Call Sign: N1WAO
John R Woodman
41 Sincock St
Caribou ME 047362309

Call Sign: KB1NLS
Derrick K Weitlich
10 Solman St Apt 20
Caribou ME 04736

Call Sign: KA1HIW
Donald T Merritt
837 Sweden St
Caribou ME 047363593

Call Sign: KA1ZTG
Zelma E Merritt
837 Sweden Street

Caribou ME 047363593

Call Sign: N1KGS
Max E Soucia
1167 Van Buren Road
Caribou ME 047360724

Call Sign: KA1ENM
Joseph M Susee
7 Violette Street
Caribou ME 04736

Call Sign: N3POZ
Tracey E Nichols
55 Washburn St
Caribou ME 04736

Call Sign: K1RLY
Robert F White
98 Washburn St
Caribou ME 04736

Call Sign: NG1F
Robert F White
98 Washburn St
Caribou ME 04736

Call Sign: KA1TIV
Mark L Westin
40 Washburn St.
Caribou ME 04736

Call Sign: N1IOZ
Joseph R Saucier
881 West Presque Isle Rd
Caribou ME 04736

Call Sign: KA1KAO
Ivan B Shaw
20 Westwind Dr
Caribou ME 04736

Call Sign: KA1ZTI
Ivan P Shaw
20 Westwind Dr

Caribou ME 04736

Call Sign: KB1MDM
Richard B Sosebee
346 York St
Caribou ME 04736

Call Sign: KC5UEQ
James T Cerrato
Caribou ME 04736

<hr>

**FCC Amateur Radio
Licenses in Carmel**

Call Sign: N1KAD
David N Smith
Rr 2 Box 1995
Carmel ME 04420

Call Sign: KB1FDN
Daniel J Holodick
Rr 1 Box 2686
Carmel ME 04420

Call Sign: N1NFP
Nicholas J Dole
Rr 1 Box 3453
Carmel ME 04419

Call Sign: KB1NDG
Ronald Kenny
134 Cook Rd
Carmel ME 04419

Call Sign: N1GAJ
Clement E Richardson
Hampden Rd
Carmel ME 04419

Call Sign: WA1IBN
Herbert P Dean
1413 Main Rd
Carmel ME 04419

Call Sign: N1TCM

Gail E Burns
Main Rd
Carmel ME 04419

Call Sign: W9AUD
Audrey J Naese
45 Plymouth Rd
Carmel ME 04419

Call Sign: N1PNJ
Wayne A Scovil
14 Preble Ln
Carmel ME 04419

Call Sign: K9QK
Kenneth L Naese Jr
Plymouth Rd Rt 69 West
Carmel ME 04419

Call Sign: K1GUP
Gerald B Burns Jr
Carmel ME 04419

Call Sign: KA1RMM
Mark W Worster
Carmel ME 04419

Call Sign: N1JLY
Julia R Soule
Carmel ME 04419

<hr>

**FCC Amateur Radio
Licenses in Carrabasset
Valley**

Call Sign: N1UVJ
GAIL M Mc GEE-
LAHAYE
1015 Carriage Road
Carrabasset Valley ME
04947

Call Sign: KB1KQX
The Loaf 13 Sugarloaf/Usa
Amateur Radio Club

6006 Mashie Ln
Carrabassett ME 04947

Call Sign: W1SLF
The Loaf 13 Sugarloaf/Usa
Amateur Radio Club
6006 Mashie Ln
Carrabassett ME 04947

Call Sign: N1URL
Richard P Lahaye
1015 Carriage Road
Carrabassett Valley ME
04947

Call Sign: KB1HQR
James P Marion
36 Tainter Corner Road
Carthage ME 04224

<hr>

**FCC Amateur Radio
Licenses in Cary
Plantation**

Call Sign: KA1EPT
Dominick J Menditto
6 Moose Lane
Cary Plantation ME 04471

<hr>

**FCC Amateur Radio
Licenses in Casco**

Call Sign: N1SNP
Mark E Jackson
31 Bass Lane
Casco ME 04015

Call Sign: N1ISW
David G Verrill
Rr 2 Box 1439
Casco ME 04016

Call Sign: KB1CQU
Alison L Green
Rr2 Box 1565

Casco ME 04015

Call Sign: KA1ZII
Leo P Bouffard
Rr 2 Box 662
Casco ME 04016

Call Sign: K9DEN
Dennis K Lennon
2 Graystone Drive
Casco ME 04015

Call Sign: KA1YX
John R Littlefield
340 Heath Road
Casco ME 04015

Call Sign: W1ANI
Richard L Holden
86 Leach Hill Road
Casco ME 04015

Call Sign: N1PJB
Miriam S Wetzel
983 Meadow Road
Casco ME 040153036

Call Sign: W1LI
Lewis D Wetzel
983 Meadow Road
Casco ME 04015

Call Sign: K1JRM
John R Manganello
84 Overlook Lane
Casco ME 04015

Call Sign: KB1LQE
Oxford County Ares
575 Poland Spring Rd
Casco ME 04015

Call Sign: W1OCA
Oxford County Ares
575 Poland Spring Rd

Casco ME 04015

Call Sign: N1WJO
Robert L Gould
572 Poland Spring Road
Casco ME 04015

Call Sign: KB1PWM
Edwin M Seckler
41 Thompson Lake Shores
Rd
Casco ME 04015

Call Sign: KB1DLH
Paul A Mitch
Casco ME 040150323

Call Sign: KB1QG
David T Sylvester
Casco ME 04015

**FCC Amateur Radio
Licenses in Castine**

Call Sign: K1UMZ
Francis X Goodwin
Hcr 79 Box 108
Castine ME 04421

Call Sign: N1EQO
Gordon B Mac Arthur
208 Castine Road
Castine ME 044213322

Call Sign: N1JMN
Lynda W Mac Arthur
208 Castine Road
Castine ME 044213322

Call Sign: KA1TPR
Gordon R Mac Arthur
13 Hatch Cove Drive
Castine ME 044210615

Call Sign: KB1CTX

Andrew N Johnson
Box 62 Maine Maritime
Academy
Castine ME 04420

Call Sign: KB1JWV
Marcus P Von Spiegelfeld
Maine Maritime Academy
Castine ME 04420

Call Sign: KB1JWU
Talal N Al-Thamna
Maine Maritime Academy
Box 192
Castine ME 04420

Call Sign: KB1JWS
Mohd S Al-Dosari
Maine Maritime Academy
Box 332
Castine ME 04420

Call Sign: KB1JWT
Ferhat Serifoglu
Maine Maritime Academy
Box C-24
Castine ME 04420

Call Sign: KB1LDB
Carl G Rhodes
Mma Box 392
Castine ME 04420

Call Sign: KB1CTU
Clarence M Young
Mma Box 506
Castine ME 04420

Call Sign: KB1CTW
David A Cunningham
Mma F 20
Castine ME 04420

Call Sign: N1RPJ
Timothy W Henderson

18 Simpson Rd
Castine ME 04421

Call Sign: KC5GRR
Robert M Womble
24 Sullivan Ln.
Castine ME 04421

Call Sign: KB1CSO
Kevin M Leeseberg
Castine ME 04421

Call Sign: KB1CTT
Leland R Dennett
Castine ME 04421

Call Sign: N1RVK
James W Warburton
Castine ME 04421

Call Sign: W1HMR
Paul E Cyr
Castine ME 044210798

Call Sign: W1ICC
E Gilman Tenney
Castine ME 04421

Call Sign: W1MMA
Maine Maritime Academy
Pleasant St Maine Maritime
Academy Amateur Radio
Club
Castine ME 04420

Call Sign: KB1JWW
Johnathan B Robichaud
Castine ME 04421

Call Sign: KB1JWX
Robert G Van Vechten
Castine ME 04420

Call Sign: KB1KMY
Jeffrey S Siegel

Castine ME 04421

Call Sign: W1ACA
Jeffrey S Siegel
Castine ME 04421

FCC Amateur Radio Licenses in Castle Hill

Call Sign: KA1YKN
Jon R Lamoreau
613 Haystack Mtn. Rd.
Castle Hill ME 047570192

Call Sign: KA1YKM
Jay R Lamoreau
591 Haystack Mtn. Road
Castle Hill ME 04757

Call Sign: KB1JJF
Tracy L Williams
2605 State Rd.
Castle Hill ME 04757

FCC Amateur Radio Licenses in Center Lovell

Call Sign: AA1UT
Timothy L Bubier
315 Foxboro Road
Center Lovell ME 04016

FCC Amateur Radio Licenses in Chamberlain

Call Sign: K1NXB
Alvin F Sproul Iii
Chamberlain ME
045410055

FCC Amateur Radio Licenses in Chapman

Call Sign: N1WRW

Kenneth N Mac Callum
708 Carvell Rd
Chapman ME 04757

FCC Amateur Radio Licenses in Charleston

Call Sign: N1WMQ
Ronald M Storer
Rr 1 Box 1030
Charleston ME 04423

Call Sign: KF4IHS
Justin M Beauvais
1223 Dover Rd
Charleston ME 04422

Call Sign: KT4NT
Robert M Beauvais
1223 Dover Rd
Charleston ME 04422

Call Sign: K1JGO
Schuyler C Burrill
Charleston ME 04422

Call Sign: KA1JZL
Richard D Trusz
Charleston ME 04422

Call Sign: WB1FXO
Rebecca R Burrill
Charleston ME 04422

FCC Amateur Radio Licenses in Charlotte

Call Sign: N1VYS
Rod B Roderick
Rr1 Box 368e
Charlotte ME 04666

Call Sign: WA1DXO
Kenneth W Carter
49 Smith Ridge Rd

Charlotte ME 04666

FCC Amateur Radio Licenses in Chebeague Island

Call Sign: NX1I
William F Armstrong
Box 126a John Small Rd
Chebeague Island ME
04017

Call Sign: W1KRH
Madeline L Craven
Rr Box 590
Chebeague Island ME
04017

Call Sign: K1VOG
Nelson D Stevens
278 South Rd.
Chebeague Island ME
04017

FCC Amateur Radio Licenses in Chelsea

Call Sign: W1CME
Michael P Bielecki
57 Beech St
Chelsea ME 043301043

Call Sign: W1QP
Michael P Bielecki
57 Beech St
Chelsea ME 043301043

Call Sign: K1HAU
Willard S Clark Jr
Rr 9 Box 4550
Chelsea ME 043309714

Call Sign: N1BCF
Phyllis E Saunders
231 River Rd

Chelsea ME 043301060

Call Sign: KA1JTP
Philip L Alexander Sr
236 River Road
Chelsea ME 04330

Call Sign: KA1JTQ
Philip L Alexander Jr
236 River Road
Chelsea ME 04330

Call Sign: KA1MLU
Carl E Morang
134 Togus Road
Chelsea ME 04330

Call Sign: N1TKF
Matthew J Corriveau
370 Windsor
Chelsea ME 04330

FCC Amateur Radio Licenses in Cherryfield

Call Sign: KA2AGG
Victor J Battaglia
53 Big Rock Lane
Cherryfield ME 046220351

Call Sign: AA1SF
Kevin J Shissler
Rfd 1 Box 116
Cherryfield ME 04622

Call Sign: KB1CKQ
Debra K Hubbard
Rr 1 Box 116
Cherryfield ME 04622

Call Sign: KB1PXT
Richard P Willey
33 Grant Rd
Cherryfield ME 04622

Call Sign: KB1CEJ
Narraguagus Bay Area
Amateur Radio Club
183 Main St
Cherryfield ME 04622

Call Sign: K1FQ
Kevin J Shissler
183 Main Street
Cherryfield ME 04622

Call Sign: N1FQ
Debra K Shissler
183 Main Street
Cherryfield ME 04622

Call Sign: KA1ZRA
Julian K Sprague
Narr Est Apt 37
Cherryfield ME 04622

Call Sign: KB1EUL
Cheryl A Brown
14 Spruce Hill Lane
Cherryfield ME 04622

Call Sign: KA1ZXV
Daniel W Ladrigan
Cherryfield ME 04622

FCC Amateur Radio Licenses in Chesterville

Call Sign: KB1JXY
Steven L Mudie
411 Chesterville Hill Rd
Chesterville ME 04938

FCC Amateur Radio Licenses in China

Call Sign: KG1O
Thomas W Beaudet
294 Maple Ridge Rd.
China ME 04358

Call Sign: NM1M
Frederic A Hayden
147 Park Lane
China ME 04358

Call Sign: WA1M
Todd N Tolhurst
China ME 04358

Call Sign: KC1JM
William J Rancourt
305 Neck Rd.
China Village ME
049260031

Call Sign: AA2KL
Robert C De Chaine
1078 Airline Rd
Clifton ME 04428

Call Sign: KB1AFB
Christopher F Roberts
299 Rebel Hill Rd
Clifton ME 04428

Call Sign: KB1AFC
Mike W Roberts
299 Rebel Hill Rd
Clifton ME 04428

Call Sign: KB1TLD
Ervin M Davis Ii
446 Rebel Hill Rd
Clifton ME 04428

Call Sign: K1DVW
Lawrence C Parlee
257 Scotts Point Rd

Clifton ME 044286019

Call Sign: KB1CXR
Susan Turner
Rr 2 Box 813
Clinton ME 04927

Call Sign: NS1U
Dale A Farrington
73 Dixon Rd
Clinton ME 049273724

Call Sign: KB1CXU
Thomas V Berry
813 Gustafson Rd
Clinton ME 04927

Call Sign: WA1HOD
Christopher L Murdock
416 Hinckley Road
Clinton ME 049273134

Call Sign: KB1RAL
Robert W Hartley
251 Mutton Lane
Clinton ME 04927

Call Sign: N1ENB
Timothy D Fuller
155 Pleasent St
Clinton ME 04927

Call Sign: KB1HOZ
Charles M Wescott Iii
33 Stoney Ridge Dr
Clinton ME 04927

Call Sign: KB1MRQ
Nicole M Wescott
33 Stoney Ridge Dr
Clinton ME 04927

Call Sign: N1ZDK
Paul J Favolise Jr
Rr 1 Box 40
Columbia ME 04624

Call Sign: N1JBI
James L Corliss
Rfd 1 Box 43b
Columbia ME 04623

Call Sign: N1XRW
Richard W Miller
55 Saco Rd
Columbia ME 04623

Call Sign: KA1QEI
Thomas A Ippolito
Rr2 Box 481
Columbia Falls ME 04623

Call Sign: N1ZPY
Dale J Look
224 Main St
Columbia Falls ME 04623

Call Sign: KB1HBP
Mary P Look
224 Main St
Columbia Falls ME 04623

Call Sign: K1ZPY
Mary P Look
224 Main St
Columbia Falls ME 04623

Call Sign: N1TSG
Vernon L Scott
343 Tibbettstown Rd
Columbia Falls ME 04623

Call Sign: N1WPQ
Gail M Scott
343 Tibbettstown Rd
Columbia Falls ME 04623

Call Sign: N1JIC
Charles L Foss
859 Tibbettstown Rd
Columbia Falls ME 04623

Call Sign: KA3CFM
Raymond F Fox
Tibbettstown Rd
Columbia Falls ME 04623

Call Sign: N6BAF
Candice L Perham
406 Tibbettstown Road
Columbia Falls ME 04623

Call Sign: KG4HRC
Elizabeth M Perham
406 Tibbettstown Road
Columbia Falls ME 04623

Call Sign: N1DP
David W Perham
406 Tibbettstown Road
Columbia Falls ME 04623

Call Sign: N1PPF
Bion B Tibbetts Iii
Columbia Falls ME 04623

Call Sign: W1HDW
Stanley W Novak Sr
Columbia Falls ME 04623

FCC Amateur Radio Licenses in Cooper

Call Sign: K1ITX
John D Howe
271 Cooper Highway

Cooper ME 04657

FCC Amateur Radio Licenses in Coopers Mill

Call Sign: N1UZD
William J Nelson
Coopers Mill ME 04341

Call Sign: KB1ABG
Bruce L Rollins Sr
Rr 1 Box 1058
Coopers Mills ME 04341

FCC Amateur Radio Licenses in Corea

Call Sign: N1YPM
Eli Brown
Po Box 103
Corea ME 04624

Call Sign: N1TDH
Robert A Leightner
The Seawall Box 13
Corea ME 04624

Call Sign: N1ZDJ
Ann N Fiedler
Corea ME 04624

Call Sign: N1ZDO
Preston R Weaver
Corea ME 04624

Call Sign: KB1UJI
Kaylee D Wheaton
Corea ME 04624

FCC Amateur Radio Licenses in Corinna

Call Sign: KB1BLV
Robert A Davis
290 Bowden Rd.

Corinna ME 04928

Call Sign: WA1AFS
Edwin J Appleton
R 1 Box 2300
Corinna ME 04928

Call Sign: N1YAR
Ann M Gustin
Rr 1 Box 2920
Corinna ME 04928

Call Sign: KB1UTE
Michael D Platt
406 Greenbush Rd
Corinna ME 04928

Call Sign: KB1UAS
Ryan P Stankevitz
57 Hemlock Rd
Corinna ME 04928

Call Sign: KB1ELQ
Robert S Hicks
9 Hicks Rd
Corinna ME 04928

Call Sign: N1VHQ
James P Hicks
23 Hicks Road
Corinna ME 04928

Call Sign: N1YAS
Robin R Gustin
32 Nokomis Rd
Corinna ME 04928

Call Sign: N1VHR
Robert A Hicks
223 Packard Rd
Corinna ME 04928

Call Sign: KB1KOR
Deborah L Hicks
223 Packard Rd

Corinna ME 04928

Call Sign: KB2UPK
Craig T Gadeberg
237 Packard Rd
Corinna ME 04928

Call Sign: KB2UPG
Vincent F Costello
218 Packard Road
Corinna ME 04928

Call Sign: N1SNE
Andre R Methot
9 Winchester Ave
Corinna ME 04928

Call Sign: KB1EQD
James M Towne
9 Winchester Ave.
Corinna ME 049283606

Call Sign: WA2GBP
Joseph A Ortolano
Corinna ME 04928

Call Sign: KB1IHK
Jack R Brown
Corinna ME 049280406

FCC Amateur Radio Licenses in Corinth

Call Sign: N1JRM
Robert G Kelliher
85 Covered Bridge Rd
Corinth ME 04427

Call Sign: KB1PT
Merland E Clark Jr
105 Exeter Rd
Corinth ME 04427

Call Sign: KD1IU
David J Plourde

678 Hudson Rd.
Corinth ME 04427

Call Sign: WB2WKZ
George A Thomas
366 Main Street
Corinth ME 04427

Call Sign: KB1ROS
Gary C Chapman
118 Oroak Rd
Corinth ME 04427

Call Sign: KB1RVP
Joan C Chapman
118 O'roak Rd
Corinth ME 04427

Call Sign: KB1PXS
Randolph R Tomasik
37 Ridge Rd
Corinth ME 04427

Call Sign: KE7CM
Jeanne L Slasor
Corinth ME 04427

Call Sign: N1TXW
Dale M Moore
Corinth ME 044270166

Call Sign: WA1RKA
John M Manter
Corinth ME 04427

FCC Amateur Radio Licenses in Cornish

Call Sign: N1XYJ
Alonzo K Wallace Iii
40 King St
Cornish ME 04020

Call Sign: N1XYK
Lisa M Wallace

40 King St
Cornish ME 04020

Call Sign: K1BKJ
Donald W Morton
28 Maple St
Cornish ME 04020

Call Sign: N1SNR
Jeffrey A Hartford
32 Maple St
Cornish ME 04020

Call Sign: KA7HPG
Daniel R Haig
1889 North Road
Cornish ME 040203801

Call Sign: KB1STA
Paul M Gilfedder
18 Pumpkinville Rd
Cornish ME 04020

Call Sign: N1SDJ
Karl R Roney
Cornish ME 04020

Call Sign: KA1YMI
Paul E Dunfee
Cornith ME 04427

FCC Amateur Radio Licenses in Cornville

Call Sign: KB1KH
Clifton H Pease
1916 East Ridge Road
Cornville ME 04976

Call Sign: N1LHI
Robert G Mc Cann
820 Eastridge Road
Cornville ME 04976

Call Sign: KB1HUG

Robert G Mc Cann
1082 Eastridge Road
Cornville ME 04976

Call Sign: N1SJZ
John S Mackenzie
75 Thurston Rd
Cornville ME 04976

Call Sign: KB1OBR
Brenda R Higgins
784 West Ridge Rd
Cornville ME 04976

Call Sign: N1SXT
Robert F Higgins Sr
784 West Ridge Road
Cornville ME 04976

FCC Amateur Radio Licenses in Cranberry Isles

Call Sign: W1WDO
Carl N Brooks
Cranberry Isles ME 04625

FCC Amateur Radio Licenses in Crawford

Call Sign: WA1WZK
Courtney E Henry
Rr 1 Box 1242
Crawford ME 04694

FCC Amateur Radio Licenses in Cumberland

Call Sign: N1RXA
Armand A Desjardins
12 Blackstrap Rd
Cumberland ME 04021

Call Sign: N1XRK
William J Barry

21 Crossing Brook Rd
Cumberland ME 04021

Call Sign: N1AO
Donald K Lockhart Jr
65 Crossing Brook Rd
Cumberland ME 04021

Call Sign: KB1DQH
Jake S Goldfield
5 Lockwood Lane
Cumberland ME 04021

Call Sign: W1SMO
Sally M Martin
248 Main St
Cumberland ME 04021

Call Sign: WB1EBC
Guy A Curtis
252 Main St
Cumberland ME 04021

Call Sign: N1HWG
Charles M Zacks
68 Mill Rd
Cumberland ME 04021

Call Sign: KB1ETE
John K Madigan
46 Pleasant Valley Road
Cumberland ME 04021

Call Sign: KB1IKP
Gary L Parker
6 Prince St
Cumberland ME 040219500

Call Sign: W1IKP
Gary L Parker
6 Prince St
Cumberland ME 040219500

Call Sign: KB1LBM
Larry J Aufiero

33 Stonewall Dr
Cumberland ME 04021

Call Sign: KB1OJX
Frank W Lavoie
37 Sunnyfield Lane
Cumberland ME 04021

Call Sign: KB1OSB
Frank W Lavoie
37 Sunnyfield Lane
Cumberland ME 04021

Call Sign: KE4WKW
Richard A Barker
24 Valley Road
Cumberland ME 04021

Call Sign: KB1NVT
Faith E Morse
Cumberland ME 04021

Call Sign: KB1NVU
Paul C Shaffer
Cumberland ME 04021

FCC Amateur Radio Licenses in Cumberland Center

Call Sign: KA1HCO
Steven L Case
8 Balsam Dr
Cumberland Center ME 04021

Call Sign: W1CIE
Mary C Campbell Barry
21 Crossing Brook Rd
Cumberland Center ME 040219369

Call Sign: KB1SDI
Patrick J Williams
13 Lawn Ave

Cumberland Center ME
04021

Call Sign: W1RPT
Wayne H Merrill
279 Main St
Cumberland Center ME
04021

Call Sign: WA2GWK
William N Taylor
7 Oak St
Cumberland Center ME
04021

Call Sign: W1IMD
Paul M Alberghini
14 Orchard Hill Rd
Cumberland Center ME
040213220

Call Sign: W1KDE
Harry F Hinckley
10 Phillips St
Cumberland Center ME
040219537

Call Sign: W1GCB
Charles W Lyford
8 Pinewood Dr
Cumberland Center ME
04021

Call Sign: N1AKR
Ira S Hartman
175 Range Rd
Cumberland Center ME
04021

Call Sign: K1JNW
James N Whipple
48 Val Halla Rd
Cumberland Center ME
04021

Call Sign: K7LZH
Richard C Semmes
40 Winterberry Ct
Cumberland Center ME
04021

Call Sign: KA1SWB
Richard C Smith
Rfd 2
Cumberland Center ME
04021

Call Sign: WH6EI
Boyd G Morse
Cumberland Center ME
04021

FCC Amateur Radio Licenses in Cumberland Foreside

Call Sign: KB1GET
Frank Adshead
23 Sturdivant Rd
Cumberland Foreside ME
041101418

FCC Amateur Radio Licenses in Cushing

Call Sign: KB1FHX
Richard B Provonchee
103 Bird Pt Rd
Cushing ME 04563

Call Sign: K1RBP
Richard B Provonchee
103 Bird Pt Rd
Cushing ME 04563

Call Sign: N1MSZ
George L Hoyt
Rt 68 Box 92
Cushing ME 04563

Call Sign: KA1HJR
Reino E Saastamoinen
76 Cross Rd
Cushing ME 045639600

Call Sign: KB1LXS
Peter T Aiken
259 Gay Island
Cushing ME 04563

Call Sign: KB1PHF
Daniel P Remian
640 Pleasant Point Rd
Cushing ME 04563

Call Sign: W1CDE
Daniel P Remian
640 Pleasant Point Rd
Cushing ME 045633425

Call Sign: KB1DSW
Scott J Ewen
408 River Rd
Cushing ME 04563

Call Sign: KB1FYY
Donald F Demmons Sr
58 Ryans Lane
Cushing ME 04563

Call Sign: KB1QEP
Brandon C Jones
80 Spear Mill Road
Cushing ME 04563

Call Sign: KB1OIL
Brandyn Grierson
Cushing ME 04563

Call Sign: KB1PXJ
Victoria D Hoffses
Cushing ME 04563

FCC Amateur Radio Licenses in Cutler

Call Sign: N1PRC
Juanita G Landry
1930 Cutler Road
Cutler ME 04626

Call Sign: KB1GOR
Bradford W Geel
Cutler ME 04626

FCC Amateur Radio Licenses in Damariscotta

Call Sign: KB1VJY
Matthew D Merritt
10 Belknap Rd
Damariscotta ME 04543

Call Sign: KA1CQA
Mary E Gallagher
6 Branch Rd
Damariscotta ME 04543

Call Sign: WA1GIN
John D Gallagher
6 Branch Rd
Damariscotta ME 04543

Call Sign: KB1ESC
Edward J Wynne Jr
58 Bristol Rd
Damariscotta ME
045434000

Call Sign: KI1B
Ernest L Bourgon
66 Bristol Rd
Damariscotta ME
045430358

Call Sign: W1BWM
Ralph C Powell
Bristol Rd
Damariscotta ME 04543

Call Sign: K1LCI
Virginia G Powell
Powell Lane 25 Bristol
Road
Damariscotta ME 04543

Call Sign: WA3UMZ
Eugene Y Neilsen
Chapman St
Damariscotta ME 04543

Call Sign: KA1LKL
Earle W Pulsifer
Hodgdon St
Damariscotta ME 04843

Call Sign: N1ZIV
Ryan A Gallagher
15 Oyster Creek Lane
Damariscotta ME 04543

Call Sign: W1RU
Richard L Baldwin
35 Schooner St Apt 316
Damariscotta ME 04543

Call Sign: WE1V
Barbara J Frederick
53 Westview Rd
Damariscotta ME 04543

Call Sign: N1UJY
Charles L Frederick
53 Westview Rd.
Damariscotta ME 04543

Call Sign: K1LX
Lincoln County Amateur
Radio Club
Damariscotta ME
045430396

Call Sign: KB1UV
Frank E Reisdorf
Damariscotta ME 04543

Call Sign: W1JVC
Robert P Marsh Jr
Damariscotta ME 04543

Call Sign: WA1CXP
James W Gallagher
Damariscotta ME 04543

Call Sign: WA1WYT
Jane N Dearborn
Damariscotta ME 04543

Call Sign: N1WY
Edward J Wynne Jr
Damariscotta ME
045430396

Call Sign: KB1PIC
Jason A Nehrboss
Damariscotta ME 04543

Call Sign: KB1PYK
Mark H Potter
Damariscotta ME 04543

Call Sign: W1AUX
Mark H Potter
Damariscotta ME 04543

Call Sign: KB1QDE
Deborah A Potter
Damariscotta ME 04543

Call Sign: K1AUX
Deborah A Potter
Damariscotta ME 04543

Call Sign: KB1WQB
Steven A Severance
Damariscotta ME 04543

Call Sign: KB1WYH
Steven A Severance
Damariscotta ME 04543

FCC Amateur Radio Licenses in Danforth

Call Sign: KB1ESE
Sherrill D Colford
186 Houlton Road
Danforth ME 04424

Call Sign: W1MDZ
Stanley E Whiteman
Danforth ME 044240099

FCC Amateur Radio Licenses in Dartmouth

Call Sign: W1CE
Lewis K Scott Jr
239 Cross Rd Apt 224
Dartmouth ME 02747

FCC Amateur Radio Licenses in Deblois

Call Sign: N1LHB
Donald E Glidden
16 Gulf Rd
Deblois ME 04622

FCC Amateur Radio Licenses in Dedham

Call Sign: W1GDO
James W Rhoads Jr
502 Green Lake Rd
Dedham ME 044294531

Call Sign: K1DZP
James M Boober
53 Harriman Pond Ln.
Dedham ME 04429

Call Sign: KA1OFM
Peter Burke

21 Hillside Dr
Dedham ME 04429

Call Sign: KB1MVO
Paul S Tomlinson
231 Lakeview Ave
Dedham ME 04429

FCC Amateur Radio Licenses in Deer Isle

Call Sign: N1CNA
Charles E Hance
Rfd 1 Box 139
Deer Isle ME 046279700

Call Sign: W1RPC
Neville D Eaton
92 Church St
Deer Isle ME 04627

Call Sign: WA1O
Norbert E Yankielun
3 Coves End Road
Deer Isle ME 04627

Call Sign: N1OWP
John T Harrington
9 Quaco Rd
Deer Isle ME 04627

Call Sign: N1TDN
Marta A Harrington
9 Quaco Rd
Deer Isle ME 04627

Call Sign: W1WM
Robert E Thompson
Rfd Box 658
Deer Isle ME 04627

Call Sign: KB1VFV
Olsen D Svend
297 Sunset Rd
Deer Isle ME 04627

Call Sign: W1IBC
Corneil S Balding
Sunshine Rd
Deer Isle ME 04627

Call Sign: W1HS
Edward B Watts
17 Watts Lane
Deer Isle ME 04627

Call Sign: KB1EZ
Patrick R Weirs
17 Woods Road
Deer Isle ME 04627

FCC Amateur Radio Licenses in Denmark

Call Sign: N1MRU
Theodore B Bishop
196 Berry Rd.
Denmark ME 04022

Call Sign: KE4TTH
Paul W Currie
Box 709
Denmark ME 04022

Call Sign: KB1PCT
Bradford Lanoue
968 Denmark Road
Denmark ME 04022

Call Sign: N1TDU
Harold A Smith
226 Hio Ridge Rd
Denmark ME 04022

Call Sign: N1HYF
Shirley R Guthrie
Holiday Shores
Denmark ME 04022

Call Sign: WJ1N

David Guthrie
Holiday Shores
Denmark ME 04022

Call Sign: W6ES
Frederic R Carlson Jr
Mountain Rd.
Denmark ME 04022

Call Sign: N1MRE
Andrew C Knightly
22 Warren Road
Denmark ME 04022

Call Sign: KA1ZIE
John M James
Denmark ME 04022

Call Sign: KB1DTJ
Richard W Wohlenberg
Denmark ME 04022

Call Sign: N1KNR
Randal H Warner
Denmark ME 04022

Call Sign: N1MCV
Frances I Warner
Denmark ME 04022

Call Sign: W1KNR
Randal H Warner
Denmark ME 04022

**FCC Amateur Radio
Licenses in Dennysville**

Call Sign: N1AH
Christopher P Guida
Box 49a Rt 1
Dennysville ME 04628

Call Sign: N1VSR
Sherrill A Haddock
Dennysville Heights 27

Dennysville ME 04628

Call Sign: N1ZCH
Dwight L Lingley
Box 183 Foster Ln
Dennysville ME 04628

Call Sign: KB1STK
David R Wilder
47 Milwaukee Rd
Dennysville ME 04628

Call Sign: KB1QFC
John L Thompson Sr
200 Shipyard Rd Apt -9
Dennysville ME 04628

Call Sign: KB1VDY
John C Prime
Dennysville ME 04628

Call Sign: W1JCP
John C Prime
Dennysville ME 04628

**FCC Amateur Radio
Licenses in Detroit**

Call Sign: N1OQO
John A Hussey
102 Basford Road
Detroit ME 04929

Call Sign: KB2GZH
Wayne R Pfeffer
168 River Rd
Detroit ME 04929

Call Sign: KB8JA
Ray F Sparrow
49 River Road
Detroit ME 04929

Call Sign: KA1QWM
Deborah B Killam

88 River Road Route 69
Detroit ME 049290099

Call Sign: N1LRM
Robert J Wright Sr
95 Troy Rd
Detroit ME 04929

Call Sign: KA1NWW
Lawrence G Burton Sr
Detroit ME 04929

**FCC Amateur Radio
Licenses in Dexter**

Call Sign: KA1KYG
Mellen A Randall
Rfd 3 Box 2080
Dexter ME 04930

Call Sign: KA1LOY
Allan R Thomas
Rfd 1 Box 2140
Dexter ME 04930

Call Sign: KA1KDS
Donald E Soule
Rr 2 Box 2510
Dexter ME 04930

Call Sign: KA1JHU
Christopher P Germano
30 Denny Drive
Dexter ME 04930

Call Sign: N1HRL
George P Nickerson Jr
522 N Dexter Rd
Dexter ME 04930

Call Sign: KB1SYH
Richard W Brenske
295 North Dexter Rd
Dexter ME 04930

Call Sign: KA1WE
Richard L Peters
6 Obrien Rd
Dexter ME 04930

Call Sign: KB1PDO
Mark A Walters
20 Park St
Dexter ME 04930

Call Sign: KA1KPK
Timothy K Soule
46 Park St Apt 2
Dexter ME 04930

Call Sign: KA1PFD
Richard A Gilbert
62 Pleasant St
Dexter ME 04930

Call Sign: N1WZL
Thomas J Zanzucchi
158 Ripley Rd
Dexter ME 04930

Call Sign: N1ZMQ
Carmen C Zanzucchi
158 Ripley Rd
Dexter ME 04930

Call Sign: KE1O
David R Farris Sr
12 Summit Rd
Dexter ME 04930

Call Sign: WA1JPW
Roger L Ross
30 Summit Rd Apt 5
Dexter ME 04930

Call Sign: W1JE
James K Edes
16 Sunrise Ave
Dexter ME 04930

Call Sign: N1KGT
Joseph A Ranagan
123 Zions Hill Road
Dexter ME 04930

Call Sign: N1CSS
Louis H Morong
Dexter ME 04930

Call Sign: N1IVZ
Michael E Nickerson
Dexter ME 04930

FCC Amateur Radio Licenses in Dixfield

Call Sign: KB1IRE
John W Menthe
Rr 1 Box 6815
Dixfield ME 04224

Call Sign: N1ITN
Richard M La Brecque
Common Rd Rr 1 Box 990
Dixfield ME 04224

Call Sign: N1UHW
Nancy D La Brecque
Rr 1 Box 990
Dixfield ME 04224

Call Sign: N1XAY
Lauren A La Brecque
Rr 1 Box 990
Dixfield ME 04224

Call Sign: KB1WPT
Tyler L Chiasson
6 Child Hollow
Dixfield ME 04224

Call Sign: KB1WRT
Lauren A Hebert
592 Common Rd
Dixfield ME 04224

Call Sign: KA1YYH
Wendell E Palmer
1097 Main
Dixfield ME 04224

Call Sign: KB1WRH
Michael R Myles
178 Merrill Rd
Dixfield ME 04224

Call Sign: W1YVN
Harold W Blaisdell
26 Pine St
Dixfield ME 042240217

Call Sign: KA1MEX
John H Byron Sr
10 Weld St
Dixfield ME 042240595

Call Sign: KA1YYI
John H Byron Jr
Dixfield ME 04224

Call Sign: N1UFO
Oliver I Blood Sr
Dixfield ME 04224

Call Sign: W1WJN
Donald O Horne
Dixfield ME 04224

Call Sign: KB1OUI
David L White
Dixfield ME 04224

FCC Amateur Radio Licenses in Dixmont

Call Sign: WA1ERI
William P Hamernick
Garland Rd
Dixmont ME 04932

Call Sign: KB1ITR
Matthew V Harzewski
306 Moosehead Trl
Dixmont ME 04932

**FCC Amateur Radio
Licenses in Dover Foxcroft**

Call Sign: KB1ELS
David Grady
773 Bearhill Rd
Dover Foxcroft ME 04426

Call Sign: K1HSD
Ronald F Coates
75 Dwelley Ave
Dover Foxcroft ME
044261040

Call Sign: W1APU
David H Bamford
107 East Main
Dover Foxcroft ME 04426

Call Sign: KB1PAG
Clay D Lane
821 Greeleys Landing Rd
Dover Foxcroft ME 04426

Call Sign: KB1NDF
Robert J Fisk
171 Grove St
Dover Foxcroft ME 04426

Call Sign: KA1CZA
Earl H Betts
11 Harrison Ave
Dover Foxcroft ME 04426

Call Sign: KB1FM
Robert W Grey
108 Highland Rd
Dover Foxcroft ME 04426

Call Sign: W1QZM

Harold F Preble
82 Lincoln
Dover Foxcroft ME 04426

Call Sign: N1BQR
James L Warner
137 Park St
Dover Foxcroft ME 04426

Call Sign: KB1OSS
Scott A Martinez
367 Pine Street
Dover - Foxcroft ME 04426

Call Sign: KB1VYW
Bryce A Royal
375 Pine St Apt C
Dover Foxcroft ME 04426

Call Sign: N1PGW
Harry A Webber
93 Pleasant St
Dover Foxcroft ME 04426

Call Sign: WA1UCP
Thomas K Lyford
121 Pleasant St
Dover Foxcroft ME 04426

Call Sign: KA1MVK
Andrew H Soule
13 Starbird Siding Road
Dover-Foxcroft ME 04426

Call Sign: KB1ORJ
Thomas F Iverson Jr
Dover - Foxcroft ME 04426

Call Sign: AB1KA
Alan D Irwin
Dover-Foxcroft ME
044260215

**FCC Amateur Radio
Licenses in Dresden**

Call Sign: KA6MOF
Timothy F Madigan
8 Birch Ct.
Dresden ME 04342

Call Sign: N1JBD
Peter J Lewis
Rfd 1 Box 320
Dresden ME 04342

Call Sign: N1LMC
Patricia I Lewis
Rfd 1 Box 320
Dresden ME 04342

Call Sign: N1RJO
Jason M Brown
790 Calls Hill Rd
Dresden ME 04342

Call Sign: N1RJP
Linda C Brown
790 Calls Hill Rd
Dresden ME 04342

Call Sign: N1RJQ
Roger L Brown
790 Calls Hill Rd
Dresden ME 04342

Call Sign: N1MHR
Gail M Blomquist
10 Gardiner Road
Dresden ME 04342

Call Sign: K1LTO
Robert S Howe
593 Gardiner Road
Dresden ME 04342

Call Sign: KA1RFC
Ralph L Ames
339 Middle Rd
Dresden ME 04342

Call Sign: KB1TGA
Roger E David
679 Middle Road
Dresden ME 04342

Call Sign: KA1NNP
Steven E Collemer
1221 Middle Road
Dresden ME 04342

Call Sign: KB1FOM
Rufus S Rich
297 Patterson Rd
Dresden ME 04342

Call Sign: K1MAX
Maxim J Jacques
Dresden ME 043420159

Call Sign: N1ZEK
Paula J Moody
Dresden ME 04321

**FCC Amateur Radio
Licenses in Dryden**

Call Sign: W1RUZ
John L Mc Gillicuddy
Box 103
Dryden ME 04225

Call Sign: WA1LZR
Helen D Bubier
Box 5
Dryden ME 04225

**FCC Amateur Radio
Licenses in Durham**

Call Sign: N1ULU
Robert D Hedgpeth Iii
7 Beechwood Ln
Durham ME 04222

Call Sign: N1XQN
Laura J Hedgpeth
7 Beechwood Ln
Durham ME 04222

Call Sign: KA1WAL
Donald S Wakeman
38b Beulah Lane
Durham ME 04222

Call Sign: KB1FYO
Delroy D Cass Jr
365 Brown Rd
Durham ME 04222

Call Sign: KC1W
Adolph E Galonski
67 David Louis Dr
Durham ME 04222

Call Sign: KC1WYL
Marie G Galonski
67 David Louis Dr
Durham ME 04222

Call Sign: WA1YZV
Joyce B La Gasse
98 Grant Rd
Durham ME 04222

Call Sign: N5GUY
Robert G Duke
132 Grant Road
Durham ME 04222

Call Sign: KB1BLM
Parker E Morse Jr
44 Haskins Rd
Durham ME 04222

Call Sign: N1ULQ
Elwin J Demchak
95 Leighton St
Durham ME 04222

Call Sign: KA1MWH
John C Le Clair
420 Newell Brook Rd.
Durham ME 04222

Call Sign: N1OMV
David M Chirnitch
14 Pleasant View Farm Rd.
Durham ME 04222

Call Sign: KB1OVV
Richard Thornton
229 Plummer Mill Rd
Durham ME 04222

Call Sign: K1RLT
Richard Thornton
229 Plummer Mill Rd
Durham ME 04222

Call Sign: KB1UFG
William S Thornton
229 Plummer Mill Rd
Durham ME 04222

Call Sign: N1LJG
Terry Fleck
242 Plummers Mill Rd
Durham ME 04222

Call Sign: K1BS
Robert M Smith Jr
31 Rangdale Rd
Durham ME 04222

Call Sign: KD1BU
John R O'reilly
47 Reed Rd.
Durham ME 04222

Call Sign: KB1SND
Campbell R Searle
344 Runaround Pond Rd
Durham ME 04222

Call Sign: KB1OBC
Alexander K Brookhouse
246 Shiloh Rd
Durham ME 04222

Call Sign: KB1WIB
Ernest E Mildrum Jr
20 St Theresa Dr
Durham ME 04222

Call Sign: KB1WRS
Ernest E Mildrum Jr
20 St Theresa Dr
Durham ME 04222

Call Sign: KB1GVV
Hollie E Frost
507 Stackpole Rd
Durham ME 04222

Call Sign: KB1FEE
Wayne D Keith
55 Woodland Rd
Durham ME 04222

Call Sign: W1WDK
Wayne D Keith Mr
55 Woodland Rd
Durham ME 04222

Call Sign: KB1HEJ
Jan E Keith
55 Woodland Rd
Durham ME 04222

FCC Amateur Radio Licenses in Dryer Brook

Call Sign: WA1PLZ
Anthony Gillotti
1244 Dyer Brook Road
Dyer Brook ME 04747

Call Sign: WA1ZDL
Timothy P Gillotti

1244 Dyer Brook Road
Dyer Brook ME 04747

FCC Amateur Radio Licenses in Eagle Lake

Call Sign: W4VR
Ronald J Grandmaison
1913 Sly Brook Road
Eagle Lake ME 04739

Call Sign: KB1ROR
Raymond T Albert
Eagle Lake ME 04739

FCC Amateur Radio Licenses in East Baldwin

Call Sign: N1TJC
Peter E Rogers
Hcr 74 Box 150
East Baldwin ME 04024

Call Sign: N1BXE
Gerald L Wood
Rr
East Baldwin ME
040240039

Call Sign: KB1RHM
Alec S Kindred
39a Wentworth Rd
East Baldwin ME 04024

FCC Amateur Radio Licenses in East Boothbay

Call Sign: WA1HHK
Stephen R Sozanski
8 Anderson St
East Boothbay ME
045440511

Call Sign: N1WZT
Leander A Guite Jr

Box 379
East Boothbay ME 04544

Call Sign: W1QCJ
Frederic C Mc Kown Jr
Meadow Cove Rd
East Boothbay ME 04544

Call Sign: KW1G
William H Kent Jr
28 Sea Surf Road
East Boothbay ME
045440430

Call Sign: N1MHC
Albert C Sirois
East Boothbay ME 04544

Call Sign: KB1OCD
Alice G Sozanski
East Boothbay ME 04544

FCC Amateur Radio Licenses in East Corinth

Call Sign: K1TOQ
Francis A Mc Laughlin
Rfd 1 Box 600
East Corinth ME 04427

Call Sign: N1XMY
Terry R Nason
Rr 2 Box 768
East Corinth ME 04427

Call Sign: K1FKO
Eddie L Eberly
East Corinth ME
044270096

FCC Amateur Radio Licenses in East Eddington

Call Sign: N1CZI

Frank V Crocker
Rt 01 Box 820
East Eddington ME 04428

Call Sign: N1LXM
Glenn M Prewitt
14 Merrill Rd
East Eddington ME
044283348

Call Sign: AA1WJ
Glenn M Prewitt
14 Merrill Rd
East Eddington ME
044283348

Call Sign: N1LX
Glenn M Prewitt
14 Merrill Rd
East Eddington ME
044283348

Call Sign: W1DLC
Walter L Dickson
28 Riverside Dr Apt 4
East Eddington ME 04428

FCC Amateur Radio Licenses in East Holden

Call Sign: KA1TAE
Bruce R Blackmer
Rr 3 Box 530
East Holden ME 04429

Call Sign: WX9T
Kristin R Hayward
Rr3 Box 815
East Holden ME 04429

Call Sign: N1AC
Alan L Cunningham Sr
350 Clark Hill Rd
East Holden ME 044299705

Call Sign: N1UYV
Theodore L Andrews
East Holden ME 04429

Call Sign: WB1CPN
Ray J De Chaine
East Holden ME 04429

FCC Amateur Radio Licenses in East Lebanon

Call Sign: WA1DRA
Charles W Dixon
Rr 2 Box 122
East Lebanon ME 04027

Call Sign: N1GVT
Charles P Sargent
Rr 2 Box 445
East Lebanon ME 04027

Call Sign: K1VRQ
Charles W Cobb
Rr 1 Box 671a
East Lebanon ME 04027

Call Sign: W1ZQ
Ralph E Parsons
Bigelow Rd Box 870 Rr 1
East Lebanon ME 04027

FCC Amateur Radio Licenses in East Machias

Call Sign: KB1BMP
William R Holmes
Hcr 69 Box 150
East Machias ME 04630

Call Sign: N1OXZ
Aaron L Johnson
Hcr 69 Box 216
East Machias ME 04630

Call Sign: KA1QCE

James D Albert
Hcr 74 Box 238a
East Machias ME 04630

Call Sign: N1MKW
David D Dirsa
Hcr 74 Box 29
East Machias ME 04631

Call Sign: N1MKX
Ruth Anne Q Dirsa
Hcr 74 Box 29
East Machias ME 04632

Call Sign: N1MKZ
Eleanor L Morse
Hcr 74 Box 32
East Machias ME 04630

Call Sign: N1PQL
Wesner R Reing
Elm St
East Machias ME 04630

Call Sign: KA1WHU
Brian K Albee
551 Hadley Lake Rd
East Machias ME 04630

Call Sign: AA1QI
Gary W Bridgham
7 Hadley Lake Road
East Machias ME
046304009

Call Sign: N1YML
Chester M Caton
297 High Head Rd
East Machias ME 04630

Call Sign: AB1LC
Chester M Caton
297 High Head Rd
East Machias ME 04630

Call Sign: WY1Q
Thomas A Mc Clure
57 Mattatall Road
East Machias ME 04630

Call Sign: N1MKY
Bernard L Morse Iii
148 Morse Mountain Lane
East Machias ME 04630

Call Sign: NL7AK
Christopher D Mooradian
Po Box 354
East Machias ME 04630

Call Sign: WA1JMY
Barry K Dean
27 Stage Coach Rd
East Machias ME 04631

Call Sign: N1MLC
Leo Shuck
Rt 1
East Machias ME 04630

Call Sign: N1MLD
Loren Shuck
East Machias ME 04630

Call Sign: N1NFV
Clinton E Gardner Jr
East Machias ME 04630

Call Sign: N1VOI
Tara G Wheeler
East Machias ME 04630

Call Sign: KB1GOT
Shawn P Bagley
East Machias ME 04630

Call Sign: KB1JAR
Jon F Mahar
East Machias ME 04630

FCC Amateur Radio Licenses in East Millinocket

Call Sign: N1IYY
Maurice E Nisbett
33 Cedar St
East Millinocket ME 04430

Call Sign: N1BUP
William D Brunette
45 Church St Lot# 6
East Millinocket ME 04430

Call Sign: KA1EZS
Leo E Fournier
17 Grove St
East Millinocket ME 04430

Call Sign: W1NHT
George R Mac Donald Sr
31 Maple St
East Millinocket ME 04430

Call Sign: WA1POO
Keith S Lowry
25 Orchard St
East Millinocket ME 04430

Call Sign: WA1ZOY
Sylvia W Lowry
25 Orchard St
East Millinocket ME 04430

Call Sign: N1LNW
James W Nisbett
8 Palm St
East Millinocket ME 04430

Call Sign: KB1TWB
George T Blackburn
23 Pine St
East Millinocket ME 04430

FCC Amateur Radio Licenses in East Newport

Call Sign: W1MFM
Everett F Campbell Sr
Box 44
East Newport ME 04933

FCC Amateur Radio Licenses in East Orland

Call Sign: N1WML
Charles M Young
East Orland ME 04431

FCC Amateur Radio Licenses in East Parsonsfield

Call Sign: KB1BGT
Memarie D Christoforo
East Parsonsfield ME 04028

FCC Amateur Radio Licenses in East Poland

Call Sign: KB1VUY
Trudy A Jacqmin
East Poland ME 04230

FCC Amateur Radio Licenses in East Sebago

Call Sign: N1UXS
Nicholas R Jones
East Sebago ME 04029

FCC Amateur Radio Licenses in East Vassalboro

Call Sign: N1THA
Galen W Gould
750 Bog Rd

East Vassalboro ME 04935

Call Sign: KA1UZN
Susan F Morris
East Vassalboro ME 04935

Call Sign: KB1BEB
Malgorzata Matusiak
East Vassalboro ME 04935

Call Sign: KC1TG
Danny A Morris
East Vassalboro ME 04935

Call Sign: N1FGH
Joyce C Sutherland
East Vassalboro ME 04935

Call Sign: NN1L
John H Sutherland
East Vassalboro ME 04935

FCC Amateur Radio Licenses in East Waterboro

Call Sign: N1QCC
Alfred L Gorey
Hcr 72 11
East Waterboro ME 04030

Call Sign: KA1ZYP
John R Murray
Hcr 72 Box 5560
East Waterboro ME 04030

Call Sign: KB1RBM
Jamie S Anderson
18 C And K Loop
East Waterboro ME 04030

Call Sign: KB1MCV
James D Richardson
143 Deering Ridge Rd
East Waterboro ME 04030

Call Sign: K1GPI
Charles R Phillips
11 Hanna Drive
East Waterboro ME 04030

Call Sign: N1SRL
Sandra E La Course
Old Alfred Rd
East Waterboro ME 04030

Call Sign: N1MIO
Eric M Webster
Roberts Ridge Rd
East Waterboro ME 04030

Call Sign: N1MIM
Michael Beavis
230 Townhouse Rd
East Waterboro ME 04030

Call Sign: KB1KJO
Michael Beavis
230 Townhouse Rd
East Waterboro ME 04030

Call Sign: KB1PCS
Margaret A Arsenault
546 Townhouse Road
East Waterboro ME 04030

Call Sign: N1UBG
Christine E Webster
East Waterboro ME 04030

Call Sign: KB1LBR
Gary A Prokey
East Waterboro ME 04030

Call Sign: KA1YPY
Gary A Prokey
East Waterboro ME 04030

FCC Amateur Radio Licenses in East Wilton

Call Sign: N1MTY
Eugene E Henderson
21 Lothrop St
East Wilton ME 04234

Call Sign: KB1EDI
Gene K Giddings
East Wilton ME 04234

FCC Amateur Radio Licenses in Eastbrook

Call Sign: N1NGM
Norman R Veillette
757 Eastbrook Rd
Eastbrook ME 046349734

FCC Amateur Radio Licenses in Easton

Call Sign: N1FCS
Jan H Larsen
273 Bangor Road
Easton ME 04740

Call Sign: K1GAO
Kevin T Higgins
Rfd 1 Box 179
Easton ME 04740

Call Sign: KA1ZTH
Kathryn K Peary
175 Easton Rd
Easton ME 04740

Call Sign: N1JHQ
John H Trask
405 Houlton Rd
Easton ME 047404033

FCC Amateur Radio Licenses in Eastport

Call Sign: N1VUB

Carlene C Bishop
8 Barren Rd
Eastport ME 04631

Call Sign: N1STM
Paul D Mc Culloch
8 Barron Rd
Eastport ME 04631

Call Sign: N1LNX
Charles W Avery
18 Clark St
Eastport ME 04631

Call Sign: KA1FUE
Ralph E Hicks Jr
87 Clark St
Eastport ME 04631

Call Sign: AA1KS
Richard C Emmert
44 Clark Street
Eastport ME 04631

Call Sign: KB1REU
Matthew S Francis
118 County Road
Eastport ME 04631

Call Sign: N1VLP
Harold R Keezer
7 Green St
Eastport ME 04631

Call Sign: N1LNV
Joseph K Lewis
Harris Point Rd
Eastport ME 04631

Call Sign: N1ZPX
Dennis M Cline
Harris Pt Rd
Eastport ME 04631

Call Sign: KB3CEU

Christopher A Scott
21 High St
Eastport ME 04631

Call Sign: KB1DQT
Andrew Seeley
24 High St
Eastport ME 04631

Call Sign: KB1FQB
Lauren A Seeley
24 High Street
Eastport ME 04631

Call Sign: N1VYR
William A Mcgarvey Jr
40 Key St
Eastport ME 04631

Call Sign: AA1ZR
William A Mcgarvey Jr
40 Key St
Eastport ME 04631

Call Sign: WB1EZU
Hollis E Matthews
29 Lincoln St
Eastport ME 04631

Call Sign: N1XHI
Stephen M Tibbetts
4 Mitchenar St
Eastport ME 04631

Call Sign: N1XHG
John C Prime
4 Mitchenor St
Eastport ME 04631

Call Sign: W3UWH
Harold I Goodman
7 Perkins Rd
Eastport ME 04631

Call Sign: KA1DKF

Charles W Mitchell Sr
Rfd Box 41a
Eastport ME 04631

Call Sign: KB1FTK
Edward A Scott
13 Snyder Road
Eastport ME 04631

Call Sign: N1ZFM
James L Cook
25 Sullivan
Eastport ME 04631

Call Sign: N1TLU
Patricia J Cook
25 Sullivan St
Eastport ME 04631

Call Sign: WA2APY
Daniel H Earley
25 Third St
Eastport ME 04631

Call Sign: N1XMJ
Helen G Archer
33 Third St
Eastport ME 04631

Call Sign: N1XPV
Roscoe E Archer Iii
33 Third St
Eastport ME 04631

Call Sign: N1IVX
Ronald D Bouchard
44 Third St
Eastport ME 04631

Call Sign: KB1UJH
John P Foster
71 Water St
Eastport ME 04631

Call Sign: K1EPM

John P Foster
71 Water St
Eastport ME 04631

Call Sign: N1IWA
Ricky R Ramsdell
Eastport ME 04631

Call Sign: KB1VQD
Jon M Mcnerney
Eastport ME 04631

FCC Amateur Radio Licenses in Ebeemee Township

Call Sign: N1MBX
John C Fournier
794 Ebeemee Lake Road
Ebeemee Township ME 04414

FCC Amateur Radio Licenses in Eddington

Call Sign: N1XTF
Rebecca M Ridlon
Rr 2 Box 2085
Eddington ME 04428

Call Sign: K1AKJ
Paul L Bunker
344 Main Rd
Eddington ME 04428

Call Sign: KB1KBO
Patricia T Wilking
1350 Main Rd
Eddington ME 04428

Call Sign: KB1DLO
Dorothy A Demyan
344 Main Rd.
Eddington ME 04428

Call Sign: N1PNI
Robert W Crosby
25 Main Road
Eddington ME 04428

Call Sign: N1UHT
David M Foster
1158 Main Road
Eddington ME 04428

Call Sign: KB1JTQ
Ann A Prewitt
14 Merrill Rd
Eddington ME 04428

Call Sign: N1AAP
Ann A Prewitt
14 Merrill Rd
Eddington ME 04428

Call Sign: KB1LUO
Edward A Cole
Po Box 222
Eddington ME 04428

Call Sign: KB1TXK
Matthew S Hebert
Eddington ME 04428

FCC Amateur Radio Licenses in Edgecomb

Call Sign: K2LOT
John S Peters
154 Boothbay Rd
Edgecomb ME 04556

Call Sign: KB1RUJ
Robert J Sorjanen
478 Boothbay Road
Edgecomb ME 04556

Call Sign: KB1TGH
Gerald C Hicks Jr
870 Boothbay Road

Edgecomb ME 04556

Call Sign: N1MGY
Gloria Neilson
Rr 1 Box 1960
Edgecomb ME 04557

Call Sign: N1SDP
Robert J Nelson
Rr 1 Box 1960
Edgecomb ME 04556

Call Sign: N1MHA
Willis S Clifford
Box 286
Edgecomb ME 04556

Call Sign: N1MGW
Frances C Mague
85 Eddy Road
Edgecomb ME 04556

Call Sign: KB1SZA
Corning Townsend Iii
86 Fort Rd
Edgecomb ME 04556

Call Sign: K2DJN
Corning Townsend Iii
86 Fort Rd
Edgecomb ME 04556

Call Sign: KA7QNP
Barbara K Carleton
106 Fort Rd
Edgecomb ME 04556

Call Sign: N1SKA
Kenneth R Gaecklein
8 Hionahil
Edgecomb ME 04556

Call Sign: N1TKD
Sharon R Gaecklein
8 Hionahil

Edgecomb ME 04556

Call Sign: W1YRW
Frederick L Kelley
111 Mc Kay Road
Edgecomb ME 045563328

Call Sign: N1SDA
Thomas R Trowbridge
3 Old County Road
Edgecomb ME 04556

Call Sign: KB1TGD
David R Nutt
113 River Rd
Edgecomb ME 04556

Call Sign: KB1TGE
David C Nutt Jr
113 River Road
Edgecomb ME 04556

Call Sign: KB1JIZ
George M Jones
33 Salt Marsh Cove
Edgecomb ME 04556

Call Sign: N1QDF
Keith A Bachelder
Edgecomb ME 04556

Call Sign: KB1PAF
Christopher Duke
Edgecomb ME 04556

**FCC Amateur Radio
Licenses in Eliot**

Call Sign: N1KVX
Edward Roche
10 Bayberry Dr
Eliot ME 03903

Call Sign: KB1IID
Richard T Sweeney

16 Bayberry Dr
Eliot ME 039031715

Call Sign: WA1ELF
Wilbur H Place
15 Beech Rd
Eliot ME 03903

Call Sign: N1LFV
Larry A Dow
23 Beech Rd
Eliot ME 03903

Call Sign: N1BGP
Ray M Richards
31 Beech Rd
Eliot ME 03903

Call Sign: KD4SIE
Kevin W Hynes
125 Beech Rd
Eliot ME 03903

Call Sign: WB1APE
Robert R Hodsdon
95 Bolt Hill Rd
Eliot ME 03903

Call Sign: KA1HDV
Allan B Dame
94 Brixham Rd
Eliot ME 03903

Call Sign: K1BM
Allan B Dame
94 Brixham Rd
Eliot ME 03903

Call Sign: WB1AOR
Earl F Johnson
29 Depot Rd
Eliot ME 03903

Call Sign: N1ZBC
Elinor F Amee

284 Depot Road
Eliot ME 03903

Call Sign: N1FUF
Orris H Scribner
8 Forest Ave
Eliot ME 03903

Call Sign: KA1TAR
Brian S Goodwin
128 Governor Hill Rd.
Eliot ME 03903

Call Sign: WO1B
Bruce A Stevens
28 Imperial Dr
Eliot ME 03903

Call Sign: W1LBG
Franklin P Waterman
3 Kings Hwy N
Eliot ME 039032208

Call Sign: N1OAX
David W Langford
1 Langley Farm Rd
Eliot ME 03903

Call Sign: W1WS
David W Langford
1 Langley Farm Rd
Eliot ME 03903

Call Sign: N1TXT
Melissa C Langford
17 Langley Farm Rd
Eliot ME 03903

Call Sign: W1WS
Constance E Owens
169 Main St
Eliot ME 03903

Call Sign: WA1NXS
Richard J Owens

169 Main St
Eliot ME 03903

Call Sign: KB1SXL
Jason W Lulek
252 Main St
Eliot ME 03903

Call Sign: KE5LQS
Steven D Holcomb
14 Maple Avenue / P.O.
Box 144
Eliot ME 03903

Call Sign: AB1TX
Debra A Holcomb
14 Maple Avenue / P.O.
Box 144
Eliot ME 03903

Call Sign: N1NDE
Gerard P Hickey Jr
10 N Crescent Dr
Eliot ME 03903

Call Sign: W1BDX
Richard C Roberts
181 Old Road
Eliot ME 039030181

Call Sign: KA1OK
Bucky Crowley
29 Osprey Cove Rd
Eliot ME 03903

Call Sign: N1KGL
Stephen Prodouz
1 Park St
Eliot ME 03903

Call Sign: WA2BWT
Richard Gross
3 Prides Crossing
Eliot ME 03903

Call Sign: N1GWZ
David T Caswell
32 Ridgewood Rd
Eliot ME 03903

Call Sign: KC1NY
Robert Cirone
172 Rollingwood
Eliot ME 03903

Call Sign: KD1RE
Dister L Deoss Jr
32 Rollingwood Dr
Eliot ME 03903

Call Sign: KD1SJ
Laurie J Deoss
32 Rollingwood Dr
Eliot ME 03903

Call Sign: N1RCD
Daniel E Dame
56 Sargeants Lane
Eliot ME 03903

Call Sign: K1ZIT
Lawrence W Allen Jr
14 Sargents Ln
Eliot ME 03903

Call Sign: KB1NVO
Brenda D Doyon
16 Spring Lane
Eliot ME 03903

Call Sign: KB1NVP
Ted M Huemmler
16 Spring Lane
Eliot ME 03903

Call Sign: N1OYO
Arthur W Hollenbeck
15 State Rd
Eliot ME 03903

Call Sign: WA1EDD
Richard E Pruett Jr
306 State Rd
Eliot ME 03903

Call Sign: W1DXP
Edward H Vetter
1266 State Rd
Eliot ME 039031829

FCC Amateur Radio Licenses in Ellsworth

Call Sign: W1GRG
Robert H Curtis
5 Addie Rd
Ellsworth ME 04605

Call Sign: N1CJS
Christopher J Stanley
14 B Beckwith Court
Ellsworth ME 04605

Call Sign: N1MXO
Albert Flower Iii
357 Bayside Rd
Ellsworth ME 04605

Call Sign: N1HQA
Elwin F Curtis Jr
Bayside Rd Rfd 1
Ellsworth ME 04605

Call Sign: N1IKO
Charles B Frank Jr
36 Bayview Ave
Ellsworth ME 04605

Call Sign: WB1DAH
Nathan A Walls
63 Beals Ave
Ellsworth ME 04605

Call Sign: KB1ATT
Lee E Sawyer

Rfd 4 Box 157
Ellsworth ME 04605

43 Court
Ellsworth ME 04605

629 Mariaville Rd
Ellsworth ME 04605

Call Sign: KB1ATU
Phillip N Sawyer
Rfd 4 Box 157
Ellsworth ME 04605

Call Sign: N1UYU
William G Salminen
8 Deane Street Apt 1
Ellsworth ME 04605

Call Sign: KB1CKR
Marsha T Carter
974 Mariaville Road
Ellsworth ME 04605

Call Sign: N3CTD
Colene E Sharkey
Rr 2 Box 271cc
Ellsworth ME 04605

Call Sign: KB1VBH
Neil A Shorey
110 Durham Ln
Ellsworth ME 04605

Call Sign: W1TEI
Henry L Stagg
Meadow View Apt 5
Ellsworth ME 04605

Call Sign: N1YDN
Matthew P Davis
Rr3 Box 31aa
Ellsworth ME 04605

Call Sign: KA1YPI
Matthew A Coffin
289 E Main St
Ellsworth ME 04605

Call Sign: WA1UGV
Fred J Rich
284 Nicolin Road
Ellsworth ME 04605

Call Sign: N1WZE
Anthony W Barnes
Rfd 3 Box 446a
Ellsworth ME 04605

Call Sign: KA0GHO
George L Schatz
75 Grand View Road
Ellsworth ME 04605

Call Sign: KA1YPH
Bruce A Farrin
North Street
Ellsworth ME 04605

Call Sign: KB1CTQ
Benjamin T Dinsmore
Rfd 1 Box 90
Ellsworth ME 04605

Call Sign: KB1DQM
Ronald F Schmitt
36 Laurel St
Ellsworth ME 046052305

Call Sign: KB1NJC
Galen R Okane
8 Okane Way
Ellsworth ME 04605

Call Sign: K1IDQ
Thomas L Pollard
Box Rfd 4
Ellsworth ME 04605

Call Sign: KE6PYU
Arthur S Bryant
36 Lundin Way
Ellsworth ME 04605

Call Sign: KB1NJD
Joseph R Okane
8 Okane Way
Ellsworth ME 04605

Call Sign: N1UPS
Gregory W Watts
Buttermilk Rd Rfd 1
Ellsworth ME 04605

Call Sign: W1KRP
Richard E Small
310 Main Street
Ellsworth ME 04605

Call Sign: KB1OTM
Lynn F Okane
8 Okane Way
Ellsworth ME 04605

Call Sign: KA1BFA
Everett A Beal Jr
394 Christian Ridge Rd
Ellsworth ME 04605

Call Sign: KB1MZV
Gregory B Dodson
629 Mariaville Rd
Ellsworth ME 04605

Call Sign: N1ZDG
Leonard C Daigle
1 Old Bangor Rd
Ellsworth ME 04605

Call Sign: K1LLN
Robert H Day

Call Sign: W1PEK
Gregory B Dodson

Call Sign: N1LAT
Dorothy Pulis

Partridge Cove Rd 2
Ellsworth ME 04605

Call Sign: N1PUL
Clifford A Pulis Sr
Partridge Cove Rd 2
Ellsworth ME 04605

Call Sign: K1FFF
Fists New England Cw Club
703 Red Bridge Rd
Ellsworth ME 04605

Call Sign: N1YUK
Perley A Urquhart
703 Red Bridge Rd
Ellsworth ME 04605

Call Sign: WA1ZVO
David W Remick
Rem Acres Box 353
Ellsworth ME 04605

Call Sign: W1BPZ
Donald E Carpenter
2 Sargent St
Ellsworth ME 04605

Call Sign: W1ZMK
Joseph P White
9 Spencer St
Ellsworth ME 04605

Call Sign: KB1PTL
Anne W Paradise
169 State St
Ellsworth ME 04605

Call Sign: KB1PTM
Earl J Paradise
169 State St
Ellsworth ME 04605

Call Sign: W1JX
Roberta P Donohue

103 Surry Rd
Ellsworth ME 04605

Call Sign: W1QU
Thomas Donohue
103 Surry Rd
Ellsworth ME 04605

Call Sign: N1WBQ
Nita C Whittemore
25 Tweedie Ln Apt 70
Ellsworth ME 04605

Call Sign: N1TDO
Mark E Albee
155 Twin Hill Rd
Ellsworth ME 04605

Call Sign: KB1NEB
Hancock County Amateur
Radio Emergency
Communications
155 Twin Hill Rd
Ellsworth ME 04605

Call Sign: N1MEA
Mark E Albee
155 Twin Hill Rd
Ellsworth ME 04605

Call Sign: KE6GUH
Darrell G Wilson
687 Winkumpaugh Road
Ellsworth ME 04605

Call Sign: K1PCG
Mark T Johnson
Ellsworth ME 04605

Call Sign: KA1YTO
Charlie K Foster Iii
Ellsworth ME 04605

Call Sign: KB1DLM
Richard E Small

Ellsworth ME 046050143

Call Sign: WA1FYA
Richard W Lindell
Ellsworth ME 04605

Call Sign: K1JHE
Jack H Erbes
Ellsworth ME 04605

Call Sign: KB1HOW
Jason E Piscitello
Ellsworth ME 04605

Call Sign: KB1IZR
Sherri Piscitello
Ellsworth ME 04605

Call Sign: W1ETE
Mark T Johnson
Ellsworth ME 04605

Call Sign: KD0KQC
Chris J Meyer
Ellsworth ME 04605

Call Sign: KB1TXL
Wendi A Meyer
Ellsworth ME 04605

**FCC Amateur Radio
Licenses in Eloir**

Call Sign: WA1AYT
David J Brunette
11 Spring Lane
Eloir ME 03903

**FCC Amateur Radio
Licenses in Embden**

Call Sign: KA1ZPC
Pamela R Stephens
682 East Shore Rd
Embden ME 04958

Call Sign: KA1ZPD
John G Stephens Jr
682 East Shore Rd
Embden ME 04958

Call Sign: WA1ZEM
John G Stephens Jr
2109 Embden Pond Road
Embden ME 04958

FCC Amateur Radio Licenses in Enfield

Call Sign: K1PM
Paul D Mayer
11 Beethoven Ln
Enfield ME 04493

FCC Amateur Radio Licenses in Estcourt Station

Call Sign: W1BTP
Louis P Dumond
Estcourt Station ME 04741

FCC Amateur Radio Licenses in Etna

Call Sign: N1FHT
Charles A Vaclavik
Box 76b Rfd 1
Etna ME 04434

Call Sign: KB1FDO
Victor M Fratello
582 Stage Road
Etna ME 044343216

FCC Amateur Radio Licenses in Exeter

Call Sign: KB1QQH

Warren R Akerblom
231 Between The Mill Rd
Exeter ME 04435

Call Sign: KB1VZD
Warren R Akerblom
231 Between The Mill Rd
Exeter ME 04435

Call Sign: N1WRA
Warren R Akerblom
231 Between The Mill Rd
Exeter ME 04435

Call Sign: N1WTO
Arlene M Rider
214 Tibbettes Rd
Exeter ME 04435

Call Sign: AA1PN
Clarence I Rider Jr
214 Tibbetts Rd
Exeter ME 04435

Call Sign: N1YJP
Clarence I Rider Iii
214 Tibbetts Rd
Exeter ME 04435

Call Sign: N1ZMN
Chrystal L Rider
214 Tibbetts Rd.
Exeter ME 04335

Call Sign: N1LFJ
Eugene H Stocker
Exeter ME 04435

FCC Amateur Radio Licenses in Fairfield

Call Sign: N1FID
James C Sammons
Rt 2 Box 3530
Fairfield ME 04937

Call Sign: K1SFB
Stephen F Bernier
Rfd 1 Box 5210
Fairfield ME 04937

Call Sign: N1ODD
Harold W Hanson
271 Center Rd
Fairfield ME 04937

Call Sign: KA1HMU
Merle C Proctor
291 Center Rd
Fairfield ME 049373319

Call Sign: W1BOZ
Lawrence E Prue
11 Cottage St
Fairfield ME 04937

Call Sign: N1UTZ
Michael L Gifford
28 Covell Rd
Fairfield ME 04937

Call Sign: N1DOW
Dean C Gifford
56 Covell Rd
Fairfield ME 04937

Call Sign: KB1QDR
Richard P Bentzel
186 Covell Rd
Fairfield ME 04937

Call Sign: N1EQ
Michael A Nadeau
274 Covell Rd.
Fairfield ME 049373136

Call Sign: KB1N
Albert T Webb
84 Davis Rd
Fairfield ME 04937

Call Sign: N1FYY
Arthur W Reed
14 Flood Ave
Fairfield ME 04937

Call Sign: N1NSU
Paul S Shorette Sr
21 Main St
Fairfield ME 04937

Call Sign: N1SWV
Marion D Foster
21 Main St
Fairfield ME 04937

Call Sign: WA1JNA
Lucien G Brousseau
269 Main St
Fairfield ME 04937

Call Sign: KB1FMB
Lynda L Foster
279 Main St
Fairfield ME 04937

Call Sign: KA1LWR
Eugene E Paradis
18 Maple St
Fairfield ME 04937

Call Sign: KB1HJE
Roderick J Potter
222 Martin Stream Rd
Fairfield ME 04937

Call Sign: KB1AWR
Frederick B Hawes
403 Middle Rd
Fairfield ME 04937

Call Sign: KB1GOX
Beverly S Ferland
124 Middle Road - Hillcrest
Apts - Apt 6

Fairfield ME 049373239

Call Sign: KB1KNT
Miles A Noonan
13 Military Ave
Fairfield ME 04937

Call Sign: KA1FYH
Marc A Le Blanc
160 Ohio Hill Rd
Fairfield ME 04937

Call Sign: KA1WMQ
Daniel P Holt
13 Osborne St
Fairfield ME 04937

Call Sign: K1PMR
John T Chen
109 Ridge Rd
Fairfield ME 04937

Call Sign: N1KQO
Joseph M Capriotti Jr
200 Ridge Rd
Fairfield ME 04937

Call Sign: N1JJZ
Deborah A Bizier
252 Ridge Rd
Fairfield ME 04937

Call Sign: N1UGX
Jeffrey W Zimba
378 Rt 201
Fairfield ME 04937

Call Sign: KE1LB
Eric J Foster
279 Upper Main St
Fairfield ME 04937

Call Sign: K1QIG
Clifford Stowers
38 West

Fairfield ME 04937

Call Sign: KB1PFJ
Randall D Clement
5 Western Ave
Fairfield ME 04937

Call Sign: N1GGZ
John R Williams Ii
43 Western Avenue
Fairfield ME 049371338

Call Sign: AB1MY
John R Williams Ii
43 Western Avenue
Fairfield ME 049371338

Call Sign: AK1O
John R Williams Ii
43 Western Avenue
Fairfield ME 049371338

Call Sign: W1ME
John R Williams Ii
43 Western Avenue
Fairfield ME 049371338

Call Sign: KA1ZTY
David T Suttie
10 Woodman Ave
Fairfield ME 04937

Call Sign: KB1EZZ
Maury E Prentiss
15 Woodman Ave
Fairfield ME 04937

Call Sign: N1VSS
James E Johansmeier
Fairfield ME 049370483

Call Sign: KB1OLJ
Ralph S Day
Fairfield ME 04937

Call Sign: KB1HMK
Gerald A Thompson
55 Applegate Lane
Falmouth ME 04105

Call Sign: N1WYQ
Sidney G Steinkeler
8 Birchwood Circle
Falmouth ME 04105

Call Sign: N1WYR
Andrew R Steinkeler
8 Birchwood Circle
Falmouth ME 04105

Call Sign: WK1R
Richard H Corey
91 Blackstrap Rd
Falmouth ME 04105

Call Sign: N1YKZ
Sonya R Banks
117 Blackstrap Rd
Falmouth ME 04105

Call Sign: N1XHA
Randolph J Lindberg
365 Blackstrap Rd
Falmouth ME 041051018

Call Sign: KU1A
Brian G Brock
Rfd 3 Blackstrap Rd
Falmouth ME 04105

Call Sign: KD1KV
Robert W Stakel
117 Blakstrap Rd
Falmouth ME 04105

Call Sign: KC1IG
Malcolm A Mackay

20 Blueberry Ln L113
Falmouth ME 041051856

Call Sign: N1SNO
George E Sanborn
20 Brookside Drive
Falmouth ME 04105

Call Sign: WZ1N
John A Bergeron
100 Clearwater Drive
Falmouth ME 04105

Call Sign: N1TBC
Darryl J Smith
100 Clearwater Drive Apt
153
Falmouth ME 04105

Call Sign: W1GAR
Charles B Peck Iii
12 Dale St
Falmouth ME 04105

Call Sign: KD1ED
Carlton E Fairbanks
328 Foreside Rd
Falmouth ME 04105

Call Sign: N1IBJ
Bryan M Fairbanks
328 Foreside Rd
Falmouth ME 04105

Call Sign: KI4DHX
Allen D Evans
3 Fox Hall Road
Falmouth ME 04105

Call Sign: K1IZA
Thomas P O Connor
14 Gray Rd
Falmouth ME 041052020

Call Sign: KB1HNW

Walter C Ladd
156 Gray Rd
Falmouth ME 04105

Call Sign: K1HKF
Jerome I Dorsky
348 Gray Rd
Falmouth ME 04105

Call Sign: KA1JFE
Richard S Sudds
24 Harding Ave
Falmouth ME 04105

Call Sign: KA1IGU
Joseph E Conboy
4 Hartford Ave
Falmouth ME 04105

Call Sign: KA1JDN
Dorothy M Conboy
4 Hartford Ave
Falmouth ME 04105

Call Sign: KA1ZVQ
Augustin A Root
5 Hemlock Cove Rd
Falmouth ME 04105

Call Sign: K1PCJ
John E Davidson Jr
41 Longwood Rd
Falmouth ME 04105

Call Sign: KB1CHY
Richard A Burner
16 Madokawando Landing
Falmouth ME 04105

Call Sign: KB1IAX
Rose M Coffin
118 Mast Rd
Falmouth ME 04105

Call Sign: KB1IAY

Richard N Coffin
118 Mast Road
Falmouth ME 04105

Call Sign: W1QIQ
Lee D Johnson
132 Middle Rd
Falmouth ME 041051223

Call Sign: KA1KAR
Butler H Pratt Jr
4 Oakland Rd
Falmouth ME 04105

Call Sign: KA1UMJ
Fred J Meyer
23 Payson Rd
Falmouth ME 04105

Call Sign: NW1A
Robert P Dyk
7 Pine Rd
Falmouth ME 041051823

Call Sign: N1ZRS
Eileen Quinn
8 Pinehurst Ln
Falmouth ME 04105

Call Sign: KB1RBL
James G Demer
10 Pineview Rd
Falmouth ME 04105

Call Sign: W1GF
Gregory C Finch
18 Poplar Ridge
Falmouth ME 04105

Call Sign: N1GF
Greg C Finch
18 Poplar Ridge Dr
Falmouth ME 04105

Call Sign: KB1AGR

Robert L Rand
23 Ramsdell Rd
Falmouth ME 04105

Call Sign: KA1TLR
Anthony C Rimkunas
12 Reg Roc Rd
Falmouth ME 04105

Call Sign: N1DEE
John A Rimkunas Jr
12 Reg Roc Rd
Falmouth ME 04105

Call Sign: KB1GBV
Tobias J Beal
7 Stagecoach Rd
Falmouth ME 04105

Call Sign: WQ1Y
Tobias J Beal
7 Stagecoach Rd
Falmouth ME 04105

Call Sign: KC1IR
Alan Lukas
16 Stapleford Dr
Falmouth ME 04105

Call Sign: N1ZOO
Peter M Davis Dmd
22 Stapleford Dr.
Falmouth ME 04105

Call Sign: N1CSY
John A Wilcox
9 Sunset Rd
Falmouth ME 041052433

Call Sign: N1CSZ
Eunice J Wilcox
49 Sunset Rd
Falmouth ME 04105

Call Sign: AC5BW

John O Vogt
10 Veronica Ln
Falmouth ME 04105

Call Sign: K1CMA
Donald A Ricker
11 Woodville Rd
Falmouth ME 04105

FCC Amateur Radio Licenses in Farmingdale

Call Sign: WA1UHF
Philip S Fessenden
29 Bowman St
Farmingdale ME 04344

Call Sign: KA1ROW
Norine N Du Pont
Rr 7 Box 1435
Farmingdale ME 04344

Call Sign: KB1CWI
Molly N Alexander
Rfd 7 Box 1601
Farmingdale ME
043449704

Call Sign: K1PPM
Joseph H Plante
2 Debra St
Farmingdale ME 04344

Call Sign: KB1BVA
Short Wave Society Of
Maine
2 Debra St
Farmingdale ME 04344

Call Sign: KB1IOK
Michelle L O Brien
1 Hasson St
Farmingdale ME 04344

Call Sign: KB1ITS

Gary J Markham
420 Litchfield Road
Farmingdale ME 04344

Call Sign: KB1JAN
Cynthia L Markham
420 Litchfield Road
Farmingdale ME 04344

Call Sign: K1NIT
William F Crowley
150 Maple St
Farmingdale ME 04344

Call Sign: W1TLC
Augusta Amateur Radio
Association
150 Maple St
Farmingdale ME 04344

Call Sign: KB1MQQ
Good Sam Club Maine-Ly
Hams Chapter
150 Maple St
Farmingdale ME 04344

Call Sign: W1MAP
Donald S Dupont
7 Marks Lane
Farmingdale ME 04344

Call Sign: KB1MJT
I Carl Mayhew
14 Merrill St
Farmingdale ME 04344

Call Sign: N1UYW
Kevin L Grant Sr
58 Northern Ave
Farmingdale ME
043442809

Call Sign: N1VKP
Pam J Grant
58 Northern Ave

Farmingdale ME 04344

Call Sign: WA1YPS
Ronald E Gagne
13 Winter Dr
Farmingdale ME 04344

**FCC Amateur Radio
Licenses in Farmington**

Call Sign: N1WSU
Myron R Moore
63 West Mills Road
Farmingtion ME 04938

Call Sign: KB1MUR
Jacob W Gerrie
108 Abbott Dr
Farmington ME 04938

Call Sign: KB1TPF
Thomas R Anderson
375 Bailey Hill Rd
Farmington ME 04938

Call Sign: KA1BNE
Mark C Frost
Bailey Hill Rd
Farmington ME 04938

Call Sign: N1MTZ
Mark L Norris
375 Bailey Hill Road
Farmington ME 04938

Call Sign: N1GWH
Thomas E Eastler
Rfd 1 Box 1043
Farmington ME 04938

Call Sign: W1RKO
Marc D Fisher
Rr 1 Box 1061a
Farmington ME 049389706

Call Sign: N1FGC
Kenneth M Fairbanks
Rfd 1 Box 1339
Farmington ME 04938

Call Sign: KA1GAA
Connie L Arness
Rfd 1 Box 1491
Farmington ME 04938

Call Sign: N1GZG
Ronald L Rowles
Rr 3 Box 3164
Farmington ME 04938

Call Sign: N1ULX
John L Haley
Rr 3 Box 3385
Farmington ME 04938

Call Sign: KB1IYP
Eric A Hinkley
183 Box Shop Hill
Farmington ME 04938

Call Sign: KB1PRS
Randall D Gauvin
156 Court St
Farmington ME 04938

Call Sign: KC7OGY
Glenn E Speight
135 Eastmont Square
Farmington ME 04938

Call Sign: KB1OMG
Marc Edwards
1050 Fairbanks Rd
Farmington ME 04938

Call Sign: W1HTG
Charles P Stenger
Edgewood Manor 221
Fairbanks Rd
Farmington ME 04239

Call Sign: KB1SCB
Gerald L Pressey
189 Fairbanks Rd Apt 8
Farmington ME 04938

Call Sign: N1SPN
Charles E Frost
534 Holley Rd
Farmington ME 04938

Call Sign: N1QJH
Jacqueline M Andrews
5 Meadow Ln
Farmington ME 04938

Call Sign: KB1SQL
Dorothy E Davis
189 Fairbanks Rd Apt 8
Farmington ME 04938

Call Sign: KB1SBT
Timothy A Hardy
133 Johnson Heights
Farmington ME 04938

Call Sign: WB1EYS
Gary H Hall
347 New Vineyard Rd
Farmington ME 04938

Call Sign: KB1SQN
Jason A Decker
129 Gilbert Ave
Farmington ME 04938

Call Sign: N1SVA
Jennifer J Henderson
154 Lower Main St Apt 4
Farmington ME 04938

Call Sign: KA1WFL
Timothy R Ketcham
328 Owen Mann Road
Farmington ME 04938

Call Sign: KB1RDG
Randall D Gauvin
140 Granite Heights
Farmington ME 04938

Call Sign: K1SEV
Robert J Lovejoy
64 Main St
Farmington ME 04938

Call Sign: WB1DHV
Lee R Gray
75 Perham
Farmington ME 04938

Call Sign: KB1SBZ
Ruth M Gauvin
140 Granite Heights
Farmington ME 04938

Call Sign: WA1JZP
Lydia G Hamlin
80 Main St
Farmington ME 049381901

Call Sign: KA1GPP
Brian L Taylor
113 Perham St
Farmington ME 04938

Call Sign: W1RUO
Richard E Davenport
139 Granite Hts
Farmington ME 04938

Call Sign: KB1TQP
Franklin County Ares
140 Main St
Farmington ME 04938

Call Sign: KB1SQK
Nancy E Teel
134 Perham St -2
Farmington ME 04938

Call Sign: KB1HTJ
Daric L Davenport
139 Granite Hts
Farmington ME 04938

Call Sign: W1FCA
Franklin County Ares
140 Main St Suite 1
Farmington ME 04938

Call Sign: KE5ISO
James A Mcdaniel
118 Perham Stree
Farmington ME 04938

Call Sign: AB1AY
Daric L Davenport
139 Granite Hts
Farmington ME 04938

Call Sign: N1RPH
Michael J Burrill
189 Maple Ave
Farmington ME 04938

Call Sign: KE5TEP
Rachel W Mcdaniel
118 Perham Street
Farmington ME 04938

Call Sign: KB1SCC
David A Starbird
155 Holley Rd
Farmington ME 04938

Call Sign: AA1SM
Gregory T Marshall
223 Marwick Road
Farmington ME 04938

Call Sign: KB1TRV
Jennings A Pinkham
142 Prescott St
Farmington ME 04938

Call Sign: KB1SBX
Gearry R Judkins
116 Quebec St
Farmington ME 04938

Call Sign: WB2TSZ
Paul R Bell
264 Ramsdell Rd
Farmington ME 04938

Call Sign: KB1WLH
Richard M Harvey
105 Sunny Hill Dr
Farmington ME 04398

Call Sign: WA1NXI
Michael H Whelpley Jr
671 Townfarm Rd
Farmington ME 04938

Call Sign: KB1TZY
Elaine N Whelpley
671 Townfarm Road Lot3
Farmington ME 04938

Call Sign: KB1SQI
Sylvia S Yeaton
50 West Shore Rd
Farmington ME 04938

Call Sign: N1LDH
Harry L Vose Sr
Farmington ME 04938

Call Sign: WA1BVD
Gary J Sweatt
Farmington ME 049380128

Call Sign: WA1JOF
Don E Stradley
Farmington ME 04938

Call Sign: WA1YEW
Robert A Marshall

Farmington ME 04938

Call Sign: KB1LWX
Michael H Whelpley Jr
Farmington ME 04992

Call Sign: KB1SBS
Gregory E Roux
Farmington ME 04938

Call Sign: KB1SBV
Michael G Warren
Farmington ME 04938

Call Sign: KB1SQO
Willaim H Gilliland
Farmington ME 04938

Call Sign: KB1VID
Bass Hill Repeater Group
Farmington ME 04938

Call Sign: W1BHR
Bass Hill Repeater Group
Farmington ME 04938

Call Sign: N1UVH
Richard E White Jr
Farmington Falls ME 04940

Call Sign: N1WTP
Leslie M White
Farmington Falls ME 04940

FCC Amateur Radio Licenses in Fayette

Call Sign: KB1SAX
Theodore A Coolidge
118 David Pond Rd
Fayette ME 04349

Call Sign: KB1JDN
Sally K Landry
287 East Rd.

Fayette ME 04349

Call Sign: KB1JRC
Justin J Landry
287 East Rd.
Fayette ME 04349

Call Sign: AA1XD
Gene K Giddings
287 East Road
Fayette ME 04349

Call Sign: KI1C
Malcolm E Davenport
124 Gile Rd
Fayette ME 04349

FCC Amateur Radio Licenses in Fort Fairfield

Call Sign: AA1OQ
Elmer Kornchuk
68 Aroostook Falls Rd
Fort Fairfield ME 04742

Call Sign: KC8FBU
Sharon E Nadeau
3 Blue Bell Court
Fort Fairfield ME 04742

Call Sign: KA1HGS
Marie B Ashby
Rfd 1 Box 1435
Fort Fairfield ME 04742

Call Sign: KA1ENL
James W Ashby
Rr 1 Box 1435
Fort Fairfield ME 04742

Call Sign: KA1RUU
Brent F Bishop
Rr 1 Box 37b
Fort Fairfield ME 04742

Call Sign: N1ZBZ
Jacquelyne C Morrow
25 Brown St Apt. B
Fort Fairfield ME 04742

Call Sign: WA1CXA
Bryce H Easter
429 Conant Road
Fort Fairfield ME 04742

Call Sign: KB1TDT
Stephanie F Beaulieu
72 Fort Hill St
Fort Fairfield ME 04742

Call Sign: KA1B
Frederick A Bowker Jr
11 Grant Road
Fort Fairfield ME 04742

Call Sign: KA1OOS
Catherine A Bowker
11 Grant Road
Fort Fairfield ME 04742

Call Sign: KB1PGY
Robert L Bixler
110 High St
Fort Fairfield ME 04742

Call Sign: KB1PGZ
Austin D Bixler
110 High St
Fort Fairfield ME 04742

Call Sign: KB1PHA
Brian I Bixler
110 High St
Fort Fairfield ME 04742

Call Sign: KB1OWV
Raymond K Huff
110 High St
Ft Fairfield ME 04742

Call Sign: KB1POJ
Stephen M Graham
567 Houlton Rd
Fort Fairfield ME 04742

Call Sign: KB1VNX
Robert H Leroux Jr
200 Limestone Rd
Fort Fairfield ME 04742

Call Sign: KB5IZZ
REBECCA D Diamond
Po Box 875
Fort Fairfield ME 04742

Call Sign: KB1JVN
Larry D French Jr
85 Presque Isle St
Fort Fairfield ME 04742

Call Sign: KB1STG
Joan I Shapiro
Fort Fairfield ME 04742

Call Sign: KB1STH
Ivan L Shapiro
Fort Fairfield ME 04742

FCC Amateur Radio Licenses in Fort Kent

Call Sign: KB1AOI
John A Daigle
497 Aroostook Road
Fort Kent ME 04743

Call Sign: KA1ZOE
Louis Albert
Rr 1 Box 1410
Fort Kent ME 04743

Call Sign: N1ZHP
Melissa T Albert
Rr 1 Box 1410
Fort Kent ME 04743

Call Sign: N1ZBY
Jessica C Boutot
Rr 3 Box 242
Fort Kent ME 04743

Call Sign: K1FK
David W Bowker
119 Bradbury Rd
Fort Kent ME 04743

Call Sign: KB1WKA
Derrick P Ouellette
6 Brookside Dr
Fort Kent ME 04743

Call Sign: KB1OWW
Joseph R Despres
12 Brookstore Dr
Fort Kent ME 04743

Call Sign: N1FRX
Charles P Zafonte
364 Charette Hill Rd.
Fort Kent ME 04743

Call Sign: WA1ZRO
Thomas G Ouellette
14 Dempsey Curve
Fort Kent ME 04743

Call Sign: N1JHT
Donald L Ouellette
103 E Main St
Fort Kent ME 04743

Call Sign: WA1ZPD
Michael S Dumond Sr
126 E. Main St
Fort Kent ME 04743

Call Sign: W1TCF
Michael S Dumond Sr
126 E. Main St
Fort Kent ME 04743

Call Sign: N1PMS
Peter P Pelletier
15 East Main Street Apt 001
Fort Kent ME 04743

Call Sign: W1TCP
Peter P Pelletier
15 East Main Street Apt 002
Fort Kent ME 04743

Call Sign: N1CGV
Cheryl A Boomhower
11 First Ave
Fort Kent ME 04743

Call Sign: N1ZLA
Jennifer L Boomhower
11 First Ave
Fort Kent ME 04743

Call Sign: N1UYA
Gale V Flagg
108 Franklin School Rd
Fort Kent ME 047432241

Call Sign: N1FG
Gale V Flagg
108 Franklin School Rd
Fort Kent ME 047432241

Call Sign: N1QWT
Alan M Susee
30 Klein Road
Fort Kent ME 04743

Call Sign: N1EVO
Carl J Pelletier
22 Municipal Drive
Fort Kent ME 04743

Call Sign: KA1ZOF
Henry L Carbone Ii
52 Pleasant St
Fort Kent ME 04743

Call Sign: KB1MNZ
Timothy D Rioux
147 Pleasant St
Fort Kent ME 04743

Call Sign: KB1TBI
Kevin J Pelletier
177 Pleasant St
Fort Kent ME 04743

Call Sign: KB1PCG
Clarence C Pittenger
9 Summer Ave
Fort Kent ME 04743

Call Sign: KA1YUS
Mark D Theriault
10 Third Ave
Fort Kent ME 04743

Call Sign: WA1ZQH
James G Thibodeau
19 Third Ave
Fort Kent ME 04743

Call Sign: KC1SE
James J Grandmaison
27 Third Ave
Fort Kent ME 04743

Call Sign: AA1CN
John P Theriault
25 Third Avenue
Fort Kent ME 04743

Call Sign: KW1C
Martin B Bernstein
Fort Kent ME 04743

FCC Amateur Radio Licenses in Fort Kent Mills

Call Sign: N1ZKB

Joseph L Paradis
Fort Kent Mills ME 04744

FCC Amateur Radio Licenses in Frankfort

Call Sign: KB1GUS
Caribou Me Nwsfo
Skywarn
5 Lily Lane
Frankfort ME 04438

Call Sign: KB1EYD
Vicki L Baack
5 Lily Ln
Frankfort ME 04438

Call Sign: KB1NDI
Joseph A Fabian Jr
345 Marsh Stream Rd
Frankfort ME 04438

Call Sign: KB1NKH
Marcia L Vertefeuille
345 Marsh Stream Rd
Frankfort ME 04438

FCC Amateur Radio Licenses in Franklin

Call Sign: KB1GVR
Mark A Austin
127 Blackswoods Rd
Franklin ME 04634

Call Sign: KB1CXT
Tammey L Bredbenner
Rt 182 Box 16
Franklin ME 04634

Call Sign: N1PNK
Ivan E Smith
Box 16
Franklin ME 04634

Call Sign: KB1AAK
Barrie L Arey
Rr 1 Box 368
Franklin ME 04634

Call Sign: N1QEF
Richard S Palmer Jr
Rfd 1 Box 455
Franklin ME 04634

Call Sign: N1RXH
Bonita A Palmer
Rfd 1 Box 455
Franklin ME 04634

Call Sign: WB1EAC
John P Dickens
Box 56
Franklin ME 04634

Call Sign: N1VYT
David H Lacey
Rfd 1 Box 80
Franklin ME 04635

Call Sign: AB1EP
Robert A Morse
8 Butlers Point Rd
Franklin ME 04634

Call Sign: W1DEM
Ross J Lane
7 Coombs Wharf
Franklin ME 04634

Call Sign: KD4ZAF
Ross J Lane
7 Coombs Wharf Road
Franklin ME 04634

Call Sign: KA1VDQ
Daniel R Miskell
118 Hog Bay Rd
Franklin ME 04634

Call Sign: K1SRM
Charles J Murch
Route 182
Franklin ME 04634

Call Sign: KA1ZXW
Dayton D Arey
Rr 368
Franklin ME 04634

Call Sign: N1LHC
Vernon Garrod
3 West Franklin Road
Franklin ME 04634

**FCC Amateur Radio
Licenses in Freedom**

Call Sign: N1CGP
David J Spencer
850 Belfast Rd
Freedom ME 04941

Call Sign: KB1FJG
Stanley Mcdonald Jr
25 Bryant Rd
Freedom ME 04941

Call Sign: N1UHR
Michael A Smith
36 Bryant Rd
Freedom ME 04941

Call Sign: KB1LDZ
Arlene F Smith
36 Bryant Rd
Freedom ME 04941

Call Sign: KA1PMI
Hilary N Fleming
139 Greeley Rd
Freedom ME 04941

Call Sign: N1HOY
Thomas J Fleming Jr

139 Greeley Rd
Freedom ME 04941

Call Sign: KD1KE
Thomas J Clay
138 Oak Ln
Freedom ME 04941

Call Sign: N1HPG
Helen M Clay
138 Oak Ln
Freedom ME 04941

Call Sign: N1YUV
Jennifer M Nerderman
138 Oak Ln
Freedom ME 04941

Call Sign: KB1HFL
Maurice B Rothrock Jr
Freedom ME 04941

Call Sign: KB1PYV
Anne G Rothrock
Freedom ME 04941

Call Sign: AB1KI
Maurice B Rothrock Jr
Freedom ME 04941

**FCC Amateur Radio
Licenses in Freeport**

Call Sign: WB1ATB
David A Darling
Rr 3 Box 266bb
Freeport ME 04032

Call Sign: KB1IW
James A Howard
Box 111 Curtis Rd
Freeport ME 04032

Call Sign: N1KAZ
Catherine M Clark

10 Di Pietro Dr
Freeport ME 04032

Call Sign: WM1T
Robert E Noyes
182 Durham Rd
Freeport ME 04032

Call Sign: N2HLD
Mary R Gallie
239 Flying Point Rd.
Freeport ME 04032

Call Sign: N1IJD
Stephen A Libby
53 Grant Rd
Freeport ME 040326861

Call Sign: N1AOI
Glenn A Sutton Jr
16 Harvey Brook Dr
Freeport ME 04032

Call Sign: W1GX
Philip E Shaw Jr
66 Hunter Rd
Freeport ME 04032

Call Sign: KB3KRH
Jon E Inman
37a Hunter Rd.
Freeport ME 04032

Call Sign: K1MPM
Donald P Child
11 Kendall Lane
Freeport ME 04032

Call Sign: KA1ZIX
Michele Rieger
11 Lajoie Dr
Freeport ME 04032

Call Sign: N1ITU
Robert H Ware

33 Linwood Rd
Freeport ME 04032

Call Sign: AA9PC
Paul D Conwell
33 Linwood Road
Freeport ME 04032

Call Sign: KA1IOP
William R Killion
291 Lower Flying Point Rd
Freeport ME 04032

Call Sign: WA1WRS
Kenneth B Segal
173 Lower Flying Point
Road
Freeport ME 04032

Call Sign: KB1DFW
Roland G Davis
15 Maiden Lane
Freeport ME 04032

Call Sign: W1KRF
Gerald W Mason
78 Maquoit Dr
Freeport ME 04032

Call Sign: KB6JRJ
Edward A Liggins Sr
9 Merrill Rd
Freeport ME 04032

Call Sign: KB1WWD
Christian B Anthony
10 Murch Rd
Freeport ME 04032

Call Sign: KA1UIY
Nicholas R Barry
36 Park St
Freeport ME 04032

Call Sign: N1VUD

John C Cantwell
17 Port Dr
Freeport ME 04032

Call Sign: N1ZSN
Alicia R Cantwell
17 Port Dr
Freeport ME 04032

Call Sign: WA2NTW
Adolph Holmes
64 Pownal Rd
Freeport ME 04032

Call Sign: W7IAD
Kent S Wilkinson
90 Ringrose Rd
Freeport ME 04032

Call Sign: KB1KJE
Christopher P Bean
9 Royal Ave
Freeport ME 04032

Call Sign: N1CPB
Christopher P Bean
9 Royal Ave
Freeport ME 04032

Call Sign: KB1UOQ
Richard T Stadnicki
162 S Freeport Rd
Freeport ME 04032

Call Sign: KA1IJH
Joseph W Ricci
4 Scribne Dr
Freeport ME 04032

Call Sign: KB1HOP
Michael J Detscher
6 Shady Ledge Ln
Freeport ME 04032

Call Sign: KB1PEC

Joseph J Souza Jr
60 Shore Dr
Freeport ME 04032

Call Sign: KB1VYU
Christy Gianios Jr
41 Somerset
Freeport ME 04032

Call Sign: K2HAE
Christy Gianios Jr
41 Somerset
Freeport ME 04032

Call Sign: KB1UOP
Susan P Stadnicki
162 South Freeport Rd
Freeport ME 04032

Call Sign: W1ZSV
Richard W Stoddard
24 South St A17
Freeport ME 04032

Call Sign: N1VNB
Timothy E Kiely Sr
2 Spencer's Ridge Road
Freeport ME 04032

Call Sign: WL7CUP
David R Rice
1576 Us Route 1
Freeport ME 04032

Call Sign: KB1NDE
David R Rice
1576 Us Route 1.
Freeport ME 04032

Call Sign: WW1F
Lawrence C Di Pietro Sr
110a Ward Town Rd
Freeport ME 04032

Call Sign: KB1IUO

John M Goran
74 Webster Rd
Freeport ME 040326228

Call Sign: K1JJS
John M Goran
74 Webster Rd
Freeport ME 040326228

Call Sign: KB1HNY
David L Knippa
412 Wolfes Neck Rd
Freeport ME 04032

Call Sign: N1HQG
Lawrence L Lunt Ii
Freeport ME 04032

Call Sign: N1KAA
Darren G Ellis
Freeport ME 04032

FCC Amateur Radio Licenses in Frenchtown Township

Call Sign: KG7ZJ
Stephania A Harvey
246 Frenchtown Road
Frenchtown Township ME 04441

FCC Amateur Radio Licenses in Frenchville

Call Sign: WA1PIO
Robert J Rogers
25 Airport Avenue
Frenchville ME 047450473

Call Sign: N1ZBW
Jody J Daigle
131 Church Ave
Frenchville ME 047456022

Call Sign: N1TOG
Cindy L Marquis
13 Pelletier Ave
Frenchville ME 04745

Call Sign: N1FRW
Kevin J Deschaine
8 Sirois Street
Frenchville ME 04745

Call Sign: K1RB
Steven R Bouchard
16 U.S. Route 1
Frenchville ME 04745

Call Sign: N1IMK
Steven R Bouchard
51 Us Rt 1 Apt 4
Frenchville ME 04746

Call Sign: KB1AOH
Dennis R Carrier
Frenchville ME 04745

Call Sign: KB1LGI
Steven R Bouchard
Frenchville ME 04745

FCC Amateur Radio Licenses in Friendship

Call Sign: WA1KAU
Ronald K Simmons
Box 430
Friendship ME 04547

Call Sign: N1XSH
Arthur L Ubry
Hc 69 Box 587a
Friendship ME 04547

Call Sign: WB7QNI
James Li
Cranberry Island
Friendship ME 04547

Call Sign: W1CIC
James Li
Cranberry Island
Friendship ME 04547

Call Sign: W1BMS
William L Hall
Box 130 Halls Wharf
Friendship ME 045470130

Call Sign: NE7O
Chester A Mitchell
44 Harobor Rd
Friendship ME 04547

Call Sign: KA1GAI
William A Case
368 Martin Point Rd
Friendship ME 04547

Call Sign: N1FIX
Walter S Foster
215 Martin Point Road
Friendship ME 045474322

Call Sign: KB1VQG
Frederick Blake
36 Oceanward Dr
Friendship ME 04547

Call Sign: KB1EHP
Raymond W Brann
59 Timber Point Rd
Friendship ME 04547

Call Sign: KB1ENL
Bonnie L Brann
59 Timber Point Rd
Friendship ME 04547

Call Sign: W1RWB
Raymond W Brann
59 Timber Point Rd
Friendship ME 04547

Call Sign: W1BLB
Bonnie L Brann
59 Timber Point Rd
Friendship ME 04547

Call Sign: KC1LS
John A Arness
Friendship ME 04547

Call Sign: NY1B
Norman R Smith Sr
Friendship ME 04547

FCC Amateur Radio Licenses in Fryeburg

Call Sign: KB1SWT
John W Chase Iv
13 Black Bear Rd
Fryeburg ME 04037

Call Sign: KB1UFF
Raymond C Lamont
82 Hemlock Bridge Rd
Fryeburg ME 040374130

Call Sign: W1BTY
Raymond C Lamont
82 Hemlock Bridge Rd
Fryeburg ME 040374130

Call Sign: KE2JM
Anthony Condello
54 Island Road
Fryeburg ME 04037

Call Sign: W1IAH
George R Kay
8 Kay Drive
Fryeburg ME 04037

Call Sign: N7FRF
Dana C Trumann
12 Mgnotomy Rd Box 352

Fryeburg ME 04037

Call Sign: KB1WJJ
Randolph S Evans
74 Oxford St
Fryeburg ME 04037

Call Sign: KC1JA
Charles A Condello
P.O.Box 584
Fryeburg ME 040371127

Call Sign: N1SKU
James F Mc Leod
10 Park St
Fryeburg ME 040371510

Call Sign: KB1NYC
John W Chase Iii
40 Raven Lane
Fryeburg ME 04037

Call Sign: KB1OKJ
David A Dunham
52 Stuart Street
Fryeburg ME 04037

Call Sign: KB1FIG
Daniel P Engstrom
217 West Fryeburg Road
Fryeburg ME 04037

Call Sign: N1ARY
Martin D Engstrom Jr
227 West Fryeburg Road
Fryeburg ME 040374334

Call Sign: KB1IMZ
Gary R Broniarczyk
27 Woodland St
Fryeburg ME 04037

FCC Amateur Radio Licenses in Gardiner

Call Sign: N1WTN
Matthew C Ghiglio
44 Adams St
Gardiner ME 04345

Call Sign: W1EFA
Harold T Dinsmore
Rfd 2 Box 34a
Gardiner ME 04345

Call Sign: WB1DPS
Jeffrey D Lewis
256 Capen Rd
Gardiner ME 04345

Call Sign: KB1ESA
Nathan A Sutherburg
53 Adams St
Gardiner ME 04345

Call Sign: KA1WJE
Kim M Vandermeulen
Rfd 5 Box 442
Gardiner ME 04345

Call Sign: N1DOV
Regina A Lewis
256 Capen Rd.
Gardiner ME 04345

Call Sign: N1EFO
Dean E Cunningham
39 Alexandra Dr Apt 14
Gardiner ME 04345

Call Sign: KB1KAS
George W Maxwell Iii
Rr 2 Box 517
Gardiner ME 04345

Call Sign: KB1HPW
Sean M Wyatt
34 Cedar St
Gardiner ME 04345

Call Sign: KB1KAU
Cassandra R Lavallee
Rr 5 Box 1250
Gardiner ME 04345

Call Sign: KA1MCH
Edwin E Alexander
Rfd 5 Box 551
Gardiner ME 04346

Call Sign: K1EYT
Richard E Lougee
101 Cobbossee Ave
Gardiner ME 04345

Call Sign: KB1HPC
Scott J Moulton
Rd 2 Box 1373
Gardiner ME 04345

Call Sign: KB1KBQ
Nathan P Rickett
Rr 5 Box 5680
Gardiner ME 04346

Call Sign: KB1JRE
Kyle F Harrigan
46 Deane St
Gardiner ME 04345

Call Sign: N1IQV
Dan Szmigulski
Rr 3 Box 180
Gardiner ME 04345

Call Sign: N1ZRT
Richard P Ashcroft
Rr 5 Box 620
Gardiner ME 04345

Call Sign: N1DZI
James F Cole Sr
74 Elm St
Gardiner ME 04345

Call Sign: N1OSV
Seth A Lawrence
Rfd 2 Box 19
Gardiner ME 04345

Call Sign: KB1IHZ
Mary E Bailey
Rfd 2 Box 67a
Gardiner ME 04345

Call Sign: WA1TFK
Robert E Abbey
79 Elm St
Gardiner ME 04345

Call Sign: N1SDN
Richard E Bodge
Rr 2 Box 19a
Gardiner ME 04345

Call Sign: KB1KAV
Aaron M Moody
Rr 4 Box 7940
Gardiner ME 04345

Call Sign: KB1FHV
Sean P Binette
57 Elm St.
Gardiner ME 04345

Call Sign: N1TKB
Christopher L Lemieux
Rr 2 Box 244
Gardiner ME 04345

Call Sign: N1NOU
Dennis E Rose
87 Brunswick Ave
Gardiner ME 04345

Call Sign: KB1JSF
Kennebec Valley Amateur
Radio Club
57 Elm Street
Gardiner ME 04345

Call Sign: KA1AWL
David L Beaulieu
17 Fountain St
Gardiner ME 04345

Call Sign: N1MNK
Donald E Purdy
86 Harrison Ave
Gardiner ME 04345

Call Sign: KB1JDM
Daniel R Mowatt
207 Harrison Ave
Gardiner ME 04345

Call Sign: N1ESW
Charles E Cole
43 Heselton St
Gardiner ME 04345

Call Sign: KA2VQH
Diane W Lavigne
90 High Holborn St
Gardiner ME 04345

Call Sign: KA2VQI
Gerard J Lavigne
90 High Holborn St
Gardiner ME 04345

Call Sign: KA1PYZ
Patricia A Palmer
122 High Holborn St
Gardiner ME 04345

Call Sign: KA1UTH
Mrs. Evelyn A Knowlton
101 Highland Ave Apt 2
Gardiner ME 04345

Call Sign: N1AYB
Jack Fitzgerald
159 Highland Ave Apt 4
Gardiner ME 04345

Call Sign: WB1GGL
Donald W Prew
28 Kingsbury St
Gardiner ME 04345

Call Sign: N1YUW
Perry L Bean
72 Libby Hill Rd
Gardiner ME 04345

Call Sign: KA1TXR
Christopher G Arnold
351 Lincoln Ave
Gardiner ME 04345

Call Sign: KE1AL
Timothy W Trott
17 Lincoln Ave A
Gardiner ME 04345

Call Sign: N1XIQ
Correne C Thibodeau
54 Maple Street Apt. 4
Gardiner ME 04345

Call Sign: W1GOD
James J Sawyer
246 Marston Rd
Gardiner ME 043459027

Call Sign: N1JPC
Michael F Knight
483 Marston Rd
Gardiner ME 04345

Call Sign: KB1QEN
Joshua R Johnson
38 Mattson Heights
Gardiner ME 04345

Call Sign: WB1HLW
John C Faulknham
57 Mt Vernon St
Gardiner ME 04345

Call Sign: KB1TLI
Daniel W Guilmette
36 Oak St
Gardiner ME 04345

Call Sign: WA1IIE
Charles W Sullivan
97 Old Brunswick Rd
Gardiner ME 043456036

Call Sign: W1WPA
Warren P Armstrong Jr
35 Smithtown Rd
Gardiner ME 04345

Call Sign: N1ZLJ
Darren K Vogel
98 Spring St
Gardiner ME 04345

Call Sign: N1LDI
Ryan C Robbins
18 Vine St
Gardiner ME 04345

Call Sign: KB1TPK
Andrew T Gilbert
20 Water St
Gardiner ME 04345

Call Sign: K1ALE
Andrew T Gilbert
20 Water St
Gardiner ME 04345

Call Sign: KB1CGO
Denison H Vina;
85 Winter St
Gardiner ME 04345

Call Sign: N1SDO
Richard E Johnson
94 Winter St
Gardiner ME 04345

Call Sign: KA1ROX
Calvin C Avery
Gardiner ME 04345

Call Sign: N1XJV
Keith R Richards Sr
362 Avenue Rd
Garland ME 04939

Call Sign: KA1UMG
Michael A Watson
133 Batchelder Rd
Garland ME 04939

Call Sign: KB1WRI
Jennifer L Boyd
133 Batchelder Rd
Garland ME 04939

Call Sign: KB1CXS
James M Lally
271 Campbell Rd
Garland ME 04939

Call Sign: W1FZN
Leatrice R Lally
Campbell Rd
Garland ME 04939

Call Sign: W1HDC
John F Lally
Campbell Rd
Garland ME 04939

Call Sign: KB1UQP
Hunter C Belanger
56 Day Rd
Garland ME 04939

Call Sign: WA3YFJ
Llewellyn E Small

490 Dexter Road
Garland ME 04939

Call Sign: KB1PTH
Vincent S Pitts
153 Garland Line Rd
Garland ME 04939

Call Sign: KB1PTG
Nathan T Pitts
154 Garland Line Rd
Garland ME 04939

Call Sign: KB1GWR
Michael S Gahris
83 High Cut Rd
Garland ME 04939

Call Sign: KB1GWS
Willa R Gahris
83 High Cut Rd
Garland ME 04939

Call Sign: KG8RK
William L White Jr
3 Highcut Rd
Garland ME 04939

Call Sign: KB1GAW
Jessica L Supp
63 Town Farm Rd
Garland ME 04939

Call Sign: KB1GAX
Michael G Supp
63 Town Farm Rd
Garland ME 04939

Call Sign: KB1PAT
Patricia L Supp
63 Town Farm Rd
Garland ME 04939

Call Sign: KB1FCU
Rachel A Kresina

137 Upper Garland Rd.
Garland ME 04939

Call Sign: KB1FCT
Roman P Kresina
137 Upper Garland Road
Garland ME 04939

Call Sign: KB1FCV
Susanna O Kresina
137 Upper Garland Road
Garland ME 04939

Call Sign: KA1LKS
Benjamin A Thomas
Garland ME 04939

Call Sign: N1WMO
Mary J Swain
Garland ME 04939

Call Sign: N1WMT
Donald R Swain
Garland ME 04939

Call Sign: N1YAT
Amanda J Swain
Garland ME 049390002

Call Sign: WA1SUU
Julia F Moulton
Rt 2 Box 274
Georgetown ME 04548

Call Sign: K1FI
Robert E Lundstrom
Five Islands Village
Georgetown ME 04548

Call Sign: AA9HX
Pedro M J Wyns
23 North End Road

Georgetown ME 045483810

Call Sign: N1GEV
Peter W Wilhelmi
23 North End Road
Georgetown ME 045483810

Call Sign: W1PWW
Peter W Wilhelmi
23 North End Road
Georgetown ME 045483810

Call Sign: KB1ERZ
Philip J Shelton
133 Williams Rd
Georgetown ME 04548

Call Sign: AA1RF
Kathleen Donovan
Georgetown ME 04548

Call Sign: KB1JFB
Daniel K North
Georgetown ME 04548

Call Sign: AB1RF
Daniel K North
Georgetown ME 04548

Call Sign: WA1ZDA
Charles R Plaisted
24 Warrenton Rd
Glen Cove ME 04846

Call Sign: KB1FJE
Simon J Rice
2811 Broadway
Glenburn ME 044011070

Call Sign: KB1FMD
Abby M Rice
2811 Broadway
Glenburn ME 044011070

Call Sign: KB1FME
Jeffrey A Rice
2811 Broadway
Glenburn ME 044011070

Call Sign: KB1FMF
Linda M Rice
2811 Broadway
Glenburn ME 04401

Call Sign: KB1JHO
Nathan J Rice
2811 Broadway
Glenburn ME 04401

Call Sign: KA1GM
Arthur J Emery
41 Phillips Rd
Glenburn ME 04401

Call Sign: N1SDS
Susan J Varney
22 Pine Acres Way
Glenburn ME 04401

Call Sign: W7EN
Brenda J Sytsma
22 Pine Acres Way
Glenburn ME 04401

Call Sign: KC1YF
E Wayne Huff
38 Roundstone Dr
Glenburn ME 044011208

Call Sign: KB1COY
Micah H Stade
3164 Union St
Glenburn ME 04401

Call Sign: WA1NLR
William H Thorpe
61 Barstow Rd
Gorham ME 04038

Call Sign: N1LCH
Roger J Lavigne
3 Blockhouse Run
Gorham ME 04038

Call Sign: W1QQY
Harland B Gower
Rr 3 Box 27
Gorham ME 04038

Call Sign: N2AIB
George A Wiseman Jr
Rr 3 Box 296
Gorham ME 04038

Call Sign: N1NOT
James C Jones
Rt 5 Box 324
Gorham ME 04038

Call Sign: W1IDA
Clifford V Nelson
Rr 5 Box 72
Gorham ME 04038

Call Sign: KA1KSQ
Robert A Parsons
322 Buck St
Gorham ME 04038

Call Sign: KG8MV
Duane H Dreger
8 College Avenue
Gorham ME 04038

Call Sign: KB1AXD
Thomas J Bahun Ii

280 County Rd
Gorham ME 04038

Call Sign: K1LMJ
Gilbert A Bineau
69 Cressey Rd
Gorham ME 040382010

Call Sign: WA1YFG
Cecile A Bineau
69 Cressey Rd
Gorham ME 040382010

Call Sign: KB1IUI
Michael P Kennedy
17 Daniel St
Gorham ME 04038

Call Sign: N1OTM
Russell Stibitz
99 Dunlap Road
Gorham ME 04038

Call Sign: N1JPO
Henry R Hinckley Iii
14 Dyer Rd
Gorham ME 04038

Call Sign: KB1HON
Hilary P Hamilton
3 Fall Ln C/O Junkins
Gorham ME 04038

Call Sign: KB1BHD
George A Eiskamp
137 Files Rd
Gorham ME 04038

Call Sign: WB1ENJ
June W Scothorne
22 Gateway Commons
Gorham ME 04038

Call Sign: KB1BXE
Martin J Jordan

45 Gateway Commons Dr
Gorham ME 04038

Call Sign: KB9MWS
Roland K Hawkes
19 Gateway Commons
Drive
Gorham ME 04038

Call Sign: WA1GAA
Jon L Stevens
10 George St
Gorham ME 04038

Call Sign: N1BQL
Richard G Portwine
19 Gloria St
Gorham ME 04038

Call Sign: N1LLB
Roland W Lunt
40 Hemlock Dr
Gorham ME 04038

Call Sign: W1WMG
Thomas W Watson
16 Hope Dr
Gorham ME 04038

Call Sign: KB1HNZ
Timothy W Watson
16 Hope Drive
Gorham ME 04038

Call Sign: WB2BMS
John J Kwoka
21 Hope Drive
Gorham ME 045300601

Call Sign: AB1GV
Richard P Abato
18 Jackies Way
Gorham ME 04038

Call Sign: KB1RHL

Christopher J Dodd
13 Joseph Dr
Gorham ME 04038

Call Sign: N1CJD
Christopher J Dodd
13 Joseph Dr
Gorham ME 04038

Call Sign: WB1FBN
Harry N Milliken Jr
9 Keene Dr
Gorham ME 040381949

Call Sign: KB1IOA
Eric J Schrowang
22 Lawn Ave
Gorham ME 04038

Call Sign: K1TZO
Roland R Racine Mr.
59 Libby Ave Lot 42
Gorham ME 04038

Call Sign: W1GOR
Lawrence M Feldman
32 Lily Lane
Gorham ME 04038

Call Sign: KB1DLI
Chadeverett E Brown
551 Main St
Gorham ME 04038

Call Sign: N1KSO
Mark D Mosher
259 Mosher Rd
Gorham ME 04038

Call Sign: N1HTZ
Martha J Richardson
359 Mosher Rd
Gorham ME 04038

Call Sign: KB1ADH

Albert W Noble Sr
178 N Gorham Rd
Gorham ME 04038

Call Sign: KB1FAW
Matthew L Arey
17 Narragansett St
Gorham ME 04038

Call Sign: W1CGJ
Irving F Ginn
86 Narragansett St
Gorham ME 04038

Call Sign: KB1VCY
Robert K Kuech
115 Narragansett St
Gorham ME 04038

Call Sign: KB1RNY
Peter K Shorey Jr
257 New Portland Rd
Gorham ME 04038

Call Sign: WA2UQD
Laurence E Bogner
50 New Portland Rd Apt
319
Gorham ME 04038

Call Sign: KB1VXC
Tyler G Semple
51 Osborne Rd
Gorham ME 04038

Call Sign: K1ZTA
John R Tebbetts
1 Overlook Dr
Gorham ME 04038

Call Sign: N1KTB
Daniel W Sullivan
15 Parker Hill Rd
Gorham ME 04038

Call Sign: KA1VPU
Timothy J Welch
19 Pleasant St
Gorham ME 04038

Call Sign: W1IMS
William G Keef
10 Preble St
Gorham ME 04038

Call Sign: NJ1O
William G Keef
10 Preble St
Gorham ME 04038

Call Sign: K1LPB
J Paul Cushman
45 Robie St
Gorham ME 04038

Call Sign: WB1BZE
Muriel H Cushman
45 Robie St
Gorham ME 04038

Call Sign: N2DHU
James P Califano Jr
25 Scroggie Way
Gorham ME 04038

Call Sign: KC8Q
Wayne L Bilodeau
18 Shamrock Dr.
Gorham ME 04038

Call Sign: N1KAS
Wayne L Bilodeau
18 Shamrock Dr.
Gorham ME 04038

Call Sign: W1UOY
Wayne L Bilodeau
18 Shamrock Dr.
Gorham ME 04038

Call Sign: WA1LTD
Ronald E Bibber
62 Shaws Mill Rd
Gorham ME 040382136

Call Sign: KB1SDE
Gary A Nealey Jr
53 Tow Path Rd
Gorham ME 04038

Call Sign: KA1AIF
Charles L Sawyer
137 Wilson Rd
Gorham ME 04038

Call Sign: N1NCB
Howard Yanik Jr
Gorham ME 04038

Call Sign: N1RWF
Ronald M Steinberg
Gorham ME 04038

Call Sign: N1VCN
William T Litchfield
Gorham ME 04038

Call Sign: KB1KNE
Sean M Arey
17 Narragansett St
Gorhan ME 04038

FCC Amateur Radio Licenses in Gouldsboro

Call Sign: W1AMX
Harold W Lothrop
Box 645 B Rfd
Gouldsboro ME 04607

Call Sign: W1EKJ
Vernal G Charles
Rr 1 Box 640
Gouldsboro ME 04607

Call Sign: KW1E
Deborah J Richardson
Rfd 1 Box 674
Gouldsboro ME 04608

Call Sign: WB6NMP
William R Fox
Hcr 60 Box 83
Gouldsboro ME 04607

Call Sign: K1QCF
James E Guyton
863 Pond Road
Gouldsboro ME 04607

Call Sign: KA1IQR
Janet L Hankins
Box 608 Rt 1
Gouldsboro ME 04607

Call Sign: KB1VVH
Cheri R Sankey
285 S Gouldsboro Rd
Gouldsboro ME 04607

Call Sign: AA1MW
Larry E Peterson
718 S. Gouldsboro Road
Gouldsboro ME 03051

Call Sign: KB1TGL
Andrew X Sankey
285 So Gouldsboro Rd
Gouldsboro ME 04607

Call Sign: W4IPB
William R Fox
204 So. Gouldsboro Rd.
Gouldsboro ME 04607

FCC Amateur Radio Licenses in Grand Isle

Call Sign: KA7VNR
Ruth H Mc Kinney

304 Grivois Rd
Grand Isle ME 047463314

Call Sign: N7GLR
Charles D Ames
304 Grivois Rd
Grand Isle ME 047463314

Call Sign: KA1YBF
Russell R Beaulieu
524 Main St
Grand Isle ME 047463232

Call Sign: KA1ZOD
Robert G Beaulieu
Grand Isle ME 04746

FCC Amateur Radio Licenses in Gray

Call Sign: N1CHV
Richard D Davol
16 Alling Dr
Gray ME 04039

Call Sign: W1VWT
Hubert F Cobb
66 Cambell Shore Rd
Gray ME 04039

Call Sign: NE1S
Laurence M Szendrei
67 Center Rd
Gray ME 04039

Call Sign: K1GWB
Gregory W Bennett
12 Daisy Ln Unit B
Gray ME 04040

Call Sign: WA1GFP
George E Maynard
Dry Mills Rd
Gray ME 04039

Call Sign: W1COG
Donald A Richardson
22 Dry Pond Road
Gray ME 04039

Call Sign: N1MGB
Matthew J Perry
112 Dutton Hill
Gray ME 04039

Call Sign: WA2RKZ
Lloyd E Garrison Jr
10 Garett Avenue
Gray ME 04039

Call Sign: K1EDG
Lloyd E Garrison Jr
10 Garett Avenue
Gray ME 04039

Call Sign: N1UJX
Mark Robinson
24 Hancock St
Gray ME 04039

Call Sign: KA1RQE
Nancy H Jensen Norris
13 Ledgewood Ln
Gray ME 04039

Call Sign: W2IOI
Charles C Norris Jr
13 Ledgewood Ln
Gray ME 04039

Call Sign: K1BKA
David L Pedersen
162 Long Hill Road
Gray ME 04039

Call Sign: KB1AFK
Ioannis Harizopoulos
11 Lower Marginal Way
Gray ME 04039

Call Sign: KB1VUW
Timothy J Bright
27 Marshview Dr
Gray ME 04039

Call Sign: N1RJA
Richard P Cabana
3 Spiro Avenue
Gray ME 04039

Call Sign: N1MMD
Jon W Brainerd
14 Verrill Rd
Gray ME 04039

Call Sign: N1NRC
Clyde W Pierce
256 W Gray Rd
Gray ME 04039

Call Sign: KB1TZC
David H Baur
260 Westwood Rd
Gray ME 04039

Call Sign: K0UXB
David H Baur
260 Westwood Rd
Gray ME 04039

Call Sign: N1FDU
William F Glennon
203 Weymouth Rd
Gray ME 04039

Call Sign: W1WFG
William F Glennon
203 Weymouth Rd
Gray ME 04039

Call Sign: N1YIK
Robert P Farrell
34 Wild Wood Ln
Gray ME 04039

Call Sign: N1XT
Paul D Proudian
16 Wilderness Way
Gray ME 04039

Call Sign: N1DCH
Thomas L Gorrill
27 Wildwood Ln
Gray ME 04039

Call Sign: N1ZAS
Andrew J Gorrill
27 Wildwood Ln
Gray ME 04039

Call Sign: KB5RKK
Lannie B Christensen
217 Yarmouth Rd
Gray ME 04039

Call Sign: KB1LSJ
Nws Gray Skywarn
Amateur Radio Club
Gray ME 04039

Call Sign: WX1GYX
Nws Gray Skywarn
Amateur Radio Club
Gray ME 04039

Call Sign: KB1NIB
John D Welch
Gray ME 040390478

Call Sign: KB1QHT
Staci L O'leary
Gray ME 04039

FCC Amateur Radio Licenses in Greenbush

Call Sign: KD1QX
Frank L Hoskins Jr
1032 Cardville Road
Greenbush ME 04418

Call Sign: KB1WLU
Bruce M Johnson
1517 Greenfied Rd
Greenbush ME 04418

FCC Amateur Radio Licenses in Greene

Call Sign: W1ZO
Carl P Anderson
47 Additon Rd
Greene ME 042363703

Call Sign: KB1OZY
Thomas D Johnson
38 April Lane
Greene ME 04236

Call Sign: KA1OMT
George F Herrick Jr
R 1 Box 10
Greene ME 04236

Call Sign: N1AXR
Timothy L Bubier
Rr 2 Box 3038
Greene ME 04236

Call Sign: N1TXA
Burton R Ham
Rfd 2 Box 840
Greene ME 04236

Call Sign: KB1DHI
Peter Altman
17 Hooper Pond Rd
Greene ME 04236

Call Sign: WA1EOJ
Adrien Leclair
146 Merrill Hill Rd
Greene ME 04236

Call Sign: KB1EMR

Derrick J Coady
35 N Mountain Rd
Greene ME 04236

Call Sign: KB1CXD
Jeremy M Albert
85 N Saunders Rd
Greene ME 04236

Call Sign: KB1EWT
Joanne L Albert
85 N Saunders Rd
Greene ME 04236

Call Sign: KB1OGO
David C Johnson
981 North River Rd
Greene ME 04236

Call Sign: KB1EWS
Michael O Albert
85 North Saunders Rd
Greene ME 04236

Call Sign: N1SVB
Earle A Gilmore
692 River Road
Greene ME 042364101

Call Sign: N1PEN
Donald R Champagne
Greene ME 042360244

Call Sign: WB1HFY
James B Pray
Greene ME 04236

FCC Amateur Radio Licenses in Greenville

Call Sign: W1NIC
Earl E Richardson
Birch St
Greenville ME 04441

Call Sign: N1RHA
Bernald D Wilber
Hcr 76 Box 595
Greenville ME 04441

Call Sign: KA1DHX
Daisy A Lowe
Box 6
Greenville ME 04441

Call Sign: KA1GBQ
Emile G Cote
Wayne Ave
Greenville ME 04441

Call Sign: WB2TIY
Robert Mc Elroy
Greenville ME 04441

FCC Amateur Radio Licenses in Grove

Call Sign: N1NGL
Helen R Oliver
Sr 68 Box 156a
Grove ME 04638

Call Sign: W1PLC
Paul K Oliver
Sr 68 Box 156a
Grove ME 04638

FCC Amateur Radio Licenses in Guilford

Call Sign: KA1UZP
Margaret L Templet
Box 209
Guilford ME 04443

Call Sign: KA1WUD
John W Watson
Rt 2 Box 75
Guilford ME 04443

Call Sign: K1BUC
Donald E Davis
Park St
Guilford ME 04443

Call Sign: KB1LOH
Patricia E White
306 Wharff Rd
Guilford ME 04443

Call Sign: KB1NRG
James L White
306 Wharff Rd
Guilford ME 04443

Call Sign: KB1PAH
Jacob C White
306 Wharff Rd
Guilford ME 04443

Call Sign: KA1VAW
Dorle K Cartwright
Guilford ME 04443

Call Sign: KA1VEF
Joseph E Cartwright
Guilford ME 044430298

Call Sign: KB1CKS
William A Littlefield
Guilford ME 04443

Call Sign: N1GTZ
Phillip J Buble
Guilford ME 04443

Call Sign: N1MTP
Michael E Dexter
Guilford ME 04443

Call Sign: N1SNT
Frank L Buble
Guilford ME 04443

FCC Amateur Radio Licenses in Hallowell

Call Sign: KB1MGF
Seth M Hardy
17 Academy St.
Hallowell ME 04347

Call Sign: KA1ROY
Eleanor M Benner
Rfd 1 Box 1575
Hallowell ME 04347

Call Sign: KA1CCD
Richard J Steinberger
7 Hackmatack Lane
Hallowell ME 04347

Call Sign: KA1LME
Claudette M White
Box 1427 Litchfield Rd
Hallowell ME 04347

Call Sign: KB1OE
Leslie A White
Box 1427 Litchfield Rd
Hallowell ME 04347

Call Sign: KA1IUK
Richard A Dolby
8 Mayflower Road
Hallowell ME 04347

Call Sign: K1ZAU
Patricia H Chadwick
Robbins
5 Perkins Ln
Hallowell ME 04347

Call Sign: N1KMV
Bruce E Robbins
5 Perkins Ln
Hallowell ME 04347

Call Sign: KB1MUS

Daniel T Crocker
31 Summer St
Hallowell ME 04347

Call Sign: KC3KV
John T Poland
61 Water A8
Hallowell ME 04347

Call Sign: N1KLY
Curtis T Combar
7 Wilder St
Hallowell ME 04347

Call Sign: KB1OUH
John Mcquarrie
270 Winthrop St
Hallowell ME 04347

FCC Amateur Radio Licenses in Hamlin

Call Sign: KB1VNZ
Theodore L Andrews
1664 Hamlin Rd
Hamlin ME 04785

FCC Amateur Radio Licenses in Hampden

Call Sign: N1UHD
Debbie L Burke
265 Bog Rd
Hampden ME 04444

Call Sign: WB1HBX
Paul H Desveaux
Box 154
Hampden ME 04444

Call Sign: N1MTS
Linda K France
Rr 1 Box 1597
Hampden ME 04444

Call Sign: KA1UME
Owen F Gaede
Rfd 1 Box 2022
Hampden ME 04444

Call Sign: KB1SYP
Kim M Hopper
1384 Carmel Rd North
Hampden ME 04444

Call Sign: K1TQK
Robert W Stairs
50 Coolidge Ave
Hampden ME 04444

Call Sign: KB1PJG
Charles L Gardner
20 Daisey Lane
Hampden ME 04444

Call Sign: KB1VEQ
Aaron C Mccollough
25 Griffin Ave
Hampden ME 04444

Call Sign: KB1MON
Robert F Daigle
822 Kennebec Rd
Hampden ME 04444

Call Sign: KB1UJT
Howard Jones
960 Kennebec Rd
Hampden ME 04444

Call Sign: KB1VEP
Craig D Harrison
1191 Kennebec Rd
Hampden ME 04444

Call Sign: N1FKL
Theodore R Littlefield
92 Main Rd N
Hampden ME 04444

Call Sign: KB1FMG
Brianna A Torrey
350 Main Rd N
Hampden ME 04444

Call Sign: W1GEE
Philip A Whitehouse
59 Main Rd S
Hampden ME 044440527

Call Sign: N1XJS
Charles K Sherman
421 Main Rd S
Hampden ME 04444

Call Sign: W1COP
David J Melochick
529 Main Road North
Hampden ME 044441707

Call Sign: W1SUE
Susan E Melochick
529 Main Road North
Hampden ME 044441707

Call Sign: N1UHC
William F Braisted
608 Main Road North
Hampden ME 04444

Call Sign: KA1RQT
Laura R Ludwig
40 Manning Mill Rd
Hampden ME 04444

Call Sign: WA1ZYT
James W Warren
241 Old County Rd
Hampden ME 04444

Call Sign: KB1FMH
Bruce W Torrey
398 Old County Rd #8
Hampden ME 04444

Call Sign: KB1PAI
Sheila M White
333 Old County Rd Apt B
Hampden ME 04444

Call Sign: KA1ZTE
Wayne G Madea
309 Papermill Rd
Hampden ME 04444

Call Sign: N1AIE
Marion S Ryder
32 Patterson St
Hampden ME 04444

Call Sign: AE4X
Rob A Whitmore
82 Rawley Drive
Hampden ME 04444

Call Sign: KB1TLH
Matthew J Athas
36 Ruth Ave
Hampden ME 04444

Call Sign: KA1RLB
Colin J Ambler
105 Sidney Blvd
Hampden ME 04444

Call Sign: KB1HFB
Andrew C Chic
2 Surrey Ln
Hampden ME 04444

Call Sign: KB1ORL
Brent A Sutherland
77 Wessnette Dr
Hampden ME 04444

Call Sign: K1DXC
Kenneth A Pomeroy
Hampden ME 04444

Call Sign: KA1RKQ

Harry A Bowen Jr
Hampden ME 044440076

Call Sign: W1MST
Matthew S Thomas
Hampden ME 04444

Call Sign: KB1WCA
Benjamin M Schrader
Hampden ME 04444

FCC Amateur Radio
Licenses in Hancock

Call Sign: KA1TKR
Hadley Parrot
Hc 77 Box 117
Hancock ME 04640

Call Sign: N1NUA
Joan D Hildreth
Hcr 77 Box 139
Hancock ME 04640

Call Sign: W1FNL
John H Wibby
Box 175
Hancock ME 04640

Call Sign: N3QOV
John L Nicolai
Hc 77 Box 263b
Hancock ME 04640

Call Sign: N3QOW
Coreen M Nicolai
Hc 77 Box 263b
Hancock ME 04640

Call Sign: WA1LZL
Harold A Bradford
Rr 1 Box 339
Hancock ME 046409636

Call Sign: N1NGU

Edward P Curtis
Hc77 Box 349aa
Hancock ME 04640

Call Sign: KB1CAA
Rr1 Downeast Amateur
Radio
Box 354
Hancock ME 04640

Call Sign: KB1ONT
Laurel L Poors
225 Franklin Rd
Hancock ME 04640

Call Sign: KB1DIE
Benjamin F Maddocks
Franklin Rd
Hancock ME 04640

Call Sign: N1TXE
James G Davis
417 Franklin Road
Hancock ME 04640

Call Sign: KB1PUK
Richard E Dickson
78 Grant St
Hancock ME 04640

Call Sign: WB1GKG
William H Ducharme
91 Harbor View Dr
Hancock ME 04640

Call Sign: W8NRB
Lawrence E Demilner
128 Jellison Cove Rd
Hancock ME 04640

Call Sign: W1TA
Lawrence E Demilner
128 Jellison Cove Rd
Hancock ME 04640

Call Sign: KB1VLT
Daniel A Morse Jr
52 Morse Ln
Hancock ME 04640

Call Sign: KA1UUK
Robert G Mundell
N Sullivan Rd
Hancock ME 04640

Call Sign: NW1P
Paul O Dyer
57 Old Rt 1
Hancock ME 04640

Call Sign: W1KMG
Robert Begley
272 Old Rte 1
Hancock ME 04640

Call Sign: KB2WPD
Michael J Towsley
56 Peaslee Road
Hancock ME 046403031

Call Sign: KB1NPY
Paul S Worcester
631 Us Highway 1
Hancock ME 04640

Call Sign: N1RGP
Gordon E Kelley
502 Us Hwy 1
Hancock ME 04640

Call Sign: N1LAQ
Harry B Nickerson
Hancock ME 04640

Call Sign: N1MZL
Martha J Nickerson
Hancock ME 04640

Call Sign: N2PZ
Daniel E Lorey

Hancock ME 04640

Call Sign: W3PRD
Peter R Dow
Hancock ME 04640

Call Sign: WA1OWN
James H Goff
Hancock ME 04640

Call Sign: KB1JQM
Mihkhail E Gaudette
Hancock ME 04640

Call Sign: K1JHG
James H Goff
Hancock ME 04640

FCC Amateur Radio Licenses in Hancock Point

Call Sign: KD1ML
S Rus Schay
Rr 77 Box 258b
Hancock Point ME 04640

FCC Amateur Radio Licenses in Hanover

Call Sign: AF1L
David S Worcester
Hanover ME 042370044

FCC Amateur Radio Licenses in Harborside

Call Sign: KB1PXP
John H Ashmore
29 Otis Gray Rd
Harborside ME 04642

FCC Amateur Radio Licenses in Harmony

Call Sign: N1SWS
Scott R Loupin
20 Bean Hill Road
Harmony ME 04942

Call Sign: WB1EDL
Freddie M Underwood Jr
3 Deam Dr
Harmony ME 04942

Call Sign: N5KRF
Oscar L Aristizabal
Rar Ofc Ministries
Harmony ME 049420008

Call Sign: N1MRT
Raymond A Roberts
Harmony ME 04942

Call Sign: KB1PDZ
Mark A Wormwood
Harmony ME 04942

FCC Amateur Radio
Licenses in Harpswell

Call Sign: KA1SAB
Robert C Johnson
Rr 1 Box 78
Harpswell ME 04079

Call Sign: K1AEZ
Kenneth G Brigham
926 Cundys Harbor Road
Harpswell ME 04079

Call Sign: KD0MVF
Archie D Woodworth
21 Doughty Point Rd
Harpswell ME 04079

Call Sign: N1OXG
Bryan C Selee
46 Eider Road
Harpswell ME 04079

Call Sign: N1DNM
George G Chandler Sr
20 Gray Osprey Lane
Harpswell ME 04079

Call Sign: N3APT
William D Monroe Iii
95 Gurnet Landing Rd
Harpswell ME 04079

Call Sign: KB1JTF
Paul J Monroe
96 Harpswell By The Sea
Harpswell ME 04079

Call Sign: KB1OPI
William H Hitchcock
610 Harpswell Neck Rd
Harpswell ME 04079

Call Sign: N1WC
Weston D Clement
261 High Head Road
Harpswell ME 04079

Call Sign: N1MW
Michael K White
9a Intervale Court
Harpswell ME 04079

Call Sign: KA9LLF
Ronald R Meyer
126 Pinkham Point Road
Harpswell ME 04079

Call Sign: KB9HPW
Sandra J Meyer
126 Pinkham Point Road
Harpswell ME 04079

Call Sign: K1MZB
Robert S Howe
138 Shore Road
Harpswell ME 04079

Call Sign: K1FSM
Francis S Mynahan
22 Stovers Cove Rd
Harpswell ME 04079

FCC Amateur Radio
Licenses in Harrington

Call Sign: N1FPG
Stephen O Plummer
321 Dorman Rd
Harrington ME 04643

Call Sign: KA1HRV
John B Whitten
398 Dorman Rd Rr 1
Harrington ME 04643

Call Sign: WB5NKJ
David P Baldwin
Oak Point Rd
Harrington ME 04643

Call Sign: WB5NKK
Mary H Baldwin
Oak Point Rd
Harrington ME 04643

Call Sign: W1LQ
Pine Hollow Amateur Radio
Society
Harrington ME 04643

FCC Amateur Radio
Licenses in Harrison

Call Sign: N3NVJ
Janet L Mahannah
Rr 2 Box 1121
Harrison ME 04041

Call Sign: KA1VXM
Joseph P Archambault
Rr 1 Box 1248

Harrison ME 04040

Call Sign: N1CPF
John H Taylor
Rr 1 Box 245
Harrison ME 04040

Call Sign: N1ILL
Herbert O Karnes
Rr 1 Box 374
Harrison ME 04041

Call Sign: KA1MXJ
Richard L Green
Rfd 1 Box 397
Harrison ME 04040

Call Sign: W1CFZ
Russell S Pitts
Box 472
Harrison ME 04040

Call Sign: KA1WRC
Clark K Gadway
Rr 1 Box 666
Harrison ME 04040

Call Sign: N1HCD
Gail A Woodward
Rr 1 Box 726
Harrison ME 04040

Call Sign: W1PWS
Parker W Spencer
144 Deer Hill Rd
Harrison ME 040403120

Call Sign: KB1CFE
Rr 2 Oxford A C Ham
Group
Box 134 Deer Hill Rd
Harrison ME 04040

Call Sign: KA1OHM
Maurice E Robbins

Deer Trls
Harrison ME 04040

Call Sign: N1RLI
Raymond J Sirois
751 Edes Falls Rd
Harrison ME 04040

Call Sign: N1RY
Raymond J Sirois
751 Edes Falls Rd
Harrison ME 04040

Call Sign: KB1FVF
Harrison Scouting Amateur
Radio Club
751 Edes Falls Rd
Harrison ME 04040

Call Sign: WJ0TA
Harrison Scouting Amateur
Radio Club
751 Edes Falls Rd
Harrison ME 04040

Call Sign: KB1AIS
David D Blue
742 Naples Rd
Harrison ME 04040

Call Sign: KB1JIN
David D Blue
742 Naples Rd
Harrison ME 04040

Call Sign: KA1NBD
James H Tarbox
745 Naples Rd
Harrison ME 04040

Call Sign: KB1SCY
Glenn D Foster
914 Naples Rd
Harrison ME 04040

Call Sign: N1MRW
Marcel F Morrissette
1187 Naples Road
Harrison ME 04040

Call Sign: N1INE
Ronald G Ruel
1232 Naples Road
Harrison ME 04040

Call Sign: K1SLG
Virginia P Taylor
Norway Rd
Harrison ME 04040

Call Sign: W1ZAK
Brian D Spaulding
32 Pitts Road
Harrison ME 040404139

Call Sign: KB1ENJ
Michael F Bradford Jr
Rfd2
Harrison ME 040409434

Call Sign: K1TBX
Arthur A Drisko
Box 849 Rr 2
Harrison ME 04040

Call Sign: KF6IVA
Roger C Larson
5 South Beech Road
Harrison ME 04040

Call Sign: KB1WKS
Karen J Mentus
27/8 Summit Hill Rd
Harrison ME 04040

Call Sign: W1FHG
Edward S Tarbox
15 Winslow St
Harrison ME 04040

Call Sign: KA1UIP
Edward O Soucy
Harrison ME 04040

Call Sign: KQ1B
Robert E Frost
Harrison ME 04040

Call Sign: WB1CCG
Donna D Pitts
Harrison ME 04040

FCC Amateur Radio Licenses in Hartford

Call Sign: N1OXC
Peter A Theriault
Rr #1 Box 330
Hartford ME 04221

Call Sign: N1PDQ
Christine L Theriault
Rr 1 Box 330
Hartford ME 04221

Call Sign: W1CFJ
William C Ricker
1661 Main St
Hartford ME 04220

FCC Amateur Radio Licenses in Hartland

Call Sign: KA2RAH
Michael J Geydoshek Sr
Rr 1 Box 1700
Hartland ME 04944

Call Sign: N1RPU
Jeffrey H Coffin
Rr 1 Box 3350
Hartland ME 04943

Call Sign: K1VCZ
Harold F Bishop

Rfd 1 Box 5730
Hartland ME 04943

Call Sign: N1QAU
Ruth S Wilber
2297 Canaan Rd
Hartland ME 04943

Call Sign: KB1FJA
Timothy J Emery
38 Crosby St
Hartland ME 049439609

Call Sign: KB1FIZ
Harlan E Emery
78 Crosby St
Hartland ME 04943

Call Sign: WA1REQ
Michael H Pushard Sr
450 Ford Hill Road
Hartland ME 04943

Call Sign: KR1F
Malcolm F Goodnow
691 Morrill Pond Rd
Hartland ME 04943

FCC Amateur Radio Licenses in Hebron

Call Sign: KA1VZL
Theresa M Saunders
797 Buckfield Rd
Hebron ME 04238

Call Sign: N1GZB
Bradley T Saunders
797 Buckfield Rd
Hebron ME 04238

Call Sign: N1UHV
ANGELA R Lafrance
797 Buckfield Rd.
Hebron ME 04238

Call Sign: KB1EWW
Lael M Saunders
797 Buckifield Rd.
Hebron ME 04238

Call Sign: KB1PME
Paul R Apollo
160 Merrill Hill Rd
Hebron ME 04238

Call Sign: N1ZRV
Patricia A Valeriani
Rte 119
Hebron ME 04238

Call Sign: KA1KYY
Gino P Valeriani
Hebron ME 04238

FCC Amateur Radio Licenses in Hermon

Call Sign: KB1TLE
Daniel L Owen
616 Billings Rd
Hermon ME 04401

Call Sign: W1DLO
Daniel L Owen
616 Billings Rd
Hermon ME 04401

Call Sign: KB1LUN
David G Parsons
422 Bog Road
Hermon ME 04401

Call Sign: N1EPP
Jack H Annis
588 Bog Road
Hermon ME 04401

Call Sign: N1NFN
Jeremy L Bemis

852 Bog Road
Hermon ME 04401

189 Klatt Rd.
Hermon ME 04401

196 Smith Rd
Hermon ME 04401

Call Sign: N1OJN
Sidney L Dole
869 Bog Road
Hermon ME 04401

Call Sign: N1CZL
Jay D Turner
22 New Boston Rd.
Hermon ME 04401

Call Sign: KA1HFM
E Fritz Day
78 Stoneybrook Way
Hermon ME 04401

Call Sign: KB1IHO
John F Anderson
200 Fuller Rd
Hermon ME 04401

Call Sign: N1JSL
Mary C Turner
22 New Boston Rd.
Hermon ME 04401

Call Sign: WA1AKV
Donald E Gaudreau
35 Swan Road
Hermon ME 04401

Call Sign: KB1KBW
Marilyn K Anderson
200 Fuller Rd
Hermon ME 04401

Call Sign: N0BGS
Kurt P Wesseling Iii
22 Reed Hill Rd
Hermon ME 04401

Call Sign: WB1DKN
Mary Ann E Gaudreau
35 Swan Road
Hermon ME 04401

Call Sign: W1WBP
William B Phelps
471 Fuller Rd
Hermon ME 044049520

Call Sign: WA1PKV
Stephen R Vose
551 Ridge Drive
Hermon ME 04401

Call Sign: K1BSA
Ksr Arc
504 Wing Rd
Hermon ME 04401

Call Sign: N1TMH
Howard R Towle
443 Fuller Road
Hermon ME 044010401

Call Sign: W0XOF
Daniel J Holodick
2833 Route 2
Hermon ME 04401

Call Sign: N1OJO
Daniel G Albert
504 Wing Rd
Hermon ME 04401

Call Sign: N1JRQ
Rodney A Perry Jr
1841 Hammond
Hermon ME 04401

Call Sign: K1EIV
Clarence A Hamilton
2902 Route 2
Hermon ME 044010228

Call Sign: N1STQ
Terry P Albert
504 Wing Rd
Hermon ME 04401

Call Sign: KB1FOI
Dorothy L Hughes
1841 Hammond Street
Hermon ME 04401

Call Sign: N1MKR
Douglas K Smith
Box 2780 Rt 2
Hermon ME 04401

Call Sign: KB1FJI
Neal R Albert
504 Wing Rd
Hermon ME 04401

Call Sign: KB1PNR
Zhongyu Yang
19 Hillcrest Dr
Hermon ME 04401

Call Sign: KB1HFY
Wayne A Kenney
83 Smith Rd
Hermon ME 04401

Call Sign: KA1TKS
Roger W Dole
852 Bog Road
Hermon, ME 04401

Call Sign: N1VDQ
Linwood A Hutchinson

Call Sign: WA1HUP
James R Jordan

Call Sign: N1PRB
Jean M Dole

852 Bog Rod
Hermon, ME 04401

FCC Amateur Radio Licenses in Hiram

Call Sign: N1TGT
Deanna L Hartford
454 Hampshire Street
Hiram ME 04041

Call Sign: W1BTY
Raymond C Cotton
5 Peqwaket Trail
Hiram ME 04041

FCC Amateur Radio Licenses in Hodgdon

Call Sign: KB1LGJ
Barrett T Quint
22 Catalina Rd
Hodgdon ME 04730

Call Sign: KB1LBP
Herbert E Carlow Jr
680 Jackins Settlement Rd
Hodgdon ME 04730

Call Sign: KB1JVS
Marcia P Bell
567 Walker Rd
Hodgdon ME 04730

FCC Amateur Radio Licenses in Holden

Call Sign: K3MBS
Ira Weissman
Box 427
Holden ME 044290427

Call Sign: WB1EMA
Kenneth C Lewis
105 Copeland Hill Rd

Holden ME 04429

Call Sign: KB1GEQ
Peter E Zelz
964 Eastern Avenue
Holden ME 04429

Call Sign: KU1Z
Ned Black
1 Larch Rd
Holden ME 04429

Call Sign: KF4IIG
Mark A Sullivan
108 Mann Hill Rd
Holden ME 04429

Call Sign: N1QJU
Lawrence A Sherwood
265 Rooks Rd
Holden ME 04429

Call Sign: KB2USA
Thomas R Colavito
55 Sarina Dr.
Holden ME 044298201

Call Sign: KB1SUT
Henry D Shumaker
3 Shamrock Circle
Holden ME 04429

Call Sign: KA1UGT
Kenneth G Christian Jr
557 South Rd
Holden ME 04429

Call Sign: N1MYU
Kenneth G Christian
557 South Road
Holden ME 04429

Call Sign: N1MYV
Jonette W Christian
557 South Road

Holden ME 04429

Call Sign: KB1WMJ
David J Burke
59 Tower Drive
Holden ME 04429

Call Sign: WA1BCJ
Gordon W Russell
503 Wiswell Rd
Holden ME 04429

Call Sign: KW1Q
Ronald E Sirois
Holden ME 04429

FCC Amateur Radio Licenses in Hollis

Call Sign: KB1BGD
Eric D Conway
Box 224a Waterboro Rd
Hollis ME 04042

Call Sign: N1ROA
David R Piche
1019 Cape Road
Hollis ME 04042

Call Sign: K1FAA
Richard L Eilinger
1274 Cape Road
Hollis ME 04042

Call Sign: W1TAZ
Richard E Keene
33 Oakwood Drive
Hollis ME 04042

Call Sign: KB1ETY
Reuben H Howard
517 River Rd
Hollis ME 04042

Call Sign: K1ANM
Monroe P Bean
Rr 1 Box 313
Hollis Center ME 04042

Call Sign: KA1SSY
Philip W Allen
Rfd 2 Box 401k
Hollis Center ME 04014

Call Sign: N1HTW
Donna A Anderson
437 Cape Rd
Hollis Center ME
040423704

Call Sign: KB1BQV
Southern Maine Amateur
Radio Club
1019 Cape Rd
Hollis Center ME 04042

Call Sign: N1FVZ
Mark L Anderson
437 Cape Road
Hollis Center ME
040429777

Call Sign: W1MLA
Mark L Anderson
437 Cape Road
Hollis Center ME
040423704

Call Sign: KB1CGN
Jay L Young
15 Dennett Rd
Hollis Center ME 04042

Call Sign: N1MUM
Richard C Huff
7 Haley Rd

Hollis Center ME 04042

Call Sign: KB1ASM
Richard A Alderette
9 High Street
Hollis Center ME 04042

Call Sign: N1AUG
William J Roche
3 Highland Ridge
Hollis Center ME 04042

Call Sign: N1FTE
Keith K Page
3 Muddy Brook Rd
Hollis Center ME 04042

Call Sign: W1CKD
Portland Repeater Group
3 Muddy Brook Rd
Hollis Center ME 04042

Call Sign: N1FTY
Sylvie F Page
3 Muddy Brook Rd
Hollis Center ME 04042

Call Sign: KB1MQK
Bruce K Page Ii
3 Muddy Brook Rd
Hollis Center ME 04042

Call Sign: W1CYY
Bruce K Page Ii
3 Muddy Brook Rd
Hollis Center ME 04042

Call Sign: KB1PLX
Kimberly C Metcalf
3 Muddy Brook Rd
Hollis Center ME 04042

Call Sign: N1TTY
Kimberly C Metcalf
3 Muddy Brook Rd

Hollis Center ME 04042

Call Sign: KB1AQF
Roland G Hannaford
Hollis Center ME 04042

Call Sign: N1FQW
John L Bastey Iii
61 Middle St
Hollowell ME 04347

Call Sign: WA1YMS
Andrew K Larrimore
573 Barnestown Rd
Hope ME 04847

Call Sign: KB1PWE
Justin S Lesage-Boutin
760 Camded Rd
Hope ME 04847

Call Sign: W1KS
Robert L Appleby
21 Chickadee Ln
Hope ME 04847

Call Sign: K1VVT
Arthur H Adolphsen Jr
351 Crabtree Rd
Hope ME 04847

Call Sign: KE1IL
Peter B Ettlinger
168 Gillette Road
Hope ME 048473240

Call Sign: KA1ZGX
Elray A Kimball
178 High St

Hope ME 048472030

Call Sign: KB1UPL
Ray O Sisk
153 Main St
Hope ME 04847

Call Sign: WA4GSB
Ray O Sisk Ii
153 Main St
Hope ME 04847

Call Sign: KB1VWB
Vaughan J Hawley
21 Mountain View Ln
Hope ME 04847

Call Sign: K2PAX
Vaughan J Hawley
21 Mountain View Ln
Hope ME 04847

Call Sign: KA1YXP
Andrew L Rowe Jr
53 Old Lane
Hope ME 04847

FCC Amateur Radio Licenses in Houlton

Call Sign: WB1AQP
Donald M Ladd
B Rd Box 243a
Houlton ME 04730

Call Sign: N1WAR
James D Crawford
77 Bangor St
Houlton ME 04730

Call Sign: W1ZUA
Terrence B Mc Gillicuddy
21 Bowdoin
Houlton ME 04730

Call Sign: W1BBS
Katherine P Hilton
Rr 2 Box 2309
Houlton ME 04730

Call Sign: W1QOK
John M Carson
Rfd 4 Box 238
Houlton ME 04730

Call Sign: KA1VHF
Rebecca S Nightingale
Rfd 1 Box 67
Houlton ME 04730

Call Sign: WB1HLT
Perley J Barrow
Rfd 1 Box 80
Houlton ME 04730

Call Sign: WA1MTT
John E Scovill
17 Brook St
Houlton ME 04730

Call Sign: KC4TGM
Michael J Surran
22 Cary St
Houlton ME 04730

Call Sign: KB1FEI
Bonita E Rairdon
5 Chandler Court
Houlton ME 04730

Call Sign: KB1FJF
Clarence L Rairdon
5 Chandler Court
Houlton ME 04730

Call Sign: W1OCU
Malcolm E York
23 Elm St
Houlton ME 04730

Call Sign: KB1OWX
Peter N Rairdon
6 Foxcroft Court
Houlton ME 04730

Call Sign: KB1DUT
Mark E Rondyke
11 Guy St
Houlton ME 04730

Call Sign: W1MER
Mark E Rondyke
11 Guy St
Houlton ME 04730

Call Sign: KB1BYV
James W Burton
79 Hillview Ave
Houlton ME 04730

Call Sign: KA1VU
Peter N White Iii
115 Main St
Houlton ME 04730

Call Sign: KB1WCP
Reginald W Curtis
106 Main Street
Houlton ME 04730

Call Sign: KB1EAM
Gary R Seamon
81 Military St
Houlton ME 04730

Call Sign: N1XPX
William D Ellis
14 N St C
Houlton ME 04730

Call Sign: KB1MGZ
Sanford C Ingraham
33 Park St
Houlton ME 04730

Call Sign: WA1YDD
Percy W Hoar
11 Pearce Ave
Houlton ME 04730

Call Sign: KD0BXR
Ken V Hayes
22 Porter Settlement Road
Houlton ME 04730

Call Sign: KB1FSN
Nathaniel U Cody
Rfd4
Houlton ME 04730

Call Sign: KB1DQL
Roger N Stairs
Box 660 RR#7
Houlton ME 04730

Call Sign: W1NSN
G H C A - 27 Ghca
Aerospace Radio Club
School St
Houlton ME 04730

Call Sign: W1AZQ
Donald W Nealey
98 Smyrna Street
Houlton ME 04730

Call Sign: WA1PWK
James H Bowen
17 Sunnyside St
Houlton ME 047301612

Call Sign: NM1R
Richard C Bell
567 Walker Rd
Houlton ME 04731

Call Sign: N1XFP
John E Folsom
15 Weeks Ave
Houlton ME 04730

Call Sign: KB1DLW
Robert A Miller
9 Weeks St
Houlton ME 04730

Call Sign: W1EP
John E Folsom
15 Weeks St
Houlton ME 047301920

Call Sign: K1ERN
Michael D Ford
Houlton ME 04730

Call Sign: KA1FWP
Steven C Hurd
Houlton ME 04730

Call Sign: KA1MTO
Paul H Smith Jr
Houlton ME 04730

Call Sign: KB6GCS
Kenneth Ross Mc Cart
Houlton ME 04730

Call Sign: N1DGR
Clarence N Snow
Houlton ME 04730

Call Sign: N1SS
Peter M Hurd
Houlton ME 047301005

Call Sign: WB1ASP
George E Mc Gillicuddy
Houlton ME 04730

Call Sign: N1RAM
Russell A Miller
Houlton ME 047300312

Call Sign: KB1MGX
Robert W Warrick

Houlton ME 04730

FCC Amateur Radio Licenses in Howland

Call Sign: N1ZFN
John D Carver
22 Argyle Rd
Howland ME 04448

Call Sign: KB1EIW
Priscilla A Clark
496 N Howland Rd
Howland ME 04448

Call Sign: KB1EIX
Gary O Clark
496 N Howland Rd
Howland ME 04448

Call Sign: KB1FSP
Lester A Bouldry Jr
Howland ME 04448

FCC Amateur Radio Licenses in Hudson

Call Sign: N1WBL
Timothy S Colfer
Rr 1 Box 900
Hudson ME 04449

Call Sign: KB1VZT
Ronald J Libby
51 Darling Rd
Hudson ME 04449

Call Sign: KB1IHL
Kevin J Cash
237 Old Town Rd
Hudson ME 04449

Call Sign: N1GOI
David A Baker Sr
36 Pine Grove Rd

Hudson ME 04449

FCC Amateur Radio Licenses in Hulls Cove

Call Sign: N1PFR
Terrance J Kelley
Hulls Cove ME 04604

FCC Amateur Radio Licenses in Industry

Call Sign: N1YTO
David J Beaudoin
555 Federal Row
Industry ME 04938

Call Sign: N1ZDI
Alton S Carter
69 New Sharon Rd.
Industry ME 04938

Call Sign: KG4MOR
Carroll S Ryder
19 Tracy Rd
Industry ME 04938

FCC Amateur Radio Licenses in Island Falls

Call Sign: N1VYN
Meredith E Corkum-
Greenlaw
44 Houlton Road
Island Falls ME 04747

Call Sign: WA1DBJ
Herman E Archer
Island Falls ME 04747

Call Sign: KB1JVP
Leon F Botting
Island Falls ME 04747

Call Sign: KB1JVQ

Judith G Botting
Island Falls ME 04747

FCC Amateur Radio Licenses in Islesboro

Call Sign: KB1KPJ
David G Sleeper
466 Ferry Rd
Islesboro ME 04848

Call Sign: K1AMV
Richard V De Grasse
508 Ferry Rd
Islesboro ME 04848

Call Sign: NR1V
Scott K Smith
156 Gull Point Road
Islesboro ME 04848

Call Sign: KB1WDX
Raymond Lillie
1228 Main Rd
Islesboro ME 04848

Call Sign: WB1FHW
Vera N Williams
Main Rd
Islesboro ME 04848

Call Sign: W1GTP
Frank F Fairfield
717 Main Road
Islesboro ME 04848

Call Sign: AL7LV
Frank J Ilardi
1505 Meadow Pond Road
Islesboro ME 04848

Call Sign: KC1VU
Joseph M Hughes
Islesboro ME 04848

Call Sign: ND1D
Thomas J Reynolds
Islesboro ME 04848

FCC Amateur Radio Licenses in Islesford

Call Sign: KB1VDB
Louis M Seigal
Islesford ME 04646

Call Sign: W2ZEN
Louis M Seigal
Islesford ME 04646

FCC Amateur Radio Licenses in Jackman

Call Sign: WA1GHV
Blair J Van Camp
Star Route 76 Box 1414
Jackman ME 04945

Call Sign: KB1OWO
Lawrence J Foster
300 Main St
Jackman ME 04945

Call Sign: KB1QIW
Mary J Foster
300 Main St
Jackman ME 04945

Call Sign: KA0UFD
Edward J Mc Call Jr
Jackman ME 04945

Call Sign: KB1UGB
Kevin F Cavanaugh
Jackman ME 04945

Call Sign: KB1UGC
David M Theis
Jackman ME 04945

FCC Amateur Radio Licenses in Jackson

Call Sign: N2FXI
Robert D Royds Jr
717 Hadley Mill Rd
Jackson ME 049213122

Call Sign: N1BTM
Robert D Royds Jr
717 Hadley Mill Rd
Jackson ME 049213122

Call Sign: AA1MS
Samuel H Davis
314 Village Rd
Jackson ME 049213112

FCC Amateur Radio Licenses in Jay

Call Sign: KB1GHS
Gary D Bryant
29 Belleview Dr
Jay ME 042391726

Call Sign: WA1QIK
Gary D Bryant
29 Belleview Dr
Jay ME 042391726

Call Sign: W1AHJ
John W Batchelder
Rr 1 Box 1660
Jay ME 04239

Call Sign: KD1UI
Gary J Therrien
Rr 1 Box 1895
Jay ME 04240

Call Sign: KB1RFN
Robert E Leigh
111 Intervale Rd
Jay ME 04239

Call Sign: N1QJV
John E Will
3 Ludden Dr
Jay ME 04239

Call Sign: KA1JGE
Steve J Maki
57 Macomber Hill Road
Jay ME 04239

Call Sign: N1PDP
Ashley Wing
278 Main St
Jay ME 04239

Call Sign: WA1ASY
Roger W Blais
185 Tessier Rd
Jay ME 04239

Call Sign: W1ASY
Roger W Blais
185 Tessier Rd
Jay ME 04239

Call Sign: KB1UBV
John L Donald Jr
49 Walker Hill Rd
Jay ME 04239

Call Sign: KB1MDJ
Justin P Snay
30 Weston Heights
Jay ME 04239

FCC Amateur Radio Licenses in Jefferson

Call Sign: WB2LCA
William W Pearce
12 Ashley Lane
Jefferson ME 04348

Call Sign: N1SJY

Thomas A Raye
Rr 1 Box 170
Jefferson ME 04348

Call Sign: K1NI
Ernest E Richards
8 Clark Point Rd
Jefferson ME 043489742

Call Sign: N1EJS
Elizabeth M Richards
8 Clark Point Rd
Jefferson ME 043489742

Call Sign: K1XK
Elizabeth M Richards
8 Clark Point Rd
Jefferson ME 043483255

Call Sign: W1HJP
Charles R Hewson
230 E Pond Rd
Jefferson ME 04348

Call Sign: KA1IUJ
David E Martin
250 East Pond Road
Jefferson ME 04348

Call Sign: KB1CWL
Daniel J Mellor Jr
149 Gardiner Rd
Jefferson ME 043480965

Call Sign: N1HPU
Benjamin J Benedetti Jr
79 King Cove Road
Jefferson ME 04348

Call Sign: KB2CC
Timothy E Packey
188 N Mountain Rd
Jefferson ME 04348

Call Sign: KB1TGC

Gary D Laweryson
377 North Clary Rd
Jefferson ME 04348

Call Sign: KQ1H
James W Allen
492 North Clary Rd
Jefferson ME 04348

Call Sign: KB1IJG
Philip E Pinkham
72 Pindo Polara Rd
Jefferson ME 04348

Call Sign: W1VLU
Blaine M Kimball
990 S Clary Rd
Jefferson ME 04348

Call Sign: KB1QER
Nicholas R Tassinari
382 Washington Rd
Jefferson ME 04330

Call Sign: KA1UZO
Frank D C Walton
Jefferson ME 04348

Call Sign: N1SDF
Ralph G Martin
Jefferson ME 04348

Call Sign: N1ZR
Paul V Gregory
Jefferson ME 04348

Call Sign: N1MLA
Steven M Pineo
Rr 1 Box 147c
Jonesboro ME 04648

Call Sign: KB1IKJ

Michael E Cassella
R R 1 Box 202
Jonesboro ME 04648

Call Sign: N1MCM
Nancy N Hayward
406 Looks Point Road
Jonesboro ME 04648

Call Sign: K1UD
Robert O Hayward
406 Looks Point Road
Jonesboro ME 04648

Call Sign: KB1ONR
Timothy C Look
42 Old Us Rt One
Jonesboro ME 04648

Call Sign: WA1FXC
Ellis F Smith
Rfd Box 155
Jonesboro ME 04648

Call Sign: N1PPH
Tracy J Watts
Jonesboro ME 046480113

Call Sign: KB1PUJ
Miles F Carpenter Iii
Jonesboro ME 04648

Call Sign: N1AMG
William R Torrey Jr
Cove St Rr 01 Box 1140
Jonesport ME 04649

Call Sign: W1PCY
Albert E Wilder
Rr 1 Box 730
Jonesport ME 04649

Call Sign: N1VLN
Harold S Floyd
Island St
Jonesport ME 04649

Call Sign: K1DGP
Ralph C Bolster
Box 221
Kenduskeag ME 04450

Call Sign: N1WZF
Jeffery L Clark
432 Clark Rd
Kenduskeag ME 04450

Call Sign: N1YUJ
Ruby N Story
523 Clark Rd N
Kenduskeag ME 04450

Call Sign: N1EZQ
Paul L Story
Clark Rd N
Kenduskeag ME 04450

Call Sign: N1IVY
Michael S Call
47 Oak St
Kenduskeag ME 04450

Call Sign: KB1NRF
David W Bernier
21 Strout Rd
Kenduskeag ME 04450

Call Sign: N1LGM
Bruce H Trundy
Kenduskeag ME 04450

Call Sign: KL7ZT
Lance C Lobo
Kenduskeag ME 04450

Call Sign: AB1ET
Lance C Lobo
Kenduskeag ME 04450

Call Sign: KB1SBN
Joshua M Rich
757 Alewive Rd
Kennebunk ME 04043

Call Sign: KB1HPS
William A Grady
21 Alfred Road
Kennebunk ME 04043

Call Sign: KB1VPC
Timothy R Moyer
2 Apple Lane
Kennebunk ME 04043

Call Sign: KB1VPD
Thomas R Moyer
2 Apple Lane
Kennebunk ME 04043

Call Sign: KB1SYK
Peter J Chiasson
26 Balsam Lane
Kennebunk ME 04043

Call Sign: KB1AOP
Cynthia L Maniatis
11 Bourne St
Kennebunk ME 04043

Call Sign: KB1AQZ
Andrew R Thomson
Rr 1 Box 1607
Kennebunk ME 04043

Call Sign: KB1ASW
William M Thomson

Rr 1 Box 1607
Kennebunk ME 04043

Call Sign: KA1LWP
Ralph A Prejean
Rfd 1 Box 2243
Kennebunk ME 04043

Call Sign: WB1FBE
George A Moran
101 Brown St
Kennebunk ME 04043

Call Sign: WB1ATD
Dianne C Nowacki
155 Brown St
Kennebunk ME 040432101

Call Sign: WB1BVH
Vernon E Jones
32 Catmousam Rd
Kennebunk ME 04043

Call Sign: N1KYN
AMANDA M Arloro
188 Cole Road
Kennebunk ME 04043

Call Sign: K1TQN
Paul D Krippendorf
8 Countryfield Cir
Kennebunk ME 04043

Call Sign: N1IYW
Hans Warner
22 Dane St
Kennebunk ME 04043

Call Sign: N3ATG
Susan L Warner
22 Dane St
Kennebunk ME 04043

Call Sign: WA1VDV
Frederick S Bancroft

73 Fletcher St
Kennebunk ME 04043

Call Sign: N1JUB
Carlton L Hutchins
96 Fletcher St
Kennebunk ME 04043

Call Sign: KC2GA
Rupert E Haley
27 Gendron Ln
Kennebunk ME 04043

Call Sign: KD1WA
Herve E Lavoie
3 Grasshopper Ln
Kennebunk ME 04043

Call Sign: KA1RUP
Jonathan P Archibald
5 Grasshopper Ln
Kennebunk ME 04043

Call Sign: K1VCR
John D Mc Cormack
46 High St
Kennebunk ME 04043

Call Sign: N1OTE
Peter G Maniatis
14 Intervale Road
Kennebunk ME 04043

Call Sign: K1ETK
Laurie Cohen
12 Kimball Ln
Kennebunk ME 040430268

Call Sign: N1YAU
Robert C Engel
39 Landing Drive
Kennebunk ME 04043

Call Sign: W1BQL
Charles P Howe

180 Lower Brown St Rfd
Kennebunk ME 04043

Call Sign: KB1NVV
Barbara A Weddleton
133 Maguire Rd
Kennebunk ME 04043

Call Sign: W1II
John M Shandorf
231 Maguire Rd
Kennebunk ME 04043

Call Sign: KA1KKF
Richard F Mc Loon
7 Oak Bluff Dr
Kennebunk ME 04043

Call Sign: N1HTT
Kenneth V Chace
11 Oak Bluff Rd
Kennebunk ME 04043

Call Sign: WB1BUJ
Lee H Masury
16 Peninsula Dr
Kennebunk ME 04043

Call Sign: N1YQV
Harvey A Lipman
123 Port Road
Kennebunk ME 04043

Call Sign: AI2Q
Alex M Mendelsohn
164 Sea Rd
Kennebunk ME 04043

Call Sign: KB1RBK
Brian D Wood
2 Settlers Way
Kennebunk ME 04043

Call Sign: W1CEQ
Danforth M Googins

15 Spiller Dr
Kennebunk ME 04043

Call Sign: WB1EGQ
Candide M Marsh
64r Storer St
Kennebunk ME 04043

Call Sign: KY1R
Louis C Mac Donald
53 Wakefield Rd
Kennebunk ME 040430890

Call Sign: N1UCB
Wilfred C Reid Jr
287 Webber Hill Rd
Kennebunk ME 040436320

Call Sign: W1UOT
Raymond P Belyea
171 Western Ave
Kennebunk ME 04043

Call Sign: KA1KBZ
William C Larrabee
187 Western Ave
Kennebunk ME 04043

Call Sign: W1GZS
Merle R Crowley
7 Willard Way
Kennebunk ME 040436588

Call Sign: AD1E
John C Nowacki
Kennebunk ME 04043

Call Sign: KA1QE
John F Kneeland
Kennebunk ME 04043

Call Sign: N1NMQ
Alfred K Roper
Kennebunk ME 04043

Call Sign: N1SKW
Daniel J Nowacki
Kennebunk ME 040430073

Call Sign: WB1CTT
John R Woodason Ii
Kennebunk ME 04043

Call Sign: W3NA
John C Nowacki
Kennebunk ME 04043

FCC Amateur Radio Licenses in Kennebunkport

Call Sign: N1GHT
Archibald A Talmage Iii
220 Beachwood Ave
Kennebunkport ME 04046

Call Sign: KA1KQL
Harry R Anderson
1875 Chestnut St
Kennebunkport ME 04046

Call Sign: KB1APJ
Benjamin C Merrill
11 Dorrance Road
Kennebunkport ME 04046

Call Sign: WB1DOO
Terry C Merrill
11 Dorrance Road
Kennebunkport ME 04046

Call Sign: KB1CQX
Amanda F Spenlinhauer
119 Marshall Pt Rd
Kennebunkport ME 04043

Call Sign: AE1A
Frank E Federman
90 Mills Rd.
Kennebunkport ME 04046

Call Sign: KA1AUQ
Linda J Federman
90 Mills Rd.
Kennebunkport ME 04046

Call Sign: K1XD
David W Shorthill
30 Mooserocks Rd
Kennebunkport ME 04046

Call Sign: KC4TDA
Robert D Rice
312 Ocean Ave
Kennebunkport ME 04046

Call Sign: W1NYL
Frederick T Van Veen
20 Sand Point Rd
Kennebunkport ME 04046

Call Sign: N1VWS
George W Cushman
43 School St
Kennebunkport ME
040462745

Call Sign: KA1NWB
Clifton H Smith
6 Seaview Ave
Kennebunkport ME 04046

Call Sign: KA1OIO
Andrew F Smith
6 Seaview Ave
Kennebunkport ME 04046

Call Sign: W1VXV
Robert C Boyd
16 Woodlawn Ave
Kennebunkport ME
040466120

Call Sign: NT1V
Robert C Boyd

16 Woodlawn Ave
Kennebunkport ME
040466120

Call Sign: KB1AKH
Jeanne M Peckiconis
Kennebunkport ME 04046

Call Sign: K1GDX
Laurence R Hill
5 North St
Kenneburnkport ME 04046

FCC Amateur Radio Licenses in Kents Hill

Call Sign: KA1CUM
Alfred H Gordon
Rfd 1 Box 1920
Kents Hill ME 04350

Call Sign: WA1RVI
John P Daley
Rr 2 Box 810
Kents Hill ME 04349

Call Sign: K1PIG
Martin W Rigoulot
427 Sandy River Rd
Kents Hill ME 04349

Call Sign: N1NFO
Lisa B Rigoulot
427 Sandy River Rd
Kents Hill ME 04349

Call Sign: W1PIG
Kennebec Amateur Radio
Society
427 Sandy River Rd
Kents Hill ME 04349

Call Sign: KB6DIL
Stephen B Hammond
Kents Hill ME 04349

Call Sign: N1BKH
Donald R Wismer
Kents Hill ME 04349

Call Sign: N1ZLK
Jeremiah V Donovan
Kents Hill ME 04349

FCC Amateur Radio Licenses in Kezar Falls

Call Sign: KA1YPZ
James M Smith Iii
Rfd 2 Box 357
Kezar Falls ME 04047

Call Sign: KA1YQW
Adam J Smith
Rfd 2 Box 357
Kezar Falls ME 04048

Call Sign: KA1YPX
Aaron J Smith
Rfd 2 Box 357
Kezer Falls ME 04047

FCC Amateur Radio Licenses in Kingfield

Call Sign: KB1JTD
Peter E Boucher
4 Old Parkway Rd
Kingfield ME 04947

Call Sign: KA5LSP
Robert J Sawyer
45 Pinnacle Pond Rd
Kingfield ME 049474139

Call Sign: KB1AQR
Arlene M Lancaster
Kingfield ME 04947

Call Sign: KB1ARH

Claude V Lancaster
Kingfield ME 04947

Call Sign: N1CTU
Wilbur J Dunphy Jr
Kingfield ME 04947

FCC Amateur Radio Licenses in Kingman

Call Sign: N1JNM
Hartley L Grant Jr
1451 Kingman Rd
Kingman ME 044519702

Call Sign: N1MTV
Edith B Grant
1451 Kingman Road
Kingman ME 04451

Call Sign: N1NKP
Glenn G O Donal
68 Park St
Kingman ME 04451

FCC Amateur Radio Licenses in Kittery

Call Sign: KB1SYG
Ryan Berry
15-1 Adams Lane
Kittery ME 03904

Call Sign: KC5HXX
James H Mc Nally
41 Bowen Rd
Kittery ME 039041355

Call Sign: KC5MHT
Nancy L Mc Nally
41 Bowen Rd
Kittery ME 039041355

Call Sign: KA1WUJ
Leland L Riley Jr

13 Bridge St
Kittery ME 03904

Call Sign: W1VEX
George T Farrow
21 Cromwell St
Kittery ME 039041125

Call Sign: W1YDX
Robert G Dawson Sr
38 Cromwell St
Kittery ME 039041126

Call Sign: K1VIP
John E Waterman
9 Cutts Rd
Kittery ME 03904

Call Sign: WD4KNO
Timothy J Mc Entee
6 Cutts Rd. Trlr. 73
Kittery ME 03904

Call Sign: WB1AOT
Stuart R Cressey
12 Dana Ave
Kittery ME 03904

Call Sign: KA1IZI
Irving L Lawrence
31 Dion Ave
Kittery ME 03904

Call Sign: NV1B
Andrew M Moore
16 George Street
Kittery ME 03904

Call Sign: N1XYM
Christopher L Young
103 Government St
Kittery ME 03904

Call Sign: W1CEK
Gary M Reuter

273 Haley Rd
Kittery ME 03904

Call Sign: N1HQV
Robert J Mellin
20 Halstead St
Kittery ME 03904

Call Sign: KB1WFL
David J Kelly Iii
7 Highpoint Circle
Kittery ME 03904

Call Sign: KE6CJV
Craig M Breverman
8 Howard Street
Kittery ME 03904

Call Sign: K1ZDF
David M Evans
12 Island Ave
Kittery ME 03904

Call Sign: KB1RDD
Donna L Mitchell
26 Island Ave
Kittery ME 03904

Call Sign: KA1ZWU
Bruce F Wiggin Jr
25 Jones Ave
Kittery ME 03904

Call Sign: N1UCZ
Bruce F Wiggin Sr
25 Jones Ave
Kittery ME 03904

Call Sign: N1OJB
Kristen J Long
61 Lewis Rd
Kittery ME 03904

Call Sign: W1GIU
John E Foye

8 Mendum Ave
Kittery ME 03904

Call Sign: KD1QL
Peter A Henderson
11 Mendum Ave
Kittery ME 03904

Call Sign: KB8OVI
FRANKIE L Rabbitts
64 Moore St
Kittery ME 03904

Call Sign: KB8OVH
Patrick M Rabbitts
64 More St
Kittery ME 03904

Call Sign: W1ZKO
George E Medcalf
89 Norton Rd
Kittery ME 03904

Call Sign: KB1AEA
Robert B Borden
78 Norton Rd 8
Kittery ME 03904

Call Sign: WA1QMU
William E Wilbur
25 Old Ferry Ln
Kittery ME 03904

Call Sign: N1ZBD
James R Eslinger
12 Picott Rd
Kittery ME 03904

Call Sign: KD1EC
Lee B Metcalf
10 Prince Ave
Kittery ME 03904

Call Sign: NT1A
John D Miller

10 Prince Ave
Kittery ME 03904

Call Sign: KC1QL
Gloria J Hostetler
10 Prince Avenue
Kittery ME 03904

Call Sign: N1TOO
Lawrence E Hansberry
4 Red Mill Ln
Kittery ME 03904

Call Sign: KB1VX
Barry M Kray
23 Ridgewood Dr
Kittery ME 03904

Call Sign: KB1SEO
Jonathan D Kray
23 Ridgewood Dr
Kittery ME 03904

Call Sign: N1HKT
Edward L Mossman
42 Rogers Rd
Kittery ME 03904

Call Sign: W1NUT
Manuel P Sousa
140 Rogers Rd
Kittery ME 03904

Call Sign: WB0RSD
Melvin W White
143 Rogers Rd 107
Kittery ME 039041447

Call Sign: N1ABE
John L Brandolini Sr.
5 Spinney Way Lot #12
Kittery ME 03905

Call Sign: N1DHX
Margaret F Brandolini

5 Spinney Way Lot #12
Kittery ME 03904

Call Sign: N3KMV
Scott E Wells
104 Whipple Road
Kittery ME 03904

Call Sign: N3KMX
Roger E Wells
104 Whipple Road
Kittery ME 03904

Call Sign: KB3ESM
Drew Terenzini
56b Whipple Road
Kittery ME 03904

Call Sign: W1XN
Clinton E Wise
27 Wilson Rd
Kittery ME 03904

Call Sign: WA1YRE
Dana A Junkins
87 Wilson Rd
Kittery ME 03904

Call Sign: N1MBK
Bruce D Alexander
15 Wilson Road
Kittery ME 03904

Call Sign: N1LHK
Elwood C Robbins
Kittery ME 03904

Call Sign: W1YTW
Frank L Dennett
Kittery ME 03904

Call Sign: KB1QPM
Josephine A Robbins
Kittery ME 03904

Call Sign: KB1TJV
Robert S Woodbury
16 Bond Rd
Kittery Point ME 03905

Call Sign: W1RSW
Robert Woodbury
16 Bond Rd
Kittery Point ME 03905

Call Sign: K1ZDG
Carroll H Evans
119 Brave Boat Harbor Rd
Kittery Point ME 03905

Call Sign: KB1IPT
Scott S Fraser
1 Captains Way
Kittery Point ME 03905

Call Sign: K1IPT
Scott S Fraser
1 Captains Way
Kittery Point ME 03905

Call Sign: N4SPP
Frank M Doerenberg
20 Captains Way
Kittery Point ME
039055306

Call Sign: WA1CMQ
Chandler O Dalzell Jr
29 Goose Pt
Kittery Point ME 03905

Call Sign: WA1PAN
Jeanne L Dalzell
29 Goose Pt
Kittery Point ME 03905

Call Sign: K1BH

William R Holly
395 Haley Rd
Kittery Point ME 03905

Call Sign: WB1EHV
Frances M Holly
395 Haley Rd
Kittery Point ME 03905

Call Sign: N1AIL
Charles A Ronnquist
611 Haley Rd
Kittery Point ME 03905

Call Sign: K1VJ
Virginia Pummer
632 Haley Rd
Kittery Point ME 03905

Call Sign: KB1AKW
James O Rike
163 Pepperrell Rd
Kittery Point ME 03905

Call Sign: KB1UWZ
Michael P Blackman
47 Seapoint Rd
Kittery Point ME 03905

Call Sign: AB1OV
Michael P Blackman
47 Seapoint Rd
Kittery Point ME 03905

Call Sign: KA1WM
Donald V O Toole
8 Wheelhouse Way
Kittery Point ME 03905

Call Sign: KA1TFX
John C Hackney
Kittery Point ME 03905

Call Sign: KA1TJR
Mike W Biasin

Kittery Point ME 03905

Call Sign: KB1TQQ
Thomas D Philbrook
Kittery Point ME 03905

Call Sign: W1EMA
Waldo County Ares Races
Assn
1688 Belfast Rd
Knox ME 04986

Call Sign: KD1O
Stephen P Curry
1688 Belfast Road
Knox ME 04986

Call Sign: N1TN
Waldo County Amateur
Radio Association
1688 Belfast Road
Knox ME 04986

Call Sign: KB1KPG
Joan J Sheldon
25 Knox Ridge South
Knox ME 04986

Call Sign: KB1HPE
Matthew T Clay
41 Weed Rd
Knox ME 04986

Call Sign: AA1AQ
Reynold J Moreau
5356 Bennoch Rd
Lagrange ME 04453

Call Sign: KC1JK

Elizabeth F Ames
5356 Bennoch Rd
Lagrange ME 04453

Call Sign: KB1GBE
Kenneth S Knightly
17 Knightly Road
La Grange ME 044535100

Call Sign: N1PHA
Frances F Robertson
306 Medford Road
Lagrange ME 04453

Call Sign: KA1QWP
Ronald M Pluth
La Grange ME 04453

Call Sign: KA1QWQ
Janet M Pluth
La Grange ME 04453

Call Sign: KC6END
Ronald I Shaw
La Grange ME 04453

Call Sign: KB1KRK
Eric W Sanborn
La Grange ME 04453

Call Sign: KB1LMM
Crystal C Sanborn
La Grange ME 04453

Call Sign: KB1LCE
Glenn W Sanborn
Lagrange ME 04453

Call Sign: KB1LDF
Inez Sanborn
Lagrange ME 04453

**FCC Amateur Radio
Licenses in Lakeville**

Call Sign: N2ATC
James A Doms
1251 Bottle Lake Rd
Lakeville ME 04487

Call Sign: N1EDB
Frederick W Burrill
66 Eagle Ridge Rd
Lakeville ME 04487

**FCC Amateur Radio
Licenses in Lamoine**

Call Sign: W3AKD
William Protzman Jr
20 Boulder Cove Way
Lamoine ME 046054475

Call Sign: N7YCX
Marie E Rand
261 Buttermilk Road
Lamoine ME 046054206

Call Sign: N1MTQ
Gary N Eaton
461 Buttermilk Road
Lamoine ME 04605

Call Sign: ND1T
James G Merritt
254 Douglas Highway
Lamoine ME 04605

Call Sign: KB1DRS
John T Lennon
10 Glen Mary Road
Lamoine ME 04605

Call Sign: KB1VVI
Christopher J Weaver
572 Lamoine Beach Rd
Lamoine ME 04605

Call Sign: KB1VVJ
John M Weaver

572 Lamoine Beach Rd
Lamoine ME 04605

Call Sign: AB1PZ
Christopher J Weaver
572 Lamoine Beach Rd
Lamoine ME 04605

Call Sign: W1SHI
Robert J Williams
44 Lorimer Road
Lamoine ME 04605

Call Sign: KI4TVU
Nils C Hokansson
88 Lydia's Lane
Lamoine ME 04605

Call Sign: KB1CQQ
Ann E Fitzgerald
504 Partridge Cove Rd
Lamoine ME 04605

Call Sign: K1RCW
Ralph C Warren
16 S Birchlawn Dr
Lamoine ME 046054215

Call Sign: WA3UDO
Robert G Sharkey
373 Seal Point Road
Lamoine ME 04605

Call Sign: KB1GBC
Frederick K Schade
1096 Shore Rd
Lamoine ME 04605

Call Sign: W1TU
Ellsworth Amateur Wireless
Association
1358 Shore Rd
Lamoine ME 04605

Call Sign: W8HAP

Robert L Collins
1358 Shore Rd
Lamoine ME 046059613

Call Sign: N1PTO
Robert W Pentland
36 Wolf Run
Lamoine ME 046054609

FCC Amateur Radio Licenses in Lebanon

Call Sign: N1XQM
John A Tuttle Jr
217 Bakers Grant Road
Lebanon ME 04027

Call Sign: KA1ZYR
James F Skeffington
Rfd 1 Box 1324
Lebanon ME 04027

Call Sign: N1OWR
Jordan H Pike
Rr 2 Box 758
Lebanon ME 04028

Call Sign: K1IEE
Richard H Mayrand
7 Conifer Drive
Lebanon ME 040279508

Call Sign: WA1OUS
Marie M Mayrand
7 Conifer Drive
Lebanon ME 040279508

Call Sign: N1FZD
Russell E Beckwith
Depot Rd
Lebanon ME 040270023

Call Sign: K1WHS
David C Olean
177 Dixon Rd

Lebanon ME 04027

Call Sign: N1RUF
Rory D Mc Gonagle
211 Gully Oven Rd
Lebanon ME 04027

Call Sign: KB1FFA
Douglas P Augustus
21 Homestead Way
Lebanon ME 04027

Call Sign: KB1COR
Wayne S Randall
565 Jim Grant Rd
Lebanon ME 04027

Call Sign: KB1EZS
David A Harriman
555 Little River Rd
Lebanon ME 04027

Call Sign: W1OML
Carl K Juhola
123 Lizotte Road
Lebanon ME 04027

Call Sign: K1RFO
Herbert D Mccarriston
146 Lizotte Road
Lebanon ME 04027

Call Sign: KB1EJQ
John A Carusone
115 Mills Road
Lebanon ME 040274447

Call Sign: KB1UVO
Thomas P Fahy
181 Oak Hill Rd
Lebanon ME 04027

Call Sign: KB0REG
Stuart P Morrison
103 Orrills Hill Road

Lebanon ME 04027

Call Sign: KB0SJD
April E Morrison
103 Orrills Hill Road
Lebanon ME 04027

Call Sign: N1LBI
Monte G Pike
73 Richardson Drive
Lebanon ME 04027

Call Sign: N1WFI
Matthew M Barrows
169 Upper Guinea Rd
Lebanon ME 04027

FCC Amateur Radio Licenses in Lee

Call Sign: N1JNN
Roger W Ek
2217 Lee Road
Lee ME 04455

Call Sign: N1ZDH
Patricia R Ek
2217 Lee Road
Lee ME 04455

Call Sign: KB1GEP
Shawn L Macdonald
2312 Lee Road
Lee ME 04455

Call Sign: N1TIR
Teisha J Priest
5 Ridge Road
Lee ME 04455

Call Sign: N1GJM
Merle E Mc Laughlin Jr
283 Skunk Hill
Lee ME 04455

Call Sign: KA1FFN
Marcel L Brillant
8 Weir Pond Rd
Lee ME 044554123

Call Sign: N1PVH
Kathy M Welch
521 Winn Road
Lee ME 04455

Call Sign: WA1ZJL
Harold M Welch
521 Winn Road
Lee ME 04455

Call Sign: KB1VFS
Sean L Macdonald
Lee ME 04455

FCC Amateur Radio Licenses in Leeds

Call Sign: K1OEW
Chester G Shepard
31 Bernie Hartford Rd
Leeds ME 04263

Call Sign: WB1DPO
Philip A Pease
Rfd 1 Box 1530
Leeds ME 04263

Call Sign: N1UVP
Mitchell R Adams
60 Bryant Rd.
Leeds ME 04263

Call Sign: W2DJX
Frank W Beatty
3935 Fish St
Leeds ME 04263

Call Sign: KB1OGQ
Pamela P Buckley
104 Leeds Jct Rd

Leeds ME 04263

Call Sign: KB1OGN
Hugh V Buckley
104 Leeds Juct Rd
Leeds ME 04263

Call Sign: WA1MOZ
William J Dubois
242 Quaker Ridge Road
Leeds ME 04263

Call Sign: KB1IKK
Daniel L Potvin
217 Summer Rd
Leeds ME 04263

Call Sign: K1DLP
Daniel L Potvin
217 Sumner Rd
Leeds ME 04263

FCC Amateur Radio Licenses in Levant

Call Sign: WA1WFC
James R White
Rr 1 Box 3875
Levant ME 044569744

Call Sign: KA1RTX
Carroll F Miller
Rfd 1 Box 94
Levant ME 04456

Call Sign: N1YUE
Richard H Eaton
40 Clubhouse Rd
Levant ME 04456

Call Sign: KB1KMX
Peter J Ness
21 Forest Hills Dr
Levant ME 04456

Call Sign: KB1PHS
Michael A Easterby
25 Forest Hills Dr
Levant ME 04456

Call Sign: N1NPK
Bradley A Gillis
183 Mt Pleasant Rd
Levant ME 04456

Call Sign: KB1QKP
Patrick L Tracy
7 Sinclair Road
Levant ME 04456

Call Sign: KB1TLF
Brian L Dort
212 South Levant Rd
Levant ME 04456

Call Sign: KB7SEA
Brian L Dort
212 South Levant Rd
Levant ME 04456

Call Sign: N1TCG
David A Therrien
Levant ME 04456

Call Sign: KB1SYJ
Linwood W Carman Jr
Levant ME 04456

FCC Amateur Radio Licenses in Lewiston

Call Sign: N1VOH
Thaxter A Roundy
111 Ash St Apt 7
Lewiston ME 04240

Call Sign: N1VVM
Raymond J B Michaud
20 Bailey Ave
Lewiston ME 04240

Call Sign: N1RXF
Paul L Michaud
31 Bailey Ave
Lewiston ME 04240

Call Sign: KA1UMW
Raymond T Bergeron
16 Church St
Lewiston ME 04240

Call Sign: KB1RQ
Ronald J Fournier
37 Franklin St
Lewiston ME 04240

Call Sign: KB1TAE
Alain J Laverdure
104 Baird Ave 3
Lewiston ME 04240

Call Sign: N1QQT
John L Kennedy
95 Crowley Rd
Lewiston ME 04240

Call Sign: N1RGO
Joseph H Masse
3 Frechette St
Lewiston ME 04240

Call Sign: N1KHQ
Alfred P Viens
107 Bartlett St
Lewiston ME 04240

Call Sign: N1ZHR
Jeffrey A Pelletier
3 Darcy Dr.
Lewiston ME 04240

Call Sign: KB1QYB
David P Stone
18 Green St Apt 1
Lewiston ME 04240

Call Sign: KB1DDR
Alexis Revilock Frost
650 Bates College
Lewiston ME 04240

Call Sign: KA1CKY
Laurent D Bachand
6 Dimsdale Ave
Lewiston ME 04240

Call Sign: N1RGX
Paul W Mc Quarrie
18 Greenwood Ln
Lewiston ME 04240

Call Sign: N1RGZ
Rebecca A Lewis Vincent
2 Bobby St
Lewiston ME 04240

Call Sign: KB1UOY
Maurice C Bonneau
67 Dyer Rd
Lewiston ME 04240

Call Sign: W1PSK
Roland A Desjardins
2 Hillview Ln
Lewiston ME 04240

Call Sign: N1OZV
Michael L Bilodeau
7 Brentwood Ave
Lewiston ME 04240

Call Sign: KB1UOZ
Andre M Bonneau
67 Dyer Rd
Lewiston ME 04240

Call Sign: KB1JTE
Stephen E Vermette
20 Homefield Street
Lewiston ME 04240

Call Sign: N1XDG
Nicholas L Bruno
191 Central Ave
Lewiston ME 04240

Call Sign: K1YXO
Andre M Bonneau
67 Dyer Rd
Lewiston ME 04240

Call Sign: N1TXD
Rock G Stevens
28 Horton St Apt 2
Lewiston ME 04240

Call Sign: W1NSF
Orville C Provost
200 Central Ave
Lewiston ME 04240

Call Sign: KB1DOI
Andrew D Martin
4 Elaine Ave
Lewiston ME 042402211

Call Sign: W1CTT
Steven E Cornett
8 Imelda St
Lewiston ME 04240

Call Sign: W1QZD
Robert L Jean
81 Charles
Lewiston ME 04240

Call Sign: W1LPS
Laurent Gagnon
11 Eustis St
Lewiston ME 04240

Call Sign: N1YWQ
Paul W Cyr
32 Irwin St
Lewiston ME 04240

Call Sign: N1ZHF
Kathy A Cyr
32 Irwin St
Lewiston ME 04240

Call Sign: KB1RUK
Derek T Faile
27 Jordan Rd
Lewiston ME 04240

Call Sign: AB1ML
Derek T Faile
27 Jordan Rd
Lewiston ME 04240

Call Sign: N1WFO
Richard R James
7 Judkin Ave
Lewiston ME 04240

Call Sign: KB1CVA
Ronald A Chartier
38 Larrabee Rd
Lewiston ME 04240

Call Sign: N1YEA
Brian A Horne
28 Lemaire Ave
Lewiston ME 04240

Call Sign: W1SCM
Norman F L Heureux
13 Libby Ave
Lewiston ME 04240

Call Sign: N1RGT
Scott M Russell
2161 Lisbon Rd 27
Lewiston ME 04240

Call Sign: KC2FHV
Russell P Mason
11 Lisbon St. Gateway Apt.
505

Lewiston ME 04240

Call Sign: KB1AWN
James E Porter
1252 Lisbon Street
Lewiston ME 04240

Call Sign: KB1WYA
Laurence D Heindl
607 Main Street
Lewiston ME 04240

Call Sign: N1XUC
Paul R Libbey
26 Manning Ave
Lewiston ME 04240

Call Sign: KB1BVI
L Elizabeth Hoy
39 Manning Ave
Lewiston ME 04240

Call Sign: N1RFS
Raymond G Desjardins
29 Mark St
Lewiston ME 04240

Call Sign: KE6PIJ
Paul N Leonard
25b Marston St 206
Lewiston ME 042406176

Call Sign: KB1EWU
Jeffrey J Fortin
11 Martha Ave
Lewiston ME 04240

Call Sign: N1LSD
Roger A Le Blanc
37 Martin Dr
Lewiston ME 04240

Call Sign: WA1CKD
James R Tardif
22 Mitchell St

Lewiston ME 04240

Call Sign: WB1DUW
Michael C Mc Fadden
14 Moreau Ave
Lewiston ME 04240

Call Sign: WB1ENK
Joline M Mc Fadden
14 Moreau Ave
Lewiston ME 04240

Call Sign: KA1NOB
Robert R Roy
36 Nichols St
Lewiston ME 042408513

Call Sign: N1TZS
Ronie K Ray
46 No Name Pond Rd
Lewiston ME 04240

Call Sign: N1CCG
Richard A Moore
232 Old Webster Rd
Lewiston ME 042401508

Call Sign: K1SJP
Richard A Moore
232 Old Webster Rd
Lewiston ME 042401508

Call Sign: N1IZR
David A Plourde
3 Orange St
Lewiston ME 04240

Call Sign: KE6JIT
Walter R Martin
6 Orchard Hts
Lewiston ME 04240

Call Sign: N1SVD
Paul S Bell
196 Park St Three Fl Front

Lewiston ME 04240

Call Sign: KB1TKR
Nathan D Kay
9 Pauline Ave
Lewiston ME 04240

Call Sign: KB1QHR
Paul S Bell
176 Pine St
Lewiston ME 04240

Call Sign: KA1ROT
Gary A Guimond
41 Pineland St
Lewiston ME 042405650

Call Sign: N1KBA
Amy G Guimond
41 Pineland St
Lewiston ME 04240

Call Sign: N1TXH
John R Clark
378 Pinewoods Road
Lewiston ME 04240

Call Sign: AA1ED
Stephen S Soucy Jr
294 Pleasant St
Lewiston ME 04240

Call Sign: KA1HWQ
Helen A Incze
9 Poulin Ave
Lewiston ME 04240

Call Sign: WB1DUU
Herbert E Cantwell
211 Randall Rd Apt 12
Lewiston ME 04240

Call Sign: N1TLZ
Ryan B Roderick
211 Randall Rd Apt 57

Lewiston ME 04240

Call Sign: N1PIY
Robert L Roberge
7 Raymond Ave
Lewiston ME 04240

Call Sign: N1RGV
Geraldine G Lynn
184 Russell St
Lewiston ME 04240

Call Sign: W9KLS
William J White
1211 Sabattus Box 97
Lewiston ME 04240

Call Sign: N1UXU
Tracie A Hall
52 Sabattus St
Lewiston ME 04240

Call Sign: N3QEB
Thomas E Hodgkiss
204 Sabattus St. #3
Lewiston ME 04240

Call Sign: KA1BHU
Ronald O Locke
969 Sabattus Street
Lewiston ME 04240

Call Sign: W1YZD
Roger H Chamberlain
8 Smith St
Lewiston ME 042403342

Call Sign: KB1RY
David L Spencer
313 Stetson Rd
Lewiston ME 04240

Call Sign: KE1I
Thomas A Poto
320 Stetson Rd

Lewiston ME 04240

Call Sign: KB1UOO
Brian K Wilson
167 Summer St
Lewiston ME 04240

Call Sign: W1JEB
John R E Bean
22 Sylvan Ave
Lewiston ME 04240

Call Sign: NA1B
John R E Bean
22 Sylvan Ave
Lewiston ME 04240

Call Sign: WA1ZLB
Robert R Roy
70 Tall Pines Drv Apt 7
Lewiston ME 042408513

Call Sign: KA1NXA
Louise Y Cote
60 Taylor Hill Road
Lewiston ME 04240

Call Sign: N1RGW
Roger M Morin
35 Walker Ave
Lewiston ME 04240

Call Sign: N1NFR
Arthur J Turley
178 Webber Ave
Lewiston ME 04240

Call Sign: N1OXA
Ivan L Lazure
440 Webber Ave
Lewiston ME 042404917

Call Sign: N1VWG
Ernest B Belanger
76 Webster St

Lewiston ME 04240

Lewiston ME 04241

Call Sign: WA1BZC
Alan L Gardner Sr
172 Pinnacle Road
Liberty ME 04949

Call Sign: N1RXG
Richard D Noyes
125 Wellman St.
Lewiston ME 04240

Call Sign: KB1OBD
Brian M Cox
Lewiston ME 04240

Call Sign: KB1KIL
Richard D Noyes
125 Wellman St.
Lewiston ME 04240

Call Sign: KB1OGS
William C Storm
Lewiston ME 04243

Call Sign: KB1TSR
Aria L Albino
109 Ridge School Rd
Liberty ME 04949

Call Sign: N1OXD
Bonnie L Gilchrist
9 Wildwood Dr
Lewiston ME 04240

Call Sign: KB1TSP
Wade D Brayman
Lewiston ME 04243

Call Sign: KC2QON
Neil A Caudill
84 W. Main St.
Liberty ME 04949

Call Sign: N1OXE
David B Gilchrist
9 Wildwood Dr
Lewiston ME 04240

Call Sign: KB1TSQ
Trilby L Brayman
Lewiston ME 04243

Call Sign: KB1KHR
Cynthia L Percy
Liberty ME 04949

Call Sign: KA1ROM
Garrett T Curry
17 Wood Street
Lewiston ME 04240

Call Sign: KB1SUD
Robert A Sessums
55 Summer St
Lewistown ME 04240

Call Sign: KB1KHS
Richard L Percy
Liberty ME 04949

Call Sign: K1GPJ
Armand I Clement
Lewiston ME 04241

Call Sign: W1LTX
Robert A Sessums
55 Summer St
Lewistown ME 04240

Call Sign: KB1MQS
Kyle H Wright
Liberty ME 04949

Call Sign: KB1CDU
Kenneth E Akerley
Lewiston ME 04243

FCC Amateur Radio
Licenses in Liberty

Call Sign: KB1TNV
Adam P Paul
Liberty ME 04949

Call Sign: N1BCS
Armand F Girard
Lewiston ME 042430202

Call Sign: WD9INQ
Elmer C Snow
Rr 1 Box 2500
Liberty ME 04949

Call Sign: K1RVN
Adam P Paul
Liberty ME 04949

Call Sign: N1OZX
Frank E Carey
Lewiston ME 04241

Call Sign: W1MUY
Elmer C Snow
Rr 1 Box 2500
Liberty ME 04949

Call Sign: KB1TRZ
Autumn M Birt
Liberty ME 04949

Call Sign: N1RXD
Sheila A Martin

Call Sign: KA1ZGI
Donald I Bartlett
Hcr 81 Box 360
Liberty ME 04949

FCC Amateur Radio
Licenses in Lille

Call Sign: KD1SQ
Lee Reynolds

31 Notre Dame Road
Lille ME 04746

FCC Amateur Radio Licenses in Limerick

Call Sign: W1GRL
Audrey S Mann
Rr 2 Box 1092
Limerick ME 04048

Call Sign: KB1BMR
Jesse A Fisk
Rfd 2 Box 1100
Limerick ME 04049

Call Sign: KB1ELC
Alfred E Standish
15 Carrie La
Limerick ME 04048

Call Sign: W1AES
Alfred E Standish
15 Carrie La
Limerick ME 04048

Call Sign: N1WFG
Winthrop L Farmer
10 Central Ave
Limerick ME 04048

Call Sign: N1HLW
Roger A Cates
138 Cottage Rd
Limerick ME 04048

Call Sign: KC2OWJ
Michael P Hanes
555 Doles Ridge Road
Limerick ME 04048

Call Sign: W1VZR
Peter W Whelpley
360 Elm St
Limerick ME 04048

Call Sign: KA1HYT
Marsha A Hodgkins
44 Johnson Rd
Limerick ME 04048

Call Sign: KA1ZWO
Jonathan S Hodgkins
44 Johnson Rd
Limerick ME 04048

Call Sign: KD1BB
Raymond S Hodgkins
44 Johnson Rd
Limerick ME 04048

Call Sign: KB1CTZ
Thomas M Osborne 111
40 Main St
Limerick ME 04048

Call Sign: WB1CIV
Larry F Taylor
71 Patterson Rd
Limerick ME 040484238

Call Sign: KA1AUE
Sandra A Taylor
71 Patterson Rd.
Limerick ME 04048

Call Sign: W1YRO
Raymond H Marcaurelle
48 Pleasant Hill Road
Limerick ME 04048

Call Sign: W1ROM
Clarence J Williams
Sokokis Trail
Limerick ME 04048

Call Sign: W1REX
Rex M Harper
36 Whiteley Road
Limerick ME 04048

Call Sign: KA1OQ
James W Davison
19 Woodridge Dr
Limerick ME 04048

Call Sign: AB1BR
James W Davison
19 Woodridge Dr
Limerick ME 04048

Call Sign: KA1ZUB
Michael L Cates
Limerick ME 04048

Call Sign: N0ENJ
Don R Lyon
Limerick ME 04048

Call Sign: N1WJC
Marian R Budzyna
Limerick ME 04048

Call Sign: W1TMT
Anthony T Tedeschi
Limerick ME 040480208

FCC Amateur Radio Licenses in Limestone

Call Sign: W1JTT
Austin Grass
Box 134 Bog Rd
Limestone ME 04750

Call Sign: N1FRS
Travis K Leighton
Bog Rd
Limestone ME 04750

Call Sign: K1MDK
James T Beahm
Rfd 1 Box 163
Limestone ME 04750

Call Sign: KB1EBE
David A Berry Sr
26b Manser Dr
Limestone ME 04750

Call Sign: KB1POI
Kristi L Ricker
26 Manser Dr Apt A
Limestone ME 04750

Call Sign: KB1POL
Jimmie L Livingston Jr
26 Manser Dr Apt A
Limestone ME 04750

**FCC Amateur Radio
Licenses in Limington**

Call Sign: N1ZOM
Peter D Roy
Hc 70 Box 216a
Limington ME 04049

Call Sign: KB1KTL
Robert J Hume
873 Cape Rd
Limington ME 04049

Call Sign: KA1FEL
Richard F Slocombe
824 Cape Road
Limington ME 04049

Call Sign: KA1VSC
Matthew E Webster
11 Farwoods Circle
Limington ME 04049

Call Sign: N1PGO
Matthew E Webster
11 Farwoods Circle
Limington ME 04049

Call Sign: N1RJ
Roger D Johnson

124 Hardscrabble Rd
Limington ME 04049

Call Sign: KA1YFC
Robert B Rogers Iv
93 Merrifield Rd
Limington ME 04049

Call Sign: KB1MDK
Mark A Millham
4 W Sand Pond Rd
Limington ME 04049

Call Sign: KA1YIZ
Gus G Perez Jr
Limington ME 04049

Call Sign: KB1AJR
Jeffrey G Sawyer
Limington ME 04049

Call Sign: KC1DI
David O Rowe
Limington ME 040490130

Call Sign: W1HZD
David L Sporre
Limington ME 04049

**FCC Amateur Radio
Licenses in Lincoln**

Call Sign: K1AQ
Gary N Steinberg
292 Bagley Mtn Rd
Lincoln ME 04457

Call Sign: N1MTU
Jane G Theoharides
Rr 2 Box
Lincoln ME 04457

Call Sign: N1ZFL
Andrew G Edwards
Rr3 Box 1600

Lincoln ME 04457

Call Sign: N1ZFI
Daniel J Le Brun
Rr 3 Box 1622
Lincoln ME 04457

Call Sign: N1LGW
Durward A Phillips
Rr 1 Box 3030
Lincoln ME 04457

Call Sign: N1LHA
Dolores A Phillips
Rr 1 Box 3030
Lincoln ME 04457

Call Sign: N1LHH
Frederick D Haskell
Rr3 Box 374
Lincoln ME 04458

Call Sign: N1JNO
Roger C Haynes
Rr 3 Box 576
Lincoln ME 0457

Call Sign: N1NUQ
George E Leighton
19 Clark St
Lincoln ME 04457

Call Sign: KB1DBK
Micheal E Mc Laughlin
33 Clark Street
Lincoln ME 04457

Call Sign: N1LGX
Darrell S Hurd Jr
15 Evergreen Dr
Lincoln ME 04457

Call Sign: N1ZFJ
Christopher M Hurd
8 High Hill Dr

Lincoln ME 04457

Call Sign: N1JNL
Steve N Zagorianakos
72 High St
Lincoln ME 04457

Call Sign: WA1YZY
Charles H Harding
6 Highland Ave
Lincoln ME 04457

Call Sign: WA1YZZ
Joyce P Harding
6 Highland Ave
Lincoln ME 04457

Call Sign: N1QWX
Arthur W Furrow
39 Main Street Apt 2
Lincoln ME 04457

Call Sign: KA1ZAV
Josephine E Loupin
685 Mohawk Rd
Lincoln ME 04457

Call Sign: AB9N
Darrell R Joiner
688 Mohawk Road
Lincoln ME 044570131

Call Sign: K1QXU
Edward Di Censo
Taylor St Extension
Lincoln ME 04457

Call Sign: KB1KBU
Ray A Goodspeed Jr
800 Transalpine Rd
Lincoln ME 04457

Call Sign: N1TTL
Ronald E Twist
930 Transalpine Road

Lincoln ME 04457

Call Sign: N1MUI
Timothy M Baker
14 Washington St
Lincoln ME 04457

Call Sign: KB1ROU
Levi J Guimond
50 Worster Way
Lincoln ME 04457

Call Sign: KB1CGK
David L Allain
Lincoln ME 045570534

Call Sign: N1XMM
Gary D Di Censo
Lincoln ME 04457

Call Sign: WB1AOQ
James T Cressey
Lincoln ME 04457

FCC Amateur Radio Licenses in Lincoln Center

Call Sign: N1NKQ
Richard C Haynes
Rr 1 Box 22a
Lincoln Center ME 04458

FCC Amateur Radio Licenses in Lincolnville

Call Sign: N1VYO
Gregory S Kilgore
2022 Belfast Road
Lincolnville ME 04849

Call Sign: KB1CWJ
Paul R Mc Cusker
Rr 1 Box 4266
Lincolnville ME 04849

Call Sign: KA1ALD
Byron H Haining Jr
Box 4730
Lincolnville ME 04849

Call Sign: KA1KBB
Cathy H Latham
Rr 1 Box 4875
Lincolnville ME 04849

Call Sign: W1CPU
Peter F Murphy
194 Ducktrap Rd
Lincolnville ME 04849

Call Sign: N1UKC
Robert E Kennedy
150 Martins Corner Road
Lincolnville ME 04849

Call Sign: N1UKD
Margaret H Kennedy
150 Martins Corner Road
Lincolnville ME 04849

Call Sign: KB1PML
Mary Lou Gallup
48 Masalin Rd
Lincolnville ME 04849

Call Sign: KB1PMM
Charles J Readinger
48 Masalin Rd
Lincolnville ME 04879

Call Sign: KB1ROW
Jacob M Cookson
360 Masalin Rd
Lincolnville ME 04849

Call Sign: KB1CVW
Nola Kosowsky
202 Masalin Road
Lincolnville ME 04849

Call Sign: KC1QX
Michael R Kosowsky
202 Masalin Road
Lincolnville ME 04849

Call Sign: KB1NUW
David L Stonehill
41 Patten Dr
Lincolnville ME 04849

Call Sign: KB1XV
David M Mc Curdy
74 Patten Drive
Lincolnville ME 04849

Call Sign: KA1RXZ
Alfred E Duffell
Lincolnville ME 04849

Call Sign: W1MSF
Bronislaw R Mikutajcis
Lincolnville ME 04849

FCC Amateur Radio Licenses in Lincolnville Beach

Call Sign: W1LDF
Richard B Gardner
Lincolnville Beach ME 04849

FCC Amateur Radio Licenses in Lincolnville Center

Call Sign: AA1AG
Jens C Ostergaard
35 Elusive Lane
Lincolnville Center ME 04850

FCC Amateur Radio Licenses in Linneus

Call Sign: N1XPW
Albert A Brennan Jr
1015 Hodgdon Mills Road
Linneus ME 047304623

Call Sign: KB1KBV
Clare E Desrosiers
406 New Limerick Rd
Linneus ME 04730

Call Sign: N1JFY
Joseph-?Tienne A
Desrosiers
406 New Limerick Road
Linneus ME 047305221

FCC Amateur Radio Licenses in Lisbon

Call Sign: KA1ZHI
Richard A Gamache
1 Bartholomew St
Lisbon ME 04250

Call Sign: KB1SDH
Eric W Schutt
40 Cotton Rd
Lisbon ME 04250

Call Sign: KB1POH
Kimbley K Johnson
12 Fairview Dr
Lisbon ME 04250

Call Sign: KA1OZQ
Ruth A Couture
179 Ferry Rd
Lisbon ME 04250

Call Sign: N1EAX
Gerard O Couture
Ferry Rd
Lisbon ME 04250

Call Sign: N1ETU

Glenn Berube
21 Grandview St
Lisbon ME 04250

Call Sign: KA1WUM
Robert M Clark
114 Lisbon Rd
Lisbon ME 04252

Call Sign: N1QWU
Clarence J Daigle
2144 Lisbon Rd Apt 208
Lisbon ME 04250

Call Sign: KB1EAR
Richard J Freve
140 Littlefield Rd
Lisbon ME 04250

Call Sign: N1MQW
Jerry H Arsenault Jr
19 Main St
Lisbon ME 04250

Call Sign: N1OGM
Joyce B Arsenault
19 Main St
Lisbon ME 04250

Call Sign: N1RLH
Sabrina T Arsenault
19 Main St
Lisbon ME 04250

Call Sign: KB1OWP
Terry Fleck
4 Marshall St
Lisbon ME 04250

Call Sign: N1LJG
Terry Fleck
4 Marshall St
Lisbon ME 04250

Call Sign: KA1NMF

Richard A Gamache
14 Mcclellan Street
Lisbon ME 04250

Call Sign: N1XHF
Justin C Cox
4 Merrill Ave
Lisbon ME 04250

Call Sign: KD1OD
Gerard A Tancrede
5 Merrill Ave
Lisbon ME 04250

Call Sign: KD1OW
David N Blethen Ii
23 Park St
Lisbon ME 04250

Call Sign: WA1FKB
David T Plummer
24 Park St
Lisbon ME 04250

Call Sign: K1PIR
Jeffrey J Parsons
3 Willow Circle
Lisbon ME 04250

Call Sign: KB1IBU
Michael W Butler
17 Winter St Lot 92
Lisbon ME 04250

Call Sign: KB1IIC
Michael W Butler
17 Winter St Lot 92
Lisbon ME 04250

Call Sign: AB1BC
Michael W Butler
17 Winter St Lot 92
Lisbon ME 04250

Call Sign: KA1USA

Roger R Cusson
2 Woodside Drive
Lisbon ME 04250

Call Sign: N1MNQ
Judy A Cusson
2 Woodside Drive
Lisbon ME 04250

Call Sign: KB1HSN
Oakley C Shedd Jr
47 Woodside Drive
Lisbon ME 042506468

Call Sign: KA1WUN
Robert J Clark
Lisbon ME 04250

Call Sign: N1LWC
Gerald H Arsenault
Lisbon ME 04250

**FCC Amateur Radio
Licenses in Lisbon Center**

Call Sign: N1FWZ
Robert G Weeks
363 Lisbon Rd
Lisbon Center ME 04251

**FCC Amateur Radio
Licenses in Lisbon Falls**

Call Sign: N1JD
John P Donahue
210 Bowdoinham Rd
Lisbon Falls ME 04252

Call Sign: KB1AEB
Jeffrey K Wakeman
Rfd 2 Box 1840
Lisbon Falls ME 04252

Call Sign: K1JFD
Janet R Beal

6 Cross St
Lisbon Falls ME 04252

Call Sign: W1CHL
Percy L Beal Jr
6 Cross St
Lisbon Falls ME 04252

Call Sign: AF4PC
William L Carter
10 Cross St
Lisbon Falls ME 04252

Call Sign: N1OGK
Dana G Farnum
8 Douglas St
Lisbon Falls ME 04252

Call Sign: N1HWN
Thomas L Whiting
5 Dumas Street
Lisbon Falls ME 042521405

Call Sign: N1TAN
Lance E Seelbach
5 Enterprise St
Lisbon Falls ME 04252

Call Sign: N1ULV
James W Conrad
7 First Street
Lisbon Falls ME 04252

Call Sign: KB1CKO
Roger D Marcotte
76 Frost Hill Ave
Lisbon Falls ME 04252

Call Sign: N1KBP
Mark A Edens
34 Grove St
Lisbon Falls ME 04252

Call Sign: N1QPS
Jeanie D Warren

26 Grove Street
Lisbon Falls ME 04252

Call Sign: N1PFW
Frank J Anicetti
63 Main St
Lisbon Falls ME 04252

Call Sign: N1OGO
Robert K Hall
18 North St
Lisbon Falls ME 04252

Call Sign: KB1DOH
Elaine A Thuotte
6 Pohle Street
Lisbon Falls ME 04252

Call Sign: N1ZRL
Peter A Thuotte
6 Pohle Street
Lisbon Falls ME 04252

Call Sign: N1TWZ
Richard A Coty
206 Ridge Road
Lisbon Falls ME 04252

Call Sign: KB1RBN
Frederick E Stacey
2 Roberts Lane
Lisbon Falls ME 04252

Call Sign: AB1MD
Frederick E Stacey
2 Roberts Lane
Lisbon Falls ME 04252

Call Sign: KA1YSR
Charles W Maletich
14 Spear St
Lisbon Falls ME 04252

Call Sign: KA1ZGY
Constance S Condon

19 Spear St
Lisbon Falls ME 04252

Call Sign: N1SZL
Ralph G Day
47 Summer St
Lisbon Falls ME 04252

Call Sign: WA4UJJ
Phillip E Kern
52 Summer St
Lisbon Falls ME 04252

Call Sign: KB1KAH
Lee W Trask
91 Upland Rd
Lisbon Falls ME 04252

Call Sign: K5LWT
Lee W Trask
91 Upland Rd
Lisbon Falls ME 04252

Call Sign: W1LWT
Lee W Trask
91 Upland Rd
Lisbon Falls ME 04252

Call Sign: KB1TZX
Brian A Laframboise
91 Upland Rd
Lisbon Falls ME 04252

Call Sign: KB1UKX
Radio Adventurers Of
Maine
91 Upland Rd
Lisbon Falls ME 04252

Call Sign: KD1XK
Kenneth E Mac Donald
Lisbon Falls ME 042520160

Call Sign: KB1HNV
Mark C Stambach

30 Summer St
Lisson Falls ME 04252

FCC Amateur Radio Licenses in Litchfield

Call Sign: KA1FKS
LYNDA M Hawke
7 Bessie Dr
Litchfield ME 04350

Call Sign: K1SFX
Robert L Williams
Rt 2 Box 1350
Litchfield ME 04350

Call Sign: N1SUZ
Rachel E Mitchell
Rfd 2 Box 1760
Litchfield ME 04350

Call Sign: WB1HKS
Norman G Kelting
Rt 1 Box 640
Litchfield ME 04351

Call Sign: KA1GPO
Mary M Whitten
19 Eternity Dr
Litchfield ME 04350

Call Sign: KB1VET
Anthony C Nuzzo
168 Huntington Hill Rd
Litchfield ME 04350

Call Sign: W1AKY
Edward R Myrbeck Jr
22 Kenway Drive
Litchfield ME 04350

Call Sign: KB1TXX
Paul F Graves
940 Plains Rd
Litchfield ME 04350

Call Sign: N1OZW
Donald R Vaillancourt
Po Box 374
Litchfield ME 043500374

Call Sign: N1POY
Alan S Kenney
43 Southside Estates
Litchfield ME 04350

Call Sign: KA1LAZ
Kevan N Morris
641 Stevenstown
Litchfield ME 04350

Call Sign: AA1KF
Joseph A Meehan
376 Stevenstown Road
Litchfield ME 04350

Call Sign: N1KG
Kenneth R Gilman
Litchfield ME 04350

Call Sign: N1YTP
Ernest R Keene
Litchfield ME 04350

Call Sign: KB1RME
Brian W Cole
Litchfield ME 04350

Call Sign: N1BWC
Brian W Cole
Litchfield ME 04350

Call Sign: KB1SMX
Michelle L Cole
Litchfield ME 04350

FCC Amateur Radio Licenses in Littleton

Call Sign: N1IGL

Sally A Henderson
1170 Us Hwy 1
Littleton ME 04730

Call Sign: W1NZ
F Gerald Henderson
1170 Us Hwy 1
Littleton ME 04730

Call Sign: N1PX
Roger N Stairs
1844 Us Hwy 1
Littleton ME 047306117

Call Sign: KB1JBL
Minabel A Stairs
1954 Us Hwy I
Littleton ME 04730

FCC Amateur Radio Licenses in Livermore

Call Sign: KB1RMF
Jason R Skeffington
363 Butter Hill Rd
Livermore ME 04253

Call Sign: N1NXM
Arnold W Bryant
501 Canton Road
Livermore ME 04253

Call Sign: KC1QE
Gustave A Zeissig
49 Israelson Road
Livermore ME 04253

Call Sign: KB1NDK
Stephen D Allen
44 Old Leavitt Rd
Livermore ME 04253

Call Sign: KB1JMZ
Robert C Allen
52 Old Leavitt Rd

Livermore ME 04253

Call Sign: N1VLZ
Brian M Martin
56 Old Leavitt Road
Livermore ME 04253

Call Sign: W4RCO
Leslie D Haskell
204 Robinson Rd
Livermore ME 04253

Call Sign: N1MUA
Dwayne H Bilodeau
144 Sanders Rd
Livermore ME 04253

Call Sign: WY1P
Aaron J St Laurent
354 Sanders Rd
Livermore ME 04253

FCC Amateur Radio Licenses in Livermore Falls

Call Sign: K5HTL
Rand B Evans
5 Pine Avenue
Livermore Falls ME 04254

Call Sign: KA3WTJ
Robert E Wilcox
12 Spring St
Livermore Falls ME 04254

Call Sign: N1RPM
David F Lemire
32 Tradition Way
Livermore Falls ME 04254

Call Sign: KB1OJE
Richard M Rush Jr
Livermore Falls ME 04254

FCC Amateur Radio Licenses in Locke Mills

Call Sign: AI1I
Michael J Grenier
51 Howe Road
Locke Mills ME 04255

Call Sign: N1JXQ
Ronald A Dorman
Locke Mills ME 04255

FCC Amateur Radio Licenses in Long Island

Call Sign: KB1OSN
Jason S Horr
45 Doughty Landing
Long Island ME 04050

Call Sign: N1LI
Long Island Dx Society
Long Island ME 04050

FCC Amateur Radio Licenses in Loring AFB

Call Sign: KB9IDR
Michael A Smith Jr
6350 Kentucky Rd Rm 339a
Loring Afb ME 04751

FCC Amateur Radio Licenses in Lovell

Call Sign: KB1DGI
Andrew E Carter
Rr 2 Box 1020
Lovell ME 040519722

Call Sign: N1WTM
Linda M Floccher
Rr 1 Box 23
Lovell ME 04051

Call Sign: KF4GCW
David J Comeau
201 Foxboro Rd
Lovell ME 04051

Call Sign: KB1RIY
Lance D Mcnerney
249 Foxboro Rd
Lovell ME 04051

Call Sign: N1DZQ
Bruce H Collins
173 Slab City Road
Lovell ME 040513111

Call Sign: WA1ARY
Eugene H Spender Jr
Lovell ME 04051

Call Sign: N1ZDM
Jeremy B Priest
98 Webb Cove Drive
Lowell ME 04493

FCC Amateur Radio Licenses in Lubec

Call Sign: N1PPI
Gilda A Mc Curdy
Rr 2 Box 1780
Lubec ME 04652

Call Sign: KB6UDH
Leonard H Ross Jr
Box 207a Rt 189
Lubec ME 04652

Call Sign: N1NFU
Richard C Erquhart
Rfd 2 Box 2110
Lubec ME 04652

Call Sign: N1NFT
Josephine A Archer

Rr 2 Box 2130
Lubec ME 04652

Call Sign: KC1DG
Robert B Reynolds
Rfd 1 Box 282
Lubec ME 04652

Call Sign: KB1SZO
Justin A Foley
850 County Rd
Lubec ME 04652

Call Sign: KA1NFF
Warren A Foley
County Rd Box 849
Lubec ME 04652

Call Sign: KA1JR
John D Rule Ii
625 County Road
Lubec ME 04652

Call Sign: KB3SII
Stephen E Silverman
308 Dixie Rd
Lubec ME 04652

Call Sign: W1BSB
Bernard M Ross
81 Dixie Road
Lubec ME 04652

Call Sign: KD1VG
Bruce L Archer
79 Jims Head Rd
Lubec ME 04652

Call Sign: WA1TQF
James H Bezanson
87 Main St
Lubec ME 04652

Call Sign: WA1NME
Robert F Swiecicki

33 Main Street
Lubec ME 046521010

Call Sign: KB2WGB
William A Daye
210 South Lubec Rd
Lubec ME 04652

Call Sign: K1WAD
William A Daye
210 South Lubec Rd
Lubec ME 04652

Call Sign: KB1UEO
Rydell J Flynn
272 South Lubec Rd
Lubec ME 04652

Call Sign: WA1OFN
Leonard H Ross
1065 Straight Bay Road
Lubec ME 04652

Call Sign: KB1UEP
Susan L Cline
531 Wilcox Rd
Lubec ME 04652

Call Sign: N1ZMR
Gray B Morrison Sr
Lubec ME 04652

Call Sign: KB1STL
Marty J Saccone
Lubec ME 04652

Call Sign: KB1UES
Kathryn J Tinker
Lubec ME 04652

Call Sign: KB1UET
Blair W Tinker
Lubec ME 04652

FCC Amateur Radio Licenses in Ludlow

Call Sign: W8MOO
David P Stone
200 Moose Brook Road
Ludlow ME 04730

Call Sign: KB1IGX
Joshua P Carr
88 Slow Ln
Ludlow ME 047307917

Call Sign: WB1AIC
Alan M Gillotti
171 Smyrna Town Line Rd
Ludlow ME 04730

FCC Amateur Radio Licenses in Lyman

Call Sign: KA1CUB
Paul M O Leary
20 Candlewood Drive
Lyman ME 04002

Call Sign: KB1UVV
James D Hathaway
638 Clarks Woods Rd
Lyman ME 04002

Call Sign: KR1B
Robert L Snowman Sr
20 Fernwood Loop
Lyman ME 04002

Call Sign: KB1BGP
Stephen D Taylor
78 Huff Rd
Lyman ME 04005

Call Sign: N1HMU
Robert L Atkins
43 John Street
Lyman ME 04002

Call Sign: N5UIT
Robert D Marchand
210 Poor Farm Rd
Lyman ME 04002

Call Sign: KA1MCD
Christopher D Farrar
14 Rollins Rd
Lyman ME 04002

Call Sign: W1DJ
Douglas J Spencer
99 Rustic Ln
Lyman ME 040026042

Call Sign: KA1VJY
Carol A Lambert
13 Ruth Ln
Lyman ME 04002

Call Sign: WJ1L
Edward C Lambert
13 Ruth Ln
Lyman ME 04002

Call Sign: KA1YCS
Paul S Pepin
145 S Waterboro Rd
Lyman ME 04002

Call Sign: KB1KSB
Darius Rad
72 Shore Rd
Lyman ME 04002

Call Sign: KB1QZM
Darius Rad
72 Shore Rd
Lyman ME 04002

Call Sign: KB1AOS
Suzanne M Coolbroth
122 Williams Rd
Lyman ME 04002

Call Sign: KA1KPA
Dennis S Coolbroth
122 Williams Road
Lyman ME 04002

Call Sign: KA1ZXH
Jean M Coolbroth
122 Williams Road
Lyman ME 04002

FCC Amateur Radio Licenses in Machias

Call Sign: K1ERM
Clayton L Hall
Rr 1 Box 131
Machias ME 04654

Call Sign: KB1EWL
Bertram J Cloney
Hc 71 Box 172
Machias ME 04655

Call Sign: N1PPL
Daniel D Bowker
Hcr 71 Box 26
Machias ME 04654

Call Sign: W1RKM
Dimitri J Margarita
Rfd 1 Box 340a
Machias ME 04654

Call Sign: W1BUA
William C Pennell
Hc 71 Box 643
Machias ME 04654

Call Sign: N1PPG
Stephen J Smith
Rr 1 Box 88
Machias ME 046543405

Call Sign: KA1JHP

Mark Adolphsen
8 Broadway
Machias ME 04654

Call Sign: KD1XR
Robert O Hayward
14 Broadway
Machias ME 04654

Call Sign: KB1BRW
Machias Valley Composite
Squadron Cap
19 Broadway
Machias ME 04654

Call Sign: N1MLB
James G Raymond
19 Broadway
Machias ME 04654

Call Sign: N1QAY
Jane L Cummings
19 Broadway
Machias ME 04654

Call Sign: WB3CPR
Frederick J Roehs
40 Broadway
Machias ME 04654

Call Sign: KA1DOD
Paul C Hoyt
10 Bruce St
Machias ME 04654

Call Sign: KB1NQY
Catherine G Hawthorne
94 Court St
Machias ME 046541005

Call Sign: K1QBI
Walter Dinsmore
96 Court St
Machias ME 04654

Call Sign: KA1LT
Kenneth P Mc Laughlin
65 Court St Apt 1
Machias ME 04654

Call Sign: KA1UEV
Thomas F Reynolds
50 Court Street
Machias ME 046540365

Call Sign: N1MLE
Peter L Stackpole
231 Dublin St
Machias ME 046543404

Call Sign: N1MCJ
Jeffrey B Currier
26 E Main St
Machias ME 04654

Call Sign: N1JZV
Mark D Burgess
14 Freemont St
Machias ME 04654

Call Sign: KB1LME
Matthew P Marshall
3 Gardner Ave
Machias ME 04654

Call Sign: KA1UFB
Philip A Roberts
8 Gardner Ave
Machias ME 04654

Call Sign: AA1XL
Philip A Roberts
8 Gardner Ave
Machias ME 04654

Call Sign: KA1UEW
William J Raye
17 Hudson Blvd
Machias ME 04654

Call Sign: KB1VQC
Michael D Shannon
17 Monaghan Lane
Machias ME 04654

Call Sign: N1TXV
James W Logan
11 North St
Machias ME 04654

Call Sign: KB1VQA
Andrew V Pierce
74 Ridge Rd
Machias ME 04654

Call Sign: W1AVP
Andrew V Pierce
74 Ridge Rd
Machias ME 04654

Call Sign: N1SCY
Michael A St Louis
20 Ridge Road
Machias ME 04654

Call Sign: W1MID
Bruce W Smith
10 Sprague Way
Machias ME 04654

Call Sign: KB1KEI
Allen J Blanchard
2 Valley View Rd Apt 15
Machias ME 04654

Call Sign: KA1YEF
Nancy J Bennett
25 Water St
Machias ME 04654

Call Sign: KB1UEW
Micah E Pascucci
27 Water St
Machias ME 04654

Call Sign: KB1P
Paul E Thompson
Machias ME 04654

Call Sign: N1LFN
Wayne C Ackley
Machias ME 04654

Call Sign: N1MKV
Stephen J Burns
Machias ME 04654

Call Sign: N1TXZ
Rhoda E Brackett
Machias ME 04654

Call Sign: N1YAX
Norman W Nelson
Machias ME 04654

Call Sign: KB1FMI
Charles Shipman Jr
Machias ME 046540500

Call Sign: KB1GOP
Patrick K Flaherty
Machias ME 04654

Call Sign: KB1GOU
Kirk M Blanchard
Machias ME 04654

Call Sign: K6CLL
Charles Shipman Jr
Machias ME 046540500

FCC Amateur Radio Licenses in Machiasport

Call Sign: KB1JOX
Carl A Hermanowski
Hc 70 Box 1080
Machiasport ME 04655

Call Sign: N1MKU

Gregory R Berry
9 Corn Hill
Machiasport ME 04655

Call Sign: KB1UFA
Daniel R Williams
13 Sprague Rd
Machiasport ME 04655

Call Sign: KB1UUA
Rose M Williams
13 Sprague Rd
Machiasport ME 04655

Call Sign: WA1JTH
Patrick D Walsh
19 Sprague Road
Machias Port ME 04655

Call Sign: KD1PT
Breunis M Verburgt
Machiasport ME 04655

Call Sign: N1JZY
Karl K Kurz
Machiasport ME 04655

FCC Amateur Radio Licenses in Macwahoc

Call Sign: N1KIZ
Donald G Pratt Sr
Hcr 62 Box 796
Macwahoc ME 04451

FCC Amateur Radio Licenses in Madawaska

Call Sign: N1HYP
David J Levesque
126 14th Ave
Madawaska ME 04756

Call Sign: KB1WQA
Andrew M Dechaine

234 19th Ave
Madawaska ME 04756

Call Sign: KB1NLQ
Paul Chasse
238 19th Ave
Madawaska ME 04756

Call Sign: N7COP
Paul Chasse
238 19th Ave
Madawaska ME 04756

Call Sign: KB1NLQ
Paul Chasse
127 20th Avenue
Madawaska ME 04756

Call Sign: KA1VTW
Daniel F Marquis
Rfd 1 Box 834
Madawaska ME 04756

Call Sign: KA1YBG
Cecile Marquis
Rfd 1 Box 834
Madawaska ME 04756

Call Sign: N1RPQ
Andre R Gendreau
5 Country Lane Road
Madawaska ME 047563044

Call Sign: KA1VXK
Dana B Bourgoin
74 Dionne St.
Madawaska ME 04756

Call Sign: N1FCV
Gilman G Bourgoin
74 Dionne St.
Madawaska ME 04756

Call Sign: N1OOP
Claudette M Bourgoin

74 Dionne St.
Madawaska ME 04756

Call Sign: N1ZKA
Krystle G Bourgoin
74 Dionne St.
Madawaska ME 04756

Call Sign: KB1GKX
Mark S Violette
498 Grandview Ave
Madawaska ME 04756

Call Sign: N1IML
Rodney A Hartt
181 Lavoie Ave
Madawaska ME 04756

Call Sign: KB1OAX
Rebecca H Harris
325 Main St Apt 205
Madawaska ME 04756

Call Sign: N1JHM
Donald D Dechaine
27 N 6th Ave
Madawaska ME 04756

Call Sign: N1POK
Michael L Tardif
123 Pleasant Ave.
Madawaska ME 04756

Call Sign: W1TCF
Finland Dumond
517 River View St Rm 220
Madawaska ME 047561024

Call Sign: K1GAV
Richard J Coltart
21 Riverview Ave
Madawaska ME 04756

Call Sign: N1XFN
Edward A Mc Henry Sr

6 Winter St
Madawaska ME 04756

Call Sign: K1FLY
Constance R Mc Laughlin
7 Winter St Apt 4
Madawaska ME 04756

Call Sign: N1LON
Leland J Roix
Madawaska ME 04756

FCC Amateur Radio Licenses in Madison

Call Sign: N1ZDD
Thresa A Hayden
R 2 Box 3470
Madison ME 04950

Call Sign: N1YUU
Carlton R Hayden
Rfd 2 Box 3470
Madison ME 04950

Call Sign: KF6AYF
Glennon E Shawcross Jr.
Rr1 Box 381
Madison ME 04950

Call Sign: KB1HT
Richard G Henderson
359 Golf Course Rd
Madison ME 04950

Call Sign: N1WSV
Craig A Pomelow
5 Hazel St
Madison ME 04950

Call Sign: KA1FXI
Ruth L Hodgdon
175 Lakewood Road
Madison ME 04950

Call Sign: KB1IMM
Peter P Clukey
13 Myrtle St
Madison ME 04950

Call Sign: W1PPC
Peter P Clukey
13 Myrtle St
Madison ME 04950

Call Sign: WB1CXX
Francis A Whittier
4 Old County Rd
Madison ME 04950

Call Sign: KB1KV
Donald L Newcomb
82 Park Street Apt 15
Madison ME 04951

Call Sign: N1XDL
Paul D Laverdiere
Box 200 Rr 2
Madison ME 04950

Call Sign: WB1CAK
Mitchell E Cole
40 Sierra Lane
Madison ME 04950

Call Sign: KB1OMA
John H Corson
659 White School House Rd
Madison ME 04950

Call Sign: WO1C
John H Corson
659 White School House Rd
Madison ME 04950

Call Sign: N1RPP
Richard T Bishop
Madison ME 04950

Call Sign: KB1LAP

Lester C Brown
Madison ME 04950

Call Sign: KB1OCY
Richard M Baumgardner
Madison ME 04950

FCC Amateur Radio Licenses in Manchester

Call Sign: WB1GOW
Gerard L Lebel
Rr 2 Box 6310
Manchester ME 04352

Call Sign: W1JHS
John H Schrader
295 Pond Road
Manchester ME 043513606

Call Sign: WB1ANB
Alfred E Poitras
564 Prescott Rd
Manchester ME 04351

Call Sign: KB1CWV
Lee A Baggott
4 Red Paint Rd
Manchester ME 043510306

Call Sign: WA1N
Pine Tree Dx Club
10 Ryan Dr
Manchester ME 04351

Call Sign: KB1HBE
Alan D Mc Gary
32 Summer Haven Rd
Manchester ME 04351

Call Sign: KB1TSS
Noli M Santos Jr
5 Summerhaven Rd
Manchester ME 04351

Call Sign: NO1Y
Noli M Santos Jr
5 Summerhaven Rd
Manchester ME 04351

Call Sign: KA1RLF
William F Crowell
98 Woodridge Drive
Manchester ME 04351

Call Sign: K1RES
Peter C Williamson
Manchester ME 04351

Call Sign: K1STB
Maurice D Dandeneau
Manchester ME 04351

Call Sign: KB1CKM
Paul C Spear
Manchester ME 043510257

Call Sign: KB1CWN
Paul P Gagnon
Manchester ME 04351

Call Sign: KB1DEA
Michael P Kozak
Manchester ME 04351

Call Sign: W1AO
Joseph M Kozak
Manchester ME 04351

Call Sign: W1RAC
David P Bridge
Manchester ME 043510245

FCC Amateur Radio Licenses in Manset

Call Sign: W1UCD
Richard W Noyes
147 Seawall Rd
Manset ME 04679

Call Sign: N1OJJ
James A Parker
Manset ME 04656

FCC Amateur Radio Licenses in Mapleton

Call Sign: K1VOR
Sherman B Packard
519 Griffin Ridge Rd
Mapleton ME 04757

Call Sign: KA1HOP
Kenneth E White
956 Mapleton Rd
Mapleton ME 04757

Call Sign: KB1JJI
Randolph S Michaud
1086 Mapleton Rd
Mapleton ME 04757

Call Sign: KB1KMF
Eric P Huoppi
3330 West Chapman Road
Mapleton ME 04757

Call Sign: KA1SJS
Bruce C Griffin
Mapleton ME 04757

Call Sign: KA1TNA
Peter S West
Mapleton ME 04757

Call Sign: KB1STF
Logan P Huoppi
Mapleton ME 04757

FCC Amateur Radio Licenses in Mars Hill

Call Sign: N1ITT
Mark D Dunfee

Box 437
Mars Hill ME 04758

Call Sign: KA1HGD
Charles D Scott
9 Church St
Mars Hill ME 047580596

Call Sign: N1ZTF
Debra L Allen
359 Fort Rd
Mars Hill ME 04758

Call Sign: AA1SW
Frank W Allen
359 Fort Road
Mars Hill ME 04758

Call Sign: KA1CQX
James W Wiggins
286 Presque Isle Rd
Mars Hill ME 04758

Call Sign: KB1EYB
Kevin A Warman
7 Scovil St Apt 18
Mars Hill ME 04759

Call Sign: KA1OOW
Ken Simons
6 York St
Mars Hill ME 047580726

Call Sign: N1UYB
Deanna L Simons
6 York St
Mars Hill ME 04758

Call Sign: N1XMR
Kenneth P Simons
14 York St
Mars Hill ME 047581164

Call Sign: KA1OOX
Arlington E Wiggins

Mars Hill ME 04758

Call Sign: KB1CUC
Adam E Pinette
Mars Hill ME 04758

Call Sign: N1WRV
Scott R Pinette
Mars Hill ME 04758

Call Sign: KB1OWY
Gordon D Anderson
Mars Hill ME 04758

FCC Amateur Radio Licenses in Marshfield

Call Sign: K1PAR
Philip A Roberts
129 Hadley Lake Rd
Marshfield ME 04654

Call Sign: KB1ONO
Washington County Ares
129 Hadley Lake Rd
Marshfield ME 04654

Call Sign: WN1EOC
Washington County Ares
129 Hadley Lake Rd
Marshfield ME 04654

Call Sign: W1SMQ
William J Raye
90 Indian Hill Rd
Marshfield ME 04654

Call Sign: KB1OTO
Kenneth A Varian
120 Old County Rd.
Marshfield ME 04654

Call Sign: KB1SAE
Arron W Mitchell
74 Ridge Rd

Marshfield ME 04654

Call Sign: W1ACP
Mark D Burgess
58 Rocky Ridge Lane
Marshfield ME 04654

Call Sign: K1HF
Mark D Burgess
58 Rocky Ridge Lane
Marshfield ME 04654

**FCC Amateur Radio
Licenses in Marshill**

Call Sign: W1BN
Robert J Koczera
6 Hillside Street Apt 1
Marshill ME 04758

**FCC Amateur Radio
Licenses in Mashpee**

Call Sign: KB1GEU
Jo Anne R Babcock
21 Scituate Rd
Mashpee ME 02649

**FCC Amateur Radio
Licenses in Matinicus**

Call Sign: K1MI
Robert P Burr
Matinicus Island
Matinicus ME 04851

**FCC Amateur Radio
Licenses in Mattawam
Keag**

Call Sign: N1XLC
Daniel F Clark
216 Hathaway Road
Mattawam Keag ME 04459

Call Sign: N1MNI
Donald G Whitney
Rt 2
Mattawamkeag ME
044590174

Call Sign: N1MTT
Carl E Sweeney
Mattawamkeag ME 04459

Call Sign: N1XKX
Fayette H Keith
Mattawamkeag ME 04459

**FCC Amateur Radio
Licenses in Maxfield**

Call Sign: KB1HLD
Steven A Rozek
474 Bunker Hill Rd
Maxfield ME 04453

**FCC Amateur Radio
Licenses in Mechanics
Falls**

Call Sign: N1JUH
Blaine L Conley
Rr 1 Box 1010
Mechanic Falls ME 04256

Call Sign: WA1YSH
Douglas L Marston
Rfd 2 Box 4670
Mechanic Falls ME 04256

Call Sign: W1EVD
Frederick Cooper
Rr 1 Box 4900
Mechanic Falls ME 04256

Call Sign: N1KAX
Richard G Daoust
81 Elm St

Mechanic Falls ME 04256

Call Sign: WA1SCQ
Albert R Stronach
32 Herrick Ave
Mechanic Falls ME
042565332

Call Sign: KA1UJE
Andrew D Frechette
40 Park St
Mechanic Falls ME
042565131

Call Sign: N1YTL
Michael E Frechette
40 Park St
Mechanic Falls ME 04256

Call Sign: N1YTM
Warren B Frechette
40 Park St
Mechanic Falls ME 04256

Call Sign: KB1PHR
Cheyenne E Robinson
230 Pigeon Hill
Mechanic Falls ME 04256

Call Sign: KB1LCD
Dee A Robinson
230 Pigeon Hill Rd
Mechanic Falls ME 04256

Call Sign: N1YDP
Kenneth E Robinson
230 Pigeon Hill Road
Mechanic Falls ME 04256

Call Sign: WA1SKP
Frederick T Skripol Jr
35 Timber Lane
Mechanic Falls ME 04256

Call Sign: N1LVM

Terry L Torbert
Mechanic Falls ME 04256

Call Sign: N1YIR
Greg A Gay
Mechanic Falls ME 04256

FCC Amateur Radio Licenses in Meddybemps

Call Sign: N1IZB
Bruce P Bailey Sr
1018 Main St
Meddybemps ME
046574121

Call Sign: K1QJJ
Eugene I Merrithew Sr
Rt 191
Meddybemps ME 04657

FCC Amateur Radio Licenses in Medway

Call Sign: N1XDT
John F Cahill
44 Birch St
Medway ME 04460

Call Sign: N1PVI
George E Stanley
Box 18
Medway ME 04460

Call Sign: N1GNO
Dell W Turner
Hrc 86 Box 2165
Medway ME 04460

Call Sign: N1TIQ
David S Van Ess
Hcr 69 Box 340
Medway ME 04460

Call Sign: N1XML

Douglas E Cramer
Hcr 69 Box 799
Medway ME 04460

Call Sign: N1JNQ
Hartley L Grant Sr
899 Medway Rd
Medway ME 04460

Call Sign: N1CFL
Jacqueline M Waterhouse
56 Wilderness Drive
Medway ME 04460

Call Sign: N1GUQ
Louis C Gantnier Jr
Medway ME 04460

FCC Amateur Radio Licenses in Mercer

Call Sign: WA1DLZ
Frederick E La Plante Jr
344 Bacon Rd
Mercer ME 04957

Call Sign: K1ACU
Wesley A Freese
Rr 2 Box 1016
Mercer ME 04957

Call Sign: N1XVD
Margaret T Freese
Rr 2 Box 1016
Mercer ME 04957

Call Sign: KA1KWO
Glenn E Carter
Rfd 2 Box 760
Mercer ME 04957

Call Sign: K1MCT
Mercer C E R T
Communications Team
9 Main St

Mercer ME 04957

Call Sign: KA1TAC
Bryant M Ayer
9 Main Street
Mercer ME 04957

FCC Amateur Radio Licenses in Mexico

Call Sign: N1BBK
Leo J Dyer
7 Brigham St
Mexico ME 04257

Call Sign: N1RNM
James R Radmore
3 Front St
Mexico ME 04257

Call Sign: N1TIF
Barbara A Radmore
3 Front St
Mexico ME 04257

Call Sign: N1ZXP
George W Lannon
81 Granite St
Mexico ME 04257

Call Sign: N4VBD
Jerry E Chambers Sr
16 Intervale Ave.
Mexico ME 04257

Call Sign: N1QDE
David W Sisk
43 Kimball Ave
Mexico ME 04257

Call Sign: N1QDD
Lisa A Wiggett
47 Kimball Ave
Mexico ME 04257

Call Sign: N1UUE
Robert J Eastman
73 Kimball Ave
Mexico ME 04257

Call Sign: KA1YCE
Hector A Thibeault
31 Pine St
Mexico ME 04257

Call Sign: KB1MEE
Mark T Beedy
7 Poplar Hill Rd
Mexico ME 04257

Call Sign: W1RMD
Ryan M Dunbar
81 Swett Ave.
Mexico ME 042571315

FCC Amateur Radio Licenses in Millbridge

Call Sign: KA1UBI
Helen H Haroutunian
Ficketts Point Rd 249a
Milbridge ME 04658

Call Sign: N1ZPV
Brenda M Duggan
195 Kansas Rd
Milbridge ME 04658

Call Sign: N1EP
Philip W Duggan
195 Kansas Rd
Milbridge ME 04658

Call Sign: N1XVE
Philip W Duggan
278 Kansas Rd
Milbridge ME 04658

Call Sign: KB1OTN
Lindsey R Tucker

521 Kansas Rd
Milbridge ME 04658

Call Sign: K1SMF
William E Halpin
356 Rays Point Road
Milbridge ME 046589732

Call Sign: KC4RPY
Joanne M Halpin
356 Rays Point Road
Milbridge ME 04658

Call Sign: KA1JMH
Joanne M Halpin
356 Rays Point Road
Milbridge ME 04658

Call Sign: KB1HFZ
George L Blackford
24 Wallace Cove Ln
Milbridge ME 04658

Call Sign: K1EXI
Dana F Kennedy
Milbridge ME 04658

Call Sign: N1ZOR
John T Bullitt
Milbridge ME 04658

Call Sign: KB1MTL
Kevin Keane
Milbridge ME 046580112

Call Sign: AB1OX
Kevin Keane
Milbridge ME 046580112

FCC Amateur Radio Licenses in Milford

Call Sign: N1ZDL
William D Bloemen
13 Curtis Ln

Milford ME 04461

Call Sign: N1SHY
Andrew E Fish
64 Henderson Lane
Milford ME 04461

Call Sign: N1WZI
William D Mackowski
444 Main Rd
Milford ME 04461

Call Sign: K1EST
Paul H Osborne
92 Sandy Pt Rd
Milford ME 04461

Call Sign: K1WXY
Robert L Stessel
Milford ME 04461

Call Sign: N1VHS
Richard L Lacadie I
Milford ME 04461

Call Sign: KA1HAO
Gerald E Mc Kay
Miford ME 04461

Call Sign: N1YCJ
Clarence E Ketch Sr
Milford ME 04461

Call Sign: W5KWY
Daniel J Bird
Milford ME 044610293

Call Sign: KB1LUM
Ryan J Bond
Milford ME 04461

Call Sign: KB1PTQ
Samuel P Stessel
Milford ME 04461

Call Sign: KB1WPS
Cody B St Louis
Milford ME 04461

**FCC Amateur Radio
Licenses in Millinocket**

Call Sign: N1TLR
Bruce F Leavitt
72 Aroostook Ave
Millinocket ME 044621303

Call Sign: N1JRK
Michael A Butler
474 Aroostook Ave
Millinocket ME 04462

Call Sign: KA1EKS
John P Barton
Hc 74 Box 590
Millinocket ME 04462

Call Sign: N4PZQ
Philip M Edwards
30 Colony Place
Millinocket ME 04462

Call Sign: W2NQW
Philip M Edwards
30 Colony Place
Millinocket ME 04462

Call Sign: N1JRP
Edwin C Nordfors Jr
49 Iron Bridge Rd
Millinocket ME 04462

Call Sign: N1PUT
Reginald W Mott Jr
102 Katadin Ave
Millinocket ME 04462

Call Sign: KD4UJU
John J Bertagni
417 Kelley Trailer Park

Millinocket ME 04462

Call Sign: K1HWM
George T Blackburn
92 Lincoln St
Millinocket ME 04462

Call Sign: W1MXT
Gerald H Leavitt
154 Maine Ave
Millinocket ME 04462

Call Sign: KA1NNZ
Stewart M Farquhar
124 Massachusetts Ave
Millinocket ME 04462

Call Sign: KA1KQH
Wilbur S Stewart
80 Michigan St
Millinocket ME 04462

Call Sign: N1NKN
Richard W Yost Sr
84 Pine St
Millinocket ME 04462

Call Sign: WN1OTV
Donald A Benson
67 State St
Millinocket ME 044621405

Call Sign: W1ISO
Wilbur D Bragdon
28 Wassau St
Millinocket ME 04462

Call Sign: N1LGY
Vincent D Staples
120 Wasson St
Millinocket ME 044621843

Call Sign: K1PQS
George C Monti
Millinocket ME 04462

Call Sign: N1PVG
Glenn L Wiley
Millinocket ME 04462

Call Sign: KB1NVY
Mark J Bossie
Millinocket ME 04462

**FCC Amateur Radio
Licenses in Milo**

Call Sign: KB1JHJ
Bobby J Byrne Sr
1 Chase Hill St
Milo ME 04463

Call Sign: W3JMB
Bobby J Byrne Sr
1 Chase Hill St
Milo ME 04463

Call Sign: W1JMB
Bobby J Byrne Sr
1 Chase Hill St
Milo ME 04463

Call Sign: N1VFL
Gary P Metilly
33 Deer Run Dr
Milo ME 044630150

Call Sign: KB1MUG
Gary P Metilly
33 Deer Run Dr
Milo ME 044630150

Call Sign: KB1MUI
Andrew G Metilly
33 Deer Run Dr
Milo ME 04463

Call Sign: KB1MUL
Isaiah M Metilly
33 Deer Run Dr

Milo ME 04463

Call Sign: KB1MUH
Josiah J Metilly
33 Deer Run Drive
Milo ME 04463

Call Sign: KB1MUJ
Jonathan D Metilly
33 Deer Run Drive
Milo ME 04463

Call Sign: N1BUG
Paul N Kelley
293 Elm St
Milo ME 04463

Call Sign: KB1ITT
Barry F Knowles Jr
54 First St
Milo ME 04463

Call Sign: KB1EIV
Dorothea E Perkins
17 High St
Milo ME 04463

Call Sign: KB1ELB
Chad R Perkins
17 High St
Milo ME 04463

Call Sign: WA1PBR
Ben W Kittredge
88 Hovey Rd
Milo ME 04463

Call Sign: KB1VTE
George S Morse
5 Morrill St
Milo ME 04463

Call Sign: KB1MUO
Joshua J L Dillon
152 Park St

Milo ME 04463

Call Sign: KA1HPJ
George W Day
410 Park Street
Milo ME 044630104

Call Sign: N1DGJ
Carolyn J Kelley
21 Pleasant Park Circle Apt
B
Milo ME 04463

Call Sign: W1ALS
Adolph B Mattson
5 Pleasant St
Milo ME 04463

Call Sign: KB1MUK
Nancy A Metilly
33 Reer Run Dr
Milo ME 04463

Call Sign: NY1E
Dick L Mc Duffie
3 Sebec Court
Milo ME 04463

Call Sign: N1KUS
Stephen D Smith
9 Willow Street
Milo ME 04463

Call Sign: K1PQ
Sargent Hill Rd Piscataquis
Amateur Radio Club
Milo ME 04463

FCC Amateur Radio Licenses in Minot

Call Sign: N1JXC
Glen A Bailey
90 Bailey Rd
Minot ME 04258

Call Sign: N3AZP
Daniel M Leclair
377 Center Minot Hill Road
Minot ME 04258

Call Sign: N1SVE
Laurie K Bailey
8 Hunter Ave
Minot ME 04258

Call Sign: N9IZQ
Gene A Bailey
8 Hunter Ave
Minot ME 04258

Call Sign: K1TVT
Jean G Thompson
384 Minot Ave
Minot ME 04258

Call Sign: N1PIZ
J Granville Chandler
40 Star Drive
Minot ME 04258

Call Sign: KB1QHS
Samuel K Barton
132 Woodman Hill Rd
Minot ME 04258

Call Sign: W1SKB
Samuel K Barton
132 Woodman Hill Rd
Minot ME 04258

Call Sign: KA1ZNI
Gordon N Barnes
Minot ME 04258

FCC Amateur Radio Licenses in Monhegan Island

Call Sign: KB1GJG

Laurence F Rollins
Monhegan Island ME 04852

Call Sign: AK1SS
Laurence F Rollins
Monhegan Island ME 04852

FCC Amateur Radio Licenses in Monmouth

Call Sign: KB1OUG
Thomas S Manduca
39 Academy Rd
Monmouth ME 04259

Call Sign: WA1LKM
Donald J Coltart
127 Academy Rd
Monmouth ME 04259

Call Sign: WA1HRR
F Phillip Prescott
256 Blue Rd
Monmouth ME 04259

Call Sign: N1YWP
Richard M Grant
249 Blvd Rd
Monmouth ME 04259

Call Sign: KB1ELR
Zane W Keeler
Rt 135 Box 197
Monmouth ME 04259

Call Sign: KA1IUA
Erma B Painter
Box 325
Monmouth ME 04259

Call Sign: KB1SDF
Kevin M Oliveira
242 Cressey Rd
Monmouth ME 04259

Call Sign: N1NYX
Mark R Bonderud
44 Karen Ave
Monmouth ME 042597702

Call Sign: N1QBC
Carol L Bonderud
44 Karen Ave
Monmouth ME 042597702

Call Sign: KB1NDD
Tamara L Bonderud
44 Karen Ave
Monmouth ME 04259

Call Sign: W1KX
William C Mann
645 Main St
Monmouth ME 042597538

Call Sign: WM1C
Michelle E Mann
645 Main St
Monmouth ME 042597538

Call Sign: K1HLG
William F Braisted
Po Box 402
Monmouth ME 04259

Call Sign: KB1JDO
John R Valonis
109 Rte 126
Monmouth ME 04259

Call Sign: KB1PEU
Patrick J Derosby
483 South Monmouth Rd
Monmouth ME 04259

Call Sign: KB1FHZ
Donald J Keeler
625 Wilson Pond Rd
Monmouth ME 04265

Call Sign: KA1BLL
Stanley L Painter Jr
Monmouth ME 04259

Call Sign: KV1K
Mark W Poole
Monmouth ME 04259

Call Sign: N1SEI
Lowell E Woodman
Monmouth ME 04259

Call Sign: N1ULN
Maxine C Wheeler
Monmouth ME 04259

Call Sign: KB1FVE
Hans L Boedeker
Monmouth ME 04259

FCC Amateur Radio Licenses in Monroe

Call Sign: K1ALX
Nolan C Gibbs
351 Curtis Rd
Monroe ME 04951

Call Sign: KB1KDX
Carol A Inman
23 Dahlia Farm Rd
Monroe ME 04951

Call Sign: KB1GBD
Gary B Daigle
23 Dahlia Farm Road
Monroe ME 04951

Call Sign: KA1TG
Robert L Neville
Frankfort Rd
Monroe ME 04951

Call Sign: K1DPD
Lawrence T Bartlett Jr

79 Jackson Rd
Monroe ME 049513000

Call Sign: KB1SEN
Jonathan S Fulford
127 Stovepipe Alley
Monroe ME 04951

Call Sign: KB1UAL
Neil A Caudill
375 Swan Lake Ave
Monroe ME 04951

Call Sign: KB1ULD
Katherine F Crowley
375 Swan Lake Ave
Monroe ME 04951

FCC Amateur Radio Licenses in Monson

Call Sign: KX2W
Freeman S Shontz
747 N Guilford Rd
Monson ME 04464

Call Sign: N2CLX
Mary L Shontz
747 N Guilford Rd
Monson ME 04464

Call Sign: KC1AU
Robert C Wilson
36 Water St
Monson ME 04464

Call Sign: N1GTY
Ernest E Copeland Jr
Monson ME 04464

Call Sign: KB1NJO
Stanley R Spoors
Monson ME 04464

FCC Amateur Radio Licenses in Monticello

Call Sign: KB1EES
Dorothy A Marshall
Rr 1 Box 1395
Monticello ME 04760

Call Sign: W1PN
Charles H Rock
503 Britton Rd
Monticello ME 047600201

Call Sign: KB1GXK
Jennifer G Ellis
274 Britton Road
Monticello ME 04760

Call Sign: K3UTH
William J Sampar
462 Fletcher Rd
Monticello ME 047603220

Call Sign: KB1DIO
Joseph T Rozecki
18 School Street
Monticello ME 04760

Call Sign: WB1CNF
Joseph M Black
Box 2820 West Rd
Monticello ME 04760

Call Sign: KA1RJK
David W Socoby
Monticello ME 04760

Call Sign: KB1DGK
Jonathan J Rozecki
Monticello ME 04760

Call Sign: KB1DIN
Peter J Rozecki
Monticello ME 04760

FCC Amateur Radio Licenses in Montville

Call Sign: KB1JOW
Uwe Langmesser
63 Choate Rd
Montville ME 04941

Call Sign: AA1H
Edmund L Melanson
1095 Halldale Rd
Montville ME 049419611

Call Sign: AB1FY
William M Johnson
682 North Ridge Rd
Montville ME 04941

Call Sign: N1ZSG
Corie L Dimmitt
141 So Mountain Valley
Hwy
Montville ME 04941

FCC Amateur Radio Licenses in Moody

Call Sign: WN1SWR
Theodore R Cunningham
42 Tatnic Rd
Moody ME 04054

Call Sign: K1NLA
Dorothy R Paine
Moody ME 04054

Call Sign: KA1DNF
Edward L Parker
Moody ME 04054

Call Sign: KA1GKO
Warren G Cousins Sr
Moody ME 04054

Call Sign: KA1QHN

Christa M Koenig
Moody ME 040540660

Call Sign: KA1ZUS
Nils F Nelson
Moody ME 04054

Call Sign: KB1BBF
Martin Fuchs
Moody ME 04054

Call Sign: N1FWU
Ferol Austen
Moody ME 040540332

FCC Amateur Radio Licenses in Moro Plantation

Call Sign: N1ALI
Edward N George
314 Town Line Rd
Moro Plantation ME 04780

FCC Amateur Radio Licenses in Morrill

Call Sign: N1RXX
Lucky Skidgell Sr
73 Brown Road
Morrill ME 04952

Call Sign: N1PGY
Peter C Hawley
13n Main St
Morrill ME 04952

Call Sign: KB1MMY
John K Tani
125 Morey Hill Rd
Morrill ME 04952

Call Sign: N1UBV
Glenice M Lear
13 N Main St

Morrill ME 04952

Call Sign: N1STN
Michael J Farris
Morrill ME 04952

FCC Amateur Radio Licenses in Mount Chase

Call Sign: WA1UDP
Phillip J Hunter
1030 Shin Pond Road
Mount Chase ME 04765

FCC Amateur Radio Licenses in Mount Desert

Call Sign: KB1WKP
Lewis E Gordon
1 Bartlett Island
Mount Desert ME 04660

Call Sign: K1RZH
Robert E Foster
Rt 198 Box 98
Mount Desert ME 04660

Call Sign: N1BTE
Ellen S Bennett
Hall Quarry
Mount Desert ME 04660

Call Sign: WB1EIS
Lowell W Bennett
Hall Quarry Rd
Mount Desert ME 04660

Call Sign: KB1HXD
Joseph P Renault Iii
77 Parker Farm Rd
Mount Desert ME 04660

Call Sign: KA1KWH
Mark D Smith
Mount Desert ME 04660

Call Sign: N4KOU
Steven J Carvajal
328 Pretty Marsh Road,
Mount Desert, ME
046606117

FCC Amateur Radio Licenses in Mount Vernon

Call Sign: KB1MEC
Raymond D Kittredge
1170 Bean Rd
Mount Vernon ME 04352

Call Sign: N1FFF
Charles A Mills
Box 41
Mount Vernon ME 04352

Call Sign: KA1DMB
Harold R Wilkey
Rr 1 Box 5130
Mount Vernon ME 04352

Call Sign: N1BVP
Alan R Dearborn
3 Demariano Road
Mount Vernon ME 04352

Call Sign: KA1HUX
Roger L Scott
893 North Rd
Mt Vernon ME 04352

Call Sign: KB1MHG
Alexis I Scott
893 North Rd
Mt Vernon ME 04352

Call Sign: K1AUQ
Russell W Dearborn
1889 North Road
Mt.Vernon ME 04352

Call Sign: N1DWU
Philip J Fleury
19 Pine Grove Drive
Mount Vernon ME 04352

Call Sign: KB1JHW
Ronald J Lockwood
78 Pond Rd
Mount Vernon ME 04352

Call Sign: WB1BYR
Keith O Power
Rfd Box 2120
Mount Vernon ME 04352

Call Sign: N1MFR
Gary Adler
Mt Desert ME 04660

**FCC Amateur Radio
Licenses in Naples**

Call Sign: KA1NUW
Patricia A Skolfield
Rr 1 Box 520
Naples ME 04057

Call Sign: N1MEA
Bryce H Skolfield
Rr 1 Box 520
Naples ME 04056

Call Sign: K1DWQ
Walter P Smith
19 Burnham Dr
Naples ME 04055

Call Sign: AA1VA
Walter P Smith
19 Burnham Dr
Naples ME 04055

Call Sign: KB1NJK
Micah J Haslett
207 Edes Falls Rd

Naples ME 04055

Call Sign: KB1IUV
Harleigh P Clukey Sr
372 King Hill Rd
Naples ME 04055

Call Sign: N1RQV
Duane R Stone
638 Lake House Rd
Naples ME 040553218

Call Sign: KA1ZVS
Earl P Portee
55 Lake Sebago Dr
Naples ME 040556507

Call Sign: W1EMJ
Lincoln T Bent
571 Lambs Mill Rd
Naples ME 04055

Call Sign: K1WEI
David E Mills
23 Melody Ln
Naples ME 04055

Call Sign: KC7SWL
Frank Kosidowski
23 Oakwood Circle
Naples ME 04055

Call Sign: K1QS
Walter P Smith
23 Oakwood Circle
Naples ME 04055

Call Sign: KB1FUD
Wayne M Smith
23 Oakwood Circle
Naples ME 04055

Call Sign: KB1UGL
Michael Dimitrakakis
23 Oakwood Circle

Naples ME 04055

Call Sign: K9CVY
Michael Dimitrakakis
23 Oakwood Circle
Naples ME 04055

Call Sign: W1EZI
Paul M Cumming
101 Pike Hill Rd
Naples ME 04055

Call Sign: N1ZEU
Edward T Lee
Rr 1 Pine Rock Rd Box 4
Naples ME 040559705

Call Sign: W1SXF
Adrian T Ward Jr
50 Pond Park Dr
Naples ME 04055

Call Sign: KC1XB
Carl R Pearson
264 River Road
Naples ME 04055

Call Sign: K1OTS
Earl P Portee
176 Rolling Hill Dr
Naples ME 040556507

Call Sign: W1GYK
Bernard B Twombly Jr
162 Rolling Hill Drive
Naples ME 04055

Call Sign: KB1MDL
Stephen M Catto
589 Roosevelt Tr
Naples ME 04055

Call Sign: WA1EIG
Gary D Begin
Rt 302

Naples ME 04055

Call Sign: KB1KXS
Blair O Watson
102 State Park Rd
Naples ME 04055

Call Sign: KB1SHF
Gregory J Fiory
51 Taylor Lane
Naples ME 04055

Call Sign: KA1NSY
Ronald L Hunt
159 Thompsons Pt Rd
Naples ME 04056

Call Sign: K1NXV
Roger H Beane
Naples ME 04055

Call Sign: KA1NWN
Warren N Kernander
Naples ME 04055

Call Sign: KA1SFQ
Bruce W Stevens
Naples ME 04055

Call Sign: KA1SFR
Luke A Stevens
Naples ME 04055

Call Sign: N1HOZ
Martin Burke
Naples ME 04055

Call Sign: N1ZNJ
Gary L Gilman
Naples ME 04055

Call Sign: KB1KNF
Caine A Wing
Naples ME 04055

Call Sign: KB1URO
John C Kilday Iii
Naples ME 04055

Call Sign: W1JCK
John C Kilday Iii
Naples ME 04055

FCC Amateur Radio Licenses in New Gloucester

Call Sign: KA1RUF
David Margolis
Rr 2 Box 1274
New Gloucester ME 04260

Call Sign: W1KDW
John N Edgerton
Rr 2 Box 1354
New Gloucester ME 04260

Call Sign: N1TMM
Fred J Crory Iii
36 Bridgeham Road
New Gloucester ME 04260

Call Sign: N1XUZ
Deborah W Crory
36 Bridgham Road
New Gloucester ME 04260

Call Sign: KB1OTJ
Shawn A Butler
19 Butler Dr
New Gloucester ME 04260

Call Sign: W1SAB
Shawn A Butler
19 Butler Dr
New Gloucester ME 04260

Call Sign: KB1OJU
Brandon M Bagley
60 Church Rd

New Gloucester ME 04260

Call Sign: KB1OKC
Michael P Bagley
60 Church Rd
New Gloucester ME 04260

Call Sign: NU1H
Michael P Bagley
60 Church Rd
New Gloucester ME 04260

Call Sign: KB1AOE
Beth L Coolbroth
51 Hillside Dr
New Gloucester ME 04260

Call Sign: KA1ISI
Edward E Ford
849 Intervale Rd
New Gloucester ME 04260

Call Sign: N1QEX
Avis T Ford
849 Intervale Rd
New Gloucester ME 04260

Call Sign: N1XMU
Lester R Watkins
943 Intervale Rd
New Gloucester ME 04260

Call Sign: N1OEL
Howard N Mikkelsen
1372 Intervale Rd
New Gloucester ME 04260

Call Sign: N1IPU
Mark N Chauvin
19 Jack Hall Rd.
New Gloucester ME 04260

Call Sign: K2ZLF
Joseph C Meyer
31 Lake View Dr

New Gloucester ME 04260

Call Sign: KA2ZKM
Marion Meyer
31 Lake View Dr
New Gloucester ME
042603025

Call Sign: KD1AK
Anthony Kariotis
15 Majestic Way
New Gloucester ME 04260

Call Sign: N1ULW
Deana L Kariotis
15 Majestic Way
New Gloucester ME 04260

Call Sign: KA1SYF
Frank J Knight
75 Mc Intire Rd
New Gloucester ME 04260

Call Sign: N1JST
Fannie V Edgerton
111 Morse Rd
New Gloucester ME 04260

Call Sign: KA1CKO
Richard B Clark
181 Peacock Hill Rd
New Gloucester ME 04260

Call Sign: N1WRU
Lewis W Corriveau
52 Shaker Rd
New Gloucester ME 04260

Call Sign: K1NND
Daniel H Mc Leod
185 Shaker Rd
New Gloucester ME 04260

Call Sign: KC2HBC
Robert E Grindle

4 Village Mission Ln
New Gloucester ME 04260

Call Sign: KB1HBK
Charles J Behounek
20 Witham Road
New Gloucester ME 04260

Call Sign: KB1AQH
Michael G Lang
225 Woodman Road
New Gloucester ME 04260

Call Sign: N1PGH
James F Ledger
New Gloucester ME 04260

FCC Amateur Radio Licenses in New Harbor

Call Sign: KB1GFK
Robert C Hutchinson
52 Drebelbis Point Road
New Harbor ME 04554

Call Sign: KA1NBZ
Leora H Robbins
Pemaquid Trl
New Harbor ME 04554

Call Sign: KA3GAB
George L Robbins
Pemaquid Trl
New Harbor ME 04554

Call Sign: KB1LXY
Troy M Benner
108 Rodgers Rd
New Harbor ME 04554

Call Sign: K1ZQC
Jonathan L Le Veen
190 Snowball Hill Road
New Harbor ME 04554

Call Sign: WA1UJQ
Carmen L Knipe
South Side Rd
New Harbor ME 04554

Call Sign: K1AZK
Robert D Williams
137 State Route 32
New Harbor ME 04554

Call Sign: N9ILM
Albert W Wehlitz
New Harbor ME 04554

Call Sign: W3XD
Stephen B Dresner
New Harbor ME 04554

FCC Amateur Radio Licenses in New Limerick

Call Sign: KA1PP
Carl R De Witt
864 County Rd
New Limerick ME 04761

Call Sign: K1CFR
Clyde L Schillinger
1233 County Rd
New Limerick ME 04761

Call Sign: N1MCL
Del M Hastey
1243 County Rd
New Limerick ME 04761

Call Sign: WA1VHZ
Bruce B Burnham
1690 County Rd
New Limerick ME 04761

Call Sign: KB1PHM
Donald G Haller
226 Drews Lake Rd
New Limerick ME 04761

Call Sign: KB1DUS
Andrew L Putnam
337 Drews Lake Road
New Limerick ME 04761

Call Sign: W1AAF
Mark F Stile
77 Jeffery Rd
New Limerick ME 04761

Call Sign: N1UYD
Paul E Macilroy
Po Box 11
New Limerick ME 04761

Call Sign: N1WAP
Wanda A Mac Ilroy
Po Box 11
New Limerick ME 04761

Call Sign: K1UVU
Jasper C Hardy
New Limerick ME 04761

Call Sign: KA1VHE
Mark L Nightingale
New Limerick ME 04761

**FCC Amateur Radio
Licenses in New Portland**

Call Sign: N1ULY
Lloyd C Dalton
40 Bog Road
New Portland ME 04961

Call Sign: K1VEQ
Robert G Kennedy
New Portland ME 04954

**FCC Amateur Radio
Licenses in New Sharon**

Call Sign: N0EIA

Justin P Snay
248 Farmington Falls Rd.
New Sharon ME 04955

Call Sign: N1KCP
Brent L Granberg
23 Kimball Pond Rd
New Sharon ME 04955

Call Sign: KB1UUD
Jeanne L Harris
147 Lane Rd
New Sharon ME 04955

Call Sign: KB1UBT
William H Colwell
21 Smith Rd
New Sharon ME 04955

Call Sign: KB1TRU
William M Hensley
32 Starks Rd
New Sharon ME 04955

Call Sign: W1DSA
David S Adam
134 Swan Road
New Sharon ME 04955

Call Sign: KA1FKC
Russell H Norris
318 Swan Road
New Sharon ME 04955

Call Sign: K1TMJ
James N Mann
New Sharon ME 04955

Call Sign: N1MRA
Jerry H Bartlett
New Sharon ME 04955

**FCC Amateur Radio
Licenses in New Sweden**

Call Sign: KB1BHJ
Erica A Mc Dougal
Box 13 Capital Hill Rd
New Sweden ME 04762

Call Sign: KB1BHK
Douglas A Mc Dougal
Box 13 Capital Hill Rd
New Sweden ME 04762

Call Sign: K1SUT
Almon R Mc Dougal
14 Capitol Hill Rd
New Sweden ME 04762

Call Sign: K1SWG
Brian D Mc Dougal
39 Capitol Hill Rd
New Sweden ME 04762

Call Sign: WA1JCN
Judith E Mann
12 Rista Rd
New Sweden ME 04762

Call Sign: KB1DLN
Larry L Lindquist
23 Rista Rd
New Sweden ME 04762

Call Sign: KB1MGY
Arnold E Thibodeau
996 Rista Road
New Sweden ME 04762

Call Sign: KA1KXP
Laurie J Spooner
9 Station Rd
New Sweden ME 04762

Call Sign: W1KXP
Laurie J Spooner
9 Station Rd
New Sweden ME 04762

Call Sign: N1EZR
Patricia A Maki
Anson Valley Rd
New Vineyard ME 04956

Call Sign: N1MNL
Sandra A Messeder
New Vineyard ME 04956

Call Sign: N1URT
Kerry T Case
New Vineyard ME 04956

**FCC Amateur Radio
Licenses in Newburgh**

Call Sign: KB1CDA
Charles D Mc Mahan
16 Babcock Rd
Newburgh ME 04444

Call Sign: K1CDA
Charles D Mc Mahan
16 Babcock Rd
Newburgh ME 04444

Call Sign: K1UO
Lawrence F Emery
2044 Carmel Road North
Newburgh ME 04444

Call Sign: N1MKO
Carrie A Getchell
2639 Kennebec Rd
Newburg ME 04444

Call Sign: W1LUC
Luc G Perin
1050 North Rd
Newburgh ME 04444

Call Sign: KB1EAU

Luc G Perin
1050 North Rd.
Newburgh ME 04444

Call Sign: AE4HL
James W Kauppila
335 Old Mudgett Road
Newburgh ME 04444

Call Sign: KA1ZGC
Thomas A Rounds
2635 Western Ave
Newburgh ME 04444

**FCC Amateur Radio
Licenses in Newcastle**

Call Sign: KA1ADF
Lawrence B Roy
190 Academy Hill Rd
Newcastle ME 04553

Call Sign: W1DW
Nahum W Morse
216 E. Old County Rd.
Newcastle ME 04553

Call Sign: N1LME
Ralph A Berticelli
40 Hassen Ave
Newcastle ME 04553

Call Sign: KM1J
James K Skilling
29 Lake Meadow Ln
Newcastle ME 04553

Call Sign: N1LOX
Roger A Wilcox
28 North Dyer Neck Rd
Newcastle ME 04553

Call Sign: KB1TGF
William P Terry
24 Pine Ledge Dr

Newcastle ME 04553

Call Sign: WB2WZE
Roger D Hathaway
12 Pond Rd
Newcastle ME 04553

Call Sign: KA1WRM
Paul L Farrington
96 Sheepscot Rd
Newcastle ME 04553

Call Sign: W1IQO
Leslie A Coffin Sr
94 Station Rd
Newcastle ME 04553

Call Sign: KA1NFS
Douglas L Roberts
Newcastle ME 04553

Call Sign: KB1DLF
Michael H Clark
Newcastle ME 04553

Call Sign: KB1OMF
Peter A Kenyon
Newcastle ME 04553

**FCC Amateur Radio
Licenses in Newfield**

Call Sign: KA1WAO
Charles F Hicks
Newfield ME 04056

**FCC Amateur Radio
Licenses in Newport**

Call Sign: KB2EVL
Donald A Seavey
Rr2 Box 1047
Newport ME 04953

Call Sign: N1VAG

Thomas P Kus
Rr 2 Box 1185
Newport ME 04953

Call Sign: N1FAX
Lincoln M Clifford
Rr 2 Box 240
Newport ME 04953

Call Sign: KB1UTC
Troy M Bagley
62 Durham Bridge Rd
Newport ME 04953

Call Sign: W1FNU
Errald N Turner
18 Elm Street
Newport ME 049533124

Call Sign: NA1K
John E Clifford
201 Elm Street
Newport ME 04953

Call Sign: N1XRG
Richard W Tibbetts Sr
22 Mc Nally Terr
Newport ME 04953

Call Sign: N1NJU
Peter M Mc Kay
12 South St
Newport ME 04953

Call Sign: KA1IE
William R Goff
670 Stetson Rd
Newport ME 04953

Call Sign: KB1GIF
Jeffrey D Scribner
Hc 61 Box 340

Newry ME

Call Sign: KA1TFD
Fayette H Branch
W Neck Rd Rr 1 Box 413
Nobleboro ME 04555

Call Sign: N1WTJ
Patricia H Winslow
353 Duck Puddle Rd
Nobleboro ME 04555

Call Sign: N1RP
Richard E Perkins
27 Evergreen Estates Rd
Nobleboro ME 045559004

Call Sign: WN1TXD
Florence H Perkins
27 Evergreen Estates Rd
Nobleboro ME 045559004

Call Sign: N1DX
John P Corson
107 Island View Dr
Nobleboro ME 04555

Call Sign: W1YZ
Ellwood Collamore
18 Nash Rd.
Nobleboro ME 04555

Call Sign: KD3WH
John E Knapp
25 Oyster Creek Lane
Nobleboro ME 04555

Call Sign: KE1LX
John E Knapp
25 Oyster Creek Lane
Nobleboro ME 04555

Call Sign: W1YB
Clayton H Sacks
W Neck Rd Box 353
Nobleboro ME 04555

Call Sign: KA1LHX
James G Olson
West Neck Rd
Nobleboro ME 04555

Call Sign: W1IPL
Wilton J Barnum
609 West Neck Rd.
Nobleboro ME 04555

Call Sign: WA1ZAX
Robert S Trial Jr
433 Westneck Road
Nobleboro ME 04555

Call Sign: KB1FJB
Joseph A Chaykowsky
180 Airport Rd
Norridgewock ME 04957

Call Sign: AA1YD
Joseph A Chaykowsky
180 Airport Rd
Norridgewock ME 04957

Call Sign: KB1JRG
Carol L Decker
180 Airport Rd
Norridgewock ME 04957

Call Sign: KB1OLR
Darrin L Gilman I
3 Becki Way
Norridgewock ME 04957

Call Sign: N1WBK
Theodore E Brown Jr

Rfd 2 Box 1570
Norridgewock ME 04957

Call Sign: KA1CNV
Victoria G Hall
Rr 2 Box 210
Norridgewock ME 04957

Call Sign: KA1LTK
Robert J Bourassa
Rfd 2 Box 2330
Norridgewock ME 04957

Call Sign: KA1DIV
Henry T Perry
Box 342
Norridgewock ME 04957

Call Sign: KA1KSP
John W Carter
Rfd 2 Box 760
Norridgewock ME 04957

Call Sign: N1TYA
Vickie L Ayer
Rr 2 Box 770
Norridgewock ME 04957

Call Sign: N1NOR
Edward A Clark
637 Madison Rd
Norridgewock ME 04957

Call Sign: N1NOQ
Irislea C Clark
637 Madison Road
Norridgewock ME 04957

Call Sign: KB1UJJ
Mercer C E R T
Communications Team
9 Main St
Norridgewock ME 04957

Call Sign: KB1VDS

Robert E Herman
13 Main St
Norridgewock ME 04957

Call Sign: KA1OFK
Robert G Crommett
Martin Stream Rd
Norridgewock ME 04957

Call Sign: KB1SBW
Jesse J Crandall
1405 Mercer Rd
Norridgewock ME 04957

Call Sign: KA1HC
John B Covert
297 River Road
Norridgewock ME 04957

Call Sign: KA1HHQ
Nancy E Covert
297 River Road
Norridgewock ME 04957

Call Sign: WA1YRO
Christiaan J Beeuwkes
Box 840 Rt 2
Norridgewock ME 04957

Call Sign: KB1AQW
Charles H R Perry
Sandy River Rd
Norridgelock ME 04957

Call Sign: KA1KMV
Renee M Perry
Sandy River Rd
Norridgewock ME 04957

Call Sign: KB1IU
Frederick G Bell
Sandy River Rd
Norridgewock ME 04957

Call Sign: N1MNJ

Frederick C Souza
29 Sophie May Lane
Norridgewock ME 04957

Call Sign: N1WGP
Doreen L Brown
229 Ward Hill Rd
Norridgewock ME 04957

Call Sign: N1NX
Gardiner W Brown Sr
Norridgewock ME 04957

Call Sign: N1TL
Thomas L Lint
Norridgewock ME 04957

Call Sign: KB1LRP
Norridgewock Area
Wireless Association
Norridgewock ME 04957

Call Sign: W1RMA
Russell A Miller
Hc 61 Box 86b
North Amity ME
044719622

Call Sign: KB1DSG
Russell A Miller
Hc 61 Box 86b Estabrook
Rd
North Amity ME
044719622

Call Sign: KD5KRU
Odel B Fields
444 Lycette Rd
North Amity ME 04471

Call Sign: K1KRU
Odel B Fields

444 Lycette Rd
North Amity ME 04471

Call Sign: KA1GYV
Louis E Weatherbee
Star Route Box 55
North Amity ME 04465

FCC Amateur Radio Licenses in North Anson

Call Sign: K1OQV
Wilbert H Hayes
Rr 1 Box 1050
North Anson ME
049589709

Call Sign: KB1CTR
Seth D Danner
Rr1 Box 3512
North Anson ME 04958

Call Sign: N1SXS
Charles R Coffren
43 Elm St
North Anson ME 04958

Call Sign: N1WSW
Brian J Pomelow
Rfd 476
North Anson ME 04958

Call Sign: KA1WOE
Gary R Morin Sr
North Anson ME 04958

Call Sign: NH6ZB
Michael L Cote Sr
North Anson ME 04958

Call Sign: WB1FKP
Robert A Mc Quillan Jr
North Anson ME 04958

Call Sign: KB1KFP

Sheri L Cote
North Anson ME 04958

Call Sign: KJ1Z
Michael L Cote Sr
North Anson ME 04958

FCC Amateur Radio Licenses in North Berwick

Call Sign: N1YXW
Edgar M Hoey Iii
460 Bauneg Beg Hill Road
North Berwick ME 03906

Call Sign: N1UHF
Edgar M Hoey Iii
460 Bauneg Beg Hill Road
North Berwick ME 03906

Call Sign: N1KSQ
Thomas R Coffin
Rr 2 Box 219
North Berwick ME 03906

Call Sign: KB1JYA
John M Bemis
32 Butler Rd
North Berwick ME 03906

Call Sign: W1CTR
John M Bemis
32 Butler Rd
North Berwick ME 03906

Call Sign: N1UJL
William L Jacques
12 Chadbourne Ln
North Berwick ME
039065135

Call Sign: W1RLB
Robert L Bean
15 Church Ave
North Berwick ME 03906

Call Sign: KF6TMR
Bror H Rinne
651 Ford Quint Rd
North Berwick ME 03906

Call Sign: KB1GIN
Sue E Fleig
113 Lebanon Rd
North Berwick ME 03906

Call Sign: K1SEF
Sue E Fleig
113 Lebanon Rd
North Berwick ME 03906

Call Sign: W1VVO
William H Fleig
113 Lebanon Rd
North Berwick ME 03906

Call Sign: K1BF
William H Fleig
113 Lebanon Rd
North Berwick ME 03906

Call Sign: KB1CQW
Shawn P Matile
40 Main St Apt 3
North Berwick ME 03906

Call Sign: N1ORS
Jason G Langelier
251 Morrells Mill Road
North Berwick ME 03906

Call Sign: N1BOK
Leo H Langelier Jr
251 Morrills Mill Rd
North Berwick ME 03906

Call Sign: KC1VY
Norman L Beaudoin Jr
12 Old Route 9
North Berwick ME 03906

Call Sign: N2MSS
Enrique J Lopez
P.O. Box 454
North Berwick ME 03906

Call Sign: N1HL
Lillian Lopez
P.O. Box 454
North Berwick ME 03906

Call Sign: KC1BS
Roger R Deroy
Pine Meadow Dr
North Berwick ME 03906

Call Sign: KB1EZR
Wayne E Snow
15 Sunset Ave
North Berwick ME 03906

Call Sign: WA1UKH
Carleton E Snow
Sunset Ave
North Berwick ME 03906

Call Sign: KB1UWX
Thomas F Martin
74 Valley Rd
North Berwick ME 03906

Call Sign: KB1DTK
Ernest D Houle
420 Valley Rd
North Berwick ME
039065920

Call Sign: KB1DTL
Shirley P Gauthier
420 Valley Rd
North Berwick ME
039065920

Call Sign: KB1PHK
Richard P Genest

North Berick ME 03906

Call Sign: KB1AAO
Shawn T Cook
North Berwick ME 03906

FCC Amateur Radio Licenses in North Berwicksanford

Call Sign: KA1ZZK
Craig W Curtis
76 Meehan Lane
North Berwicksanford ME
03904073

FCC Amateur Radio Licenses in North Bridgton

Call Sign: W1FZQ
Richard A Allen
52 Browns Mill Rd
North Bridgton ME 04057

Call Sign: KA1QKN
Jerry W Gardner
221 Chadbourne Hill Rd - P
O Box 212
North Bridgton ME
040570212

Call Sign: KA1IPF
Susan L Allen
North Bridgton ME 04057

Call Sign: N1ADT
Clyde W Pierce Iii
North Bridgton ME 04057

Call Sign: N1EKW
Walter W Allen
North Bridgton ME 04057

FCC Amateur Radio Licenses in North Haven

Call Sign: W1MGP
Samuel H Beverage
163 Middle Road
North Haven ME
048533116

FCC Amateur Radio Licenses in North Lebanon

Call Sign: K0ZK
Arnold F Olean
North Lebanon ME
040270073

FCC Amateur Radio Licenses in North Monmouth

Call Sign: N1VNN
William H Wood Sr
202 Annabessacook Rd
North Monmouth ME
04265

Call Sign: W1QMK
Richard W Merrill
34 Blaisdell Rd
North Monmouth ME
04265

Call Sign: N1UOF
Peter G Kelley
157 N Main St
North Monmouth ME
04265

Call Sign: KB1RNZ
Edward G Kreiton
27 Turner Dr
North Monmouth ME
04265

Call Sign: KB1GVT
Steven T Hall
672 Wilson Pond Rd
North Monmouth ME
04265

Call Sign: KB1IEG
Daleen Hall
672 Wilson Pond Rd
North Monmouth ME
04265

FCC Amateur Radio Licenses in North Temple

Call Sign: KF4OTI
Richard F Mc Carthy
North Temple ME
049840514

FCC Amateur Radio Licenses in North Vassalboro

Call Sign: N1QAS
Allen R Rowe
R 1 Box 1235
North Vassalboro ME
04962

Call Sign: W1PXE
Charles J Pitman
Rr 1 Box 50
North Vassalboro ME
049629701

Call Sign: KA1VKI
Bernadette L Peaslee
5 Dearborn Hill
North Vassalboro ME
04962

Call Sign: WA1BFO
Thomas M O'keefe

Priest Hill Rd.
North Vassalboro ME
04962

Call Sign: K1QVH
Lloyd F Cutting
North Vassalboro ME
04962

Call Sign: N1XTC
Robert J Carroll
North Vassalboro ME
04962

Call Sign: KB1IBV
Douglas W Grosso
North Vassalboro ME
04962

FCC Amateur Radio Licenses in North Waterboro

Call Sign: K1KWU
Joseph F Caron
6 Allview Ter
North Waterboro ME 04061

Call Sign: KA1SZS
Robert C Fisher
32 Back St
North Waterboro ME 04061

Call Sign: KA1QW
Frank R Allen Jr
365 Chadbourne Ridge
North Waterboro ME 04061

Call Sign: KA1VNW
Nancy A Bennison
13 Evergreen Dr
North Waterboro ME 04061

Call Sign: KB1RDT
Thomas C Witham

121 Lone Pine Rd
North Waterboro ME 04061

Call Sign: KB1SYQ
Syvella A Kalil
116 Old Portland Rd
North Waterboro ME 04061

Call Sign: KB1JRD
Robert H Brasil
168 Old Portland Rd.
North Waterboro ME 04061

Call Sign: N1XIF
Mark A Johnstone Jr
246 Old Portland Rd.
North Waterboro ME 04061

Call Sign: KA1ZYG
Brian A White
21 Rosemont Ave
North Waterboro ME 04061

Call Sign: KB1MSA
Mark Ford
103 Thyngs Mill Road
North Waterboro ME 04061

Call Sign: WA1PLD
Frank R Allen Jr
North Waterboro ME 04061

Call Sign: WB5RKH
Rhonda K Kelly
North Waterboro ME 04061

FCC Amateur Radio Licenses in North Waterford

Call Sign: W4QBR
Carl L Coleman Sr
Rr 1 Box 2005
North Waterford ME 0

Call Sign: N1CFK
Ella T Button
Rr 1 Box 2800
North Waterford ME 04267

Call Sign: KA1WQX
Jennifer L Kist
Box 2582 Higgins Rd
North Waterford ME 04267

Call Sign: W1SQC
Wilbur H Button
5 Kezar Lakes
North Waterford ME 04267

FCC Amateur Radio Licenses in North Whitefield

Call Sign: AF1G
Joseph J Mayer
Rfd 1 Box 544
North Whitefield ME 0

Call Sign: KA1IUC
David A Chase
Box 150 Townhouse Rd
North Whitefield ME 04353

FCC Amateur Radio Licenses in North Yarmouth

Call Sign: KB1VFT
Carl Hinsman
83 Christopher Rd
North Yarmouth ME 04097

Call Sign: WB1CTV
Charles W Weaver Iii
19 Conifer Ln
North Yarmouth ME 04097

Call Sign: W1QFM
David De Bree

32 Cumberland Rd
North Yarmouth ME 04097

Call Sign: KD1ZY
Warren F Whitney
215 Cumberland Rd
North Yarmouth ME 04097

Call Sign: KB1UOW
George A Fogg
56 Deer Run Rd
North Yarmouth ME 04097

Call Sign: N1GAF
George A Fogg
56 Deer Run Rd
North Yarmouth ME 04097

Call Sign: KL7OI
David A Price
75 Farms Edge Rd
North Yarmouth ME 04097

Call Sign: K1EQG
Evelyn R Baldwin
80 Gray Rd
North Yarmouth ME 04097

Call Sign: W1EFF
Caryl P Baldwin
80 Gray Rd
North Yarmouth ME 04097

Call Sign: N1TUU
Michael T Hassey
83 Haskell Rd
North Yarmouth ME 04097

Call Sign: W2BHE
James C Conrad
85 Mountfort Road
North Yarmouth ME 04097

Call Sign: N1FJR
Eleanor E Cyr

1185 North Rd
North Yarmouth ME 04097

Call Sign: N1HHW
Robert J Cyr
1185 North Rd
North Yarmouth ME 04097

Call Sign: KB1OKD
Roscoe G Dennison Iii
17 Rocky Rd
North Yarmouth ME 04097

Call Sign: K1MV
Steven F Freeman
118 Royal Rd
North Yarmouth ME 04097

Call Sign: KS1F
Steven F Freeman
118 Royal Rd
North Yarmouth ME 04097

Call Sign: K1MV
Steven F Freeman
118 Royal Rd
North Yarmouth ME 04097

Call Sign: KA1QYZ
Richard I Cottle
71 Walnut Hill Rd
North Yarmouth ME 04021

Call Sign: KB1IAW
Paul V Dunn
361 West Pownal Rd
North Yarmouth ME 04097

Call Sign: KB1IUJ
Lise G Dunn
361 West Pownal Rd
North Yarmouth ME 04097

Call Sign: W2EMT
James W W Wilmerding
Cove End Rd
Northeast Harbor ME 04662

Call Sign: W1EMT
James W W Wilmerding
4 Huntington Road
Northeast Harbor ME 04662

Call Sign: W1WNP
James W W Wilmerding
4 Huntington Road
Northeast Harbor ME 04662

Call Sign: W1EMT
James W W Wilmerding
4 Huntington Road
Northeast Harbor ME 04662

Call Sign: KB2LNX
William P Stewart
32 Sergeant Dr
Northeast Harbor ME 04662

Call Sign: WA1DJK
Joseph P Renault Jr
18 Sylvan Road
Northeast Harbor ME 04662

Call Sign: W1JPR
Joseph P Renault Jr
18 Sylvan Road
Northeast Harbor ME 04662

Call Sign: WB0YJP
William L Hodgkins
3 Tracy Rd
Northeast Harbor ME
046620989

Call Sign: N1MCN
Susan P Hodgkins
3 Tracy Road
Northeast Harbor ME 04662

Call Sign: WB0YSU
Earl L Hodgkins
Northeast Harbor ME
046620708

**FCC Amateur Radio
Licenses in Northfield**

Call Sign: KB1IKI
Christopher S Skinner
6 Holway Drive
Northfield ME 04654

Call Sign: KB1IMW
Susan M Chessa
6 Holway Drive
Northfield ME 04654

**FCC Amateur Radio
Licenses in Northport**

Call Sign: KB1AES
Harold D Pendleton Iii
1158 Atlantic Hwy
Northport ME 04849

Call Sign: KS0E
Charles R Grossman
248 Bluff Rd.
Northport ME 04849

Call Sign: W1LMO
Linwood M Pattee
Rr 1 Box 873
Northport ME 04915

Call Sign: KG6CQX
Edward R Lord
5 Park Row
Northport ME 048494407

Call Sign: WA6CWM
Michael S Bowden
218 Priest Rd
Northport ME 04849

Call Sign: AB1MC
Michael S Bowden
218 Priest Rd
Northport ME 04849

**FCC Amateur Radio
Licenses in Norway**

Call Sign: N1WOV
David A Burnham Jr
32 Alpine St Apt 3
Norway ME 04268

Call Sign: KB1SSD
Allyson S Hill
155 Ashton Rd
Norway ME 04268

Call Sign: N1SEN
Richard L Abbott
57 Beal St
Norway ME 04268

Call Sign: KA1WIE
Jason F Meserue
Rfd 1 Box 3520
Norway ME 04268

Call Sign: N1ZAT
Michael J Grenier
10 Cottege St
Norway ME 04268

Call Sign: KB1PHV
Kyle S Ivey
90 Country Club Rd
Norway ME 04268

Call Sign: K1NAJ

Norman A Jackson
350 Dunn Rd
Norway ME 04268

Call Sign: KA1NBC
Victoria S Jackson
350 Dunn Rd
Norway ME 04268

Call Sign: KB1BOG
Diane P Zutter
340 Dunn Road
Norway ME 04268

Call Sign: N1VOT
Mimi G Bell
180 Emerson Road
Norway ME 04268

Call Sign: N1XAZ
Stephen A Bell
180 Emerson Road
Norway ME 04268

Call Sign: KB1SSF
Stephen R Kimball
14 Fair St
Norway ME 04268

Call Sign: W1RWG
Clevis O Laverty
17 Fair St
Norway ME 04268

Call Sign: KB1KDY
Joseph M Grace
28 Huntington Ave
Norway ME 04268

Call Sign: N1JUG
Ernest E Dunham
3 Lee St
Norway ME 04268

Call Sign: WA4QYC

Robert L Godwin
62 Main St
Norway ME 04268

Call Sign: KB1ECN
Maurice J Arsenault
196 Main St
Norway ME 04268

Call Sign: KA1SHB
Clyde L Clark
202 Main St
Norway ME 04268

Call Sign: KB1AUP
David P Hilton
499 Maine St
Norway ME 04268

Call Sign: KB1PHJ
Roland G Blake Jr
40 Pikes Hill Rd Apt -1
Norway ME 04268

Call Sign: KB1SSG
Freya A Kory
565 Pleasant St
Norway ME 04268

Call Sign: KB1COW
Freya A Kory
565 Pleasant St
Norway ME 04268

Call Sign: W1HLK
Freya A Kory
565 Pleasant St
Norway ME 04268

Call Sign: KB1MEF
Brian B Button
491 Pleasant St .
Norway ME 04268

Call Sign: KB1KPU

Rowena M Palmer
286 Round The Pond Rd
Norway ME 04268

Call Sign: KB1VXO
Randy R Hallock
153 Sodom Rd
Norway ME 04268

Call Sign: KA4UOK
George C Byrd
24 T & C Mobilehome Pk
Norway ME 04268

Call Sign: KA1LUN
Tom J Winsor
107 Thurston Rd
Norway ME 04268

Call Sign: KA1NAZ
Patricia A Winsor
107 Thurston Rd
Norway ME 04268

Call Sign: KB1WKV
Paula J Cox
144 Waterford Rd
Norway ME 04268

Call Sign: KB1MKT
John R Hersey
6 Windy Dr
Norway ME 042684177

Call Sign: WB1FAK
Tere K Porter
Norway ME 04268

FCC Amateur Radio Licenses in Oakfield

Call Sign: WB1CLR
Ronald G Browne
Rr 1 Box 946
Oakfield ME 047639713

Call Sign: W1RSN
Robert C Fisher
Smyrna St
Oakfield ME 04763

Call Sign: KB1JVO
Joy C Botting
Oakfield ME 04763

**FCC Amateur Radio
Licenses in Oakland**

Call Sign: KA1LSH
Jon M Morrison
31 Belgrade Rd.
Oakland ME 04963

Call Sign: W0LWA
Thomas R Berger
102 Birch Meadows
Oakland ME 049634255

Call Sign: K1TRB
Thomas R Berger
102 Birch Meadows
Oakland ME 049634255

Call Sign: W1PDN
Alan R Works
Rfd 2 Box 4305
Oakland ME 04964

Call Sign: KA1ZXA
Deanne M King
Rfd 1 Box 5825
Oakland ME 04963

Call Sign: W1ANR
Charles S Lewis
Rd 1 Box 5870
Oakland ME 04963

Call Sign: KB1ABC
Ivy L Latendresse

Rfd 1 Box 6470
Oakland ME 04963

Call Sign: KA1ZVF
Samuel I Williams
Rt 1 Box 6510
Oakland ME 04963

Call Sign: KB1BDB
Mackenzie L Rackleff
Rfd 1 Box 7185
Oakland ME 04963

Call Sign: KA1TQZ
Raymond D Smith
30 Church St
Oakland ME 04963

Call Sign: KB1ULC
Stuart S Mairs
31 Church St
Oakland ME 04963

Call Sign: KC4BOO
Sharon M Conover
41 Heritage Rd
Oakland ME 04963

Call Sign: KK4QO
Charles W Conover Iii
41 Heritage Rd
Oakland ME 04963

Call Sign: KB1EQE
Edward R Ringel
119 Highland Dr
Oakland ME 04963

Call Sign: AA1WZ
Edward R Ringel
119 Highland Dr
Oakland ME 04963

Call Sign: K1FUY
Almond R Merrill

15 Middle St
Oakland ME 04963

Call Sign: N1RCS
Richard T Morrison
237 Oak St
Oakland ME 04963

Call Sign: N1UHM
Jane E Morrison
237 Oak St
Oakland ME 04963

Call Sign: KB1MQT
Bonnie L Kouletsis
122 S Alpine St
Oakland ME 04963

Call Sign: KB1MUM
Lydia M Kouletsis
122 S Alpine St
Oakland ME 04963

Call Sign: KB1MFY
Antonia M Smith
20 S Greenridge Hts
Oakland ME 04963

Call Sign: N1MUN
Eugene S Roy
12 Sawdust Trail
Oakland ME 04963

Call Sign: N1SDR
Chad T Smith
20 South Greenridge
Heights
Oakland ME 04963

Call Sign: W1MAE
Michael A Ellis
90 Tukey Rd.
Oakland ME 04963

Call Sign: KB1MFX

William G Fiedler
338 Willey Point Rd
Oakland ME 04963

Call Sign: WA1GWE
Michael S Willey
215 Willey Point Road
Oakland ME 04963

Call Sign: N1MBB
Blaine A Ellis
Oakland ME 04963

Call Sign: N1MNN
Alan L Lape
Oakland ME 04963

Call Sign: N1UFP
Michael A Ellis
Oakland ME 04963

Call Sign: WT1N
Jeffrey W Finkel
Oakland ME 04963

Call Sign: KB1WPR
Colby A Fischang
Oakland ME 04963

FCC Amateur Radio Licenses in Ocean Park

Call Sign: K1ZNU
Lona L Mills
10 Temple Ave
Ocean Park ME 04063

FCC Amateur Radio Licenses in Ogunquit

Call Sign: KA1YNJ
Debbie L Tower
31 Frazier Pasture Rd
Ogunquit ME 03907

Call Sign: KA1YNO
William R Tower Iii
93 Frazier Pasture Rd
Ogunquit ME 03907

Call Sign: WA1DEP
John J Choroszy
85 Riverbank Road
Ogunquit ME 03907

Call Sign: AB4OJ
Adam M Farson
Ogunquit ME 03907

Call Sign: K1XR
Bruce E Marton
Ogunquit ME 03907

Call Sign: KB1UXB
Jason R Andrews
Ogunquit ME 03907

FCC Amateur Radio Licenses in Old Orchard

Call Sign: KB1FOR
David N Lovejoy
Old Orchard ME
040641002

FCC Amateur Radio Licenses in Old Orchard Beach

Call Sign: K1OK
Jeffrey W Jenks
4 Banks Brook Rd
Old Orchard Beach ME
040644352

Call Sign: N1HLU
Janet R Psonak
27 Date St
Old Orchard Beach ME
04064

Call Sign: K1LWK
Robert J Yamartino Jr
191 E Grand Ave Unit 206
Old Orchard Beach ME
04064

Call Sign: KB1GDH
Robert Bertrand
44 Foote St
Old Orchard Beach ME
04064

Call Sign: N1GRI
Raymond Psonak
General Delivery
Old Orchard Beach ME
04064

Call Sign: KB1WOQ
Eber K Weinstein
20 Lewis Ave
Old Orchard Beach ME
04064

Call Sign: KB1BTA
James E Chadbourne
14 Maplewood Ave
Old Orchard Beach ME
04064

Call Sign: N1NZF
Glenace B Brown
14 Mc Callum Dr
Old Orchard Beach ME
04064

Call Sign: KA1VVO
Andrew D Ledger
12 Mccallum Drive
Old Orchard Beach ME
04064

Call Sign: N8UOQ
Robert L Dougherty Jr

103 Ocean Avenue
Old Orchard Beach ME
040641731

Call Sign: N1UCE
Dale R Berube
6 Oregon Ave 12
Old Orchard Beach ME
04064

Call Sign: KB1HUR
Barbara J Sykes
50 Park Ave
Old Orchard Beach ME
04064

Call Sign: KB1HUU
David R Francoeur
50 Park Ave
Old Orchard Beach ME
04064

Call Sign: N1BJZ
Roderick E Johnson
23 Pine Cone Drive
Old Orchard Beach ME
040641443

Call Sign: W1DFC
Martin S Murphy
166 Portland Ave
Old Orchard Beach ME
04064

Call Sign: K1KBX
Wesley L Curtis
37 Reggio Ave
Old Orchard Beach ME
04064

Call Sign: WB1FRF
Robert E Croston Sr
9 Rockland Drive
Old Orchard Beach ME
04064

Call Sign: W1GJ
F Norman Davis
27 Ross Rd
Old Orchard Beach ME
04064

Call Sign: W1BCV
Charles N Davis
33 Ross Rd
Old Orchard Beach ME
04064

Call Sign: AA1GA
Mark W Andrews
98 Ross Rd
Old Orchard Beach ME
04064

Call Sign: N1CFT
Neal L Weinstein
32 Saco Ave
Old Orchard Beach ME
04640

Call Sign: KA1ARG
Rene L Cote
188 Saco Ave
Old Orchard Beach ME
04064

Call Sign: KC1YB
King H Weinstein
198 Saco Ave
Old Orchard Beach ME
04064

Call Sign: W1YMD
Robert J Couri
7 Smith Ave
Old Orchard Beach ME
040642316

Call Sign: KB1GVI
Timothy A Hogan

25 Smith Wheel Rd Unit 23
Old Orchard Beach ME
04064

Call Sign: K2XM
Peter C Thomas
18 Smithwheel Rd #27
Old Orchard Beach ME
04064

Call Sign: KC8WAB
Maurice E Cox Iii
51 Smithwheel Rd #B15
Old Orchard Beach ME
04064

Call Sign: WX4WTF
Jason S Cote
26 Staples St Apt C
Old Orchard Beach ME
04065

Call Sign: K3GUW
Howard L Nielsen
105 Union Ave
Old Orchard Beach ME
04064

Call Sign: N4GQB
Richard E Platt
105 Union Ave
Old Orchard Beach ME
04064

Call Sign: WA1YGY
Eugene P Pierotti Jr
99 W Grande Ave 2
Old Orchard Beach ME
04064

Call Sign: W1TAS
Chester J Littlefield
50 W Old Orchard Ave
Old Orchard Beach ME
04064

Call Sign: N1LKY
Michael E Labbe
9 Washington Ave
Old Orchard Beach ME
04064

Call Sign: W1IV
Robert J Perlstein
2 Wavelet Ave
Old Orchard Beach ME
040640642

Call Sign: W1XZ
Gregory E Hanson
1 Woodland Avenue
Old Orchard Beach ME
04064

**FCC Amateur Radio
Licenses in Old Town**

Call Sign: WI1Z
Edward L Paradis
266 4th St.
Old Town ME 04468

Call Sign: N8HGW
Cynthia L Wilcox
65 7th St
Old Town ME 04468

Call Sign: KD1RR
Roderick E Blue
2120 Bennoch Rd
Old Town ME 04468

Call Sign: WB1GKD
Paul N Nadeau
2444 Bennoch Road
Old Town ME 04468

Call Sign: KD1MY
Phillip E Tibbetts
Rfd 1 Box 478

Old Town ME 04468

Call Sign: KB1WNA
Stanley W Rediker Jr
333 Brunswick St - Apt 2
Old Town ME 04468

Call Sign: W1AYX
Lawrence W Caron
9 Fifth St
Old Town ME 04468

Call Sign: KB1VCW
Joel M Castro
112 Fourth St Apt 1
Old Town ME 04468

Call Sign: N1STO
Carroll V Emery Iii
317 Fourth Street
Old Town ME 044681516

Call Sign: N1WBS
Galen L Malenfant
40 Hildreth St
Old Town ME 04468

Call Sign: KB1WPY
Adam Nickerson
59 Karen Circle
Old Town ME 04468

Call Sign: N1QKM
Christine M Spencer
461 Main St
Old Town ME 044681726

Call Sign: N1ME
Pine State Amateur Radio
Club
467 Main St
Old Town ME 04468

Call Sign: KB1VER
Nicholas J Bouchard

183 Main St Apt 5
Old Town ME 04468

Call Sign: N1OJD
Carroll A Spencer
467 Main Street
Old Town ME 044681726

Call Sign: N1UAM
Cassandra M Abbott
467 Main Street
Old Town ME 044681726

Call Sign: N1JHA
Edward L Paradis
81 N 4th St
Old Town ME 04468

Call Sign: W1GIB
Ray Gibouleau
233 N 4th St
Old Town ME 04468

Call Sign: KA1URG
Juan Condori
5 Oak St
Old Town ME 04468

Call Sign: N1QJB
Beth C Bunker
719 Stillwater Ave
Old Towne ME 04468

Call Sign: N2FEN
Rosalie B Welch
Lot 15 Pine Haven Tp
Stillwater Ave
Old Town ME 04468

Call Sign: KB1VFO
Chad M Paradis
152 Poplar St
Old Town ME 04468

Call Sign: KB1WPV

Casey M Clark
282 Poplar St
Old Town ME 04468

Call Sign: KB1FYB
Joseph T Prekop Ii
141 Southgate Road
Old Town ME 04468

Call Sign: W1EBJ
Amos L Hadley
395 Stillwater Ave
Old Town ME 04468

Call Sign: KB1WLT
Asgeir J Whitney
98 Veazie St
Old Town ME 04468

Call Sign: KA1URH
Alton F Herbest Jr
456 W Old Town Rd
Old Town ME 044685709

Call Sign: AB6PJ
Gary M Attean
Old Town ME 04468

Call Sign: N1IAT
Christian A Gagnon
Old Town ME 04468

FCC Amateur Radio Licenses in Oquossoc

Call Sign: W3OOU
William F Hughes
Box 245 Bemis Rd
Oquossoc ME 04964

Call Sign: N1HDT
Leon A Duchesne Jr
Oquossoc ME 04964

FCC Amateur Radio Licenses in Orchard Beach

Call Sign: KB1QZW
Charles L Largay
215 East Grand Ave Apt 312
Orchard Beach ME 04064

FCC Amateur Radio Licenses in Orient

Call Sign: NO1B
Walter M Zakupowsky
45 Maxell Settlement Rd
Orient ME 044710183

Call Sign: KB1CZF
Stephen J Martin
1049 Us Route One
Orient ME 04471

FCC Amateur Radio Licenses in Orington

Call Sign: KA1DX
Jackson L Williams
655 River Rd
Orington ME 04474

FCC Amateur Radio Licenses in Orland

Call Sign: N1NJB
Clifford E Gray
264 Backridge Rd
Orland ME 04472

Call Sign: WA1TVQ
John M Peckenham
1599 Bald Mountain Rd
Orland ME 04472

Call Sign: KQ1P
John M Peckenham
1599 Bald Mountain Rd
Orland ME 04472

Call Sign: KB1TPE
Margaret O Peckenham
1599 Bald Mountain Rd
Orland ME 04472

Call Sign: KB1VEJ
Nathaniel B Bray-Marks
727 Castine Rd
Orland ME 04472

Call Sign: KB1IMV
Daivd R Hopkins
37 Hopkins Rd
Orland ME 04472

Call Sign: KB1MYE
Everett L Saunders
212 Upper Falls Road
Orland ME 04472

FCC Amateur Radio Licenses in Orneville

Call Sign: KB1LML
Jonathan G Harmon
261 John Dean Rd
Orneville ME 04463

FCC Amateur Radio Licenses in Orneville Township

Call Sign: KB1LJS
Susan W Harmon
261 John Dean Rd
Orneville Twp ME 04463

Call Sign: KB1LOJ
Gary R Harmon
261 John Dean Rd

Orneville Twp ME 04463

**FCC Amateur Radio
Licenses in Orono**

Call Sign: N1YIP
Andrew K Sheaff
28 A Crosby St
Orono ME 04473

Call Sign: W1YA
University Of Maine Ama
Rad Club
5708 Barrows Hall
Orono ME 044695708

Call Sign: N1GAW
Beat P Bruegger
120 Boardman Hall
Orono ME 04469

Call Sign: KB1PTN
Joshua C Gaylin
21 Centre Dr Apt 7g
Orono ME 04474

Call Sign: N1ZAQ
C Bronson Crothers
17 Charles St
Orono ME 04473

Call Sign: AA1ZB
C Bronson Crothers
17 Charles St
Orono ME 04473

Call Sign: KB1WPU
John J Brosnan Iv
95 College Ave
Orono ME 04473

Call Sign: KB1VJZ
Richard J Pierce
66 College Ave Apt 2
Orono ME 04473

Call Sign: WI1J
Brett Grandchamp
65 College Avenue
Orono ME 04473

Call Sign: N1JIE
Susan R Thomas
1 College Heights
Orono ME 04473

Call Sign: N1OJK
Malin L Pinsky
21 College Heights
Orono ME 04473

Call Sign: KB1NDL
Ali Shareef
6 Cross Dr Apt B1
Orono ME 04473

Call Sign: N1KEU
Leila A Bowen
33 E University Pk
Orono ME 04473

Call Sign: KB1EYC
David G Kleinschmidt
18 Elm St
Orono ME 04473

Call Sign: WB1CVU
Stephen A Fadel
1 Fernald Road #3
Orono ME 04473

Call Sign: KB1IHM
Terence J Jason Jr
11 Forest Ave
Orono ME 04473

Call Sign: N1XMP
Lubomir A Ribarov
34 Forest Ave
Orono ME 044731415

Call Sign: KB1ATK
John G Riley
97 Forest Ave
Orono ME 04473

Call Sign: WA1TNH
Robert C Bayer
99 Forest Ave
Orono ME 04473

Call Sign: WZ1M
Gary K Brown
478 Forest Ave
Orono ME 04473

Call Sign: K1UP
Masaki Koizumi
595 Forest Ave
Orono ME 04473

Call Sign: KB1VFW
Pierric Guiral
595 Forest Ave
Orono ME 04473

Call Sign: AB1OM
Pierric Guiral
595 Forest Ave
Orono ME 04473

Call Sign: KB1WPO
Thomas Eismann
595 Forest Ave
Orono ME 04473

Call Sign: AA1PJ
Richard O Eason
595 Forest Ave.
Orono ME 044733008

Call Sign: N1YMN
Mary A Eason
595 Forest Ave.
Orono ME 044733008

Call Sign: N1XMN
Richard P Eason
595 Forest Avenue
Orono ME 044733008

Call Sign: KA1NP
Walter J Harris Jr
63 Forrest Ave
Orono ME 04473

Call Sign: KB1WPW
Andrew R Cote
3 Founders Pl Apt 1a
Orono ME 04473

Call Sign: N1VTP
Elaine S Gershman
6 Frost Ln
Orono ME 04473

Call Sign: WA1YGX
Melvin Gershman
6 Frost Ln
Orono ME 04473

Call Sign: W8NDI
Kenneth D Fox
7 Glenwood
Orono ME 04473

Call Sign: KB1FYR
Alexander D French
5 Harris Road
Orono ME 04469

Call Sign: N1YLT
Andrea S Mishou
23 Harrison Ave
Orono ME 04473

Call Sign: N1YIQ
Michael L Tipping Spitz
14 Kell St
Orono ME 04473

Call Sign: WB9RWQ
Thomas L Spitz
14 Kell St
Orono ME 04473

Call Sign: N1LFK
Gregory S Perkins
167 Kelley Rd
Orono ME 04473

Call Sign: N1YPK
Geremy M Chubbuck
142 Kelly Road
Orono ME 04473

Call Sign: KB1WPP
Aman K Maskay
5739 Knox Hall Rm 229
Orono ME 04469

Call Sign: W1KHW
Karl H Wichmann
10 Lexington Dr
Orono ME 04473

Call Sign: KA1WKW
Sascha L Deri
167 Main St
Orono ME 04473

Call Sign: KB1QYD
David E Kotecki
431 Main St
Orono ME 04473

Call Sign: KB1RAN
Hetty L Richardson
431 Main St
Orono ME 04473

Call Sign: AI1J
David E Kotecki
431 Main St
Orono ME 04473

Call Sign: KB1ORN
Noelle Keyser
188 Main St Apt - 1
Orono ME 04473

Call Sign: KB1ONV
4rf.Org Amateur Radio
Club
188 Main St Apt 1
Orono ME 044733866

Call Sign: KW4RF
4rf.Org Amateur Radio
Club
188 Main St Apt 1
Orono ME 044733866

Call Sign: KD6KUI
Christopher E Russell
188 Main Street Apt 1
Orono ME 04473

Call Sign: KB1VJV
Ali Abedi
31 Mainewood Ave
Orono ME 04473

Call Sign: KB1VJW
Masoumeh Esfahani
31 Mainewood Ave
Orono ME 04473

Call Sign: WB1DQK
Dennis W Martin
1 Marsh Ln Apt 1f
Orono ME 04473

Call Sign: WA4SWM
John F Hackney Jr
51 N Main Ave
Orono ME 04473

Call Sign: N1ZMO
Ronald J Bryant

20 N Main St
Orono ME 04473

Call Sign: N1ZMP
Benjamin H Bryant
20 N Main St
Orono ME 04473

Call Sign: K1MJC
Francis R Wihbey
16 Noyes Dr
Orono ME 044733671

Call Sign: N1QAR
Caroline R Tjepkema
25 Old Kelly Ave
Orono ME 04473

Call Sign: KD1OC
Benjamin K Pickering
2 Park Ln
Orono ME 04473

Call Sign: N1NSW
Christopher J Chilelli
156 Park St
Orono ME 04473

Call Sign: N1XJU
Joseph E Leavitt
40 Penobscot St
Orono ME 04473

Call Sign: N1XJW
Anita M Leavitt
40 Penobscot St
Orono ME 04473

Call Sign: N1CNB
Paul J Farr
199 Stillwater Ave
Orono ME 044731017

Call Sign: N1SES
Lloyd H Stitham Jr

73 Stillwater Ave Lot 21
Orono ME 04473

Call Sign: WA1VXP
Charles H Whorton
14 Whorton Rd
Orono ME 04473

Call Sign: KB1DCU
Michael C Dudley
5783 York Hall Rm 412
Orono ME 04474

Call Sign: N1OJG
Damon M Kiesow
Orono ME 04473

Call Sign: N1UTG
Edward R Lyon
Orono ME 04473

FCC Amateur Radio Licenses in Orrington

Call Sign: N1IEA
John K Watters
Route 1 Box 156
Orrington ME 04474

Call Sign: N1OWJ
Peter J Swett
Rt 2 Box 35
Orrington ME 04474

Call Sign: W1EXD
Edwin W Hadley
Rfd 1 Box 517
Orrington ME 04474

Call Sign: KA1JEZ
Arlan E Hurd
Rt 1 Box 588
Orrington ME 04474

Call Sign: K1EEP

Donald C Ernst Sr
Rfd 2 Box 716
Orrington ME 04474

Call Sign: K1ADY
Mary C Hadley
898 Brewer Lake Rd
Orrington ME 04474

Call Sign: AF4XF
Burton K Snowman
1019 Brewer Lake Road
Orrington ME 04474

Call Sign: AB1IK
Burton K Snowman
1019 Brewer Lake Road
Orrington ME 04474

Call Sign: K1IKI
Reginald C Faulkingham
506 Dow Rd
Orrington ME 04474

Call Sign: W1SG
Scott E Bates
521 Dow Road
Orrington ME 04474

Call Sign: N1KVI
David S Armstrong
14 Fields Pond Road
Orrington ME 04474

Call Sign: W1CN
Bonnie F Lufkin
14 Fields Pond Road
Orrington ME 04474

Call Sign: W1WL
Colby W Lufkin
14 Fields Pond Road
Orrington ME 04474

Call Sign: N1PRD

Allan H Elkin
28 Johnson Mill Rd
Orrington ME 04474

Call Sign: W1ANR
Allan H Elkin
28 Johnson Mill Rd
Orrington ME 04474

Call Sign: N1MCT
James R Sturgeon
141 Johnson Mill Rd
Orrington ME 04474

Call Sign: K1SIV
Merrill P Richardson
136 Richardson Rd
Orrington ME 04474

Call Sign: N1LAS
Charles M Kennedy
865 River Road
Orrington ME 04474

Call Sign: WB1CUD
Mark R Buongirno
1365 River Road
Orrington ME 04474

Call Sign: KA1BWG
Paul W Bouchard
38 Settlers Way
Orrington ME 044743642

Call Sign: N1MKQ
Hazen E King
Rfd 2 Swetts
Orrington ME 04474

Call Sign: N1OXW
Jonathan W Bemis
20 Turkey Lane
Orrington ME 04474

FCC Amateur Radio Licenses in Orrs Island

Call Sign: N1MQX
Bruce A Freeman
1713 Harpswell Islands Rd
Orrs Island ME 04066

Call Sign: KA1BIV
Douglas L Skillin
Orrs Island ME 04066

Call Sign: KB1JBP
Raymond A Dixon Jr
Orrs Island ME 04066

FCC Amateur Radio Licenses in Otis

Call Sign: WB1DEG
Gary G Wheaton
445 Point Rd
Otis ME 04605

FCC Amateur Radio Licenses in Otisfield

Call Sign: KB1IKL
Melissa A Pelletier
273 Bean Rd
Otisfield ME 04270

Call Sign: KB1PZR
Jack L Eaton
474 Bolsters Mills Rd
Otisfield ME 042707020

Call Sign: KB1GWT
Jesse L Cottingham
819 Bolsters Mills Rd
Otisfield ME 04270

Call Sign: KB1JZW
John Cottingham
819 Bolsters Mills Rd

Otisfield ME 04270

Call Sign: K1GRO
Ernest G Mason
497 Bolsters Mills Rd.
Otisfield ME 04270

Call Sign: WB2RRP
Kai A Pedersen
223 Rayville Rd
Otisfield ME 042706009

Call Sign: N1XRH
Nicolette T Spear
188 Scribner Hill Rd
Otisfield ME 04270

Call Sign: N1RPG
Rhonda A Beaudet
541 Scribner Hill Road
Otisfield ME 04270

Call Sign: N1RPI
Tarain L Beaudet
Scribner Hill Road
Otisfield ME 04270

FCC Amateur Radio Licenses in Otter Creek

Call Sign: N1XJT
Robert C Voisine
57 Otter Creek Drive
Otter Creek ME 04660

FCC Amateur Radio Licenses in Owls Head

Call Sign: KB1CLJ
Paul Klainer
533 Ash Point Dr
Owls Head ME 04854

Call Sign: N1MGQ
Robert S Pratt

4 Beach St
Owls Head ME 04854

Call Sign: KA1RIW
Alfred W Young
Hc 32 Box 2147
Owls Head ME 048549603

Call Sign: KC5ZPK
Sandra D Lovley
64 Crocketts Beach Rd
Owls Head ME 04854

Call Sign: KD5ADD
Shane B Lovley
64 Crocketts Beach Rd
Owls Head ME 04854

Call Sign: WH6CT
Sandra D Lovley
64 Crocketts Beach Rd
Owls Head ME 04854

Call Sign: K3LLC
Larry L Choate
43 Freedom Drive
Owls Head ME 04854

Call Sign: K1NOX
Larry L Choate
43 Freedom Drive
Owls Head ME 04854

Call Sign: W1LYX
Reino O Kangas
66 Hendrickson Point Road
Owls Head ME 048543331

Call Sign: KB1IOJ
Jason A Philbrook
111 Lucia Beach Rd
Owls Head ME 04854

Call Sign: KB1URB
Thomas S Ames

17 Meadowbrook Lane
Owls Head ME 04854

Call Sign: W1OWL
David W Darnell
178 South Shore Drive
Owls Head ME 04854

Call Sign: K1OWL
Andrew M Sheppe
15 Weeks Rd
Owls Head ME 04854

Call Sign: KB1VDK
Joseph M Gamage
3 Woodmans Trailer Park
Owls Head ME 04854

Call Sign: KB1TCE
Stephen P Hansen
Owls Head ME 04854

**FCC Amateur Radio
Licenses in Oxbow**

Call Sign: N1FCM
David A Dow
Main Rd
Oxbow ME 04764

**FCC Amateur Radio
Licenses in Oxford**

Call Sign: KB1LJB
Jacob J Knight
13 Allen Hill Rd
Oxford ME 04270

Call Sign: KB1LBI
Yvette L Rheault
14 Allen Hill Rd
Oxford ME 04270

Call Sign: KB1LBJ
David L Davidson

14 Allen Hill Rd
Oxford ME 04270

Call Sign: KB1LBK
Kelsie J Davidson
14 Allen Hill Rd
Oxford ME 04270

Call Sign: KB1LJA
Ethan D Davidson
14 Allen Hill Rd
Oxford ME 04270

Call Sign: KB1UHU
Raymond A Hanson
288 Allen Hill Rd
Oxford ME 04270

Call Sign: K1RAH
Raymond A Hanson
288 Allen Hill Rd
Oxford ME 04270

Call Sign: N1MTA
Robert R Ivey
119 Aspen Ave
Oxford ME 04270

Call Sign: KA2FHU
Joel H Dulberg
241 Black Island Rd
Megquier Island
Oxford ME 04270

Call Sign: N1VCM
Robert E Leigh
Rr 2 Box 1790
Oxford ME 04270

Call Sign: KA1FOU
Carroll W Parsons
Box 286
Oxford ME 04270

Call Sign: W1IF

Robert A Albrightson
556 East Oxford Road
Oxford ME 04270

Call Sign: N1JTH
Douglas E Rugg
127 Fore St.
Oxford ME 04270

Call Sign: N1ZIR
Gerri B Rugg
127 Fore Street
Oxford ME 04270

Call Sign: KB1KNC
Damian D Auger
26 Gary Street
Oxford ME 04270

Call Sign: W1CWP
Carroll W Parsons
1008 Gore Rd
Oxford ME 04270

Call Sign: N1TYB
Robert A Libby
13 Independence Dr
Oxford ME 04270

Call Sign: KB1NJL
Aaron J Haslett
25 Jenny Lane
Oxford ME 04270

Call Sign: N1WFP
Marshall S Douglass
664 Maine St
Oxford ME 04270

Call Sign: WB2ORY
Richard F Maloon
Box 2845 Otisfield Gore Rd
Oxford ME 04270

Call Sign: KA1VFR

Doug J Bourque
35 Penley Ln
Oxford ME 04270

Call Sign: KB1UDC
Daniel J Cooper
30 Record Lane
Oxford ME 04270

Call Sign: N1LNY
David T Mc Kay
Box 2832 Rfd 1
Oxford ME 04210

Call Sign: KB1IJJ
James A Tufts
28 Robinson Hill Rd
Oxford ME 04270

Call Sign: KB1IJK
Anita J Tufts
28 Robinson Hill Rd
Oxford ME 04270

Call Sign: AA1PD
George A Spear
188 Scribner Hill Rd
Oxford ME 04270

Call Sign: N1MBY
James L Packard Jr
89 Webber Brook Rd.
Oxford ME 04270

Call Sign: N1MNS
Betty J Packard
89 Webber Brook Road
Oxford ME 04270

Call Sign: N1XKW
Bertrand W Rugg Iii
254 Webber Brook Road
Oxford ME 04270

Call Sign: KB1IIA

Frances L Rugg
254 Webberbrook Rd
Oxford ME 04270

Call Sign: KB1CKL
Scott J Pelletier
Oxford ME 04270

Call Sign: N1VVJ
Dennis R Anderson
Oxford ME 04270

Call Sign: N1XKZ
Christine H Anderson
Oxford ME 042700216

Call Sign: KB1GCY
Timothy E Douglas
Oxford ME 04270

Call Sign: KB1WKU
George B Gardner Iii
Oxford ME 04270

FCC Amateur Radio Licenses in Palermo

Call Sign: KB1UTD
Michael O Coulombe
200 Gore Rd
Palermo ME 04354

Call Sign: KB1NNJ
Peter S Cote
1032 Parmenter Rd
Palermo ME 04354

Call Sign: K1ACO
Peter S Cote
1032 Parmenter Rd
Palermo ME 04354

Call Sign: WB1DPM
John A Bradstreet
1640 Route 3

Palermo ME 04354

Call Sign: KB1HZU
Michael E Mccarty
20 Turner Ridge
Palermo ME 04354

Call Sign: KA1AJA
Deborah L Leavitt
Rr 1 Turner Ridge Rd
Palermo ME 04270

FCC Amateur Radio Licenses in Palmyra

Call Sign: N1XMK
Beverly N Breau
364 Ell Hill Rd
Palmyra ME 04965

Call Sign: KB1CWK
Joann L Brown
140 Gee Rd
Palmyra ME 04965

Call Sign: N1OPU
Darrin S Dyer
53 Raymond Road
Palmyra ME 04965

Call Sign: WA1SZN
Clyde G Whitten
374 St Albans Rd
Palmyra ME 04965

Call Sign: KB1PTS
Daniel P Mouland
290 Warren Hill Rd
Palmyra ME 04965

Call Sign: N1QPD
Edward A Blake
617 Warren Hill Rd
Palmyra ME 04965

Call Sign: N1NKE
Warren P Blake
641 Warren Hill Rd.
Palmyra ME 04965

Call Sign: KA1FDS
J Robert Le Blanc
Palmyra ME 04965

Call Sign: N1XTG
Dean M Wilber
Palmyra ME 049650139

Call Sign: KB1SBY
Frederick A Campbell
Palmyra ME 04965

FCC Amateur Radio Licenses in Paris

Call Sign: K1SKI
William H Bowman
56 Tremont St
Paris ME 04271

FCC Amateur Radio Licenses in Parkman

Call Sign: KB1IHI
David M Hession
65 Landers Rd
Parkman ME 04443

Call Sign: N1SYW
Marvin S Wilhite
32 Sate Hwy 150
Parkman ME 04443

FCC Amateur Radio Licenses in Parsonsfield

Call Sign: W1VCL
David Mooers
328 Federal Rd
Parsonsfield ME 040470202

Call Sign: N1HCQ
Thomas W Yoder Jr
42 Hammond Road
Parsonsfield ME 04047

Call Sign: KB1WEX
Thomas A Searway
635 North Rd
Parsonsfield ME 04047

Call Sign: KB1PZU
Clement J Schaffer
1594 North Rd
Parsonsfield ME 04047

Call Sign: KB1PZV
Kim J Gray
1594 North Road
Parsonsfield ME 04047

Call Sign: KC1CS
James F Sheehan
4 Robins Ln
Parsonsfield ME 04047

Call Sign: KA1OPP
Steven H Simpson
Parsonsfield ME 040470282

FCC Amateur Radio Licenses in Parsonsfield Road

Call Sign: KC1YH
Bo T Yoder
42 Hammond Road
Parsonsfield Road ME 04047

FCC Amateur Radio Licenses in Passadumkeag

Call Sign: N2DKJ
Clinton Gaskill Jr

Fire Lane 5
Passadumkeag ME 04475

Call Sign: N1JNP
Tadeusz Kajkowski
268 Main Rd
Passadumkeag ME
044753109

Call Sign: N1JNR
Sylvia M Cockburn
Passadumkeag ME 04475

Call Sign: N1NPL
Erik D Cockburn
Passadumkeag ME 04475

Call Sign: WA1JGO
Edward H Cockburn
Passadumkeag ME
044750106

FCC Amateur Radio Licenses in Patten

Call Sign: W1FKJ
Maynard W Bray
Finch Hill
Patten ME 04765

Call Sign: N1XQJ
Robert A Mycroft
218 Happy Corner Rd
Patten ME 04765

Call Sign: KB1CMJ
Michael E Arbo
Shin Pond Rd
Patten ME 04765

Call Sign: K1EQD
Darryl F Smallwood
40 South Patten Rd
Patten ME 04765

Call Sign: W1PRS
Ty W Rodenizer
Patten ME 04765

Call Sign: KB1RQI
Robert A Mycroft Jr
Patten ME 04765

FCC Amateur Radio Licenses in Peaks Island

Call Sign: KA1QYY
Albert J Mc Cann
4 Greenwood St
Peaks Island ME 04108

Call Sign: KB1HUH
William J Desmond
33 Seashore Ave
Peaks Island ME 04108

Call Sign: AB1AS
William J Desmond
33 Seashore Ave
Peaks Island ME 04108

Call Sign: N1WJ
William J Desmond
33 Seashore Ave
Peaks Island ME 04108

Call Sign: W1YKR
Donald A Newcombe
94 Torrington Ave
Peaks Island ME 04108

Call Sign: N1NRD
Alexander Mills Jr
Peaks Island ME 04108

FCC Amateur Radio Licenses in Pemaquid

Call Sign: KF4NZD
Graham E W Searle

440 Old County Rd
Pemaquid ME 04558

Call Sign: KA1MUY
Duncan R Cameron
38 Riverview Rd
Pemaquid ME 04558

FCC Amateur Radio Licenses in Pembroke

Call Sign: KB1VDX
Joshua M Brown
1343 Ayers Jct
Pembroke ME 04666

Call Sign: N9IGA
Debra L Eckert
547 Ayers Jct Rd
Pembroke ME 04666

Call Sign: N9KC
Louis A Eckert
547 Ayers Jct Rd
Pembroke ME 04666

Call Sign: KT1R
Louis A Eckert
547 Ayers Jct Rd
Pembroke ME 04666

Call Sign: KN1TME
Debra L Eckert
547 Ayers Jct Rd
Pembroke ME 04666

Call Sign: KB1RQE
Allen C Weickers
597 Ayers Junction Rd
Pembroke ME 04666

Call Sign: KB1RQG
Troy L Palmeter Jr
1345 Ayers Junction Rd
Pembroke ME 04666

Call Sign: WB1EKS
Deborah M Jamieson
Rt 1 Box 289
Pembroke ME 04666

Call Sign: N1PPJ
Shasta D Knox
Rr 1 Box 88
Pembroke ME 04666

Call Sign: N1QJW
Steven L Knox
Rr 1 Box 88
Pembroke ME 04666

Call Sign: KB1UEX
Donald W Ross Jr
75 Clarkside Rd
Pembroke ME 04666

Call Sign: KB1VKL
Houston A Ross
75 Clarkside Rd
Pembroke ME 04666

Call Sign: KA1TSD
Charles Mitchell
13 Countryview Lane Apt 104
Pembroke ME 04666

Call Sign: AB1JH
Charles Mitchell
13 Countryview Lane Apt 104
Pembroke ME 04666

Call Sign: W1TSD
Charles Mitchell
13 Countryview Lane Apt 104
Pembroke ME 04666

Call Sign: KE1LG

Steven B Hanson
235 Garnet Head Road
Pembroke ME 04666

Call Sign: K1CFJ
Robert W Mackintire
399 Garnet Head Road
Pembroke ME 04666

Call Sign: NL7IR
Alfred L Van Sickel
448 Garnet Head Road
Pembroke ME 04666

Call Sign: KA1VKQ
Kevin E Stanhope
91 Hardy Point Road
Pembroke ME 04666

Call Sign: WA2MIS
Gary L Portnow
12 Loon Lane
Pembroke ME 04666

Call Sign: N8SAH
Deborah D Shields
344 Old County Road
Pembroke ME 046664625

Call Sign: N8SAI
Ralph E Shields
344 Old County Road
Pembroke ME 046664625

Call Sign: KB1RQF
Andrew D Hatton
35 Sandy Beach Ln
Pembroke ME 04666

Call Sign: KB1RQH
Ann M Carter
49 Smith Ridge Rd
Pembroke ME 04666

Call Sign: W1SFG

Paul E Thompson
Pembroke ME 04666

FCC Amateur Radio Licenses in Penobscot

Call Sign: KB1CTY
Laurier R Martel
Rr 1 Box 1270
Penobscot ME 04476

Call Sign: N1SMH
Alta A Harrison
Rr 1 Box 195
Penobscot ME 04476

Call Sign: KB1LDC
William R Mize
68 C Dunbar Rd
Penobscot ME 04476

Call Sign: KB1MDN
Sandra P Bendixen
68a Dunbar Rd
Penobscot ME 04476

Call Sign: KA1GFD
Steven P Belyea
North Penobscot Road
Penobscot ME 04476

Call Sign: KC1PP
Andrew L Abrams
P.O. Box 29
Penobscot ME 04476

Call Sign: KA1BC
David B Gross
Rfd Box 197
Penobscot ME 04476

Call Sign: KI6FL
William F Bromley
87 Seal Ledge Lane
Penobscot ME 044760138

Call Sign: KB1JQJ
Heather E Thompson
797 Southern Bay Rd
Penobscot ME 04476

Call Sign: NY1C
Philip R Leonard
825 Southern Bay Road
Penobscot ME 04476

Call Sign: KB1TGM
Justin C Willis
Penobscot ME 04476

FCC Amateur Radio Licenses in Perham

Call Sign: KA1IWX
Henry J Nutting
371 Nutting Rd
Perham ME 04766

Call Sign: N1MQP
Ethel M Nutting
371 Nutting Rd
Perham ME 04766

Call Sign: K1ASJ
Robert S Wilk
757 Perham Rd
Perham ME 04766

Call Sign: KB1TDS
Tina R Bogdanovic
792 Tangle Ridge Rd
Perham ME 04766

Call Sign: KB1CLC
David L Garey
793 Tangle Ridge Rd
Perham ME 04766

Call Sign: KB1EBH
Sylvia K Garey

793 Tangle Ridge Rd
Perham ME 047664008

FCC Amateur Radio Licenses in Perry

Call Sign: KB1UEV
Andrew M Perna
510 Cannon Hill Rd
Perry ME 04667

Call Sign: K1FSL
Leslie W Gross
520 Old Eastport Rd.
Perry ME 04667

Call Sign: W1SMQ
Harry J Raye
Rr 1 Shore Rd Box 28
Perry ME 04667

Call Sign: WA1LBS
Austin E Townsend Jr
1813 Us Route 1
Perry ME 04667

Call Sign: N1QPM
Richard F Goggin
Perry ME 04667

Call Sign: N1XHH
Donald L Calebaugh
Perry ME 04667

Call Sign: KB1HFC
Dennis W Dineen
Perry ME 04667

Call Sign: KB1HFE
Cynthia L Dineen
Perry ME 04667

Call Sign: KB1IVK
Christopher M Sullivan
Perry ME 04667

FCC Amateur Radio Licenses in Peru

Call Sign: KB1IEJ
Jean P Maurais
136 Auburn Rd
Peru ME 04290

Call Sign: KA1ZRB
Jason R Skeffington
Rfd 1 Box 1255
Peru ME 04290

Call Sign: W1LPZ
Ronald C Bryant
277 E Shore Rd
Peru ME 04290

Call Sign: KB1QHD
Joseph D Quirion
15 Hutchinson Rd
Peru ME 04290

Call Sign: WA1RKR
Robert F Skeffington
38 Packard Rd
Peru ME 04290

Call Sign: N1TIH
John W Dalzell
Peru ME 042900129

FCC Amateur Radio Licenses in Phillips

Call Sign: WA1KLI
John S Tarbox
20 Main Street
Phillips ME 04966

Call Sign: N1VHG
Dennis J Atkinson
459 Park St
Phillips ME 04966

Call Sign: N1QQQ
Bruce A Wilcox
112 Weld Road
Phillips ME 04966

Call Sign: W1GLG
Gerald L Grant
Phillips ME 049660103

Call Sign: KA1LFN
John E Halpin
27 Darling Lane
Phippsburg ME 04562

Call Sign: K1ZMB
John E Halpin
27 Darling Lane
Phippsburg ME 04562

Call Sign: KB1HSO
Joseph E Dauphin
3 Echo Ln
Phippsburg ME 04562

Call Sign: KB1PHT
Thomas O Jones Jr
11 Fred Brigham Rd
Phippsburg ME 04562

Call Sign: KA1SNP
Peter J Havens
441 Main Rd
Phippsburg ME 04562

Call Sign: KD1OG
James E Rounds Jr
454 Main Rd
Phippsburg ME 04562

Call Sign: N1MA
R Michael Adair

60 Parker Head Rd
Phippsburg ME 04562

Call Sign: KA1IPY
Alison S Adair
Parker Head Rd
Phippsburg ME 04562

Call Sign: KS1R
Merrymeeting Amateur
Radio Association
1 Smithfield Crossing
Phippsburg ME 045624047

Call Sign: W1ZE
Joseph B Randall
1 Smithfield Crossing
Phippsburg ME 04562

Call Sign: N1PAA
Donald E Dauphin Jr
124 Stoney Brook Rd
Phippsburg ME 04562

Call Sign: KB1IEF
Louise M Dauphin
124 Stoney Brook Rd
Phippsburg ME 04562

Call Sign: WD1F
Donald E Dauphin Jr
124 Stoney Brook Rd
Phippsburg ME 04562

Call Sign: N1YTJ
James R Loney
190 Th Boulevard
Phippsburg ME 04562

Call Sign: KB1SDD
Gordon D Nash
Phippsburg ME 04562

Call Sign: KB1NLD
William Doane
4623 Beans Corner Rd
Pittsfield ME 04967

Call Sign: W1GWF
Louise H Wright
Box 2100r1
Pittsfield ME 04967

Call Sign: W1SRQ
Doris M Mac Gown
Rfd 1 Box 4990
Pittsfield ME 04967

Call Sign: W1HYH
Lester W Mac Gown
Rfd 1 Box 4990
Pittsfield ME 04967

Call Sign: N1UAK
Sandra S Mac Gown
Rr 1 Box 4990
Pittsfield ME 04968

Call Sign: K1HAQ
Jasper A Farrington Jr
775 Canaan Rd
Pittsfield ME 049675543

Call Sign: KA1HRZ
William H Booth
24 Chester St
Pittsfield ME 04967

Call Sign: N1QLK
David R Lessard
13 Davis St
Pittsfield ME 04967

Call Sign: KB1OBQ
Bernard C Williams
7 First St
Pittsfield ME 04967

Call Sign: W1HYH
Richard H Mac Gown
40 Grant Road
Pittsfield ME 04967

Call Sign: KB1MAD
Dianne T Osgood
1610 Grove Hill Road
Pittsfield ME 04967

Call Sign: N1JSD
Christopher H Weymouth
100 Hussey Road
Pittsfield ME 04967

Call Sign: W1MES
Joseph W Hohn
199 Main Street
Pittsfield ME 04967

Call Sign: W7WWA
Jeff W Stevens
119 Manson Street
Pittsfield ME 04967

Call Sign: KA1YIN
Edovidio Carranza
4 Pittsfield Gardens
Pittsfield ME 04967

Call Sign: N1JYC
Malcolm M Burrell
Rfd 2
Pittsfield ME 04967

Call Sign: WA1RGQ
Edward E Sprague
39 Sebasticook St
Pittsfield ME 04967

Call Sign: N1KHU
Cathleen H Knox
593 Snake Root Rd
Pittsfield ME 04967

Call Sign: N1JRO
Kenneth L Knox
593 Snakeroot Rd
Pittsfield ME 04967

Call Sign: KB1NYE
Levi K Ladd
125 So Main St
Pittsfield ME 04967

Call Sign: KB1PAD
Helen E Campbell
292 Somerset Ave
Pittsfield ME 049671432

Call Sign: W1PYY
Guy L Wood
8 South St
Pittsfield ME 04967

Call Sign: N1RCV
William E Hathaway Ii
7 Union St
Pittsfield ME 04967

Call Sign: N1TSK
Jeffrey S Becker
5 Waverly Ave
Pittsfield ME 04967

Call Sign: KB1TBE
George W Yarbrough
Pittsfield ME 049670048

FCC Amateur Radio Licenses in Pittston

Call Sign: N1SDQ
Peter E Pinkham
Rr#4 Box 7520
Pittston ME 04345

Call Sign: KA1IIC
Vincent G Werber

137 Hunts Meadow Rd
Pittston ME 043455941

Call Sign: N1YUX
Harriet S Werber
137 Hunts Meadow Rd
Pittston ME 043455941

Call Sign: K1FYD
Jack Fitzgerald
691 Nash Road
Pittston ME 04345

Call Sign: N1XRB
William L Baxter
59 Old County Road
Pittston ME 04345

Call Sign: KB1HPD
Aaron D Moody
12 Ripley Rd
Pittston ME 04345

Call Sign: KB1TIY
Warren P Armstrong Jr
35 Smithtown Rd
Pittston ME 04345

Call Sign: KB1ABH
Richard L Hanson
43 Turner Drive
Pittston ME 04345

Call Sign: KA1RFD
Rodney L Scribner
72 Turner Road
Pittston ME 04345

Call Sign: KB1EKY
Thomas D Bailey
30 Webb Rd
Pittston ME 04345

Call Sign: KK5RR
Barney M Price

623 Wiscasset Rd
Pittston ME 04345

FCC Amateur Radio Licenses in Plymouth

Call Sign: N1YMM
Lawrence W Raymond Jr
733 Clark Road
Plymouth ME 04969

Call Sign: KB1KPI
Lisa A Chase
733 Clark Road
Plymouth ME 049693224

Call Sign: KB1NGK
Calvin J Cobb
733 Clark Road
Plymouth ME 049693224

Call Sign: N1XIM
Drew D Northup
88 Condon Rd
Plymouth ME 049693024

Call Sign: K1TES
Cyrus R Currier
69 Etna Rd W
Plymouth ME 049690060

Call Sign: WA3GHL
Frank P Swan
404 Loud Rd
Plymouth ME 04969

Call Sign: W1GHL
Frank P Swan
404 Loud Rd
Plymouth ME 04969

Call Sign: W1NOV
Thomas Novak
379 Ridge Rd
Plymouth ME 04969

Call Sign: N1OJF
Barbara B Swan
Plymouth ME 04969

Call Sign: KB1NDH
Sally R Currier
Plymouth ME 04969

Call Sign: N1TES
Sally R Currier
Plymouth ME 04969

FCC Amateur Radio Licenses in Poland

Call Sign: N1ART
Roger Sklar
Hc 33 Box 426-5
Poland ME 04275

Call Sign: N1SEL
William R Force
110 Brown Rd
Poland ME 04274

Call Sign: KB1RSD
Jason A Gawenus
23 Chestnut Dr
Poland ME 04274

Call Sign: KB1SSB
Jessica M Gawenus
23 Chestnut Dr
Poland ME 04274

Call Sign: K1GUR
Harold J Goss Sr
24 Goss Way
Poland ME 02474

Call Sign: N1ZNK
Robbie L Walker
21 Lakewood Lane
Poland ME 04274

Call Sign: KB1FWB
Poland Regional High
School Radio Club
1457 Maine St
Poland ME 04274

Call Sign: KB1KAG
Carolyn D Limerick
28 Maple Ln
Poland ME 04274

Call Sign: WB1GBC
David R Guay
14 Mark St
Poland ME 04274

Call Sign: N1XDI
Erland N Tucker
38 Megquier Hill Rd
Poland ME 04274

Call Sign: N1XUB
Esther A Tucker
38 Megquier Hill Rd
Poland ME 04274

Call Sign: KB1ECG
Andrew J Fogg
344 Schellinger Rd
Poland ME 04274

Call Sign: KB1CHI
Roger T Landry
97 Verrill Rd
Poland ME 04274

Call Sign: KB1OWB
Mary Karren- Landry
97 Verrill Rd
Poland ME 042745315

Call Sign: N1SDH
Marc R Bilodeau
Poland ME 042740180

FCC Amateur Radio Licenses in Poland Spring

Call Sign: N1RWO
Normand A Groleau
Rt 2 Box 540
Poland Spring ME 04274

Call Sign: W1JD
Donald S Winslow
8 Cardinal Ln
Poland Spring ME 04274

Call Sign: W1UPQ
Wanda M Winslow
8 Cardinal Ln
Poland Spring ME 04274

Call Sign: K1GMV
Harold J Goss Jr
23 Goss Way
Poland Spring ME 04274

Call Sign: W1CUW
Salvatore J Aliano
25 Julie St
Poland Spring ME 04274

Call Sign: KA1GHF
Peter B Magee
203 North Raymond Rd
Poland Spring ME
042749716

Call Sign: KB1ARD
Gretchen A Dutkiewicz
293 Schellinger Road
Poland Spring ME
042746129

Call Sign: KC5HN
Rodney W Winslow
57 Walker Point Rd
Poland Spring ME 04274

FCC Amateur Radio Licenses in Port Clyde

Call Sign: KR1E
Patricia Wakefield
Glenmere Rd
Port Clyde ME 04855

Call Sign: KB1DDF
Cherie A Yattaw
Port Clyde ME 048550117

Call Sign: N1UYT
Clifton W Yattaw Jr
Port Clyde ME 04855

Call Sign: W4SHE
Richard Laubly Ii
Port Clyde ME 04855

Call Sign: W9AMY
George H Krauss Iii
Port Clyde ME 04855

Call Sign: WA1SAZ
Nathan D Marvin
Port Clyde ME 04855

FCC Amateur Radio Licenses in Portage

Call Sign: KA1AOK
Freeland D Skidgel
West Lake Rd
Portage ME 04768

FCC Amateur Radio Licenses in Porter

Call Sign: N1ZEE
Christopher E Caouette
495 Bickford Pond Rd
Porter ME 04068

Call Sign: W1DQY
Peter J Mc Manus
Box 38
Porter ME 04068

Call Sign: W1ISI
Charles E Miller
88 Hoover Pt.
Porter ME 04068

Call Sign: K1WTZ
Arthur G Dullinger Jr
381 Ossipee Trail
Porter ME 04068

Call Sign: N1DGF
Neil B Walker
468 Porterfield Rd
Porter ME 04068

Call Sign: KA1CNG
Dennis R Whitten
8 Whitten Way
Porter ME 04068

FCC Amateur Radio Licenses in Portland

Call Sign: KB1HQS
Stuart H Thomas
Po Box 9739 #1102
Portland ME 04104

Call Sign: W1PMC
Peter M Carpenter
244 Bancroft St
Portland ME 041021729

Call Sign: N1KTA
Thomas E Berman
25 Bartlett St
Portland ME 04103

Call Sign: KA1KLS
Marc E Drabik

7 Bayview Terrace
Portland ME 04103

Call Sign: KA1KXA
Bethany K Drabik
7 Bayview Terrace
Portland ME 04103

Call Sign: KD1ZI
Donald B Wildes Jr
23 Bayview Terrace
Portland ME 04103

Call Sign: KA1NXJ
Harry L Marsters Ii
9 Belden St
Portland ME 041031203

Call Sign: KB1VCX
Jefferson Gaynor
44 Berkeley St Apt 1
Portland ME 04103

Call Sign: KB1BOC
Denise W Paige
32 Bernard Rd
Portland ME 04103

Call Sign: N1ZPB
Edwin E Paige
32 Bernard Rd
Portland ME 04103

Call Sign: KC1UX
John M Ney Sr
19 Birchwood Dr
Portland ME 04102

Call Sign: KB1MVQ
Matthew R Lapointe
262 Brackett St Apt - 1
Portland ME 04102

Call Sign: K3XX
Kenneth E Grossweiler

935 Brighton Avenue
Portland ME 04102

Call Sign: KB1JY
Kenneth H Wickwire
167 Caleb Street
Portland ME 04102

Call Sign: W1KB
Daniel F Bowen
257 Canco Rd - Apt 327
Portland ME 04103

Call Sign: W1IOK
Zenon J Litwinowich
257 Canco Road #307
Portland ME 04103

Call Sign: WA1YNN
Francis G Fortin
63 Carleton St
Portland ME 04102

Call Sign: KB1IBA
Arnold G Peterson
105 Carlyle Rd
Portland ME 041033427

Call Sign: NX1C
George F Leahy
53 Carter St
Portland ME 04103

Call Sign: K1GAX
Bryce P Rumery
37 Casco Street Apt. 513
Portland ME 04101

Call Sign: KB1MQJ
Igor Begovic
131 Chadwick St Apt 53
Portland ME 04102

Call Sign: KA1ZIG
Gary J Anderson

Chandlers Wharf Marina
Portland ME 041127952

Call Sign: N1BNB
David G Bailey
39 Chesley Ave
Portland ME 04103

Call Sign: KB1FHL
Matthew J Mueller
92 Clifton St
Portland ME 04103

Call Sign: WA1CVU
Michael L Ward
169 Clinton St
Portland ME 04103

Call Sign: KA1PLU
Richard A Norton
24 Cobbert Rd
Portland ME 04102

Call Sign: WB2JLE
Bernard J Gordon
94 Codman St
Portland ME 04103

Call Sign: N1UXT
Gibbs M Zabot Hall
243 Congress St
Portland ME 04101

Call Sign: KB1DNB
Kenneth P Kelly
743 Congress St
Portland ME 04102

Call Sign: N1ON
Peter B Hayward
1239 Congress St
Portland ME 04102

Call Sign: KB1PRJ
Michael J Davis

764 Congress St 3
Portland ME 04102

Call Sign: KB1JBD
William E Soares Iii
684a Congress St Apt 4
Portland ME 04101

Call Sign: K1SA
Bernard G Cohen
194 Craigie St
Portland ME 04102

Call Sign: KB1RUR
Maine FOC
194 Craigie St
Portland ME 04102

Call Sign: WA1FOC
Maine FOC
194 Craigie St
Portland ME 04102

Call Sign: WB9NZN
Matthew J Mueller
341 Cumberland Ave Apt
17
Portland ME 04101

Call Sign: KB1GLX
Paul P Clark
158 Cumberland Ave Apt 3
Portland ME 04101

Call Sign: KM5XV
Robert S Heiser
25 Cushman St Unit 2
Portland ME 04102

Call Sign: KE1MH
Robert S Heiser
25 Cushman St Unit 2
Portland ME 04104

Call Sign: KG2IC

Bruce J Howes
29 Cushman Street
Portland ME 04102

Call Sign: N1WGO
John D Hodges Ii
416 Danforth St.
Portland ME 04092

Call Sign: KB1GLV
Donald W Littlefield
63 Deane St
Portland ME 04102

Call Sign: KB1GRV
Heather A Treadwell
63 Deane St 1
Portland ME 04102

Call Sign: W1ZW
Robert S Thing
22 Deblois St
Portland ME 041033010

Call Sign: W1LNI
Russell H Lowd
28 Dennett St
Portland ME 04102

Call Sign: N1ZSY
Elizabeth B Trice
100 Dorset St
Portland ME 04102

Call Sign: AB1HX
Julie R Ellis
116 Douglass St
Portland ME 04102

Call Sign: W1HWP
Frank M Ingerowski
6 Edwards St
Portland ME 04102

Call Sign: KB3FUR

Zdenka S Griswold
46 Federal Street
Portland ME 04101

Call Sign: N0DBI
Scott F Enos
70 Forest Ave
Portland ME 04101

Call Sign: KB1GLY
Paul W Clark Jr
335 Forest Ave 503
Portland ME 04101

Call Sign: N1IYV
Robert A Harriman
1350 Forest Ave 7
Portland ME 04103

Call Sign: N1UDD
James E Lamoin
774 Forest Ave Apt 2
Portland ME 04103

Call Sign: KB1IKQ
Jeremy L Gayette
1390 Forest Ave Apt 4a
Portland ME 04103

Call Sign: KB1LIQ
John W Sommer
51 Garrison St
Portland ME 04102

Call Sign: KB1ZV
David S Palmer
35 Garsoe
Portland ME 04103

Call Sign: K1SIW
David S Palmer
35 Garsoe Drive
Portland ME 04103

Call Sign: KD4PWG

Aaron M Sigel
124 Grant St #1
Portland ME 04101

Call Sign: W1EIL
Robert Checkoway
72 Gray St
Portland ME 04102

Call Sign: W1ODA
Nathan J Copeland
72 Groveside Rd
Portland ME 04102

Call Sign: WA1AW
John J Kwoka
92 Hamblet Ave
Portland ME 04103

Call Sign: K1DRL
David R Lawson
35 Harris Ave
Portland ME 04103

Call Sign: N1BBY
Samantha E Darling
100 Harris Ave
Portland ME 04103

Call Sign: N1YTH
Elizabeth Darling
100 Harris Ave
Portland ME 04103

Call Sign: W9WBA
Dale M Darling
100 Harris Ave
Portland ME 04103

Call Sign: KB1GLW
Patricia A Littlefield
33 Hawthorne St
Portland ME 04103

Call Sign: KA1BER

Lloyd M Moss
49 Heather Rd
Portland ME 04103

Call Sign: K1LSJ
Bennett C Webber
106 Hersey St
Portland ME 04103

Call Sign: KA1NTZ
Joan D Robertson
180 High St 54
Portland ME 04101

Call Sign: KB1QDQ
Andrew S Marshall
198 High St Apt 9
Portland ME 04101

Call Sign: KB1STE
Laura K Welles
21 Holly St
Portland ME 04103

Call Sign: KB1FWF
Robert J Dailey
46 Irving St
Portland ME 04103

Call Sign: KB1JWL
Wellington E Lazette
96 Irving St
Portland ME 041033405

Call Sign: W1TBF
F Roger Butterfield
78 Lane Ave
Portland ME 04103

Call Sign: K2IPH
Marvin C Sachs
12 Lewis Street
Portland ME 04102

Call Sign: N1LWJ

Gerald J Buotte Sr
30 Libby St
Portland ME 04103

Call Sign: KB1PLY
Rory H Mcewen
14 Lloyd Ave
Portland ME 04103

Call Sign: KB1SHG
Joseph M Mcewen
14 Lloyd Ave
Portland ME 04103

Call Sign: KB1UPU
Wireless Society Of
Southern Maine
14 Lloyd Ave
Portland ME 04103

Call Sign: WS1SM
Wireless Society Of
Southern Maine
14 Lloyd Ave
Portland ME 04103

Call Sign: WA1KPZ
Margaret E Hutchins
388 Ludlow St
Portland ME 04102

Call Sign: W1GXI
Harold S Stitham
53 Mabel St
Portland ME 04103

Call Sign: K0VIY
Carl J Haney
14 Mackworth St
Portland ME 04103

Call Sign: KD4CAJ
Richard P Umbel Sr
45 Mackworth Street
Portland ME 04103

Call Sign: KB1GRW
Silver C Woodward
18 Mayland St
Portland ME 04103

Call Sign: KB0WZQ
Jordan D Palmer
14 Montrose Ave #3
Portland ME 04103

Call Sign: N1TYC
Steven B Grindle
115 Murray St
Portland ME 04103

Call Sign: KA1UDM
Richard L Fischer
31 Nevada Ave
Portland ME 04103

Call Sign: WA2TKT
Robert D Carlson
152 North St G04
Portland ME 04101

Call Sign: N1PEO
Roger A Emmons
68 Northwood Dr
Portland ME 041032063

Call Sign: N1VTQ
Kenneth B Mitchell
602 Ocean Avenue
Portland ME 04103

Call Sign: KB1HGA
Peter L Fulton
1050 Ocean Avenue
Portland ME 041034703

Call Sign: KA1JFD
Charles G Carswell
26 Panoramic View Dr
Portland ME 04103

Call Sign: KB1AJG
Robert D Smiley
120 Park Ave Apt 10
Portland ME 04101

Call Sign: WA2HLM
Jeffrey S Barkin
105 Parsons Rd
Portland ME 04103

Call Sign: KB1AXX
Louisa S Rocha Mc Carthy
129 Pine St
Portland ME 04102

Call Sign: KB1UOV
Peter C Harmon
77 Pine St Suite 2-2
Portland ME 04102

Call Sign: KG7XD
Gene P Mc Avoy
175b Pine Street
Portland ME 04102

Call Sign: KB1LIU
Cheryl F Jensen
169 Pinecrest Rd
Portland ME 04103

Call Sign: N1OAH
Philip J Kemp
87 Pleasant Ave
Portland ME 04103

Call Sign: N1PEM
Jeffrey A Campbell
254 Pleasant Ave
Portland ME 04102

Call Sign: KA1DSY
Jon D Soule
71 Plymouth St
Portland ME 04103

Call Sign: KA0KSL
Marilyn J Maggi
19 Range St
Portland ME 04103

Call Sign: K1PPM
Short Wave Society Of
Maine
20 Range St
Portland ME 041031136

Call Sign: K1PPN
William J Plante
20 Range Street
Portland ME 04103

Call Sign: W1CWW
William J Plante
20 Range Street
Portland ME 04103

Call Sign: W1RSX
Stephen J White
88 Read St
Portland ME 04103

Call Sign: K1QKW
Richard L Scott
128 Read St
Portland ME 041033483

Call Sign: KA1ODS
Irene M Scott
128 Read St
Portland ME 04103

Call Sign: N1CUK
Juergen W Bolte Jr
99 Revere St
Portland ME 04103

Call Sign: KB1FIE
Jeffrey J Parsons
723 Riverside St Apt 436

Portland ME 04103

Call Sign: N1ZQV
Shirley J Slauenwhite
15 Riverview St
Portland ME 041021721

Call Sign: KL0IT
Aaron E Werner
26 Rustic Lane
Portland ME 04103

Call Sign: W1AAA
Aaron E Werner
26 Rustic Lane
Portland ME 04103

Call Sign: KB1IAZ
Craig R Treadwell
6 Sara Ln
Portland ME 041033623

Call Sign: N1LLD
Clifton H Whitten
247 Sherwood St
Portland ME 04103

Call Sign: KB1EMQ
Edward M Domas
237 Sherwood St #1
Portland ME 04103

Call Sign: WB1EQY
Phillips H Prince
73 Skylark Rd
Portland ME 04103

Call Sign: W1DNY
William R Lairsey
40 Spar Lane
Portland ME 04102

Call Sign: KA1YEK
Joshua A Dolby
210 St. John Street

Portland ME 04101

Call Sign: KB1UQL
David L Michaud
62 State St 41
Portland ME 04101

Call Sign: AA1ZY
Donald W Littlefield
48 State St Apt 23
Portland ME 04101

Call Sign: KB1FIB
Paul A Leblond
55 Stevens Ave
Portland ME 04102

Call Sign: WA1ZAV
Patricia A Duncan
605 Stevens Ave
Portland ME 04103

Call Sign: WA1ZQI
Sr Mary D Schwartz
605 Stevens Ave
Portland ME 04103

Call Sign: AA4SN
Charles C Elliott
34 Summit Park Ave
Portland ME 04103

Call Sign: KA1IJT
Robert M Rodgers
216 Summit St
Portland ME 041032916

Call Sign: N9KWS
Andrew Whitcroft
147 Tarbell Ave
Portland ME 04103

Call Sign: N1HSB
Herbert Payson
Trust Dept Casco N Bank

Portland ME 04104

Call Sign: KA1RY
Frank J Amabile Sr
119 Tucker Ave
Portland ME 04103

Call Sign: N1CHL
William Fitz Jr
54 Turner St Apt 1
Portland ME 04101

Call Sign: N1FPT
Mark A Hathaway
248 Valley St
Portland ME 04102

Call Sign: KB1LIR
Matthew J Rooney
188 Vaughan St
Portland ME 04102

Call Sign: KB1PNB
Jeffrey B Ferland
91 Vesper St 1
Portland ME 04101

Call Sign: KB1IUN
Cary P Clements
63 Vesper St 3rd Floor
Portland ME 04101

Call Sign: KB1IKR
Michael J Fletcher
34 W Commonwealth Dr
Portland ME 04103

Call Sign: K1UC
Michael J Fletcher
34 W Commonwealth Dr
Portland ME 04103

Call Sign: N1SCR
Kenneth L Jack
145 Warren Ave

Portland ME 04103

Call Sign: KB1LIS
Gregory M Murphy
1969 Washington Ave
Portland ME 04103

Call Sign: KB1MQI
Christos V Christolow
1614 Washington Avenue
Portland ME 04103

Call Sign: W1GFO
Christos Christolow
1614 Washington Avenue
Portland ME 04103

Call Sign: N1SD
Jonathan A Taylor
12 Wayne St
Portland ME 04102

Call Sign: KA1ZVU
John W Bogner
90 Wayside Rd
Portland ME 041021831

Call Sign: W1JLB
John W Bogner
90 Wayside Rd
Portland ME 041021831

Call Sign: K1OEV
Dana B Estabrook
57 Wellstone Dr
Portland ME 041032761

Call Sign: N1GLQ
William T Webster Jr
25 West St
Portland ME 04102

Call Sign: KA1WBU
Robin M Fagan
34 West St

Portland ME 04102

Call Sign: WB1FNB
Charles W Wordell Jr
20 West St Apt 34
Portland ME 041023443

Call Sign: KC1HB
Frank L Chamberlain
94 Westland Ave
Portland ME 04102

Call Sign: KA1RDH
Anita Balzano
28 Westminister Ave
Portland ME 04103

Call Sign: KX1E
Robert W Coakley
34 Whitney Ave
Portland ME 04102

Call Sign: KB1LTI
Mary E Petersen
53 Whitney Ave
Portland ME 04102

Call Sign: K1MEP
Mary E Petersen
53 Whitney Ave
Portland ME 04102

Call Sign: KB1IRC
James R Jones
110 Whitney Ave
Portland ME 04102

Call Sign: N1OTD
Carolyn B Mills
76 Winter St 1
Portland ME 04102

Call Sign: KB1UOA
Roy L Ouellette
18 Wolcott St

Portland ME 04102

Call Sign: KA1LIZ
Keith L Savage
59 Woodford St
Portland ME 04103

Call Sign: K1JB
Joseph S Blinick
Portland ME 04104

Call Sign: KA1KKH
Stephen S Turbovsky
Portland ME 04104

Call Sign: KA1NKA
James M Quinn
Portland ME 04104

Call Sign: KA1QVN
Arthur J Di Rocco
Portland ME 041127542

Call Sign: N1LWB
Anthony R Lewis
Portland ME 04101

Call Sign: W1UMU
Alan A Ames Sr
Portland ME 04104

Call Sign: WX1U
Gary C W Nelson
Portland ME 04104

Call Sign: K4JAG
Joel A Glass
Portland ME 041041001

Call Sign: KB1HTR
Kimberly L Volk
Portland ME 041127711

Call Sign: KB1LBN
Daniel L Silliman

Portland ME 04104

Call Sign: KB1MSM
Alfred E Piombino
Portland ME 04104

Call Sign: KB1UOT
Art Vandelay
Portland ME 04112

Call Sign: KC1VAN
Art Vandelay
Portland ME 04112

Call Sign: KB1VZE
Francis C Brooks
Portland ME 04104

FCC Amateur Radio Licenses in Pownal

Call Sign: KA1RVT
Madelyn M Best
15 Allen Rd
Pownal ME 04069

Call Sign: KA1RWV
Emma R Condon
Rr 4 Box 4169
Pownal ME 04070

Call Sign: KA1RTW
Michael J Grace
24 Dows Ln
Pownal ME 04069

Call Sign: KA1BPJ
Donald H Ward
111 Hodsdon Rd
Pownal ME 040696410

Call Sign: KG4ODG
Stacie A Hanes
49 Hodsdon Road
Pownal ME 04069

Call Sign: W8MBD
Richard K Kinney
79 Hodson Rd
Pownal ME 04069

Call Sign: KB1VLB
Steven D Pettengill
595 Lawrence Rd
Pownal ME 04069

Call Sign: WB1GYL
Ellsworth Mc Donald
916 Lawrence Rd
Pownal ME 04069

Call Sign: N1YKY
Bradley P Burgess
181 Verrill Rd
Pownal ME 04069

FCC Amateur Radio Licenses in Prentiss Township

Call Sign: WA1JAS
Michael L Ward
693 Tar Ridge Rd
Prentiss Twp ME 04487

FCC Amateur Radio Licenses in Presque Isle

Call Sign: KB1WCB
Michael D Schrader
2 Airport Dr
Presque Isle ME 04769

Call Sign: N1JHR
Joshua M Spiers
95 Allen Rd
Presque Isle ME 04769

Call Sign: KA1CNC
Harold L Delano

15 Barton St
Presque Isle ME 047692421

Call Sign: N5IAA
Paula J Barrett
52 Barton St
Presque Isle ME 04769

Call Sign: WA5RPP
Samuel M Barrett Ii
52 Barton St
Presque Isle ME 04769

Call Sign: W5KF
Samuel M Barrett Ii
52 Barton St
Presque Isle ME 04769

Call Sign: KA1KME
Ronald R Beaulieu
10 Bridgeport Ct
Presque Isle ME 04769

Call Sign: KY1L
Peter M Underwood
29 Burlock Rd
Presque Isle ME 04769

Call Sign: KA1ETN
Milton P Mahaney
56 Caribou Rd
Presque Isle ME 04769

Call Sign: KB1JJG
Dale W Drost
37 Cedar St
Presque Isle ME 04769

Call Sign: KB1JJH
Leah J Drost
37 Cedar St
Presque Isle ME 04769

Call Sign: KB1MGV
Luke W Blackstone

379 Centerline Rd
Presque Isle ME 04769

Call Sign: KB1MGW
Gregory M Blackstone
379 Centerline Rd
Presque Isle ME 04769

Call Sign: KA1JC
Phyllis K Davis
43 Centerline Road
Presque Isle ME 04769

Call Sign: N1BJX
Elmer H Davis Jr
43 Centerline Road
Presque Isle ME 04769

Call Sign: KA1OEM
Harold A Lyford
4 City View Dr
Presque Isle ME 04769

Call Sign: KA1YKL
Eric D Burdo
26 Crestview Dr
Presque Isle ME 04769

Call Sign: KB1KZD
Daniel E Castle
28 Delmont St.
Presque Isle ME 04769

Call Sign: N1RUA
Leonard G Bragdon
Demerchants Tlr Pk Lot 15
Presque Isle ME 04769

Call Sign: KA1VHD
Carl H Doughty
96 Fleetwood St
Presque Isle ME 04769

Call Sign: K1TFX
George W Holst

379 Fort Fairfield Rd
Presque Isle ME 04769

Call Sign: K1TFW
Jacquelyne F Holst
379 Fort Fairfield Road
Presque Isle ME 04769

Call Sign: KB1IGV
Tammy L Deschesne
426 Fort Rd
Presque Isle ME 047691895

Call Sign: N1WAQ
Karl W Kornchuk
51 Hillside St
Presque Isle ME 04769

Call Sign: KB1VNY
Jeffrey R Nault
58 Hillside St
Presque Isle ME 04769

Call Sign: KA1TLC
Ronald H Soucier
18 Howard St
Presque Isle ME 04769

Call Sign: N1HSQ
Orel D Wiggins
56 Lakeshore Dr
Presque Isle ME 04769

Call Sign: KB1VNW
Maynard L Mcewen
56 Lombard St
Presque Isle ME 04769

Call Sign: KB1POK
Timothy W Duda
103 Lombard St
Presque Isle ME 04769

Call Sign: KA1QNB
Gregory C Daniels

97 Marston Rd
Presque Isle ME 04769

Call Sign: KB1GKY
Michael G Brown Ii
63 Oak Street
Presque Isle ME 04769

Call Sign: KA1YEY
Juergen A L Lochner
281 Parkhurst Siding Road
Presque Isle ME 04769

Call Sign: N1NGN
Randall W Harper
281 Parkhurst Siding Road
Presque Isle ME 04769

Call Sign: KA1KYJ
Harold J Morrissette Sr
9 Parsons St
Presque Isle ME 04769

Call Sign: N1UWZ
Sylvia A Bean
11 Sherwin St
Presque Isle ME 04769

Call Sign: N1SII
David A Morrow
9 Skyview Dr
Presque Isle ME 04769

Call Sign: N1QYU
Eric P Huoppi
205 Spragueville Road
Presque Isle ME 04769

Call Sign: KA1ZTJ
Wade E Woodworth
12 Spring St
Presque Isle ME 04769

Call Sign: N1MDV
Joyce L B Harper

79 State Park Rd
Presque Isle ME 04769

Call Sign: KB1QIB
Chris A Markey
17 State St
Presque Isle ME 04769

Call Sign: N1NXU
Steven Sandelier Sr
31 State St
Presque Isle ME 04769

Call Sign: KB1NLR
Michele H Lombard-Fowler
319 State St
Presque Isle ME 04769

Call Sign: K1FS
Aroostook Amateur Radio
Assn
31 State Street
Presque Isle ME 047692313

Call Sign: KA1PCP
Norman F Carlow Jr
8 Turner St
Presque Isle ME 04769

Call Sign: K1JCX
Earl D Bates
Presque Isle ME 04769

Call Sign: KA1TMZ
Brian L Jacobs Jr
Presque Isle ME 04769

Call Sign: KA1VDF
Clay V King
Presque Isle ME 04769

Call Sign: KB1ATN
Christine C Peary
Presque Isle ME 04769

Call Sign: KB1ATO
Hollis R Porter
Presque Isle ME 04769

Call Sign: KB1EBG
David R Deschesne
Presque Isle ME 047691310

Call Sign: WA1UPK
Stephen D Lord
Presque Isle ME 04769

Call Sign: KB1OWU
Zachary C Dow
Presque Isle ME 04769

FCC Amateur Radio Licenses in Princeton

Call Sign: KA1WZC
Mark E Dwelley
Box 407
Princeton ME 04668

Call Sign: KA1WZD
Michael J Dwelley
Box 407
Princeton ME 04668

Call Sign: WB1FOU
Ronald Tupper
937 Main St
Princeton ME 04668

Call Sign: WB1CZP
Charlotte M Hitchings
Box 145 Main St
Princeton ME 04668

Call Sign: K1HHC
Harland S Hitchings
Main St Box 145
Princeton ME 04668

Call Sign: N1OXY

James F Greenlaw Sr
131 Main Street
Princeton ME 046680008

FCC Amateur Radio Licenses in Prospect

Call Sign: N1ECP
William A Sneed Jr
38 Moody Rd
Prospect ME 049819720

FCC Amateur Radio Licenses in Prospect Harbor

Call Sign: WR1E
Mike H Summerer
32 Main Street
Prospect Harbor ME 04669

FCC Amateur Radio Licenses in Randolph

Call Sign: KA1IUD
Carl M Edwards
7 Fairview St
Randolph ME 04345

Call Sign: N1CVZ
Gary R Frost
9 Lincoln St
Randolph ME 043465140

Call Sign: KB1HZT
Kingsley Adams
11 Middle St
Randolph ME 04346

Call Sign: KB1IJE
Michael J Miller
18 Middle St Apt 1
Randolph ME 04346

Call Sign: K1JMM

Robert D Porter
63 Ridge Rd
Randolph ME 04346

Call Sign: WA1DXU
Robert V Burke
52 School Street
Randolph ME 04346

Call Sign: NS1Q
Marshall M White
1 Stevens Ave
Randolph ME 04356

Call Sign: N1GLW
Leigh K Walton
57 Windsor St
Randolph ME 04345

Call Sign: KB1FHY
James R Risch
201 Windsor St
Randolph ME 04346

Call Sign: K1HAR
Richard S Weeks
249 Windsor St
Randolph ME 043469701

Call Sign: NX1B
Paul H Hebb
267 Windsor St
Randolph ME 04346

Call Sign: KB1GXP
Josh H Barrett
29 Woodlawn Circle
Randolph ME 04346

FCC Amateur Radio Licenses in Rangeley

Call Sign: W1HPW
Henry P Wozniak
Box 444

Rangeley ME 04970

Call Sign: WA9TSS
Richard N Gacki
231 Dallas Hill Rd.
Rangeley ME 04970

Call Sign: W1PBE
Robert P Thayer
General Delivery
Rangeley ME 04970

Call Sign: W1UZZ
Richard E White Jr
2398 Main St Apt. #2
Rangeley ME 04970

Call Sign: KD4TAT
Robert R Freihoff-Lewin
Mr
247 Mingo Loop Rd
Rangeley ME 04970

Call Sign: KD4TAU
Patricia D Freihoff-Lewin
247 Mingo Loop Rd.
Rangeley ME 04970

Call Sign: KB1HBW
Francis F Jandreau
Winston Road
Rangeley ME 04970

Call Sign: K1FFJ
Francis F Jandreau
Winston Road
Rangeley ME 04970

Call Sign: WA1FDI
William H Epstein
Rangeley ME 04970

FCC Amateur Radio Licenses in Raymond

Call Sign: N1FJG
Rodney F Lebrun Jr
207 Aquila Rd
Raymond ME 04071

Call Sign: N1JRR
Chris W Applebee
3 Baker Street
Raymond ME 04071

Call Sign: W1SPJ
Paul S Hopkins
4 Brads Way
Raymond ME 04071

Call Sign: KB1RC
Jeffrey S Mac Kinnon
6 Brads Way
Raymond ME 040715522

Call Sign: KB1GWU
Albert W Knight
1 Brook Rd
Raymond ME 04071

Call Sign: N1CPL
Stuart W Mac Kinnon
Brown Rd Box 173
Raymond ME 04071

Call Sign: KB1HQT
Stephen C Perry
13 Casselton Rd
Raymond ME 04071

Call Sign: KB1VCV
John M Murray
5 Damon Rd
Raymond ME 04071

Call Sign: KB1GWV
William E Shively
70 Deep Cove Rd
Raymond ME 04071

Call Sign: KB1GWW
John W Shively
70 Deep Cove Rd
Raymond ME 04071

Call Sign: W1KVB
Donald F Gordan
Deep Cove Rd
Raymond ME 04071

Call Sign: N1ZQW
Kevin K Woodbrey
20 Egypt Rd
Raymond ME 04071

Call Sign: KB1GVL
Kyle K Woodbrey
20 Egypt Road
Raymond ME 04071

Call Sign: WB7AGY
Glen A Gisel
7 Main St
Raymond ME 040716518

Call Sign: KA1NUZ
Leonard S Noyes Jr
51 Martin Heights
Raymond ME 04071

Call Sign: KB1DSV
James M Waligora
384 N Raymond Rd
Raymond ME 040716007

Call Sign: N1XBM
Robert N Newberry
6 Outlaw Ridge Rd
Raymond ME 04071

Call Sign: KB1UOS
Breena M Newberry
6 Outlaw Ridge Rd
Raymond ME 04071

Call Sign: W1AND
Melvin A Heath Iii
3 Panther Pond Pines Rd
Raymond ME 04071

Call Sign: N1XYQ
Herbert L Jones
31 Pond Rd
Raymond ME 04071

Call Sign: W1RKM
Herbert L Jones
31 Pond Rd
Raymond ME 04071

Call Sign: KD1OB
Dean C Bridges
4 Ridge Rd
Raymond ME 04071

Call Sign: KE1T
Dean C Bridges
4 Ridge Rd
Raymond ME 04071

Call Sign: N1IZV
Ditson Welch
8 Ridge Rd
Raymond ME 04071

Call Sign: K1MJN
Charles L Cragin
85 Spring Valley Road
Raymond ME 040710248

Call Sign: N1BQT
Ralph A Estes
43 Tower Rd
Raymond ME 04071

Call Sign: KA1ZJO
J Richard Bodge
Raymond ME 04071

Call Sign: N1LTQ

Leslie J Stephenson Jr
Raymond ME 04071

Call Sign: W1NDH
Keith C Morton
Raymond ME 04071

**FCC Amateur Radio
Licenses in Readfield**

Call Sign: KA4HMB
Kostas P Papadakis
48 Harmony Hill
Readfield ME 04355

Call Sign: W1WYX
Peter D Stengel
30 Harmony Hills Rd
Readfield ME 04355

Call Sign: N1TXF
Richard A Smith
1520 Main St.
Readfield ME 04355

Call Sign: W1BFA
Ernest L Bracy
North Rd Readfield Corner
Readfield ME 04355

Call Sign: N2CGW
Robert S Bistrais
21 Rodrigue Ln
Readfield ME 04355

Call Sign: KB1VLC
Ryan D Freise
7 Stanley Rd
Readfield ME 04355

Call Sign: WA1FDU
Philip H Matthews Jr
525 Sturtevant Hill Rd
Readfield ME 04355

Call Sign: KB1OUJ
Lynn W Mecham
29 Wings Mills Rd
Readfield ME 04355

Call Sign: KA1CNS
Thomas H Jewett
Readfield ME 043550298

Call Sign: KB1WXZ
Claude E Rounds
Readfield ME 04355

Call Sign: WA1YZP
Steve D Gurin
59 Sturtevant Hill Rd
Readfield, ME 04355

**FCC Amateur Radio
Licenses in Richmond**

Call Sign: N1LVP
Craig J Deveau
Rr 1 Box 548
Richmond ME 04357

Call Sign: N1WZU
William Ruane
Rr 1 Box 770
Richmond ME 04358

Call Sign: N1XPY
Suzanne M Ruane
Rr 1 Box 770a
Richmond ME 04357

Call Sign: NO1H
Frank Thelen Iii
74 Brunswick Road
Richmond ME 043579700

Call Sign: KD1VN
Dana S Sullivan
21 Chestnut St
Richmond ME 04357

Call Sign: KA1DWO
Dana W Sullivan
3 Church St
Richmond ME 04357

Call Sign: KB1TFZ
Bruce L Arsenault
278 Front St
Richmond ME 04357

Call Sign: KA1QYU
Wilber A Cooper
Hillside St
Richmond ME 04357

Call Sign: N1ACK
Russell A Hudon
31 Kimball St. 1f
Richmond ME 04357

Call Sign: K1WGI
Bernard J Wisda
293 Langdon Road
Richmond ME 04357

Call Sign: W1SDA
Bernard J Wisda
293 Langdon Road
Richmond ME 04357

Call Sign: N1RCL
Eugene Vermillion
20 Lena Rd.
Richmond ME 04357

Call Sign: N1LJH
Marcia E Costello
21 Lincoln St
Richmond ME 04357

Call Sign: N1UME
John H Dailey
289 Main St
Richmond ME 04357

Call Sign: N1VY
John H Dailey
289 Main St
Richmond ME 04357

Call Sign: KA1MWG
Paul V Le Clair Jr
453 Main Street
Richmond ME 04357

Call Sign: N1KGB
Paul A Berry Jr
11 North Pleasant St.
Richmond ME 04357

Call Sign: KA1FTL
Michael C Bodge
129 Parks Rd
Richmond ME 04357

Call Sign: WA1ZJZ
Terrence M Dowd
166 Pitts Center Road
Richmond ME 04357

Call Sign: KJ6QO
Jeffrey B Herbster
12 Springer St
Richmond ME 04357

Call Sign: N1GLV
Richard D Ridenour
12 Springer St
Richmond ME 04357

Call Sign: WA1IVI
Alexander G Mac Donald
12 Tallman Street
Richmond ME 04357

**FCC Amateur Radio
Licenses in Robbinston**

Call Sign: KB1QFA

E Heather Sargent
232 Brewer Rd
Robbinston ME 04671

Call Sign: KB1QFB
Donald R Sargent
232 Brewer Rd
Robbinston ME 04671

Call Sign: K1QFB
Donald R Sargent
232 Brewer Rd
Robbinston ME 04671

Call Sign: KB1KBJ
Ellen J Johnson
187 Us Rt 1
Robbinston ME 04671

Call Sign: N1SCM
Bernard J Mc Nulty Jr
Robbinston ME 046710009

Call Sign: KB1KEJ
Dean Ingham
Robbinston ME 04671

Call Sign: KB1KIH
Dale H Wing
Robbinston ME 04671

Call Sign: KB1RQD
Edward F Harris
Robbinston ME 04671

FCC Amateur Radio Licenses in Rockland

Call Sign: KB1OGY
John P Bagley
65 Acadia Dr
Rockland ME 04841

Call Sign: N1MIN
Charles R Monteith Jr

11 Beech St
Rockland ME 04841

Call Sign: N1DXN
Harry W Baker
27 Birch St
Rockland ME 04841

Call Sign: KA1HGI
Charles F Bruce Jr
Rfd 1 Box 1490
Rockland ME 04841

Call Sign: N1QAW
Paul A Cole
148 Broadway 102
Rockland ME 04841

Call Sign: N1CTT
Otto C Bennett
148 Broadway Apt 208
Rockland ME 04841

Call Sign: W1RJP
Kenneth I Orcutt
68 Cedar St
Rockland ME 04841

Call Sign: W1TFK
Charles R Beals
78 Cedar St
Rockland ME 04841

Call Sign: KB1DKX
Dean W Buckley
11b Center St
Rockland ME 04841

Call Sign: N1UAL
Ann L Chase
26 Chestnut St
Rockland ME 04841

Call Sign: KB1PVU
Erwin K Lohner

3 Clayton Ln
Rockland ME 04841

Call Sign: AB1IR
Erwin K Lohner
3 Clayton Ln
Rockland ME 04841

Call Sign: KB1VJX
David H Mcguire
35 Dodge Mt Rd
Rockland ME 04841

Call Sign: W1QKK
Charles M Currier
11 Franklin
Rockland ME 04841

Call Sign: KC1EK
John S Taylor
22 Grove St
Rockland ME 04841

Call Sign: W1QJW
John Leech
45 Highland St
Rockland ME 04841

Call Sign: K1CNC
Ernest H Hammond
19 Highland Street
Rockland ME 04841

Call Sign: WB1CLM
Steven L Waterman
35 Holmes Street
Rockland ME 04841

Call Sign: N1UYY
Todd M Philbrook
91 Lawn Ave
Rockland ME 04841

Call Sign: KB1QLI
John J Blair

546 Main St
Rockland ME 04841

Call Sign: W1NNN
Mark K Marston
387 Main Street - Apt 204
Rockland ME 048410304

Call Sign: KA1GQG
Philip J Marcoux
39 Mechanic St
Rockland ME 04841

Call Sign: N1DFG
Milton F Eaton
35 Mountain View Ext
Rockland ME 048415721

Call Sign: KA1UL
William C Mutch
100 New County Rd
Rockland ME 04841

Call Sign: WA1RPN
Henry J Kennedy
4 Oliver Wood S
Rockland ME 04841

Call Sign: KB1SDJ
Marion L West Jr
59 Park St Apt A
Rockland ME 04841

Call Sign: KX1I
Francis L Weaver
1 Rankin St Apt 205
Rockland ME 04841

Call Sign: KB0VUE
Matthew D Murphy
39 Rankin Street
Rockland ME 04841

Call Sign: N1JMU
Bradford C Grindle Sr

15 Robinson St
Rockland ME 04841

Call Sign: KB1DQK
Elroy W Nash
39 Summer St Apt 3n
Rockland ME 04841

Call Sign: KB1IQB
Danica D Cowan
157 Talbot Ave
Rockland ME 04841

Call Sign: K1RPE
Wendell B Lewis
208 Talbot Ave
Rockland ME 048412260

Call Sign: WB2NNL
Richard J Korzenowski
222 Talbot Ave
Rockland ME 048415524

Call Sign: N1ZVO
Beverly J Cowan
157 Talbot Avenue
Rockland ME 048412211

Call Sign: N1WPR
Robert A Collins Jr
37 Willow Street
Rockland ME 04841

Call Sign: K1BGE
George Dedekian
Rockland ME 04841

Call Sign: K1FQE
Philip E Robinson
Rockland ME 04841

Call Sign: K1JFF
Paul W Moran
Rockland ME 048410684

Call Sign: N1NWV
Arvo G Salo
Rockland ME 04841

Call Sign: W1CR
Andrew J Staiano
Rockland ME 04841

Call Sign: KB1WBJ
Donna F Allen
Rockland ME 04841

FCC Amateur Radio Licenses in Rockport

Call Sign: WB1ATJ
Suzanne S Eichacker
4 Bristol Dr
Rockport ME 04856

Call Sign: WB1ATK
Richard F Eichacker
4 Bristol Dr
Rockport ME 04856

Call Sign: W1GLP
Gene L Piken
1 Lexington Ln
Rockport ME 04856

Call Sign: N1XGQ
Joshua D M Jinno
61 Main St
Rockport ME 04856

Call Sign: N1MGX
Kathrine M Pease
250 Meadow St
Rockport ME 04856

Call Sign: N1MGZ
Daniel M Pease
250 Meadow St
Rockport ME 04856

Call Sign: KA1VUL
Fred E Kneedler
126 Mistic Ave
Rockport ME 04856

Call Sign: KC1IL
Edward A Rowe
160 Mistic Ave
Rockport ME 04856

Call Sign: KA1NUQ
Peter M Slobogin
171 Mistic Ave
Rockport ME 04856

Call Sign: KB1FEH
Joel D Powers
126 Mistic Avenue
Rockport ME 04856

Call Sign: N1ZVP
Winfred K Stanley
19 Old County Rd
Rockport ME 04856

Call Sign: K1IRK
Philip R Gaudet Jr
81 Pascal Ave
Rockport ME 048565916

Call Sign: AA1DL
Lloyd Roberts
140 Porter St
Rockport ME 04856

Call Sign: WA1ZGH
Calvin W Maddox
22 Summer St
Rockport ME 04856

Call Sign: KA1ISG
Carter R Mann
Rockport ME 04856

Call Sign: KA1THJ

Douglas S Cole
Rockport ME 04856

Call Sign: N1PDS
Lorraine B Knight
Rockport ME 04856

Call Sign: W1GK
Homer F Trautmann
Rockport ME 048560810

Call Sign: WA6AAB
James R Huning
Rockport ME 04856

Call Sign: KB1JHN
Chris Kimball
Rockport ME 048561133

FCC Amateur Radio Licenses in Rockwood

Call Sign: N1CAR
Robert Bader
224 Drinkwater Road
Rockwood ME 04478

Call Sign: N1TXY
Edward J Cadett Sr
#28 Mooseriver Ln
Rockwood ME 04478

FCC Amateur Radio Licenses in Rome

Call Sign: KD0DYW
Caelin B Kelsey
517 Rome Rd Apt 1
Rome ME 04963

Call Sign: KD0DJF
Robert B Kelsey
517 Rome Road
Rome ME 04963

FCC Amateur Radio Licenses in Round Pond

Call Sign: KB1TCD
Jose P Douglas
254 Elliott Hill Rd
Round Pond ME 04564

Call Sign: KB1TCG
Nancy A Douglas
254 Elliott Hill Rd
Round Pond ME 04564

Call Sign: KE1EY
Steven Bixby
Po Box 180
Round Pond ME 04564

Call Sign: KB1HTY
Robert T Loney
12887 State Route 32
Round Pond ME 04564

Call Sign: KD7FGE
Nathan B Dyer
Round Pond ME 04564

Call Sign: KD7FGF
Jonathan F Dyer
Round Pond ME 04564

Call Sign: WO1M
Dana D Dyer
Round Pond ME 04564

FCC Amateur Radio Licenses in Roxbury

Call Sign: N1RLR
Steven F Bell
General Delivery
Roxbury ME 04275

Call Sign: W1FUZ
Henry H Bell Sr

General Delivery
Roxbury ME 04275

Call Sign: KB1OVY
Richard N Doughty
Roxbury ME 04275

FCC Amateur Radio Licenses in Rumford

Call Sign: KB1EWV
Clayton L Bartlett
2 Bernadine Street
Rumford ME 04276

Call Sign: N1RGS
Robert P Desgrosseilliers
Rr 1 Box 3500
Rumford ME 04276

Call Sign: K1LCE
James W Sherburne
20 Congress St
Rumford ME 04276

Call Sign: KB1UBS
Michael S Richards
205 Cumberland St
Rumford ME 04276

Call Sign: KB1YL
James N Robertson
724 Forest Ave
Rumford ME 04276

Call Sign: K1TQX
Alan T Gerace
133 Hall Hill Rd
Rumford ME 04276

Call Sign: N1JSE
Thomas F Trice
2 Holyoke Ave
Rumford ME 04276

Call Sign: N1OZY
Clifford R Haynes
240 Maple Street
Rumford ME 04276

Call Sign: N1OZZ
Irene F Haynes
240 Maple Street
Rumford ME 04276

Call Sign: N1WOW
Clifford R Haynes Ii
240 Maple Street
Rumford ME 04276

Call Sign: K1UNQ
Carl W Ellis
630 Piscataquis
Rumford ME 04276

Call Sign: K1PV
Mountain Valley Amateur
Radio Club
871 Route 120
Rumford ME 042763836

Call Sign: KB1BSC
Western Maine Packet
Association
871 Route 120
Rumford ME 042763836

Call Sign: KB1BWW
Oxford County Digital
Association
871 Route 120
Rumford ME 042763836

Call Sign: KB1OUK
Charles J Hoff
423 Swain Rd
Rumford ME 042763804

Call Sign: N1PSV
Shirley C Arsenault

Swain Rd
Rumford ME 04276

Call Sign: KA1YXL
Benny U Arsenault
439 Swain Rd.
Rumford ME 04276

Call Sign: KD1XL
Lawrence D Sutton
614 Waldo Street
Rumford ME 04276

Call Sign: N1TXG
Nicholas J Puiia Iii
620 Washington St
Rumford ME 04276

Call Sign: WA1JPL
Walter J Hutchins
80 Wyman Hill Rd
Rumford ME 04276

FCC Amateur Radio Licenses in Sabattus

Call Sign: N1SEK
Donald A Gensure
3 Beaver Rd.
Sabattus ME 04280

Call Sign: K1WTX
Ernest L Huckabey
Rfd 2 Box 2470
Sabattus ME 04280

Call Sign: N1AZE
Paul E D Amour
Rfd 1 Box 3065
Sabattus ME 04280

Call Sign: KA1ROU
Bonnie J Bickford
Rfd 2 Box 3825
Sabattus ME 04280

Call Sign: KA1RQM
George L Bickford
Rfd 2 Box 3825
Sabattus ME 04280

Call Sign: N1BHQ
Neal G Bluhm
Rfd 1 Box 610
Sabattus ME 04280

Call Sign: N1RWZ
Frank S Carey
124 Crowley Road
Sabattus ME 04280

Call Sign: N1RGU
Philip B Lewis
81 Furbush Rd
Sabattus ME 04280

Call Sign: WA1GOU
Raymond M Poirier
60 Greene St
Sabattus ME 042800056

Call Sign: N1URA
Cory M Golob
63 Jordan Bridge Rd
Sabattus ME 042804200

Call Sign: KB1IRZ
Rebecca A Curran
63 Jordan Bridge Rd
Sabattus ME 042804200

Call Sign: KU1U
Cory M Golob
63 Jordan Bridge Rd
Sabattus ME 042804200

Call Sign: KB1SCW
Glenn T Connell
105 Jordan Bridge Rd
Sabattus ME 04280

Call Sign: W7IRX
Glenn T Connell
105 Jordan Bridge Rd
Sabattus ME 04280

Call Sign: KB1SCX
Patrick D Curran
216 Jordan Bridge Rd
Sabattus ME 04280

Call Sign: KB1JBR
Geneva S West
151 Middle Rd
Sabattus ME 04280

Call Sign: KB1NHA
Diana L Getchell
871 Middle Rd
Sabattus ME 04280

Call Sign: KB1NHB
Walter N Getchell
871 Middle Rd
Sabattus ME 04280

Call Sign: K1WXX
Walter N Getchell
871 Middle Rd
Sabattus ME 04280

Call Sign: KB1WHZ
Gregory S Larsen
294 Pond Rd
Sabattus ME 04280

Call Sign: N1MDK
David W Martin
33 W Ridge Rd
Sabattus ME 04280

Call Sign: K1DXX
David W Martin
33 W Ridge Rd
Sabattus ME 04280

Call Sign: N1ZAR
Raymond Lebrun
Sabattus ME 04280

Call Sign: KB1GVU
Geoffrey S Caron
Sabattus ME 04280

Call Sign: KB1JBQ
Anita L Bouffard
Sabattus ME 042801093

Call Sign: KA1JEF
Geoffrey S Caron
Sabattus ME 04280

FCC Amateur Radio Licenses in Saco

Call Sign: KB1UNT
Augustine Martel
18 Ash Swamp Rd
Saco ME 04072

Call Sign: N1MVB
Edward P Blais
63 Bay View Rd
Saco ME 04072

Call Sign: KB1AWA
William G Nelson Jr
162 Beach St.
Saco ME 04072

Call Sign: WA1AHY
Rene W Binette
2 Boom Rd
Saco ME 04072

Call Sign: KB1HUQ
R Michael Hoitt
453 Boom Rd
Saco ME 04072

Call Sign: N1OXH
Michael E Buck
259 Bradley St
Saco ME 04072

Call Sign: N1CCY
Harry E Jenkins Sr
75 Burnham Rd
Saco ME 04072

Call Sign: N1WEZ
Leo J Labrecque
36 Buxton Rd
Saco ME 04072

Call Sign: KB1UDF
Matthew S Simonds
14 Caryn Dr
Saco ME 04072

Call Sign: KB1TPM
Tyler J Walsh
26 Cherryfield Ave
Saco ME 04072

Call Sign: KA1VZM
Matthew D Wood
48 Elm St Apt A
Saco ME 04072

Call Sign: KB1JZX
Charles W Talbot
8 Elmwood Dr
Saco ME 04072

Call Sign: W1JKL
Charles W Talbot
8 Elmwood Dr
Saco ME 04072

Call Sign: N1IZT
Gordon H Sears
23 Ferry Rd
Saco ME 04072

Call Sign: KB1TUR
Stephen K Ewing
573 Ferry Rd
Saco ME 04072

Call Sign: K1FA
George S Caras
15 Foley Ave
Saco ME 04072

Call Sign: N1MNU
Joseph T Pupecki
67 Foxhill Lane
Saco ME 04072

Call Sign: N1PSU
Ralph L Jewell Jr
123 Franklin St
Saco ME 04072

Call Sign: W1AHM
Arthur J Brymer
24 Hall Ave
Saco ME 04092

Call Sign: KB1AOF
John Mazeiko
16 Harrison Ave
Saco ME 04072

Call Sign: K1GTG
Lawrence T Dolby
60 Harrison Ave
Saco ME 04072

Call Sign: KB1IBW
John F Mckinnon
74 Hearn Rd
Saco ME 04072

Call Sign: KB1SE
James W Hinkley Jr
57b Hill St
Saco ME 04972

Call Sign: WA1WPN
Keith C Munson
9 Inland View Ave
Saco ME 040722309

Call Sign: N1OMZ
Robert D Stone
40 Jenkins Rd
Saco ME 04072

Call Sign: N1WAD
Henry B Rose Jr
6 Labonte Ave. West
Saco ME 04072

Call Sign: WA1KBD
Andrew W Delekto
304 Lincoln St
Saco ME 04072

Call Sign: WB1FSJ
Reginald C Grenier
40 Locke
Saco ME 04072

Call Sign: KA1UUO
Martha M Lostrom
7 Locke St
Saco ME 04072

Call Sign: KA1WRX
Adri A Lostrom
7 Locke St
Saco ME 04072

Call Sign: KA1WRY
Erik S Lostrom
7 Locke St
Saco ME 04072

Call Sign: KB1SSZ
Gerald E Gerlach Jr
24 Lord Rd
Saco ME 04072

Call Sign: KB1UHT
Alexander C Gerlach
24 Lord Rd
Saco ME 04072

Call Sign: N1OXB
Bradley E Emery
6 Lyman Ave
Saco ME 04072

Call Sign: N1BRS
Ralph F Sweet
380 Main St
Saco ME 04072

Call Sign: W1RWD
Robert W Dudley
408 Main St.
Saco ME 04072

Call Sign: WB1EIG
Raymond A Roberts
41 Mast Hill Rd
Saco ME 04072

Call Sign: N1IZX
John N Tillyer Sr
64 Middle St
Saco ME 04072

Call Sign: KB1UUU
George E Hamilton
29 Miranda Circle
Saco ME 04072

Call Sign: KB1PWI
James A Caruthers
10 New County Rd
Saco ME 04072

Call Sign: KA2GTI
Ronald H Cobb
162 New County Road
Saco ME 04072

Call Sign: N1MIK
Michael Beavis
342 North St Apt 503
Saco ME 04072

Call Sign: N1XR
Barry J Daniels
342 North St Apt 702
Saco ME 040721850

Call Sign: KD4HEE
Kevin L Bridges
24 Nye St
Saco ME 04072

Call Sign: WA1MLM
Linwood A Knight
14 Oceon Park Rd
Saco ME 04072

Call Sign: K1FXR
Donna G Harrison
149 Old Orchard Rd Buxton
Saco ME 04072

Call Sign: KD1IE
Richard R Libby
2 Oweymouth St
Saco ME 04072

Call Sign: N1JSR
Lee H Jones Jr
10 Pheasant Rd
Saco ME 04072

Call Sign: N1TKE
Thomas E Drew Jr
83 Pheasant Road
Saco ME 04072

Call Sign: WB1FSH
Robert J Petit Sr
126 Pleasant St
Saco ME 040722753

Call Sign: KA1UQA
Ann M Patterson
36 Plymouth Dr
Saco ME 04072

Call Sign: KB1TCF
William P Lessard
903 Portland Rd
Saco ME 04072

Call Sign: WB1DPH
Gregory R Madore
49 Rosewood Dr
Saco ME 04072

Call Sign: N1IGK
Michael C Morneault
36 Ross Road
Saco ME 04072

Call Sign: K9CV
Curt J Vainio
89 Route 202
Saco ME 04073

Call Sign: KB1NLC
Roger M Blanchette
14 Shepard Ave
Saco ME 04072

Call Sign: KB1DRA
Joseph L Sirois
6a Spring Rd
Saco ME 04072

Call Sign: KB1PCR
John J Arsenault
54 Storer Street
Saco ME 04072

Call Sign: KB1TPL
Gabriel J Letourneau
7 Sullivan Lane
Saco ME 04072

Call Sign: W1LGV
Harold L Cole
130 Surf St
Saco ME 04072

Call Sign: N1HLY
William H Chase
49 Washington Ave
Saco ME 04072

Call Sign: KB1TPJ
Robert W Dudley
62 Washington Ave
Saco ME 04072

Call Sign: WB1GER
Alexander B Cumming
16 Wendy Way
Saco ME 04072

Call Sign: KB1DII
Sally C Rose
6 West Labonte Avenue
Saco ME 04072

Call Sign: KB1IBX
Raymond W Pilotte
Saco ME 04072

FCC Amateur Radio Licenses in Saint Agatha

Call Sign: N1IMM
Charles E Pelletier
Rfd Box 84 Mountain Rd
Saint Agatha ME 04772

Call Sign: WB1FTK
Don C Elrich
174 Hillside Rd
St Agatha ME 04772

Call Sign: KA1SJV
Diane M Elrich
174 Hillside Rd

St Agatha ME 04772

Call Sign: K1FTK
Don C Elrich
174 Hillside Rd
St Agatha ME 04772

Call Sign: KB1PMR
Kenneth Cyr
178 Hillside Rd
St Agatha ME 04772

Call Sign: KB1PMS
Theresa B Cyr
178 Hillside Rd
St Agatha ME 04772

FCC Amateur Radio Licenses in Saint Albans

Call Sign: KB1LOI
Edward L Shuman
115 Bubar Rd
St Albans ME 04971

Call Sign: N1GNN
Karl J Smith
184 Bubar Rd
Saint Albans ME 04971

Call Sign: KB1ULA
Diane M Smith
184 Bubar Rd
Saint Albans ME 04971

Call Sign: N1WST
Martin J Orloski
173 Denbow Rd
Saint Albans ME 04971

Call Sign: KB1NJB
Travis J Lyssy
135 Pond Rd
Saint Albans ME 04971

Call Sign: KA1ORJ
George H Perkins
243 Webb Ridge
Saint Albans ME 04971

Call Sign: KB1PJF
David R Scamman
St Albans ME 04971

Call Sign: KF6LSI
Ronald L Spurlock
Saint Albans ME 04971

Call Sign: WT1K
William N Keating
Saint Albans ME 04971

FCC Amateur Radio Licenses in Saint Francis

Call Sign: N1JHD
Gilford Daigle
Rr 1 Box 67
Saint Francis ME 04774

Call Sign: N1ZHQ
Caralynne Daigle
Rr 1 Box 67
Saint Francis ME 04774

Call Sign: N1QMC
Sandra A Daigle
1370 Main St
Saint Francis ME 04774

Call Sign: N1RDE
Philip J Daigle
1370 Main St
Saint Francis ME 04774

Call Sign: N1PMU
Curtiss J Daigle
1370 Main Street
Saint Francis ME 04774

Call Sign: N1ZBX
Noelle Daigle
1370 Main Street
Saint Francis ME 04774

Call Sign: WJ1D
James P Delancy Jr
50 Rankin Rapids Rd.
Saint Francis ME 04774

FCC Amateur Radio Licenses in Saint George

Call Sign: KB1DRH
Ralph H Robinson
Hc 61 Box 298
St George ME 04857

Call Sign: KB1PXL
Owen T Carlson
12 Carlson Ln
Saint George ME 04860

FCC Amateur Radio Licenses in Salem Township

Call Sign: W1OKQ
Jack J Komisarek
5 Reed Rd
Salem Twp ME 04983

FCC Amateur Radio Licenses in Sandy Point

Call Sign: KA1QGQ
Susan K Viano
Sandy Point ME 04972

FCC Amateur Radio Licenses in Sanford

Call Sign: KB1TPZ
Tobey V Worrall

17 - B Kimball St
Sanford ME 04073

Call Sign: KB1NZX
Jessica Phillips
46 A Hutchinson St
Sanford ME 04073

Call Sign: WA1ETT
Jessica Phillips
46 A Hutchinson St
Sanford ME 04073

Call Sign: N1VEV
William C Sheldrake
132 Airport Rd Apt E17
Sanford ME 04073

Call Sign: N1KGI
Jonathan W Peare I
Alfred Rd.
Sanford ME 04073

Call Sign: KA1UFF
Debra J Reagan
11 Bennett St.
Sanford ME 04073

Call Sign: KA1ZYQ
Ludger J Martin
20 Beulah St
Sanford ME 04073

Call Sign: WB1EIM
William J Winslow
Rr 1 Box 2100
Sanford ME 04073

Call Sign: N1UCD
Robert T Durgin
Rr 1 Box 2217
Sanford ME 04073

Call Sign: KA1UCV
Lionel J Lamontagne

Rr 1 Box 2238
Sanford ME 04073

Call Sign: KB1VEV
Derek D Cormier
9 Breton Ave
Sanford ME 04073

Call Sign: KB1ROV
Daniel B Simpson
16 Chancery Ln
Sanford ME 04073

Call Sign: N1ZED
Arthur H Roy
29 Charles St
Sanford ME 04073

Call Sign: KB1SXN
John R Dunning
83 Country Club 1
Sanford ME 04074

Call Sign: WW1M
Bruce D Herrick
103 Country Club Rd 3
Sanford ME 040735202

Call Sign: N1YHG
James E Roberts
38 Elm St
Sanford ME 04073

Call Sign: KB1ARG
Dolly R Egan
39 Emery St
Sanford ME 04073

Call Sign: KA1APA
Joseph L Lelievre
31 Errol St
Sanford ME 040732509

Call Sign: KE1GO
William S Burnham

79 Farview Dr
Sanford ME 040734221

Call Sign: KA1ZWD
John J Mac Cormack Jr
16 Gerrish Dr
Sanford ME 04073

Call Sign: KA1ZZI
Hayden R Sevey
16 Gerrish Dr
Sanford ME 04073

Call Sign: N1ULT
Joshua C Martell
166 Grammar Rd
Sanford ME 04073

Call Sign: KA1NWA
Harvey J Arsenault
17 Grandview Ave
Sanford ME 04073

Call Sign: KB4CWF
Letty E Davis
382 Harry Howes Rd
Sanford ME 04073

Call Sign: N4BBZ
Charles G Davis
382 Harry Howes Rd
Sanford ME 04073

Call Sign: WB1GGI
Marden L Pride
254 Harry Howes Road
Sanford ME 04073

Call Sign: WM1P
Marden L Pride
254 Harry Howes Road
Sanford ME 04073

Call Sign: N1YUB
Patricia E Zerfoss

58 Jackson St
Sanford ME 04073

Call Sign: N1TTJ
Craig P Normand
97 Jackson St
Sanford ME 04073

Call Sign: N1YOO
Kevin F Hager
58 Jackson Street
Sanford ME 04073

Call Sign: N1UGB
Kenneth E Owens
64 Jagger Mill Rd
Sanford ME 04073

Call Sign: KB1RCZ
Lawrence M Floyd
3a Jellerson Rd
Sanford ME 04073

Call Sign: KB1MI
Michel A Demers
84 June St
Sanford ME 04073

Call Sign: N1UGC
Kevin P Worden Sr
12 Kilby St
Sanford ME 04073

Call Sign: KB1VUE
Crystal M Tripp
17b Kimball St
Sanford ME 04073

Call Sign: KB1AAN
Joseph R St Laurent
14a Lavin Ct
Sanford ME 04073

Call Sign: AA1LQ
Gary G Benoit

416 Lebanon Street
Sanford ME 04073

Call Sign: KB1BMB
Gary C Ford
598 Lebanon Street
Sanford ME 04073

Call Sign: N1XRO
Jason C Ford
598 Lebanon Street
Sanford ME 04073

Call Sign: W1SEA
Gary C Ford
598 Lebanon Street
Sanford ME 04073

Call Sign: KA1RLI
Christie A Blakely
9 Madison St
Sanford ME 040732028

Call Sign: N1UJH
John R Owens
1 Malden Ave
Sanford ME 04073

Call Sign: KB1PWL
William G Lefebvre Jr
Manor Circle
Sanford ME 04073

Call Sign: WA1BMG
Gerard J Maurais
3 Mitchell St
Sanford ME 04073

Call Sign: W1FNI
Louis P Normand
Rd Box 1541 New Dam Rd
Sanford ME 04073

Call Sign: WB1EJT
Robert A Ege

23 North St
Sanford ME 04073

Call Sign: N1YHH
Thomas F Quinn
86 Old Falls Road
Sanford ME 040735539

Call Sign: KA1ZRT
Ronald P Genest
110 Old Mill Rd
Sanford ME 04073

Call Sign: N1RDP
Barbara I Genest
110 Old Mill Rd
Sanford ME 04073

Call Sign: KB1ONC
Peter C Davis
8 Park St
Sanford ME 04073

Call Sign: W1SLP
Peter C Davis
8 Park St
Sanford ME 04073

Call Sign: N1HNC
David N Theoharides
68 Payeur Circle
Sanford ME 04073

Call Sign: N3YAT
Michael Derricks
34 Ridgeway Ave
Sanford ME 04073

Call Sign: KC9TUS
William S Shuey Jr
3a Seneca Avenue
Sanford ME 04073

Call Sign: KC9UEY
Katrice A Shuey

3a Seneca Avenue
Sanford ME 04073

Call Sign: KA1OHV
David L Wendel
13 Stony Brook Rd
Sanford ME 04073

Call Sign: KA1VOB
Jonathan L Martell
25 Trafton St
Sanford ME 04073

Call Sign: KB1NYN
Alexander J Hammerle
77 Twombley Rd
Sanford ME 04073

Call Sign: N1FNY
Alfred Bonti
Sanford ME 04073

Call Sign: W1ERW
Richard M Moroney
Sanford ME 04073

Call Sign: W1LSD
William A TRUE
Sanford ME 04073

Call Sign: WA1VOH
Earl J Charak
Sanford ME 04073

Call Sign: WB1HBV
Wayne G Depew
94 Anderson Rd
Sangerville ME 04479

Call Sign: KB1DZE
Randy A Green
36 Douty Hill Rd.

Sangerville ME 04479

Call Sign: AA1JR
Joseph A Ranagan
394 Frenchs Mill Rd
Sangerville ME 044793544

Call Sign: NE2O
Charles R Plumeri Jr
119 Grant Rd
Sangerville ME 04479

Call Sign: N1PGX
Harold C Rolfe
Rfd 1 Mb 518a
Sangerville ME 04479

Call Sign: N1XRJ
Arnold R Corson
Sangerville ME 04479

Call Sign: KB1UCU
Sarah V Jarnecki
Sangerville ME 04479

Call Sign: KB1JAM
David J Pert
9 White Pine Ln
Sargentville ME 04673

Call Sign: N1QFH
John D Cole
40 Arbor View Lane
Scarborough ME 04074

Call Sign: KB1LXV
Ronald W Brown
31 Beech Ridge Rd
Scarborough ME 04074

Call Sign: KB1LXW
Raven A Brooke
31 Beech Ridge Rd
Scarborough ME 04074

Call Sign: WA1RB
Ronald W Brown
31 Beech Ridge Rd
Scarborough ME 04074

Call Sign: KB1U
Mitchel A Kosoff
290 Beech Ridge Rd
Scarborough ME 04074

Call Sign: W1OZ
Mitchel A Kosoff
290 Beech Ridge Rd
Scarborough ME 04074

Call Sign: KD1UQ
Thomas E Filieo
99 Beechridge Rd
Scarborough ME 04074

Call Sign: WA1TPH
Joseph G Rokowski
309 Black Point Rd #76
Scarborough ME 04075

Call Sign: KA1GWF
Eugene E Fitzpatrick
309 Black Point Rd Unit 59
Scarborough ME 04074

Call Sign: N6XLR
Steven B Sidman
22 Black Point Road 4e
Scarborough ME 04074

Call Sign: KA1CVR
James P Paras
Box 598
Scarborough ME 04074

Call Sign: N1FZL
Michael L Waye
90 Broadturn Rd A4
Scarborough ME 04074

Call Sign: WA1YGT
Peter G Romano
154 Broadturn Rd
Scarboro ME 040749227

Call Sign: KB1JWP
Eric A Duntley
16 Clearview Dr
Scarborough ME 04074

Call Sign: W1VYA
Eric A Duntley
16 Clearview Dr
Scarborough ME 04074

Call Sign: KF4CFQ
Bre Amateur Radio Assn
72 Coach Lantern Ln E
Scarborough ME 04074

Call Sign: KA1RUB
Portland Repeater Group
72 Coach Lantern Ln E
Scarborough ME 04074

Call Sign: KB1EXB
Sylvie F Page
72 Coach Lantern Ln E
Scarborough ME 04074

Call Sign: N1BMB
Daryl W Cook
49 County Road
Scarborough ME 04074

Call Sign: KA1PRB
William E Kennedy
23 Downeast Ln
Scarborough ME 04074

Call Sign: AB1AZ
William E Kennedy
23 Downeast Ln
Scarborough ME 04074

Call Sign: W1UMQ
Ronald V Dubay
11 Dunstan Ave 2
Scarborough ME
040749733

Call Sign: KA1MQR
Harriet N Whitten
7 Dunstan Landing Rd
Scarborough ME 04074

Call Sign: W1CBQ
Wendell R Whitten
7 Dunstan Landing Rd
Scarborough ME 04074

Call Sign: WA1JTT
James O Cobb
19 Estate Dr
Scarborough ME 04074

Call Sign: W1JTT
James O Cobb
19 Estate Dr
Scarborough ME 04074

Call Sign: N1ZTA
Randall T Farr
144 Fogg Rd
Scarborough ME 04074

Call Sign: KA1VSC
Matthew E Webster
38 Foxcroft Drive
Scarborough ME 04074

Call Sign: W1UTD
Vincent E Roderick
169 Gorham Rd

Scarborough ME 04074

Call Sign: N1CSQ
Wayne H Reynolds
365 Gorham Rd
Scarborough ME
040749578

Call Sign: N1KTJ
Blanche C Reynolds
365 Gorham Rd
Scarborough ME 04074

Call Sign: KB1VPG
Christopher J Dyer
3 Higgins St
Scarborough ME 04074

Call Sign: K1GVX
Henry W Wentworth
154 Highland Ave
Scarborough ME
040748628

Call Sign: WB1COP
Horace E Davenport
174 Holmes Rd
Scarborough ME 04074

Call Sign: KB1UDE
Thomas M Osborne
227 Holmes Rd
Scarborough ME 04074

Call Sign: AA2PL
Anthony Lacertosa
11 Lancaster Lane
Scarborough ME 04074

Call Sign: NW1B
Troy W Dennen
4 Leah Ln
Scarborough ME 04074

Call Sign: KB1NQV

Susan L J Smith
24 Meeting House Rd
Scarborough ME 04074

Call Sign: KB1CNK
Philip C Gage
50 Mussey Rd
Scarborough ME
040748918

Call Sign: WA2PFJ
Robert B Hoy Sr
26 Ocean Ave
Scarborough ME 04074

Call Sign: WB2NOU
Marianne J Hoy
26 Ocean Ave
Scarborough ME 04074

Call Sign: K1ACT
James W Greenleaf
16 Oceanwood Drive
Scarborough ME 04074

Call Sign: W1SMR
Edward Valente
30 Old County Rd
Scarborough ME 04074

Call Sign: W1ZOU
Andrew T Armstrong
30 Old Neck Road
Scarborough ME 04074

Call Sign: N1ULM
Andrew T Armstrong
30 Old Neck Road
Scarborough ME 04074

Call Sign: N1XHD
Rick N Ingram
9 Ole Ironside Ln
Scarborough ME 04074

Call Sign: KB1GLU
Gary N Odonnell
19 Pine Ledge Dr
Scarborough ME 04074

Call Sign: KC1SN
Keith A Peaco
193 Pine Point Rd
Scarborough ME 04074

Call Sign: NW1H
Richard E Senghas
15 Piper Road Apt J320
Scarborough ME
040747555

Call Sign: KB1VPF
James M Connolly
7 Rays Circle
Scarborough ME 04074

Call Sign: WN1F
David B Feeney
1 Ridgeway Rd
Scarborough ME
040748210

Call Sign: KB1UEM
Downeast Hf Rovers Club
1 Ridgeway Rd
Scarborough ME
040748210

Call Sign: KZ1I
Downeast Hf Rovers Club
1 Ridgeway Rd
Scarborough ME
040748210

Call Sign: KA3AAE
R Rex Thornton
8 River Woods Dr
Scarborough ME 04074

Call Sign: KI1A

R Rex Thornton
8 River Woods Dr
Scarborough ME 04074

Call Sign: KB1BQA
Down East Dx Assn
7 Rocky Hill Rd
Scarborough ME 04074

Call Sign: K1EU
Michael J Russo
8 Rocky Hill Rd
Scarborough ME 04074

Call Sign: W1KVI
Portland Amateur Wireless
Assoc
8 Rocky Hill Rd
Scarborough ME 04074

Call Sign: KC1ME
Down East Dx Association
8 Rocky Hill Rd
Scarborough ME 04074

Call Sign: K1OYB
Martin J Feeney Jr
99 Running Hill Rd
Scarborough ME
040748934

Call Sign: KA1MQP
Roberta J Lockard
99 Running Hill Rd
Scarborough ME
040748934

Call Sign: K1MQP
Roberta J Lockard
99 Running Hill Rd
Scarborough ME
040748934

Call Sign: K1RSA
Harry J White

135 Running Hill Rd
Scarborough ME 04074

Call Sign: KA1ZMC
David B Boober
31 Saco St
Scarborough ME 04074

Call Sign: KB1MQG
Kenneth A Kennedy
14 Saco Street
Scarborough ME 04074

Call Sign: WA1YNB
John P Thurlow
1 Starpine Lane
Scarborough ME 04074

Call Sign: KB1NIA
Douglas A Knight
6 Stonebrooke Rd
Scarborough ME 04074

Call Sign: K1DAK
Douglas A Knight
6 Stonebrooke Rd
Scarborough ME 04074

Call Sign: W1HVO
Freeman M Santos
17 Thomas Dr
Scarborough ME 04074

Call Sign: KB1EHC
David M Pino
1 Two Rod Rd
Scarborough ME
040749764

Call Sign: W1CLL
Leslie A Cohen
201 Us Rt 1 Pmb 227
Scarborough ME 04075

Call Sign: WA1WFE

Libby G Cohen
201 Us Rt 1 Pmb 227
Scarborough ME 04076

Call Sign: KB1TRO
Daniel B Bell
17 W Beech Ridge Rd
Scarborough ME 04074

Call Sign: AA1FJ
Michael A Cunniff
21 Waldron Drive
Scarborough ME 04074

Call Sign: KA1SSZ
George E Caswell Jr
16 Westwood Ave
Scarborough ME 04074

Call Sign: W1ME
George Caswell Sr
16 Westwood Ave
Scarborough ME 04074

Call Sign: WA1MER
Caroline P Caswell
16 Westwood Ave
Scarborough ME 04074

Call Sign: K1PUR
John A Anderson Iii
106 Winnocks Neck Road
Scarborough ME 04074

Call Sign: AA1FR
James S Hatch
Scarborough ME
040702334

Call Sign: KA1VQQ
David M Wood
Scarborough ME 04074

Call Sign: KB1FGF
David M Wood

Scarborough ME 04074

Call Sign: KB1LRE
Philip B Hamilton
Scarborough ME 04070

Call Sign: KB1ONF
Matthew R Albrecht Mr
Scarborough ME 04070

Call Sign: KD1ID
James T Farr
Scarboro ME 04074

Call Sign: KB1OWA
Brian Romage
Scarborough ME 04070

FCC Amateur Radio Licenses in Seal Cove

Call Sign: KB1WRX
Joshua A King
Seal Cove ME 04674

FCC Amateur Radio Licenses in Seal Harbor

Call Sign: W2IHP
Robert W Hipkens
6 Champlain Dr
Seal Harbor ME 04675

Call Sign: WA1PKO
James W Wood Jr
11 Main St
Seal Harbor ME 046750062

Call Sign: KB1IQL
Ellen Y Stanley
Seal Harbor ME 04675

FCC Amateur Radio Licenses in Searsmont

Call Sign: W1HHO
Calder B Latham
52 Crie Rd
Searsmont ME 04973

Call Sign: KE6LXK
Ronald B Collins
44 Fowles Road
Searsmont ME 04973

Call Sign: KC1VA
A Bradford Drawbridge
3 French Rd N
Searsmont ME 04973

Call Sign: W1ONE
Glenn E Graichen
451 Main St. South
Searsmont ME 04973

Call Sign: N1YUG
Diana C Laing
467 Muzzy Ridge Road
Searsmont ME 04973

Call Sign: N1YUH
Peter H Laing
467 Muzzy Ridge Road
Searsmont ME 04973

Call Sign: KB1RVO
Robert K Hoey
81 Peters Rd
Searsmont ME 04973

Call Sign: W1EBA
Robert E Hoey
81 Peters Rd
Searsmont ME 04973

Call Sign: KB9VTT
Stephen R Bow
20 Pines Rd
Searsmont ME 04973

Call Sign: KB9VTU
Cheryl A Bow
20 Pines Rd
Searsmont ME 04973

FCC Amateur Radio Licenses in Searsport

Call Sign: N1ZUR
Philip J Millette Sr
67 Bowen Rd
Searsport ME 04974

Call Sign: N1RCY
Robert W Brochu
Box 506
Searsport ME 04974

Call Sign: N1MTW
Florence N Gilmore
136 Brock Rd
Searsport ME 04974

Call Sign: N1MTX
Charles R Gordon
138 Brock Rd
Searsport ME 049740551

Call Sign: N4EDL
Montgomery C Hart
C/O V Hart Smith E Main
St Box 355
Searsport ME 04174

Call Sign: KB1UPK
Matthew J Partridge
438 E Main St
Searsport ME 04974

Call Sign: KA1LPP
Howard L Ruben
Green Valley Rfd 1
Searsport ME 04974

Call Sign: AA1OY

Amanda Reynolds
161 Mt Ephraim Rd
Searsport ME 04974

Call Sign: KA1AIL
Rick A Glidden
199 Mt Ephraim Rd
Searsport ME 04974

Call Sign: KA1ZAF
Julie A Glidden
199 Mt Ephraim Rd
Searsport ME 04974

Call Sign: KA1OLU
James R Babb
Mt Ephraim Rd
Searsport ME 04974

Call Sign: N1UHQ
Lawrence E Reynolds
161 Mt Ephriam Rd
Searsport ME 04974

Call Sign: N1YIN
Gloria A Mason
7 Osprey Ln
Searsport ME 04974

Call Sign: N1YIO
Charles E Mason
33 Prospect St Apt 9
Searsport ME 04974

Call Sign: N1VNK
Daniel R Gaecklein
16 Prospect Street
Searsport ME 04974

Call Sign: KB1OF
Lionel L Merrill Jr
32 Turnpike Rd
Searsport ME 04974

Call Sign: KB1HCQ

Michael A Housman
316 W Main St
Searsport ME 04974

Call Sign: KA1LPO
Palmer B Pearson
23 Water St
Searsport ME 049740273

Call Sign: KA1ZMT
Edward F Anthonis Jr
Searsport ME 04974

Call Sign: KA1ZMU
Gail W Anthonis
Searsport ME 04974

Call Sign: WA1KKB
Everett M Gilmore Jr
Searsport ME 04974

Call Sign: KB1NRH
George B Kerper Jr
Searsport ME 04974

FCC Amateur Radio Licenses in Sebago

Call Sign: W1SQA
Anthony B Fisher
837 Anderson Road
Sebago ME 04029

Call Sign: W1GQD
Richard H Keighley
Hc 75 Box 231b Peabody
Pond Rd
Sebago ME 04029

Call Sign: K1UCU
Millis C Pelton
Hc 75 Box 309a
Sebago ME 04029

Call Sign: N4INP

Glenn F Wilson
354 Bridgton Road
Sebago ME 04029

Call Sign: KB4IPK
Trudy G Wilson
Bridgton Road
Sebago ME 04029

Call Sign: N6QWI
Robert D Greene
21 Fitch Road
Sebago ME 04029

Call Sign: KA1ZFY
Steven R Eisenberg
694 Sebago Road Unit 8
Sebago ME 04029

Call Sign: KA1ZRZ
John I Cumming Sr
63 Shore Rd
Sebago ME 04029

Call Sign: KB1UDD
Paul M Cumming
63 Shore Rd
Sebago ME 04029

Call Sign: WB1GZF
Frank S Merritt
7 Spring Lane
Sebago ME 040290314

Call Sign: WB2DPF
Rolf Ramseyer
Sebago ME 040290298

FCC Amateur Radio Licenses in Sebago Lake

Call Sign: N1KAB
Woodrow P Billington
Route 35 Box 85
Sebago Lake ME 04076

Call Sign: W1GFP
Thomas F Mannetto
34 Carroll Ave
Sebago Lake ME 04075

Call Sign: KB1BVX
Ellis V O Brien Jr
Cottage St
Sebago Lake ME 04075

Call Sign: W1SD
E C Titcomb
Shore Rd
Sebago Lake ME 04075

FCC Amateur Radio Licenses in Sebasco Estates

Call Sign: KA1YYU
Jason A C Marshall
Long Cove Rd
Sebasco Estates ME 04565

FCC Amateur Radio Licenses in Sebec

Call Sign: KB1WEA
William N Welsh
427 Downs Rd
Sebec ME 04481

Call Sign: KA1CYY
Donald A Ambler
92 North Rd.
Sebec ME 04481

Call Sign: W1GHH
Daniel C Newcome
Sebec ME 04481

FCC Amateur Radio Licenses in Sedgwick

Call Sign: WA8EPS
Thomas R Koontz Jr
R R 1 - Box 2920
Sedgwick ME 04676

Call Sign: K3OZP
Donald S Bowes
9 Alder Lane
Sedgwick ME 04676

Call Sign: KB1JQL
Kathie J Koontz
Rfd 1 Box 2920
Sedgwick ME 04676

Call Sign: N1DYR
Robert H Colburn
Rr1 Box 3115
Sedgwick ME 04677

Call Sign: KB1TLG
Thomas L Poole
342 Graytown Rd
Sedgwick ME 04676

Call Sign: KB1PHD
Trevor H Colburn
373 Sedgwick Ridge Rd
Sedgwick ME 04676

Call Sign: N1QBB
Gardiner L Schneider
Sedgwick ME 04676

Call Sign: W1HFP
Charles E Greenwood
Sedgwick ME 04676

FCC Amateur Radio Licenses in Shapleigh

Call Sign: KA1ING
Catherine B Pike
Box 1
Shapleigh ME 04076

Call Sign: N1SRK
Jesse P L Esperance
Rfd 1 Box 2650
Shapleigh ME 04076

Call Sign: KB1FS
Danny R Merrifield
259 County Road
Shapleigh ME 04076

Call Sign: KB1SYI
Laurence P Cable Iii
964 Goose Pond Rd
Shapleigh ME 04076

Call Sign: KB1PLW
Rodney E Miller
288 Hooper Rd
Shapleigh ME 04076

Call Sign: N1TZT
Scott G Hopkins
426 Shapleigh Corner Road
Shapleigh ME 04076

Call Sign: KA1TFS
Nina E Knapp
79 Twenty-First St
Shapleigh ME 04076

Call Sign: N1TJD
John Hj Skillings
Shapleigh ME 04076

Call Sign: KB1LYV
Robert M Pike
Shapleigh ME 04076

Call Sign: KB1NZK
Lynnette D Munson
Shapleigh ME 04076

Call Sign: KB1NUT
Lynnette D Munson

Shapleigh ME 04076

Call Sign: W1BIR
Robert M Pike
Shapleigh ME 04076

**FCC Amateur Radio
Licenses in Sidney**

Call Sign: KB1TPI
Joel M Dudley
2323 Belgrade Rd
Sidney ME 04330

Call Sign: KB1JHX
Kenneth A Gotreau
46 Blue Ridge Drive East
Sidney ME 04330

Call Sign: W1GCX
Leigh C Alexander
R 3 Box 555
Sidney ME 04331

Call Sign: KC1EL
Everett F La Porte
61 Howard Circle
Sidney ME 04330

Call Sign: K1RWN
Lawrence E Parlin Sr
12 Larry Way
Sidney ME 04330

Call Sign: KB1WWI
Robert H Morrison Ii
31 Lendall Forest
Sidney ME 04330

Call Sign: KB1QOI
Jeffrey A Campbell
2531 Middle Rd
Sidney ME 04330

Call Sign: AB1JG

Jeffrey A Campbell
2531 Middle Rd
Sidney ME 04330

Call Sign: W5JEF
Jeffrey A Campbell
2531 Middle Rd
Sidney ME 04330

Call Sign: K1JEF
Jeffrey A Campbell
2531 Middle Rd
Sidney ME 04330

Call Sign: N1IFP
Philip A Downes
49 Mt Vista Dr
Sidney ME 04330

Call Sign: KB1UZK
Barton J Newhouse
313 Pond Rd
Sidney ME 04330

Call Sign: N1UB
Barton J Newhouse
313 Pond Rd
Sidney ME 04330

Call Sign: KG4COV
Eric W Barry
683 Pond Road
Sidney ME 04330

Call Sign: N1HRX
Brenda J Stevens
484 Quaker Rd
Sidney ME 04330

Call Sign: N1VLW
Samuel J Stevens
484 Quaker Rd
Sidney ME 04330

Call Sign: WX1V

Dennis R Stevens
484 Quaker Rd
Sidney ME 04330

Call Sign: KB1FAZ
Elizabeth A Stevens
484 Quaker Rd
Sidney ME 04330

Call Sign: KA1BVV
Richard A Downe
114 Quaker Road
Sidney ME 04330

Call Sign: K1LIZ
Elizabeth A Stevens
484 Quaker Road
Sidney ME 04330

Call Sign: KB1KJZ
Edwin K Lee
36 Rebecca Dr
Sidney ME 04330

Call Sign: KB1LEE
Edwin K Lee
36 Rebecca Dr
Sidney ME 04330

Call Sign: KB1PNL
Richard L Peary
218 Shepard Rd
Sidney ME 04330

Call Sign: KB1IUC
Eric N Welch
55 Sunset Ridge
Sidney ME 04330

Call Sign: KB1FAY
Charlie R Wood
2913 West River Rd
Sidney ME 04330

Call Sign: KB1FAX

Jessica L Fay
3646 West River Road
Sidney ME 04330

FCC Amateur Radio Licenses in Sinclair

Call Sign: WA1ZOR
Mark L Peterson Jr
Long Lake Sporting Club
Sinclair ME 04779

Call Sign: WA1ZOS
Pierrette T Peterson
Long Lake Sporting Club
Sinclair ME 04779

Call Sign: KA1QOV
Roland W Fortin Jr
Sinclair ME 04779

Call Sign: KA1QPC
Albert L Watt
Sinclair ME 047790231

FCC Amateur Radio Licenses in Skowhegan

Call Sign: KB1OWT
Seymour W Charles
475 Back Rd
Skowhegan ME 04976

Call Sign: KA1YBH
Wayne K Provost
16 Bailey St
Skowhegan ME 04976

Call Sign: N1ULR
Charles R Mc Gray
18 Beauford St
Skowhegan ME 04976

Call Sign: N1STK
Lera A Mc Gray

18 Beauford Street
Skowhegan ME 04976

Call Sign: N1STL
Charles R Mc Gray Sr
18 Beauford Street
Skowhegan ME 04976

Call Sign: WA1RMC
Theodore N Parker
47 Bennett Ave
Skowhegan ME 04976

Call Sign: WD8OGU
Willard M Hammann
525 Bigelow Hill Rd.
Skowhegan ME 04976

Call Sign: KA1KKZ
Steve A Demo
Rt 3 Box 15
Skowhegan ME 04976

Call Sign: W1MQI
Francis E Croteau Jr
Rfd 4 Box 1580
Skowhegan ME 04976

Call Sign: W1HHV
Robert H Nicholson
Rfd 1 Box 5180
Skowhegan ME 04976

Call Sign: KA1LQH
Charles J Carpenter
Rfd 1 Box 5340
Skowhegan ME 04976

Call Sign: K1LMQ
Elmer J Frace Sr
Rd 2 Box 645
Skowhegan ME 04977

Call Sign: KA1CLF
Thomas A Crowley

Rfd 3 Box 755
Skowhegan ME 04977

Call Sign: N1IOS
Henry A Gates
Rfd 4 Box 7725
Skowhegan ME 04976

Call Sign: N1UGV
John A Sincyr
10 Dawes St
Skowhegan ME 04976

Call Sign: KC1N
James A Holland
184 East River Road
Skowhegan ME 04976

Call Sign: N1TSJ
William A Burkhart
7 Forrest Greene St
Skowhegan ME 04976

Call Sign: KB1OMB
David W Corson
20 Hanover St
Skowhegan ME 04976

Call Sign: K1DWC
David W Corson
20 Hanover St
Skowhegan ME 04976

Call Sign: KB1SSV
Somerset County Emcomm
Group
20 Hanover St
Skowhegan ME 04976

Call Sign: K1SOM
Somerset County Emcomm
Group
20 Hanover St
Skowhegan ME 04976

Call Sign: N1TIG
Gerald K Mc Clintick
79 Hill Top Dr Ames
Trailer Park
Skowhegan ME 04976

Call Sign: KA1C
Stephen A Roderick
81 Hilton Hill Road
Skowhegan ME 04976

Call Sign: KA1EMK
Merlene C Roderick
81 Hilton Hill Road
Skowhegan ME 04976

Call Sign: N1FIZ
Wayne A Cook
22 Maple St
Skowhegan ME 04976

Call Sign: WA1CQL
Malcolm O Bennett
25 Middle St
Skowhegan ME 04976

Call Sign: N1UMB
Aric M Gott
49 Middle St
Skowhegan ME 04976

Call Sign: N1UMC
Melissa L Gott
49 Middle St
Skowhegan ME 04976

Call Sign: KB1RNX
James A Richard
67 Mount Pleasant Ave
Skowhegan ME 04976

Call Sign: NR1W
Francis L La Fratta
177 North Ave
Skowhegan ME 079762150

Call Sign: KB1UUV
Richard K Smith
98 Palmer Rd
Skowhegan ME 04976

Call Sign: N1SGL
Richard K Smith
98 Palmer Rd
Skowhegan ME 04976

Call Sign: WB1FMX
Lawrence A Fruzzetti
34 Parkman Hill Road
Skowhegan ME 04976

Call Sign: ND1A
Hatherly L Souther
8 Pennell St
Skowhegan ME 049761115

Call Sign: KB1OCZ
Ralph E Mcafee
14 Riverside Dr
Skowhegan ME 04976

Call Sign: KA1BHF
George N Cannell
65 Summer St
Skowhegan ME 04976

Call Sign: K1BXI
John H Phillips
21 Summer Street
Skowhegan ME 04976

Call Sign: WA1HLR
Timothy M Smith
49 Tower Drive
Skowhegan ME 04976

Call Sign: KA1LQJ
Vernard E Elliott Jr
10 W Front St
Skowhegan ME 04976

Call Sign: W1GBM
Robert A Lyons
10 W Front St
Skowhegan ME 04976

Call Sign: KA1DIO
Jane Lyons
Skowhegan ME 04976

Call Sign: KA1ZZC
Gilles A Chouinard
Skowhegan ME 04976

Call Sign: N1JAK
Russell P Denis
Skowhegan ME 04976

Call Sign: N1PRO
Seth R Lewis
Skowhegan ME 04976

Call Sign: N1SKT
William A Lashon
Skowhegan ME 049760142

Call Sign: KB1ORK
Harry D Oneil
Skowhegon ME 04976

**FCC Amateur Radio
Licenses in Smithfield**

Call Sign: KC2FW
Mary C Ostrowski
32 Joly Lane
Smithfield ME 04978

Call Sign: N2NA
Richard J Ostrowski
32 Joly Lane
Smithfield ME 04978

Call Sign: KB1OBO
Stephen Crowe

565 Village Rd
Smithfield ME 04978

Call Sign: N1NCR
Kenneth D Landry
668 Wilder Hill Rd
Smithfield ME 04978

Call Sign: N1NEX
Michele C Landry
668 Wilder Hill Rd
Smithfield ME 04978

FCC Amateur Radio Licenses in Smyrna

Call Sign: KB1LOG
Herb F Boutilier
Smyrna ME 04780

Call Sign: K1LOG
Herb F Boutilier
Smyrna ME 04780

FCC Amateur Radio Licenses in Smyrna Mills

Call Sign: K1FLO
Daniel L Russell
Box 5
Smyrna Mills ME 04780

FCC Amateur Radio Licenses in Solon

Call Sign: N1RVL
Rosalie D Walker
Rr 1 Box 560
Solon ME 04979

Call Sign: N1RVM
Donald B Walker
Rr 1 Box 560
Solon ME 04979

Call Sign: KB1JAS
Jan Kloub
3367 French Hill Rd
Solon ME 04979

Call Sign: WB1HIK
George D Munroe
Main St Box 102
Solon ME 04979

Call Sign: W1ZNL
Clayton E Adams
11 N Main St
Solon ME 04979

Call Sign: N1ROT
Everett H Day
159 N Main St
Solon ME 04979

Call Sign: KB1OBS
David A Spencer
60 South Main St
Solon ME 04979

Call Sign: N1ONA
Dennis W Lafont
Solon ME 04979

FCC Amateur Radio Licenses in Somerville

Call Sign: KB1IJH
Michelle A Hisler
12 Brann Rd
Somerville ME 04348

Call Sign: KB1IJI
Martin D Hisler
12 Brann Rd
Somerville ME 04348

Call Sign: KB1DFX
David E Stanley
599 Crummett Mtn Rd

Somerville ME 04348

Call Sign: KB2EYX
Robert L Scherlacher
3348 Turner Ridge Road
Somerville ME 043483015

FCC Amateur Radio Licenses in Sorrento

Call Sign: N1NM
Albert D Spain Jr
24 Kearsarge Pob 83
Sorrento ME 04677

Call Sign: N1LG
Letia C Spain
24 Kearsarge / Pob 83
Sorrento ME 04677

Call Sign: KB9TQC
Raymond H Reckamp
25 Lipton Rd
Sorrento ME 046773001

Call Sign: KB1TQC
Raymond H Reckamp
25 Lipton Rd
Sorrento ME 046773001

Call Sign: WB1APD
John P Murnane
503 West Shore Road
Sorrento ME 046773040

Call Sign: KB1DXB
Dennis E Perry
Sorrento ME 04677

FCC Amateur Radio Licenses in South Berwick

Call Sign: KB1VLA
Jacob C Mayo
13 Alder Dr

South Berwick ME 03908

Call Sign: KB1FZS
Glen A Sansoucie
7 Beaver Dam Rd
South Berwick ME 03908

Call Sign: KB1GEN
Glen A Sansoucie
7 Beaver Dam Rd
South Berwick ME 03908

Call Sign: N1XF
Glen A Sansoucie
7 Beaver Dam Rd
South Berwick ME 03908

Call Sign: KA1LJE
Stephen P Zinck
25 Bennett Lot Rd
South Berwick ME 03867

Call Sign: N1JLM
Wallace S D Mills
22 Chestnut Dr
South Berwick ME 03908

Call Sign: N4CQC
Ralph W Dame
30a Clarks Lane
South Berwick ME 03908

Call Sign: KB1CRX
Kevin E Dawson
23 Dover Eliot Rd
South Berwick ME 03908

Call Sign: N1WZK
Matthew D Small
5 Earls Rd
South Berwick ME 03908

Call Sign: KB1QPF
Beth A Flanagan
71 Earls Road

South Berwick ME 03908

Call Sign: KB1KGK
Nathan H Mayer
23 Elizabeth Rd
South Berwick ME 03908

Call Sign: AA1CM
Robert Miranda Iii
563 Emery's Bridge Road
South Berwick ME 03908

Call Sign: K1EPO
Cary R Wallace
46 Flynns Ln
South Berwick ME 03908

Call Sign: N1XPM
Charles S Nadeau
12 Knights Pond Road
South Berwick ME 03908

Call Sign: KB1CJG
Michael B Cobb
139 Knights Pond Road
South Berwick ME 03908

Call Sign: N1YSU
Robert C Prewitt
12 Nealley St
South Berwick ME 03908

Call Sign: WB1DMO
Richard J Coughlin
17 Old South Rd
South Berwick ME 03908

Call Sign: WA1ZUZ
Elizabeth L Snow
27 Old South Rd
South Berwick ME 03908

Call Sign: KB1SPS
Peter M Howell
68 Old South Rd

South Berwick ME 03908

Call Sign: N1TFQ
Peter Greenblatt
37 Quarry Dr
South Berwick ME 03908

Call Sign: N1XIC
Nicholas R Hamel
2 Railroad Ave Apt 109
South Berwick ME 03909

Call Sign: N1JLL
Paul F Klebaur
24 Ross St
South Berwick ME 03908

Call Sign: KA1JUK
Manfred R Griesemer
23 Stevens St
South Berwick ME 03908

Call Sign: W1OPA
Manfred R Griesemer
23 Stevens St
South Berwick ME 03908

Call Sign: KA1JUL
Charlene J Griesemer
25 Stevens St
South Berwick ME 03908

Call Sign: N1OMA
Charlene J Griesemer
25 Stevens St
South Berwick ME 03908

Call Sign: KB1POQ
Gary F Wechter
57 Tamarack Drive
South Berwick ME 03908

Call Sign: N0IZE
Kenneth D Hasenbank
128 Wild Rose Lane

South Berwick ME 03908

Call Sign: N0LFM
Irene K Hasenbank
128 Wild Rose Lane
South Berwick ME 03908

Call Sign: KB1SOD
George C Bloomberg
250 Witchrot Rd
South Berwick ME 03908

Call Sign: WT1P
David L Callanan
104 Witchtrot Rd
South Berwick ME 03908

Call Sign: WA1TDA
Neal R Gordon
142 Witchtrot Rd
South Berwick ME
039082151

Call Sign: KC4ETF
Sheryl L Cornell
137 York Woods Rd
South Berwick ME 03908

Call Sign: N1UBF
Robert J Hunter
South Berwick ME 03908

Call Sign: NQ4F
Jeffrey B Greenfield
South Berwick ME 03908

Call Sign: KB1WIF
Charles Downing
South Berwick ME
039080125

Call Sign: W1CSD
Charles Downing
South Berwick ME
039080125

FCC Amateur Radio Licenses in South Bristol

Call Sign: KB1KFY
Daniel D Mac Cready
161 Holmes Rd
South Bristol ME 04568

Call Sign: KJ1A
Peter E Mac Cready
161 Holmes Rd.
South Bristol ME 04568

Call Sign: KB1ATM
Maurice A House
27 Thompson Inn Rd.
South Bristol ME 04568

Call Sign: KA1JRR
George E Lewis
50 W Side Rd Rutherford
Island
South Bristol ME 04568

Call Sign: KB1ADF
James T Davis
South Bristol ME 04568

FCC Amateur Radio Licenses in South Casco

Call Sign: N1IYX
Martin G Greco
P.O. Box 9
South Casco ME 04077

FCC Amateur Radio Licenses in South China

Call Sign: N1TCK
James I Macfarland
8 29th Fire Rd
South China ME 043580116

Call Sign: KB1AWD
Paul D Memmer
Rfd 1 Box 1270
South China ME 04359

Call Sign: N1BPT
Arthur A Poulin
Box 174
South China ME 04358

Call Sign: KA1NTQ
Priscilla L Chapman
Rr 1 Box 4330
South China ME 04358

Call Sign: KA1IVH
Beatrice E Towne
Rr 1 Box 733
South China ME 04358

Call Sign: N1ZVS
Charles H Allen
16 Fire Road 55
South China ME 04358

Call Sign: KA1JTN
William H Morgan
184 Hanson Rd
South China ME 04358

Call Sign: WB1DXB
Jon M James
52 Hobbit Ln
South China ME 04358

Call Sign: KB1LZX
Matthew J James
52 Hobbit Ln
South China ME 04358

Call Sign: KB1HFF
David B Van Wickler Jr
Box 1101 Lake View Dr
South China ME 04358

Call Sign: KB1AWC
Maribeth Memmer
Box 1270 Lakeview Dr
South China ME 04358

Call Sign: WA1VGB
Ronald W Carr
880 Lakeview Drive
South China ME 04358

Call Sign: K1VFG
Nathan E Hall
514 Pleasant View Ridge
Rd
South China ME 043584419

Call Sign: KB1LQL
Jeromy J Carey
939 Route 3 Apt 1
South China ME 04359

Call Sign: NB1T
Alexander L Clifford
937 Rt 3
South China ME 04358

Call Sign: KB1UAO
Steven A Uhlman
206 Village St
South China ME 04358

Call Sign: KB1EKX
Stephen M Page
South China ME 04358

Call Sign: N1SCH
Stephen M Page
South China ME 04358

**FCC Amateur Radio
Licenses in South Freeport**

Call Sign: NW1Z
James M Klick
Po Box 767

South Freeport ME
040780767

Call Sign: KA1QG
Jack E Conner
South Freeport ME
040780726

Call Sign: WA1WFF
Mark A Curry
South Freeport ME 04078

Call Sign: KB1HXM
Richard A Merrick
South Freeport ME 04078

Call Sign: KB1SLD
Ronald A Hames
South Freeport ME 04078

**FCC Amateur Radio
Licenses in South
Gardiner**

Call Sign: KE2KK
James C Ziegler
69 Riverview Dr
South Gardiner ME 04359

Call Sign: N1PNH
David R Potter
South Gardiner ME 04359

Call Sign: N1TLV
William C De Guisto
South Gardiner ME 04359

**FCC Amateur Radio
Licenses in South
Harpswell**

Call Sign: N1FLN
Harland R Alexander
Ash Cove
South Harpswell ME 04079

Call Sign: N1EUI
Ronald B Davis
Rr 2 Box 338
South Harpswell ME 04079

Call Sign: W1SJN
Robert S Thing
Box 376
South Harpswell ME 04079

Call Sign: K1YJB
Barbara P Knedler
South Harpswell ME 04079

**FCC Amateur Radio
Licenses in South Paris**

Call Sign: KB1CUY
Clifford E Foss
294 Alpine St
South Paris ME 04281

Call Sign: W7CAP
Clifford E Foss
294 Alpine St
South Paris ME 04281

Call Sign: KB1CUY
Clifford E Foss
294 Alpine St
South Paris ME 04281

Call Sign: KA1LVJ
Jonathan A Wilcox
Rr 1 Box 1312
South Paris ME 04281

Call Sign: KA1BRY
Richard I Turner Sr
386 Christian Ridge Rd
South Paris ME 04281

Call Sign: K1LYC
Richard R Cylik Jr

53 East Oxford Road
South Paris ME 04281

23 Mink Farm Rd
South Paris ME 04281

257 Parsons Rd
South Paris ME 04281

Call Sign: KA1WHC
Lyle J Engle
810 Elm Hill Rd
South Paris ME 04281

Call Sign: N1PJA
William H MARSHALL
91 Oxford St
Southparis ME 04281

Call Sign: KC1FE
Russell A Michaud
11 Penley St
South Paris ME 04281

Call Sign: KB1PLA
Cherith R Reyes
67 Gothic St
South Paris ME 04281

Call Sign: KA1VHH
Laurene L Moore
101 Old Route 26
South Paris ME 04281

Call Sign: KB4WFT
Michael T Craig Ii
Quail Ridge Apts 25
South Paris ME 04281

Call Sign: KF4ORY
David P Randall
53 Gothic Street
South Paris ME 04281

Call Sign: N1MNT
Timothy J Packard
315 Oxford Street
South Paris ME 04281

Call Sign: N1ZAO
John M Shannon
3 Russell Ave
South Paris ME 04281

Call Sign: N1OWZ
Stephen D Verrill
74 High St
South Paris ME 04281

Call Sign: KA1TNT
Richard G Young
159 Paris Hill Rd
South Paris ME 04281

Call Sign: KA1ILJ
Richard A Wendell
8 Stock Farm Rd
South Paris ME 04281

Call Sign: NT1P
Harry E Trask Jr
223 High St Lot 5c
South Paris ME 04281

Call Sign: KA1VOS
Richard R Young
159 Paris Hill Rd
South Paris ME 04281

Call Sign: KB1CAC
Harvey R Lord
10 Streaked Mountain Rd
South Paris ME 04281

Call Sign: KA1FTQ
Margaret S Berryment
33 Hill St Apt 7
South Paris ME 04281

Call Sign: W2EP
Arthur C Holub
269 Paris Hill Rd
South Paris ME 04281

Call Sign: KB1FIF
Mary A Lord
10 Streaked Mtn Rd
South Paris ME 04281

Call Sign: KA1ADK
Larry A Moore
7 Mc Keen St
South Paris ME 04281

Call Sign: KA3VCH
William H Miller
546 Paris Hill Road
South Paris ME 042810143

Call Sign: KB1CDM
Muriel S Lord
10 Streaked Mtn Rd
South Paris ME 04281

Call Sign: WB1HBJ
Olive B Moore
7 Mc Keen St
South Paris ME 04281

Call Sign: KB1EJI
Sidney L Berry
889 Park St
South Paris ME 042816441

Call Sign: N1XAF
Robert L Whittemore
15 Thurlow Ave
South Paris ME 04281

Call Sign: KA1RUC
Eugene J Corriveau

Call Sign: KA1UGV
Lawrence J Curtis Sr

Call Sign: K1PWG
Kerry E Phelps

40 Town Farm Estates
South Paris ME 04281

Call Sign: KB1PKZ
Luke B Woodman
2 Upper Swallow Rd
South Paris ME 04281

Call Sign: WC1ABA
Oxford County Emergency
Management Agency
26 Western Ave
South Paris ME 04281

Call Sign: KA1NAY
Kenneth H Whitman
South Paris ME 04281

Call Sign: KB1DZH
Sandra J Morin
South Paris ME 042810331

Call Sign: KD1XA
Jon L Morin
South Paris ME 04281

Call Sign: KF1F
Armand E Bonneau
South Paris ME 04281

Call Sign: W1ZPK
Jon N Morin
South Paris ME 042810331

FCC Amateur Radio Licenses in South Portland

Call Sign: KA1DPA
Merrill C Kaiser
150 Alfred St
South Portland ME
041066701

Call Sign: N1BIE
Harold W Janson

11 Allen Rd
South Portland ME 04106

Call Sign: KA1UTC
Paul A Hutchinson
33 Bayberry Way
South Portland ME 04106

Call Sign: KE7VOM
Kenneth R Mayes
2 Bennett St Unit 4
South Portland ME 04107

Call Sign: N1EXD
Douglas R P Greer
15 Beverly St
South Portland ME
041063820

Call Sign: KB1JBE
Eric P Greer
15 Beverly St
South Portland ME 04106

Call Sign: N1HTY
Craig H Skelton
94 Bonnybank Rd
South Portland ME 04106

Call Sign: KB1IQ
William M Branscomb
16 Brigham St
South Portland ME 04106

Call Sign: KB1FOL
Don V Clayton Jr
132 Brigham St
South Portland ME 04106

Call Sign: K1JKT
Thomas P Duran
1700 Broadway Apt #210
South Portland ME
041063336

Call Sign: KB1JWM
Dolores C Williams
58 Carignan Ave
South Portland ME 04106

Call Sign: N1HZW
Richard N Gosselin
34 Carroll St
South Portland ME 04106

Call Sign: K1TNF
Victor R Montanese
40 Carroll St
South Portland ME 04106

Call Sign: K1AXO
Sewall Y Austin
122r Clifford St
South Portland ME 04106

Call Sign: KE1BB
Frederick A Stuart
4 Cole St
South Portland ME 04106

Call Sign: W1WAS
Maine Yankee Ssb Radio
Club
4 Cole St
South Portland ME 04106

Call Sign: W1LZT
Francis E Malia
51 Cole St
South Portland ME 04106

Call Sign: K1DPM
Richard R Small
37 Coolidge Ave
South Portland ME 04106

Call Sign: N1NOH
Marie I Jordan
32 Crestview Dr
South Portland ME 04106

Call Sign: N1BCY
Fred B Gordon
66 Cumberland Rd
South Portland ME 04106

Call Sign: KB1VYV
Robert S Hatch
9 E St
South Portland ME 04106

Call Sign: N1FKF
James R Veinot
44 E St
South Portland ME 04106

Call Sign: N1EJM
Philip A Bower
10 Elmwood Ave
South Portland ME 04106

Call Sign: KB1SDK
James S Fraser
97 Elsmere Ave
South Portland ME 04106

Call Sign: KA1VPX
Edward E Foster
22 Everett Ave
South Portland ME 04106

Call Sign: W1XAW
Edward E Foster
22 Everett Ave
South Portland ME 04106

Call Sign: K1HAX
William F Ingraham
102 Fessenden Ave
South Portland ME
041064636

Call Sign: KB1NLZ
Robert K Golder
20 Fickett St

South Portland ME 04106

Call Sign: W1WYZ
Robert K Golder
20 Fickett St
South Portland ME 04106

Call Sign: KB1QKE
H Buschhorn Jon
3 Florence St
South Portland ME 04106

Call Sign: KA1ZZJ
David E Chandler
29 Grand St
South Portland ME 04106

Call Sign: KB1KSC
David E Chandler
29 Grand St
South Portland ME 04106

Call Sign: KB1CID
David E Chandler
29 Grand St
South Portland ME 04106

Call Sign: K1DPM
Richard R Small
88 Hamilton St
South Portland ME 04106

Call Sign: W1PWM
Richard R Small
88 Hamilton St
South Portland ME 04106

Call Sign: KB1GLT
Robert A Sobczak
26 Haskell Ave
South Portland ME 04106

Call Sign: WB1EIL
Harry L Phillips
67 Haven Rd

South Portland ME 04106

Call Sign: KD1KG
Bartley L Cardon
49 Hawthorne Lane
South Portland ME
041066935

Call Sign: KA1PRC
Bruce W Green
465 Highland Ave
South Portland ME 04106

Call Sign: N1ULZ
Clifton W Edgerton
41 Hill St 8
South Portland ME 04106

Call Sign: KA1ULS
Christina A Howe
41 Hillside Ave
South Portland ME 04106

Call Sign: N1DNY
Robert D Kendall
52 Hillside Ave
South Portland ME 04106

Call Sign: KB1WJG
Robert D Kendall
52 Hillside Ave
South Portland ME 04106

Call Sign: N1DNY
Robert D Kendall
52 Hillside Ave
South Portland ME 04106

Call Sign: WV2R
Nicholas Benfaremo
72 Hobart St
South Portland ME 04106

Call Sign: KD1WH
Paula J Roberts

91 Huntress Ave
South Portland ME 04106

Call Sign: WA2PGN
Jack Purdy
8 Kenneth Rd
South Portland ME 04106

Call Sign: KA1VPT
John C Hartley
24 Keswick Rd
South Portland ME 04106

Call Sign: W1DVP
Dexter W Freese
72 Keswick Rd
South Portland ME 04106

Call Sign: K1TEV
Peter E Sterling
39 Latham St
South Portland ME 04106

Call Sign: W1WNU
Winston W Brown
9 Lawn Ave
South Portland ME 04106

Call Sign: KD7PJY
Toni D Ferger
1 Long Wharf
South Portland ME 04116

Call Sign: N1SDI
Scott A Mc Donald
69 Mac Arthur Cir E
South Portland ME 04106

Call Sign: N1GLE
George W Adamczyk
751 Main St 87
South Portland ME 04106

Call Sign: N3TCT
Karen C Pience

469 Main Street
South Portland ME 04106

Call Sign: KB1SHE
David A Sherbs Jr
91c Margaret St
South Portland ME 04106

Call Sign: N6TPZ
Scott A Ouillette
31 Mc Kinley St
South Portland ME 04106

Call Sign: N1HPD
William C Googins
54 Memory Ln
South Portland ME 04106

Call Sign: KB1CJH
Jeffrey D Berry
88 Mitchell Rd
South Portland ME 04106

Call Sign: N1UXV
John M Green
97 Mussey St
South Portland ME 04106

Call Sign: N1QHX
David N Boynton
106 Mussey St
South Portland ME 04106

Call Sign: N1ZIT
Judy A Simpson
16 Mussey St 108
South Portland ME
041062033

Call Sign: WA1TNJ
Herman E Ferland
45 Oakdale Ave
South Portland ME 04106

Call Sign: WM1SPN

Jeffrey D Berry
273 Ocean Street
South Portland ME 04106

Call Sign: KA1TXH
Michael D Grimmett
28 Pearl St
South Portland ME 04106

Call Sign: KB1OND
Ross M Drivas
208 Pine St
South Portland ME 04106

Call Sign: KA1ZEZ
Roy P Dufour
33 Ridgeland Ave
South Portland ME 04106

Call Sign: KB3DRD
Kambiz B Makoui
10 Riverplace Dr Unit
10206
South Portland ME
041062083

Call Sign: W2YA
Robert F Wall
149 Sandy Hill Rd
South Portland ME 04106

Call Sign: KB1ORZ
Richard E Colson
440 Sawyer St
South Portland ME 04106

Call Sign: KB1KIN
Ronald M Lussier
945 Sawyer
South Portland ME 04106

Call Sign: KB1DSZ
Deborah Pfeffer
Beausang 585 Sawyer St
South Portland ME 04106

Call Sign: N1UOG
John C Boisvert
71 Scamman Street
South Portland ME 04106

Call Sign: WA1ZEM
Gary C Stephens
27 Simmons Rd
South Portland ME 04106

Call Sign: KA1JFF
Victor Turkewitz
38 Skillings St
South Portland ME 04106

Call Sign: KA1XX
Benjamin A Hubley
103 South Richland St
South Portland ME 04106

Call Sign: N1HPB
William Fenton Jr
70 Springwood Rd
South Portland ME 04106

Call Sign: KB1FDI
Albert A Ingraham
77 Thadeus St
South Portland ME 04106

Call Sign: K1HAX
Albert A Ingraham
77 Thadeus Street
South Portland ME 04106

Call Sign: WB1FSI
Ludger J Guimont
87 Thirlmere Ave
South Portland ME 04106

Call Sign: WB1FSK
Jane M Guimont
87 Thirlmere Ave
South Portland ME 04106

Call Sign: KB7SVI
Joseph S Hatvany
555 Westbrook St Apt 12
South Portland ME
041061925

Call Sign: KB1QZV
Swapna Cherukuri
593 Westbrook St Apt 303h
South Portland ME 04106

Call Sign: KB1QZU
Mahan K Acharyabhatta
593 Westbrook St Apt
303hh
South Portland ME 04106

Call Sign: KB1FGE
Timothy C Kimball
50 Western Ave
South Portland ME 04106

Call Sign: K1EOC
Cumberland County Ares
405 Western Avenue -252
South Portland ME 04106

Call Sign: KB1CPB
Ross F Beale
71 Willard St
South Portland ME 04106

Call Sign: KB1RFB
Ross F Beale
71 Willard St
South Portland ME 04106

Call Sign: N1QZF
Ryan P Morse
South Portland ME 04116

Call Sign: N1UXR
Michael L Howell

South Portland ME
041162811

Call Sign: N1XP
Roger D Pience
469 Main Street
South Potrland ME 04106

FCC Amateur Radio Licenses in South Thomaston

Call Sign: W1FKC
John A Mitchell
Rt 33 Box 647
South Thomaston ME
04859

Call Sign: K1SAM
Samuel L Godfrey
227 Dublin Rd
South Thomaston ME
04858

Call Sign: N1XTE
Karen L Godfrey
227 Dublin Rd
South Thomaston ME
04858

Call Sign: N1WLT
Gary C Muzzey
Elm St
South Thomaston ME
04858

Call Sign: N2BUW
Francis C Stokes
37 Ledge Rd
South Thomaston ME
04858

Call Sign: KA1EJ
Karl W Niemi
358 St George Rd

South Thomaston ME
04858

Call Sign: N1XDH
Robert W Powell
621 St George Rd
South Thomaston ME
04858

Call Sign: KB1AIA
Thomas R Stewart
2 Westbrook St
South Thomaston ME
04858

Call Sign: N1ZVQ
Kennedy L Wilson
South Thomaston ME
04858

FCC Amateur Radio Licenses in South Windham

Call Sign: KA1YMB
Janice L Welch
19 Pleasant St
South Windham ME 04062

Call Sign: KB1HOD
Daniel J Wing
South Windham ME 04082

FCC Amateur Radio Licenses in Southberwick

Call Sign: WA1TOL
Richard C Owens
30 Clarks Ln
Southberwick ME 03908

FCC Amateur Radio Licenses in Southport

Call Sign: KB1UOU

Maureen H Kinsey
98 Cross Rd
Southport ME 04576

Call Sign: KA1RXO
Edward W Kent
Southport ME 04576

Call Sign: N1MQV
Robert W Cronk
Southport ME 04576

Call Sign: WB2LII
William T Fearnside
Southport ME 04576

FCC Amateur Radio Licenses in Southwest Harbor

Call Sign: KB1PMB
David P Lary
115 Clark Point Road
Southwest Harbor ME
04679

Call Sign: KB1VZ
Prentice Strong Jr
Box 68 Main St
Southwest Harbor ME
04679

Call Sign: KA1BNF
Janet B Perry
Main St
Southwest Harbor ME
04679

Call Sign: W1TFV
Wendell D Perry
Main St Box 262
Southwest Harbor ME
04679

Call Sign: W1UWG

Samuel T Chisholm
100 Seal Cove Road
Southwest Harbor ME
046790456

Call Sign: W1JOB
Samuel T Chisholm
100 Seal Cove Road
Southwest Harbor ME
046790456

Call Sign: WB1BQJ
Francis C Soares Jr
17 Seawall Pt Ln
Southwest Harbor ME
046794063

Call Sign: KB1VBI
James A Chalmers
324 Seawall Rd
Southwest Harbor ME
04679

Call Sign: KB1CCU
Carolyn J Parks
Southwest Harbor ME
046790829

Call Sign: KU4BZ
Robert H Zinn
Southwest Harbor ME
04679

Call Sign: KC2JRS
Alex H Efron
Southwest Harbor ME
04679

Call Sign: KB1IZT
Angela C Spurling
Southwest Harbor ME
04679

FCC Amateur Radio Licenses in Springfield

Call Sign: KA1AAK
Stephen R Sawyer
301 Park Street
Springfield ME 044874516

Call Sign: N5ERG
John W Bice
Springfield ME 04487

Call Sign: NN1J
Alphonse J Longo
Springfield ME 04487

FCC Amateur Radio Licenses in Springvale

Call Sign: KB1DHX
Robert G Stephenson
Rr 1 Box 1255
Springvale ME 040839716

Call Sign: KB1WDL
Edward E Baker
7 Heidi St
Springvale ME 04083

Call Sign: W1HEZ
Hugh C Crouch
7 Kirk St
Springvale ME 04083

Call Sign: N1GEW
Robert W Lalime
6 Mousam Street
Springvale ME 04083

Call Sign: KB1GYG
Allister B Banks
18 Pine St Apt 3
Springvale ME 04084

Call Sign: WS1D
Warren A Roberts
16 Sawyer Lane

Springvale ME 04083

Call Sign: KB1AAF
Donald R Labbe
5 Witham St
Springvale ME 04083

Call Sign: AJ1M
Jake R Marsh
Springvale ME 04083

Call Sign: K1UIF
Sidney F Mason
Springvale ME 04083

Call Sign: N1XRV
Robert W Ferguson
Springvale ME 04083

Call Sign: WB1HKY
Scott E Mitchell
Springvale ME 04083

Call Sign: K1DQ
Danny R Merrifield
Springvale ME 04083

FCC Amateur Radio Licenses in Spruce Head

Call Sign: W1GPQ
Richard C Hopkins
Hcr 33 Box 284
Spruce Head ME 04859

Call Sign: KB1ORI
Trevor Reiff
22 Caven Ln
Spruce Head ME 04859

Call Sign: KB1MUT
Russell J Gray
50 Cline Rd
Sprucehead ME 04859

Call Sign: KB1LXT
Kyle P Rolerson
304 Dennison Rd
Spruce Head ME 04839

Call Sign: KB1QNA
Jesse E Ellis
111 Dennison Road
Spruce Head ME 04859

Call Sign: KB1OIO
Eric J Caswell
14 Fuller Road
Spruce Head ME 04859

Call Sign: N5BNA
Stuart B Robinson
Box 206 Rackcliff Rd
Spruce Head ME 04859

Call Sign: W1VJ
James C Elwell Sr
754 Spruce Head Road
Spruce Head ME 04859

Call Sign: N1TMJ
Gary M Post
Spruce Head ME 04859

FCC Amateur Radio Licenses in Standish

Call Sign: KB1OFB
Dana R Perry
163 B Cape Rd
Standish ME 04084

Call Sign: KA1EN
Russell M Ingalls Jr
14 Busque Blvd
Standish ME 04084

Call Sign: KB1MVR
David A Perry
163 Cape Rd

Standish ME 04084

Call Sign: KA1KAX
Carl C Robinson
19 Carroll Ave
Standish ME 040845606

Call Sign: AB1GK
Joseph A Peralta
3 Deer Acres Rd
Standish ME 04084

Call Sign: KE4SEP
Edward L Smith
42 Deer Hill Ave
Standish ME 04084

Call Sign: K1HXE
Herschel A Ward
48 Fort Hill Rd
Standish ME 04084

Call Sign: KB1CRF
Herschel A Ward
48 Fort Hill Rd
Standish ME 04084

Call Sign: KB1KRZ
Jean D Irish
11 Fox Run Rd
Standish ME 04084

Call Sign: KB1SZ
Robert G Fuller
11 Fox Run Road
Standish ME 040845514

Call Sign: WA3CQW
David S Goldfield
10 Gilman Rd Ext
Standish ME 04084

Call Sign: KD1FQ
James F Waters Jr
184 Highland Rd

Standish ME 04084

Call Sign: KA1APM
William L Wilkins
2 Lakeview Ln S
Standish ME 04084

Call Sign: K1APM
William L Wilkins
2 Lakeview Ln S
Standish ME 04084

Call Sign: KA1PXH
Lois A Gelzer
20 Libby Pines Rd.
Standish ME 04084

Call Sign: K1ME
Gregory L Dean
20 Meadow Ln
Standish ME 04084

Call Sign: WB1ALF
Eugene F Terwilliger
7 Oak Hill Rd
Standish ME 04084

Call Sign: W1ZLR
Walter S Gray
17 Oak Ridge Dr
Standish ME 04084

Call Sign: N1NCC
Steven E Sidelinker
60 Pine Grove Dr
Standish ME 04084

Call Sign: N1PS
Peter F Sturdivant
7 Pond View Rd
Standish ME 04084

Call Sign: KB1PYL
Stephan H Titcomb
1554 Richville Rd

Standish ME 04084

Call Sign: KB1BMA
David R Gryskwicz
Rt35
Standish ME 04084

Call Sign: WA1WIJ
Alton G Dyer
12 Westside Sebago
Standish ME 04084

Call Sign: KB1TTJ
Christine A Dyer
12 Westside Sebago
Standish ME 04084

Call Sign: KB1TCC
George D Johnston
179 Whites Point Rd
Standish ME 04084

Call Sign: N1VVV
George D Johnston
179 Whites Point Rd
Standish ME 04084

Call Sign: N1DZJ
David E Wilkie
2 Whitney Pines Dr
Standish ME 04084

Call Sign: K1AAM
Brian J Lashua
Standish ME 04084

Call Sign: N1GAX
Sara A Boutin
Standish ME 04084

**FCC Amateur Radio
Licenses in Starks**

Call Sign: N1ZUC
Darrell A Dyke

Rr 1 Box 1116
Starks ME 04911

Call Sign: KB1OVX
Leland F Dyke
Rr 1 Box 1116
Starks ME 04913

Call Sign: WA1YJY
Craig Comstock
Rfd 1 Box 1160
Starks ME 04912

Call Sign: KB1DBJ
Cora I Comstock
58 Comstock Farm Rd.
Starks ME 04911

Call Sign: WA1LJC
William A Fox
1115 New Sharon Road
Starks ME 04911

Call Sign: N1YJS
Charles L G Comstock
Box 1160 Rfd 1
Starks ME 04912

Call Sign: KA1WEZ
Tobin M Carson
Rr1
Starks ME 04911

FCC Amateur Radio Licenses in Steep Falls

Call Sign: KA1ZZG
Carolyn J Brown
Hcr 70 Box 413
Steep Falls ME 04086

Call Sign: KB1AOR
Clarence A Brown
Hcr 70 Box 413
Steep Falls ME 04085

Call Sign: N1FRZ
Ronald E Palmer
1 Deborah Lane
Steep Falls ME 04085

Call Sign: KC1OD
Ernest M Roma
175 Manchester Road
Steep Falls ME 04085

Call Sign: KB1SDC
Eric P Melanson
565 Pequawket Trail
Steep Falls ME 04085

Call Sign: W1VFO
Eric P Melanson
565 Pequawket Trail
Steep Falls ME 04085

Call Sign: WA1LBR
Charles R Lewis
1076 Pequawkette Trl
Steep Falls ME 04085

Call Sign: KF1G
Leroy A Jason Jr
6 Steven Lane
Steep Falls ME 04085

Call Sign: N1PQY
Mary Ann Jason
6 Steven Lane
Steep Falls ME 04085

Call Sign: K3CXL
James T Hill Sr
Steep Falls ME 04085

Call Sign: WA1HWS
Harry H Minehart Iii
Steep Falls ME 04085

Call Sign: KB1HOO

Gregory L Allard
Steep Falls ME 04085

FCC Amateur Radio Licenses in Stetson

Call Sign: N1PWM
Robert W Semple
Rr 2 Box 3490
Stetson ME 04488

Call Sign: KB1ATS
Wendell W Harriman
67 Burleigh Rd
Stetson ME 04488

Call Sign: KB1AWH
Sally J Harriman
67 Burleigh Rd
Stetson ME 04488

Call Sign: N1XPZ
Merrill W Harriman
Box 460 Burleigh Rd
Stetson ME 04488

Call Sign: WB0BS
Robert W Semple
1015 Mullen Rd.
Stetson ME 04488

Call Sign: AE4GZ
Donald W Kozerow
280 Village Rd.
Stetson ME 04488

FCC Amateur Radio Licenses in Steuben

Call Sign: W1SXQ
Donald A Elderkin
Rr 1 Box 71d
Steuben ME 04680

Call Sign: KA1CCG

Alma A Gordon
1119 Pigeon Hill Rd
Steuben ME 04680

Call Sign: KA1CFO
Lewis L Gordon
1119 Pigeon Hill Rd
Steuben ME 04680

Call Sign: KA1MKI
Edward C Hart
35 Wilderness Shore Rd
Steuben ME 04680

Call Sign: KA1MKJ
Karen L Hart
35 Wilderness Shore Rd
Steuben ME 04680

Call Sign: N1WU
Karen L Hart
35 Wilderness Shore Rd
Steuben ME 04680

FCC Amateur Radio Licenses in Stillwater

Call Sign: KA1URF
Bruce L Oberg
Stillwater ME 04489

Call Sign: N1PNL
Thomas J Crocker
Stillwater ME 04489

Call Sign: WB1E
Mark A Mac Kinnon
Stillwater ME 04489

Call Sign: KB1TNU
Seth A Bolduc
Stillwater ME 04489

FCC Amateur Radio Licenses in Stockholm

Call Sign: N1EYG
Harry O Roth
Donworth St
Stockholm ME 047830117

Call Sign: WL7CD
Alton N Ketch Ii
317 Lake Shore Dr
Stockholm ME 047835530

Call Sign: KB1WMG
Alton N Ketch Ii
317 Lake Shore Dr
Stockholm ME 047835530

Call Sign: WL7DE
Jana L Ketch
317 Lake Shore Dr.
Stockholm ME 04783

Call Sign: KB1TDR
Carl S Seccomb
245 Main St
Stockholm ME 04783

FCC Amateur Radio Licenses in Stockton Springs

Call Sign: N1WPU
John T Bean
101 Blanket Ln
Stockton Springs ME 04981

Call Sign: N1XMV
Robert E Webster Sr
Rr 1 Box 2140
Stockton Springs ME 04981

Call Sign: KB1MUP
Keith E Bradley
50 Church St
Stockton Springs ME 04981

Call Sign: KB1WKO
Robert J Hanish
49 Harbor View Dr
Stockton Springs ME 04981

Call Sign: KA1MBU
Granville H Bowden
617 Harris Rd
Stockton Springs ME 04981

Call Sign: WA8YIG
Harvey R Smith
128 Lighthouse Road
Stockton Springs ME 04981

Call Sign: K1VJI
Walter M Fife Jr
Stockton Springs ME 04981

Call Sign: KA1DYV
Lolinda F Fife
Stockton Springs ME 04981

Call Sign: N1OJE
Douglas W Stover
Stockton Springs ME 04981

Call Sign: N1UDM
Cindy S Bulkley
Stockton Springs ME 04981

Call Sign: N1UDN
Chad E Bulkley
Stockton Springs ME 04981

Call Sign: WA1PGB
Lorin D Hollander
Stockton Springs ME 04981

Call Sign: KC2GXQ
Ruth L Lind
Stockton Springs ME 04981

FCC Amateur Radio Licenses in Stoneham

Call Sign: KB1RSB
Dennis K Boutilier
Stoneham ME 04231

Call Sign: K1OLD
Dennis K Boutilier
Stoneham ME 04231

FCC Amateur Radio Licenses in Stonington

Call Sign: KA1YMT
Jeremy M Rissi
Rfd 1 Box 1779
Stonington ME 04681

Call Sign: N1XVH
Erlene E Davis
Rfd 1 Box 1810
Stonington ME 04681

Call Sign: W1HSO
Wendell D Davis
Rfd 1 Box 1810
Stonington ME 04681

Call Sign: KA1PXT
Lowell A Kent
103 Thurlows Hill
Stonington ME 04681

Call Sign: KB1HBG
Joseph W Sullivan
Stonington ME 04681

Call Sign: KB1VHU
Erik A Walter
Stonington ME 04681

FCC Amateur Radio Licenses in Stow

Call Sign: KB1LRN
Marcel D Bernier

302 Stow Rd
Stow ME 04037

Call Sign: W1WAY
Marcel D Bernier
302 Stow Rd
Stow ME 04037

Call Sign: W1MDB
Marcel D Bernier
302 Stow Rd
Stow ME 04037

Call Sign: KB1MRL
Catherine G Bernier
302 Stow Rd
Stow ME 04037

Call Sign: K1COD
Marcel D Bernier
302 Stow Rd
Stow ME 04037

Call Sign: W1MDB
Marcel D Bernier
302 Stow Rd
Stow ME 04037

FCC Amateur Radio Licenses in Stratton

Call Sign: KB1HSP
John G Labonte
14 Appalachain Rd
Stratton ME 04982

Call Sign: KB1VTM
James F Boyle Jr
51 Main St
Stratton ME 04982

Call Sign: KA1YYG
Charles E Gagne
Stratton ME 04982

Call Sign: N1XDF
Rori L Caldwell
Stratton ME 04982

FCC Amateur Radio Licenses in Strong

Call Sign: KA1OAI
Roger E Martel
Rr 1 Box 220
Strong ME 04983

Call Sign: N1GFZ
Lee D Anderson
Rr 1 Box 563
Strong ME 049839715

Call Sign: KB1VSI
Thomas A Mauzaka
21 Hartwell Rd
Strong ME 04983

Call Sign: N1PRN
Gary R Beedy
High St
Strong ME 04983

Call Sign: KB1TRS
Bradley T Barrie
220 Pillsbury Rd
Strong ME 04983

Call Sign: KB1TRT
Rhona G Barrie
220 Pillsbury Rd
Strong ME 04983

Call Sign: KB1UBU
Aaron E Marden
163 True Hill Rd
Strong ME 04983

Call Sign: KE1LA
Joel M Denison Sr
Strong ME 049830542

Call Sign: N1GND
Charles W Staier Sr
Strong ME 04983

Call Sign: N1SEM
Michael C Darnell Sr
Strong ME 04983

Call Sign: N1UIA
Dena M Darnell
Strong ME 04983

Call Sign: KB1SBU
Michael S Carleton
Strong ME 04983

FCC Amateur Radio Licenses in Sullivan

Call Sign: W1GHS
Wayne E Snow
207 Bert Gray Road
Sullivan ME 04664

Call Sign: WB4LPZ
Hugh R Williams Jr
Hog Bay Rd
Sullivan ME 046640039

Call Sign: K1LOV
Harris L Mc Lean Jr
Little Island Cove Box 32
Sullivan ME 04664

Call Sign: N1MTN
James W Cormier
21 Sand Beach Rd
Sullivan ME 04664

Call Sign: W1DTX
Steven A Montague
Sullivan ME 046640158

FCC Amateur Radio Licenses in Sumner

Call Sign: WB9EWP
Susan J Simpson
431 Black Mountain Rd
Sumner ME 04292

Call Sign: W1COM
Charles L Tripp
162 Gammon Rd
Sumner ME 04292

Call Sign: KB1SSI
Lana E Pratt
1142 Main St
Sumner ME 042923000

Call Sign: KB1SSE
George P Jones Iii
Sumner ME 04292

Call Sign: W2GPJ
George P Jones Iii
Sumner ME 04292

FCC Amateur Radio Licenses in Sunset

Call Sign: KA1NS
Edmund H Kendrick
Sunset ME 04683

FCC Amateur Radio Licenses in Surry

Call Sign: W1ISH
Michael J Gallo
Rfd 1 Box 2260
Surry ME 046849714

Call Sign: KB1BEP
Virginia B Grogean
Rr 1 Box 72a Newbury
Neck Rd

Surry ME 04684

Call Sign: KB1HHB
Bryan T Mclellan
37 Cross Cut Road
Surry ME 04684

Call Sign: AK1W
Minot P Hubbell
4e Harborview Rfd 1
Surry ME 04684

Call Sign: N1VYU
Russell I Smith
20 Murphy Rd
Surry ME 04684

Call Sign: KB1VDW
Jonathan L Thomas
19 Newbury Neck Rd
Surry ME 04684

Call Sign: N5HMX
Jerry W Dunn
88 Ring Bolt Lane
Surry ME 04684

Call Sign: KB1FJJ
Alexander G Smith
Surry ME 04684

FCC Amateur Radio Licenses in Swans Island

Call Sign: KA1SAE
Ronald H Rowland
29 Scofield Lane
Swans Island ME 04685

Call Sign: N1RCM
Robert G Mattsen
Steamboat Hill Rd
Swans Island ME 04685

Call Sign: AB1V

Ralph V Hagopian
Swans Island ME 04685

FCC Amateur Radio Licenses in Swanville

Call Sign: KD1HH
Fred F Carroll Sr
6 Dx Drive
Swanville ME 04915

Call Sign: KB1LOK
Kyle A Dow
153 Webster Rd
Swanville ME 04915

FCC Amateur Radio Licenses in Sweden

Call Sign: N3JLQ
William E Jones Iii Iii
105 Marr Rd
Sweden ME 04040

Call Sign: N1ISZ
Robert A Rice
307 Plummer School Rd
Sweden ME 04040

FCC Amateur Radio Licenses in Temple

Call Sign: KA1JGF
Kathleen S Lynch
23 Center Hill Rd
Temple ME 049843200

Call Sign: KB1SQJ
George E Lynch Iii
23 Center Hill Rd
Temple ME 04984

Call Sign: KA1GPQ
George E Lynch Iii
Rfd Box 92

Temple ME 04984

FCC Amateur Radio Licenses in Tenants Harbor

Call Sign: KA1AGH
Suzanne M Billheimer
Cr 35 Box 455
Tenants Harbor ME 04860

Call Sign: KB1RQC
Austen J Hupper
274 Port Clyde Rd
Tenants Harbor ME 04860

Call Sign: KB1OIK
Joshua A Mitchell
235 Ridge Rd
Tenants Harbor ME 04860

Call Sign: KB1RQB
Zachariah A Mitchell
235 Ridge Rd
Tenants Harbor ME 04860

Call Sign: N1XDM
William J Knowlton Ii
190 River Rd
Tenants Harbor ME 04857

Call Sign: KB1UXC
Michael E Ansart
478 River Rd
Tenants Harbor ME 04860

Call Sign: KB1DKW
Robert T Niland Sr
Tenants Harbor ME
048600268

Call Sign: KB1LXQ
Timothy S Crockett
Tenants Harbor ME 04860

Call Sign: KB1LXR
Garrett J Thorbjornson Jr
Tenants Harbor ME 04860

Call Sign: KB1VCE
Hans K Akselsen Ii
Tenants Harbor ME 04860

Call Sign: KB1VCG
Benjamin R Oakes Boynton
Tenants Harbor ME 04860

FCC Amateur Radio Licenses in Thomaston

Call Sign: KB1TOG
Samantha J Crowell
25 Beechwood St
Thomaston ME 04861

Call Sign: KB1OIN
Zach S Quint
296 Beechwood St
Thomaston ME 04861

Call Sign: KB1KSM
Jonathan T Grout
41 Booker St
Thomaston ME 04861

Call Sign: KB1LXP
Shannon C Grout
41 Booker St
Thomaston ME 04861

Call Sign: KB1LYI
Tyler R Fish
44 Booker St
Thomaston ME 04861

Call Sign: KB5BGT
Marshall N Spear
10 Brooklyn Heights Rd
Thomaston ME 048613515

Call Sign: KB1RQA
Rosemary A Mcgeady
28 Dunn St
Thomaston ME 04861

Call Sign: N1ZVT
Edward O Hahn
20 Gleason St
Thomaston ME 04861

Call Sign: KB1LXO
Nathan N Robertson
38 Green St
Thomaston ME 04861

Call Sign: KB1UXD
Jacob O Hyatt
11 Hyler St
Thomaston ME 04861

Call Sign: KB1TNZ
Drew T Townsend
331 Main St
Thomaston ME 04861

Call Sign: KB1TNY
Deven K Peters
499 Main St
Thomaston ME 04861

Call Sign: KB1TNW
Caitlin M Schesser
22 Main St Mall Apt -1
Thomaston ME 04861

Call Sign: KB1DCV
John W Robinson
23 New County Rd
Thomaston ME 04861

Call Sign: KB1TNX
Kendra L Finnegan
20 Ols County Rd
Thomaston ME 04861

Call Sign: N3JAZ
Roderick H Grindell
65 Oyster River Rd
Thomaston ME 048613304

Call Sign: N3KRK
Catherine D Grindell
65 Oyster River Rd
Thomaston ME 048613304

Call Sign: KB1ROQ
John E Grindell
65 Oyster River Rd
Thomaston ME 04861

Call Sign: KB1PXK
Matthew J Shields
14 Ridgeview Dr
Thomaston ME 04861

Call Sign: WA1MJS
Matthew J Shields
14 Ridgeview Dr
Thomaston ME 04861

Call Sign: KB1HZS
Henry R Grubb
41 Ridgeview Dr
Thomaston ME 04861

Call Sign: WA1WFB
Henry R Grubb
41 Ridgeview Dr
Thomaston ME 04861

Call Sign: W1MCX
Henry R Grubb
41 Ridgeview Dr
Thomaston ME 04861

Call Sign: KB1OIP
Summer L Temple
7 Sawyer St
Thomaston ME 04861

Call Sign: KB1TGB
Charles B Fleming
30 Serenity Lane
Thomaston ME 04861

Call Sign: KA1AGG
Lawrence S Dearborn
26 Sunset St
Thomaston ME 04861

Call Sign: KB1OIM
Matthew J Morse
90 Thomaston Street
Thomaston ME 04861

Call Sign: KB1UVX
Noah H Nedderman
18 Toll Bridge Rd
Thomaston ME 04861

Call Sign: KB1OUF
Dana R Lear
55 West Meadow Rd
Thomaston ME 04861

Call Sign: KB1VCF
Alex R Arsenault
274 West Meadow Rd
Thomaston ME 04861

Call Sign: KA1PPK
Edith S Harding
Thomaston ME 04861

Call Sign: KD1VI
Ralph S Burckes
Thomaston ME 04861

Call Sign: KB1LGP
Eric G Martin
Thomaston ME 04861

Call Sign: AB1GT
Eric G Martin
Thomaston ME 04861

FCC Amateur Radio Licenses in Thorndike

Call Sign: WB2MCD
Douglas R Fox
Rr 1 Box 11
Thorndike ME 04986

FCC Amateur Radio Licenses in Togus

Call Sign: KH6IGD
Jerry A Maske
Togus ME 04330

FCC Amateur Radio Licenses in Topsham

Call Sign: KD1JM
David E Fournier
40 Atwood Rd Apt C
Topsham ME 04086

Call Sign: K1WNC
Barry J Daniels
40 Atwood Road Apt E
Topsham ME 04086

Call Sign: AE1ME
Barry J Daniels
40 Atwood Road Apt E
Topsham ME 04086

Call Sign: KB1JBH
Howard S Truesdell
286 Augusta Rd
Topsham ME 04086

Call Sign: KB1HOB
Katharine C Schmidt
6 Baxter Lane
Topsham ME 04086

Call Sign: W1WEW

Wayne E Wood
13 Blueberry Ln
Topsham ME 04086

Call Sign: N1JWM
Cheryl D Galuza
Rr 1 Box 222
Topsham ME 04086

Call Sign: KA1AME
Kenneth P Caron
33 Carons Corner
Topsham ME 04086

Call Sign: KA1NGO
Fulton E Hunt
18 Cathance Road
Topsham ME 040865500

Call Sign: NG1P
Bill A Richardson
47 Clearview Lane
Topsham ME 04086

Call Sign: N1VVI
John J Chonko
3 Cleave St
Topsham ME 040869728

Call Sign: KB1OGI
Mid Coast Red Cross Radio Club
16 Community Way
Topsham ME 04086

Call Sign: N1TRC
Mid Coast Red Cross Radio Club
16 Community Way
Topsham ME 04086

Call Sign: N1YMO
William H Tracy Jr
37 Eider Ln
Topsham ME 04086

Call Sign: KA1BNL
Richard P Leveille
39 Eider Ln
Topsham ME 04086

Call Sign: N1RPL
Richard P Leveille
39 Eider Ln
Topsham ME 04086

Call Sign: N1VYM
William D Geoghegan Ii
6 Elm St
Topshom ME 04086

Call Sign: KA1RGD
Dale M Stewart
16 Godeneye Drive
Topsham ME 04086

Call Sign: KC1VN
John D Light
37 Golden Eye Dr
Topsham ME 04086

Call Sign: N3JYH
Wellington Yaple
30 Governors Way Unit 578
Topsham ME 04086

Call Sign: KB1CRU
Darren B Theberge
15 Green St
Topsham ME 04086

Call Sign: KD1FO
Gregory J Siska
2 Jersey Cir
Topsham ME 04086

Call Sign: AA1QZ
Gary A Weaver
9 Junco Dr
Topsham ME 04086

Call Sign: KC7LIF
Michele C Briggs
55 Katie Lane
Topsham ME 04086

Call Sign: W1UL
Philip C Hintz
12 Katie Ln
Topsham ME 04086

Call Sign: AK1L
Raymond W Tabloski
21 Kent Circle
Topsham ME 04086

Call Sign: KA1X
Shirley R Tabloski
21 Kent Circle
Topsham ME 04086

Call Sign: KB1JBO
Sandy J Mauro
865 Lewiston Rd
Topsham ME 04086

Call Sign: N1POU
Daniel W Oden
61 Main St
Topsham ME 04086

Call Sign: N1GVF
Gilbert L Barbour
62 Main St
Topsham ME 04086

Call Sign: KA1RVD
Virginia L Davis
6a Main St
Topsham ME 04086

Call Sign: KA1NYN
Eric D Brousseau
58 Main Street Apt. 101
Topsham ME 04086

Call Sign: N1HOV
James L Hoover
56 Mallett Dr
Topsham ME 040861321

Call Sign: N1YWR
Anthony E Bush
63 Mallett Dr.
Topsham ME 04086

Call Sign: N1VNP
Marguerite E Larrabee
50 Marc Ave
Topsham ME 04086

Call Sign: N1IPA
James W A Mc Irvin
414 Meadow Cross Rd
Topsham ME 04086

Call Sign: WA1YIH
John F Best Sr
162 Meadow Rd
Topsham ME 04086

Call Sign: WB1CIW
Douglas G Mcgraves
329 Meadow Rd
Topsham ME 04086

Call Sign: KA1UZZ
Jay G Gaudette
85a Meadow Rd
Topsham ME 04086

Call Sign: KB1ERX
Andy F Estes
8 Merganser Ln
Topsham ME 04086

Call Sign: N1ZDE
Stephen A Sinclair
10 Merganser Ln
Topsham ME 04086

Call Sign: KB1CGJ
Andre L Cote
15 Middle St
Topsham ME 04086

Call Sign: N1JOV
Dj Merrill
149 Middlesex Rd
Topsham ME 04086

Call Sign: KB1SUW
David S Zelno
82 Munroe Lane
Topsham ME 04086

Call Sign: N1TZV
Robert J Rizzo
32 Munroe Ln
Topsham ME 04086

Call Sign: KA1SLC
Walter W Anderson
55 Munroe Ln
Topsham ME 04086

Call Sign: KB1JJC
Andrew R Sylvia
18 Old Farm Rd
Topsham ME 04086

Call Sign: N1UVG
Pamela W Bird
63 Old Lisbon Rd
Topsham ME 04086

Call Sign: WA1YKH
Raymond T West
10 Pinewood Dr
Topsham ME 04086

Call Sign: N1QQU
Christopher W Dickinson
11 Spruce Ln
Topsham ME 04086

Call Sign: N1RLG
Daniel J Mc Carthy
9 Thomas Ave
Topsham ME 040861828

Call Sign: KA1RXN
Duncan G Wood
6 Union St
Topsham ME 04086

Call Sign: W1VRY
James W Wilkes Jr
5 Veery Lane
Topsham ME 04086

Call Sign: KB1KRX
Alan J Aliberti
122 W Merrill Rd
Topsham ME 04086

Call Sign: N1LJI
Chester D Rowe
64 Ward Rd
Topsham ME 04086

Call Sign: KQ1A
Robert G Ackley
2 Western Ave
Topsham ME 040861706

Call Sign: N1TGU
John N Nordby
19 Western Ave
Topsham ME 04086

Call Sign: KB1SYM
Lori A Enos
15 Williams Dr
Topsham ME 04086

Call Sign: KA1OR
Michael D Evringham
16 Williams Dr
Topsham ME 04086

Call Sign: N1ROG
Michael I Atwood
24 Winter St
Topsham ME 04086

Call Sign: KA1PRW
Joel E Sommers
Topsham ME 04086

Call Sign: KA1PTT
Dwight S Sommers
Topsham ME 04086

FCC Amateur Radio Licenses in Trenton

Call Sign: KC7UNK
Kristian J Bearscove Mr.
1117 Bar Harbor Rd Apt 2
Trenton ME 04605

Call Sign: AA1PI
Robert A Carter
829 Bar Harbor Road
Trenton ME 04605

Call Sign: W1FF
Raymond P Midura
15 Lupine Lane
Trenton ME 04605

Call Sign: W1CCN
Elmer P Yates
764 Oak Point Rd
Trenton ME 04605

FCC Amateur Radio Licenses in Trescott

Call Sign: N1PET
Michael K Paquette
92 Wilcox Rd
Trescott ME 04652

FCC Amateur Radio Licenses in Trescott Township

Call Sign: KB1VQB
Wayne C Jones Jr
445 Dixie Rd
Trescott TWP ME 04652

FCC Amateur Radio Licenses in Trevett

Call Sign: KA1DXN
Vernon F Lewis
Barters Island Rd
Trevett ME 04571

Call Sign: N1DAA
William C Eberhardt
Mainstay Box 13
Trevett ME 04571

FCC Amateur Radio Licenses in Troy

Call Sign: K1DY
Stuart W Olson
502 Barker Rd
Troy ME 04987

Call Sign: WP2AEI
Stephen R Kramar
49 Myrick Road
Troy ME 049873406

Call Sign: WP2AEM
Phyllis J Kramar
49 Myrick Road
Troy ME 049873406

Call Sign: K2YSY
Peter A Sneed
28 Rutland Road
Troy ME 04987

Call Sign: K1YSY
Peter A Sneed
28 Rutland Road
Troy ME 04987

Call Sign: N1OZU
Robert W Greenwood
464 Whitaker Road
Troy ME 04987

FCC Amateur Radio Licenses in Turner

Call Sign: N1VCC
Heather M Adams
Rfd 1 Box 183
Turner ME 04282

Call Sign: N1VVG
Robert Blackwood
Rfd 2 Box 354
Turner ME 04282

Call Sign: K1TOL
Paul F Clement
153 Bryant Rd
Turner ME 042820068

Call Sign: N1SIE
David R Youland
280 Fish St
Turner ME 04282

Call Sign: KB1OSM
Michael L Soucy
39 Holbrook Rd
Turner ME 04282

Call Sign: KA1WKE
Jeffrey J Houser
167-2 Howes Corner Rd
Turner ME 04282

Call Sign: K1HZU
Peter L Norris

50 Jordan Ln
Turner ME 042824300

Call Sign: KB1JQS
Andrew A Goyette
539 Lower St
Turner ME 04282

Call Sign: KC1KU
Linwood J Swett Jr
86 Mason Road
Turner ME 04282

Call Sign: KB1SDA
Jeffrey R Kirouac
23 Mill Hill Rd
Turner ME 04282

Call Sign: N1FCM
James D Dow Sr
191 North Parish Road
Turner ME 04282

Call Sign: N1MBZ
Gerard J Ouellette
23 Oakwood Drive
Turner ME 04282

Call Sign: KB1LAM
Martin V Fournier
97 Potato Rd
Turner ME 04282

Call Sign: K1EMW
Donald L Shields
72 Tidswell Rd
Turner ME 04282

Call Sign: N1ZLI
Roland L Gaumont
9 Water Way
Turner ME 04282

Call Sign: K1YSK
Scott L Williams

Turner ME 04282

Call Sign: KA1NWK
Paula J Grimard
Turner ME 04282

Call Sign: N1DOT
Kenneth V Grimard
Turner ME 04282

Call Sign: N1OWX
David C Gagnon
Turner ME 04282

Call Sign: W2IRY
Hector L Creamer
Turner ME 04282

Call Sign: KB1NHD
Gerald E Hume
Turner ME 04282

Call Sign: KB1NHE
James D Dow Sr
Turner ME 04282

Call Sign: K1WTX
Gerald E Hume
Turner ME 04282

Call Sign: W1BOX
Paula J Grimard
Turner ME 04282

Call Sign: KB1VFA
Maine Digital Users Group
Turner ME 04282

FCC Amateur Radio Licenses in Union

Call Sign: K1BEA
Kenneth L Orne
632 Appleton Rd
Union ME 04862

Call Sign: KB1QYC
Jonathan N Powers
282 Barrett Hill Rd Apt 2
Union ME 04862

Call Sign: K1VEB
Edna L Bennett
Rr 3 Bdox 6700
Union ME 04862

Call Sign: KA1WIJ
Karen E Pulsifer
Rr 1 Box 1730
Union ME 04862

Call Sign: KA1WEH
Harry E Freeman
Rr 1 Box 555
Union ME 04862

Call Sign: W1CFY
Neal F Fogg
Rt 2 Box 557
Union ME 04862

Call Sign: N1KIW
Glenn C Abel
Rt 3 Box 8390
Union ME 04862

Call Sign: N1MXZ
Eli R Spooner
Rr 3 Box 9693
Union ME 04862

Call Sign: N1MYA
Denise B Spooner
Rr 3 Box 9693
Union ME 04862

Call Sign: N1DXM
Carleton C Ingerson
7 Browns Ln
Union ME 048629559

Call Sign: N1XDJ
Cathy D Cole
48 Browns Ln
Union ME 04862

Call Sign: W2BFE
Tomm B Shockey
1069 Clarry Hill Rd
Union ME 04862

Call Sign: N1YTI
Scott A Wheelis
844 Depot St
Union ME 04862

Call Sign: KB1POG
Monica R Tofield
803 Sennebec Rd
Union ME 04862

Call Sign: KA1OHN
John S Snow
Rt 235 South
Union ME 04682

Call Sign: KB1HBF
Robert R Bilodeau
369 Stone Rd
Union ME 04862

Call Sign: WC1W
Wilbur M Chadwick
Wottons Mill Rd
Union ME 04862

Call Sign: K8PO
Paul T Obert
Union ME 04862

Call Sign: KA1TBP
Mary R Bragan
Union ME 04862

Call Sign: KB1LIB

Mildred H Grindle-Orne
Union ME 04862

FCC Amateur Radio Licenses in Unity

Call Sign: KB1LDE
Joshua S Van Deventer
1058 Albion Rd
Unity ME 04988

Call Sign: W1HVW
Ivan A King
Fisher Farm Rd
Unity ME 04988

Call Sign: KB1KOQ
Glen H Van Deventer
29 Grady Place
Unity ME 04988

Call Sign: KB1FAJ
Robert A Van Deventer
35 Grady Place
Unity ME 04988

Call Sign: W1HFE
Michael Koziupa
533 Thorndike
Unity ME 04988

Call Sign: KA1AKS
Daniel A Toto Sr
Box 8 Vickery Ln
Unity ME 04988

Call Sign: N1CHO
Thelma L Whitehouse
4 Vickery Ln Box 84
Unity ME 04988

Call Sign: KC1IB
Robert W Curry
520 Waning Road
Unity ME 04988

Call Sign: N1FMA
Pamela M Proulx Curry
520 Waning Road
Unity ME 04988

Call Sign: KB1WQC
Matthew A Converse
63 Wesley Rd
Unity ME 04988

Call Sign: KB1WYI
Matthew A Converse
63 Wesley Rd
Unity ME 04988

Call Sign: N1NFQ
David B Kingsbury
Unity ME 04988

Call Sign: KB1RAM
Robert W Powell Ii
Unity ME 04988

FCC Amateur Radio Licenses in Van Buren

Call Sign: N1RTZ
Guy R Cormier
22 Bridge St
Van Buren ME 04785

Call Sign: KD5DXU
Charles S Paul
104 Poplar Street
Van Buren ME 04785

Call Sign: N1IMP
Nelson Lebel
83 State St
Van Buren ME 04785

Call Sign: K7OP
Jeff M Potter
Van Buren ME 04785

Call Sign: KB1BHL
Joshua G Levesque
Van Buren ME 04785

Call Sign: KB1NIC
Luke R Dyer
Van Buren ME 04785

Call Sign: K1NIC
Luke R Dyer
Van Buren ME 04785

FCC Amateur Radio Licenses in Vassalboro

Call Sign: WA1YBZ
Robert L Whittemore
19 Baker Rd
Vassalboro ME 04989

Call Sign: N1UMD
Joey B Leathers
Bog Rd
Vassalboro ME 04989

Call Sign: KA1YBK
Kelly A Paquette
Rfd 1 Box 1630
Vassalboro ME 04989

Call Sign: KB1CTS
Wallace R Pooler Iii
Rr1 Box 2890
Vassalboro ME 04989

Call Sign: N1EBC
Maud I Peterson
Rr 2 Box 951-15
Vassalboro ME 049899270

Call Sign: KB1INF
Shaun C O Brien
7 Brock Rd
Vassalboro ME 04989

Call Sign: KB1JRF
Timothy O Brien
7 Brock St
Vassalboro ME 04989

Call Sign: KA1YBJ
Douglas P Perry
18 Cemetary Street
Vassalboro ME 04989

Call Sign: N1UMG
Troy O La Breck
Box 2040 Cross Hill Rd
Vassalboro ME 04989

Call Sign: KB1RDH
Mona M Park-Allen
177 Cushnoc Rd
Vassalboro ME 04989

Call Sign: K1WWT
Richard Ociepka
142 Cushnoc Rd.
Vassalboro ME 04989

Call Sign: KR1I
Norma R Ociepka
142 Cushnoc Rd.
Vassalboro ME 049899721

Call Sign: N1NOW
Jon K Rowe Sr
162 Cushnoc Road
Vassalboro ME 04989

Call Sign: KA1LPW
Arnold P Smith Sr
171 Cushnoc Road
Vassalboro ME 04989

Call Sign: KA1MLF
Pauline M Smith
171 Cushnoc Road
Vassalboro ME 04989

Call Sign: KB1OVW
Arnold P Smith Jr
177 Cushnoc Road
Vassalboro ME 04989

Call Sign: N1ANG
Evelyn R Parsons
176 Holman Day Rd
Vassalboro ME 049894147

Call Sign: N1CVT
David A Parsons
176 Holman Day Rd
Vassalboro ME 049894147

Call Sign: KA1SRB
JULIE L Harding
311 Legion Park Rd.
Vassalboro ME 04989

Call Sign: KB1OGV
Richard T Lafountain
592 Nelson Rd
Vassalboro ME 04989

Call Sign: N1XKC
Richard H Claudio Mr
2486 Riverside Drive
Vassalboro ME 04989

Call Sign: N1JBF
Frederick W Naborowsky
196 Stone Rd
Vassalboro ME 04989

Call Sign: KB1LAO
Nathaniel H Dunlap
722 Webber Pond Rd
Vassalboro ME 04989

Call Sign: N1ODX
Michael J Bossie
54 Whitehouse Rd
Vassalboro ME 049893631

FCC Amateur Radio Licenses in Veazie

Call Sign: WB1DKS
Richard J Stevenson
20 Arbor Dr
Veazie ME 04401

Call Sign: N1XMX
Mike Foster
1185 Chase Rd
Veazie ME 04401

Call Sign: AA1QS
James A Jenkins
1285 Chase Rd
Veazie ME 044017067

Call Sign: KA1JUJ
Larry M Zibilske
7 Highview Ter
Veazie ME 04401

Call Sign: KA1OGG
Tammy P Olson
5 Prouty Drive
Veazie ME 044016961

Call Sign: KE1JH
Robert H Jackson Iii
7 Prouty Drive
Veazie ME 04401

Call Sign: WB1GUF
Francis B Webster
1600 State
Veazie ME 04401

Call Sign: N1WTQ
Andrew J Brown
1233 State Street
Veazie ME 04401

FCC Amateur Radio Licenses in Verona Island

Call Sign: N1ZFH
Paul H Webster
249 Eastside Drive
Verona Island ME 04416

FCC Amateur Radio Licenses in Vienna

Call Sign: N1YJQ
Dylan S Archard
Rr 1 Box 615
Vienna ME 04360

Call Sign: KA1EBJ
Charles A Brossy
15 North Woods Rd
Vienna ME 04360

Call Sign: KB1LAN
Mark Rains
101 Town House Rd
Vienna ME 04360

Call Sign: K1PGF
Roger C Plaisted
522 Town House Road
Vienna ME 04360

FCC Amateur Radio Licenses in Vinalhaven

Call Sign: KA1DEI
Patricia A Sheppard
Atlantic Ave
Vinalhaven ME 04863

Call Sign: N1FMD
Robert K Jenner
Rr 1 Box 483
Vinalhaven ME 04863

Call Sign: N2CGY

J Gerhardt Torborg
Rr 1 Box 549
Vinalhaven ME 04863

Call Sign: N1QMQ
Nathaniel J Littlefield
Cottage St
Vinalhaven ME 04863

Call Sign: KC1CW
Robert L Watts Jr
77 York Road
Vinalhaven ME 04863

Call Sign: N1CMS
Frederick A Dyer
Vinalhaven ME 04863

FCC Amateur Radio Licenses in Vinalhaven Island

Call Sign: K1KJC
Leo Demers
446 Calderwood Neck Road
Vinalhaven Island ME 04863

FCC Amateur Radio Licenses in Waldo

Call Sign: N1ECC
Robert Fish
717 Waldo Station Rd
Waldo ME 04915

Call Sign: N1HFL
Margaret R Fish
717 Waldo Station Rd
Waldo ME 04915

Call Sign: N1CBJ
Philip W Cunningham
1235 Waldo Station Rd
Waldo ME 04915

Call Sign: KC2ENR
Earl Slack
1400 Waterville Road
Waldo ME 04915

FCC Amateur Radio Licenses in Waldoboro

Call Sign: N1ZQJ
Sandra D Webster
1607 Atlantic Hwy
Waldoboro ME 04572

Call Sign: N1ZQK
Gordon E Webster
1607 Atlantic Hwy
Waldoboro ME 04572

Call Sign: W1CET
Warren A Wick
Rfd 3 Box 178a
Waldoboro ME 04572

Call Sign: N1KEK
David E Koubek
Rfd 3 Box 345
Waldoboro ME 04572

Call Sign: WG1T
Edgar R Canavan Jr
975 Bremen Rd
Waldoboro ME 04572

Call Sign: N1XDD
Robert C Morse
41 Cross St
Waldoboro ME 04572

Call Sign: W1GQL
David W Billheimer
110 Deer Run Ln
Waldoboro ME 04572

Call Sign: WB1DGR

Donald E Nutter
720 Depot St
Waldoboro ME 04572

Call Sign: N1ZAP
Leona J Farrin
795 Feylars Corner Road
Waldoboro ME 04572

Call Sign: K1KF
Kenneth G Farrin Jr
795 Feylers Corner Rd.
Waldoboro ME 04572

Call Sign: KL7IEY
Donald W Tewksbury
745 Finntown Rd
Waldoboro ME 045726312

Call Sign: K1VYE
Frederick E Thompson
549 Flanders Corner Rd
Waldoboro ME 045725628

Call Sign: N6JL
John S Lawrence
455 Flanders Corner Rfd
Waldoboro ME 04572

Call Sign: W1QS
John S Lawrence
455 Flanders Corner Road
Waldoboro ME 04572

Call Sign: K1NYY
Richard W Glidden
Box 65 Friendship
Waldoboro ME 04572

Call Sign: KB1IVL
Michael L Wile
1011 Friendship Rd
Waldoboro ME 04572

Call Sign: N1FJC

Robert E Pooler
92 George Luce Rd
Waldoboro ME 04572

Call Sign: KB1KLH
Jenna M Tolman
447 Goshen Rd
Waldoboro ME 04572

Call Sign: KB1KLI
Julia F Tolman
447 Goshen Rd
Waldoboro ME 04572

Call Sign: N1OLX
David E Hungerford Ii
940 Gross Neck Rd
Waldoboro ME 04572

Call Sign: N1EML
Henry P Groth
Groths Hill
Waldoboro ME 04572

Call Sign: KA1AFT
Galen R Harkins
196 Kaler Corner St
Waldoboro ME 045726003

Call Sign: WA1JFX
Russell W Anderson
1301 Manktown Rd
Waldoboro ME 04572

Call Sign: KF4BWV
Alexander S Zelinski Iv
262 N Nobleboro Rd
Waldoboro ME 04572

Call Sign: W1AFT
Galen R Harkins
78 Nash Road
Waldoboro ME 045726003

Call Sign: KB1GDW

Tabatha M Abel
598 Old Augusta Road
Waldoboro ME 04572

Call Sign: KC1RK
Carl L Hammond
71 Old Route One
Waldoboro ME 04572

Call Sign: KB1VKZ
Robert H Kanewske
3 Orffs Corner Rd
Waldoboro ME 04572

Call Sign: WA1ZAW
Robert S Trial Iii
Friendship Rd Rt 220 Rfd 3
Waldoboro ME 04572

Call Sign: N1BFO
Bruce F Offhaus
20 Shady Avenue
Waldoboro ME 045720786

Call Sign: KB1DRI
Stephen T Farnum
1819 Union Rd
Waldboro ME 04572

Call Sign: KA1DDI
David A Lawrence
1403 Wagner Bridge Rd
Waldoboro ME 045720364

Call Sign: W1DAL
David A Lawrence
1403 Wagner Bridge Rd
Waldoboro ME 045720364

Call Sign: N1DHO
Peter W Douglas
1318 Washington Rd
Waldoboro ME 04572

Call Sign: W1BDL

Charles Kigel
176 Winslow Mills Rd
Waldoboro ME 04572

Call Sign: N1IEJ
Alan M Johnson
2312 Winslow Mills Road
Waldoboro ME 04572

Call Sign: K1JHN
Earle T Maxcy Jr
1421 Winslows Mills Rd
Waldoboro ME 04572

Call Sign: N1DOZ
Scott E Harding
Waldoboro ME 04572

Call Sign: N1NMS
Thomas J Ford
Waldoboro ME 045721283

Call Sign: N1RQI
Harold G Sears
Waldoboro ME 04572

Call Sign: KB1KSN
William H Watson
Waldoboro ME 04572

FCC Amateur Radio Licenses in Wales

Call Sign: N1YIW
Heath A Blier
197 Andrews Road
Wales ME 04280

Call Sign: N1VVO
Timothy A Blake
Rr 1 Box 1895
Wales ME 04280

Call Sign: KB1DOJ
Elizabeth J Leighton

241 Centre Rd
Wales ME 042803306

Call Sign: N1TXC
Stanton E Leighton
241 Centre Rd
Wales ME 042803306

Call Sign: K1SEL
Stanton E Leighton
241 Centre Road
Wales ME 04280

Call Sign: KB1ENK
James L Miller
369 Pond Rd
Wales ME 04280

Call Sign: K1BGW
Elbert O Derick Sr
502 Pond Rd
Wales ME 04280

Call Sign: W1CFQ
Elbert O Derick Sr
502 Pond Rd
Wales ME 04280

Call Sign: N1YLH
Dana V Robidoux
8 Ruby Lane
Wales ME 04280

FCC Amateur Radio Licenses in Wallagrass

Call Sign: KB4K
Gary L Striker
2127 Aroostook Road
Wallagrass ME 04781

FCC Amateur Radio Licenses in Walpole

Call Sign: N1TEE

Robin M Mac Cready
Hcr 64 Box 126
Walpole ME 04573

FCC Amateur Radio Licenses in Warren

Call Sign: N1VAS
Forrest L Hooper Jr
51 Cooper Rd
Warren ME 04864

Call Sign: WB1GEN
Robert T Niland Sr
1294 Finntown Rd
Warren ME 04864

Call Sign: KA1AFV
Dyson T Jameson
317 Four Rod Rd
Warren ME 04864

Call Sign: N1AFV
Gordon L Jameson
317 Four Rod Rd
Warren ME 04864

Call Sign: W4FIX
Luther V Yonce Jr
211 Hart Road
Warren ME 04864

Call Sign: W1LVY
Luther V Yonce Jr
211 Hart Road
Warren ME 048644524

Call Sign: KB1FUL
Donald F Demmons Jr
51 North Pond Road
Warren ME 04864

Call Sign: KB1DBL
Michael L Courtenay
238 Oyster River Rd

Warren ME 04864

Call Sign: N1YQD
Lyndon M Gresham
401 Patterson Mill Road
Warren ME 04864

Call Sign: KA1VUM
George W Scott Jr
Warren ME 04864

Call Sign: N1SKB
Russell F Smith
Warren ME 048640262

Call Sign: KB1GER
Ralph Demmons Jr
Warren ME 04864

Call Sign: KB1IOI
Matthew D York
Warren ME 04864

Call Sign: KB1LCG
Norman E Meyer
Warren ME 04864

FCC Amateur Radio Licenses in Washburn

Call Sign: KA1IPW
Troy G Hartley
Box 99
Washburn ME 04786

Call Sign: WA1YNZ
Wilburn A Scott
36 Cross Road
Washburn ME 04786

Call Sign: N1WRX
Dwayne D Dow
Washburn ME 047860018

Call Sign: N1WRY

Evelyn M Dow
Washburn ME 047860018

Call Sign: N1YQU
Donald R Peary
Washburn ME 04786

Call Sign: KB1IGW
Robert D Ewing
Washburn ME 047860174

Call Sign: KB1JVR
Eric A Johnson
Washburn ME 04786

**FCC Amateur Radio
Licenses in Washington**

Call Sign: KA1SLY
Philip A Scribner
Rr 1 Box 654
Washington ME 04574

Call Sign: N1MSD
Charles W Robinson
93 Fitch Road
Washington ME 04574

Call Sign: KB1WBK
Donald L Grinnell
74 Liberty Rd
Washington ME 04574

Call Sign: N6ERK
Richard D Bernhardt
369 Old Union Rd
Washington ME 04574

Call Sign: N1CSR
Mark G Day
81 Waldoboro Rd
Washington ME 04574

Call Sign: KC1CG
Edward C Rotch

Washington ME 04574

Call Sign: W1PBR
Pen Bay Amateur Radio
Club Inc
Washington ME 04574

**FCC Amateur Radio
Licenses in Waterboro**

Call Sign: KB1BVH
Anthony N Altieri
Rr 1 296
Waterboro ME 04087

Call Sign: W2HQO
Charles H Heller
Rr1 Box 462
Waterboro ME 040879715

Call Sign: KA1KAE
Candace M Coan
Rr 1 Box 735a
Waterboro ME 04087

Call Sign: KA1KAF
Russell F Coan
Rr 1 Box 735a
Waterboro ME 04087

Call Sign: WB1CIM
Lawrence W Latulip
328 Federal St
Waterboro ME 040873228

Call Sign: N1LAW
John B Griffin
435 Main St
Waterboro ME 04087

Call Sign: N1NIW
Emily M Griffin
435 Main St
Waterboro ME 04087

Call Sign: N1JPD
Daniel B Abraham
Box 540 Middle Rd
Waterboro ME 04087

Call Sign: N1SKV
Scott F Walker
610 Middle Road
Waterboro ME 04087

Call Sign: KB1SDB
Gerard R Lapierre
667 Ossipee Hill Rd
Waterboro ME 04087

Call Sign: KB1OVZ
Donna G Basile
1306 West Rd
Waterboro ME 04087

Call Sign: W3RWA
Donna G Basile
1306 West Rd
Waterboro ME 04087

Call Sign: N1ZUT
Christopher P Hodgdon
179 West Rd.
Waterboro ME 04087

Call Sign: N1NBU
Roland P Basile
1306 West Road
Waterboro ME 04087

Call Sign: KA1VMJ
Jeremy C Smart
Waterboro ME 04087

Call Sign: N1JSQ
Josefa B Abraham
Waterboro ME 04087

Call Sign: KB1PRG
Timothy H Wilkins

Waterboro ME 04087

Call Sign: N1MNR
Thomas M Fanning
11 Baldpate Mountain Dr
Waterford ME 04267

Call Sign: KB1SSC
Gerald Geisler
15 Mcwain Rd
Waterford ME 04088

Call Sign: KU1H
Gerald Geisler
15 Mcwain Rd
Waterford ME 04088

Call Sign: KA1PPY
James E Rose
479 Norway Rd.
Waterford ME 04088

Call Sign: N1YBI
Jacob T St Hilaire
Rice Rd
Waterford ME 04088

Call Sign: N1YBJ
Joseph E St Hilaire Jr
Rice Rd
Waterford ME 04088

Call Sign: NV6V
C Chapin Cutler Sr
1 Rice Road
Waterford ME 040880094

Call Sign: N1JTG
Diana D Taylor Wright
114 Sweden Rd
Waterford ME 040880243

Call Sign: N1MHJ
Lee S Wright
Sweden Rd
Waterford ME 040880205

Call Sign: W1SWW
Stanley W Wright Jr
114 Sweden Road
Waterford ME 04088

Call Sign: NA8M
John C Huffman
30 Valley Road
Waterford ME 04088

Call Sign: K1ESE
John C Huffman
30 Valley Road
Waterford ME 04088

Call Sign: N1NYW
Richard G Knight
1110 Waterford Rd
Waterford ME 040880165

Call Sign: K1ELB
Gordon C Lovell
330 Waterford Rd.
Waterford ME 04088

Call Sign: KA1FTT
Reynold E Jordan
Waterford ME 04088

Call Sign: N1NYV
Virginia M Knight
Waterford ME 04088

Call Sign: N1ZRU
George H Knight
Waterford ME 040880165

Call Sign: KB1TBF
Michael S Brochu
14 Ann St
Waterville ME 04901

Call Sign: K9NCO
William A Lindie Jr
88 B Oakland St
Waterville ME 049015239

Call Sign: N1AII
Lenwood J Pinkham
R4 Benton Ave Box 2280
Waterville ME 04901

Call Sign: KB1QVI
Christopher M Ganza
7 Cherry Hill Terrace
Waterville ME 04901

Call Sign: KB1UPM
Weldon R Black
4 Chesley Dr
Waterville ME 04901

Call Sign: N1ODY
Reed C Bolduc
142 College Ave
Waterville ME 04901

Call Sign: N1HLE
David P Carpenter
189 College Ave
Waterville ME 04901

Call Sign: N1MNM
Gordon L Jones
52 Cool St
Waterville ME 04901

Call Sign: W1BAK
Gordon L Jones
52 Cool St
Waterville ME 04901

Call Sign: WX1F
Gordon L Jones
52 Cool St
Waterville ME 04901

Call Sign: WA1UZA
Gerald A Dessent Sr
11 Donald
Waterville ME 04901

Call Sign: KB1TZZ
Paul M Bilodeau Jr
8 Elmhurst St
Waterville ME 04901

Call Sign: W1PMB
Paul M Bilodeau Jr
8 Elmhurst St
Waterville ME 04901

Call Sign: KB1LNQ
Andrew R Jones
67 Eustis Parkway
Waterville ME 04901

Call Sign: N1NAF
Michael R Francoeur
17 Gilbert St
Waterville ME 04901

Call Sign: W1DPC
David P Carpenter
13 Hathaway St
Waterville ME 04901

Call Sign: WT1J
Malcolm N Kenniston
50 High St
Waterville ME 04901

Call Sign: KA1TCD
Harry E Wing Jr
77 High St
Waterville ME 049015641

Call Sign: N1EYC
Daniel M Hutchinson
1 Highland Ave
Waterville ME 04901

Call Sign: N1KVC
David S Shea
60 Johnson Heights
Waterville ME 04901

Call Sign: N1YX
David S Shea
60 Johnson Heights
Waterville ME 04901

Call Sign: KV1C
David S Shea
60 Johnson Heights
Waterville ME 04901

Call Sign: N1ENA
Michael A Nadeau
28 King St
Waterville ME 049016320

Call Sign: K1DAP
Frederick J Mc Collor
7 Lawrence St
Waterville ME 04901

Call Sign: KY1K
Art Allen
14 Lloyd Road
Waterville ME 04901

Call Sign: NK1I
Barbara C Shutt
14 Lloyd Road
Waterville ME 04901

Call Sign: KA1IPP
Brian A Bourque
16 Mae Ter
Waterville ME 04901

Call Sign: KA1YBM
Robert V Flanagan
260 Main St
Waterville ME 04901

Call Sign: KA1SQH
Richard A Maxwell
294 Main St
Waterville ME 04901

Call Sign: KA1UOH
Pauline G Maxwell
294 Main St
Waterville ME 04901

Call Sign: KA1UOI
Edmund E Saucier
19 Mathews Ave
Waterville ME 04901

Call Sign: KA1YZB
Joanne I Saucier
19 Mathews Ave
Waterville ME 04901

Call Sign: KA1HXK
Kerry A Clark
6 Maude St
Waterville ME 04901

Call Sign: KA1SVO
Roger E Pooler
48 Merryfield Ave
Waterville ME 04901

Call Sign: N1CTD
Donald W Loud
50 Merryfield Ave
Waterville ME 04901

Call Sign: KB1MFW
Doris Bennett
11 Messalonskee Ave Apt 3
Waterville ME 04901

Call Sign: N1EVM
Dorin Zohner
4 Morrill Avenue
Waterville ME 04901

Call Sign: N1TAT
Daniel M Mac Donald
6 Myrtle St 2
Waterville ME 04901

Call Sign: N1TDP
Albert J Vigue
23 Pleasant St
Waterville ME 04901

Call Sign: KA1PZW
Donald J Hamlin
7 Punky Meadows 667
Waterville ME 04901

Call Sign: N1XVG
Paul M George
7 Ryan Drive
Waterville ME 04901

Call Sign: W1NIA
Miles T Brookes
4 Spring Street Apt 1
Waterville ME 049016530

Call Sign: N1IYH
James E Boivin
13 Spruce St
Waterville ME 04901

Call Sign: KB1MRR
Matthew J Moholland
77 Summer St Apt 3
Waterville ME 04901

Call Sign: KB1IOL
Jack E Swicker Jr
20 Veteran Court
Waterville ME 04901

Call Sign: KB1IRD
Morris E Prentiss Iii
21 Victoria Dr
Waterville ME 04901

Call Sign: K1BBJ
Francis W Chase
15 Violette Ave
Waterville ME 04901

Call Sign: N1JID
Theodore M Alpert
8 Waterville Commons
Drive #123
Waterville ME 04901

Call Sign: KA1UNO
Gerald B Lachance
266 West River Rd
Waterville ME 04901

Call Sign: KB1GOS
Hillary J Lister
28 Winter St
Waterville ME 04901

Call Sign: KA1ZZL
Lawrence Lauzon
47 Winter Street
Waterville ME 04901

Call Sign: KA1PMD
Ethyl A Merrick
15 Yeaton St
Waterville ME 049015153

Call Sign: KW1N
David M Merrick
15 Yeaton St
Waterville ME 049015153

Call Sign: N1XHB
Charles J Creamer
Waterville ME 04903

Call Sign: NB1W
Ellery J Borow
Waterville ME 04901

Call Sign: WB1DOY
Eileen S Gould
Waterville ME 04901

FCC Amateur Radio Licenses in Wayne

Call Sign: N1YJR
Gary W Carr
22 Berry Road
Wayne ME 04284

Call Sign: N1EBR
Deborah R Crosby
Rfd 1 Box 2740
Wayne ME 04284

Call Sign: W1IJW
Alexander F Smith
Rfd 1 Box 3323
Wayne ME 04284

Call Sign: N1ZIU
Carroll Paradis
607 Main St
Wayne ME 04284

Call Sign: KA1MVB
Duane R Crosby
Wayne ME 04284

FCC Amateur Radio Licenses in Wayterville

Call Sign: KA1IEQ
Joyce F Dessent
11 Donald St
Wayterville ME 04901

FCC Amateur Radio Licenses in Week Mills

Call Sign: KB1FA
Russell D Cram
Weeks Mills ME 04361

**FCC Amateur Radio
Licenses in Weld**

Call Sign: KA1SIZ
Dorothy R Skolfield
349 Phillips Road
Weld ME 04285

Call Sign: N1XNO
Thomas H Skolfield Mr.
349 Phillips Road
Weld ME 04285

Call Sign: N1LQH
Duncan P Hutchinson
Weld ME 04285

Call Sign: KB1FAI
Shirley J Hutchinson
Weld ME 04285

**FCC Amateur Radio
Licenses in Wellington**

Call Sign: KA1DYN
Mary E Ward
5 Huff Corner Road
Wellington ME 04942

Call Sign: N1UVK
James K Karanis
10 Reed Road
Wellington ME 04942

Call Sign: KB1VAV
Bryant R Garrett
27 Zion Rd
Wellington ME 04942

Call Sign: WA1GYK
Harry D James
Rr 2 Box 1407
Wells ME 04091

Call Sign: N1AYF
Alvin N Smith
102 Burnt Mill Rd
Wells ME 04090

Call Sign: W1KVF
Thomas E Chretien
45 Fern St
Wells ME 040904427

Call Sign: KB1MVP
Peter D Carmel Sr
26 Glen Circle
Wells ME 04090

Call Sign: WR1C
Arthur N Gately
72 Libby Lane
Wells ME 04090

Call Sign: KB1PYG
Steve J Inscore
286 Littlefield Rd
Wells ME 04090

Call Sign: N1XCF
John R Cacciato
50 Morison Ave
Wells ME 04090

Call Sign: WA1EBE
Benjamin K Wildes
78 Natanis Ridge Circle
Wells ME 04090

Call Sign: AB1EB
Benjamin K Wildes

78 Natanis Ridge Circle
Wells ME 04090

Call Sign: AA1LO
David A Johnson
114 Newhall Rd
Wells ME 04090

Call Sign: K1STY
Joseph M Bonica
466 Ocean Ave
Wells ME 04090

Call Sign: KB1GVJ
William L Cotter
1820 Post Rd
Wells ME 04090

Call Sign: KA1DLV
Rose E Perry
6 Robinson Rd
Wells ME 04090

Call Sign: KA1HD
William R Perry
6 Robinson Rd
Wells ME 04090

Call Sign: N1XHZ
John A Dennett
750 Sanford Rd Unit 3
Wells ME 04091

Call Sign: KB1QXD
Brianna F Dennett
750 Sanford Rd Unit 3
Wells ME 04090

Call Sign: N3KIE
Peter P Des Roches
971 Sanford Rd.
Wells ME 04090

Call Sign: W1LBH
Carter B Hart

163 Spinnaker Ridge Drive
Unit 53
Wells ME 040905000

Call Sign: KA1CJN
David A Kiwak
562 Tatnic Rd
Wells ME 04090

Call Sign: WA1ETV
James E Elwell Sr
821 Tatnic Rd
Wells ME 04090

Call Sign: KB1NQC
Leon A Chamblee
61 Valley Rd
Wells ME 04090

Call Sign: N1BPS
David L Collins
Wells ME 04090

Call Sign: WA1YWO
Bruce D Marshall
Wells ME 04090

Call Sign: W1MWB
Mike W Biasin
Wells ME 04090

FCC Amateur Radio Licenses in Wells Highlands

Call Sign: WB1DPX
Floyd E Rutledge
Rr 1 57
Wells Highlands Wells
04090

FCC Amateur Radio Licenses in Wesley

Call Sign: W1EL

Eric F Lowell
48 Loon Road
Wesley ME 04686

Call Sign: KB1ERY
Steven L Ramsey
64 Loon Road
Wesley ME 04686

FCC Amateur Radio Licenses in West Baldwin

Call Sign: KA1UIZ
Brendan T Adelman
Rr 1 Box 341
West Baldwin ME 04091

Call Sign: WA1IVB
Norman B Blake
135 Douglas Hill Rd
West Baldwin ME 04091

Call Sign: W1ITT
Norman B Blake
135 Douglas Hill Rd
West Baldwin ME 04091

Call Sign: KB1UWY
Allen B Jordan
126 Wards Hill Rd
West Baldwin ME 04091

Call Sign: W1PTO
Allen B Jordan
126 Wards Hill Rd
West Baldwin ME 04091

FCC Amateur Radio Licenses in West Bath

Call Sign: KB1FMC
Leo R Maurer
395 B Fosters Point
West Bath ME 04530

Call Sign: KA1WWI
George E Hoskin
Rfd 1 Box 841
West Bath ME 04530

Call Sign: WA1GYM
Herman Merkord Jr
153 Fosters Pt Rd
West Bath ME 04530

Call Sign: KB1INH
Jeffrey O Moore
298 Fosters Pt Rd
West Bath ME 04530

Call Sign: WA1WOR
Jeffery A Jacobs
300 Houghton Pond Rd
West BATH ME 04530

Call Sign: WB1DNO
Catherine M Jacobs
300 Houghton Pond Road
West Bath ME 04530

Call Sign: K1NPO
Leroy C Neilson
428 Kings Pt Box 428
West Bath ME 04530

Call Sign: KB1TGG
Ronald D Vachon
80 Shoal Cove Rd
West Bath ME 04530

Call Sign: KB1IAV
Darlene M Mackinnon
14 Steam Boat Landing
West Bath ME 04530

Call Sign: KB1CNF
George P Swanton
45 Windy Hill Rd
West Bath ME 04530

Call Sign: AB1BO
George P Swanton
45 Windy Hill Rd
West Bath ME 04530

Call Sign: WK1X
George P Swanton
45 Windy Hill Rd
West Bath ME 04530

Call Sign: KB1JXX
Deborah D Swanton
45 Windy Hill Rd
West Bath ME 04530

Call Sign: KB1EDH
Michael J De Sisto
West Boothbay Harbor ME 04575

Call Sign: N1UXW
Margaret S Dalton
4 Ledge Road
Westbaldwin ME 04091

Call Sign: K1IAA
David A Brooks
131 Western Avenue
West Boothbay Harbor ME 04575

Call Sign: N1DHV
Evert N Fowle
West Boothbay Harbor ME 04575

Call Sign: N1XQA
Frederick A Pelletier

Rr 1 Box 108a
West Buxton ME 04093

Call Sign: KB1CKP
Ryan H Bethel
Rr 1 Box 264
West Buxton ME 04093

Call Sign: N1URN
Richard E Keene
Rr 2 Box 464
West Buxton ME 04093

Call Sign: KB1AAV
Erica L Crossman
Box 540 Rr 2
West Buxton ME 04093

Call Sign: N1GFA
Scott H Crossman
Box 540 Rr 2
West Buxton ME 04093

Call Sign: KB1CKN
David S Hubley
35 Tall Pines Acres
West Buxton ME 04093

Call Sign: KA1MQO
Edwin D Mooers Sr
West Buxton ME 04093

Call Sign: KA1VOA
Aaron P Senechal
West Buxton ME 04093

Call Sign: KA1YNN
Paul D Senechal
West Buxton ME 04093

Call Sign: KB1IEE
Damon F Gentile
West Buxton ME 040930337

Call Sign: K1ZPV
John M Caron
188 LOWELL Road
West Enfield ME 04493

Call Sign: KB1VFP
Ian E La Forge
1346 Main Rd
West Enfield ME 04493

Call Sign: KB1LIT
Court L Mccrea
2277 Main Road
West Enfield ME 04493

Call Sign: N1CRT
Court L Mccrea
2277 Main Road
West Enfield ME 04493

Call Sign: W1RKZ
Robert G Harris
8 Victoria Ln
West Falmouth ME 04105

Call Sign: W1WST
Willis E Lane
17 Winn Rd
West Falmouth ME 04105

Call Sign: KY1E
Thomas R Knight
West Farmington ME 04992

FCC Amateur Radio Licenses in West Gardiner

Call Sign: N1SVC
Ronald P Cote
Rr5 Box 198aa
West Gardiner ME 04345

Call Sign: KB1PYU
Lawrence J Hall Jr
31 Brann Ave
West Gardiner ME 04345

Call Sign: KA1PMF
Barbara A Murray
6 Dunn St
West Gardiner ME
043453561

Call Sign: N1EWS
Llewellyn A Murray
6 Dunn St
West Gardiner ME
043453561

Call Sign: KB1FDG
Robert A Brayley Iii
14 Dunn St
West Gardiner ME 04345

Call Sign: KA1JTR
Francis A Malinowski
616 High St
West Gardiner ME
043453201

Call Sign: KB1KWE
Down East Maine Radi
Association
1117 High St
West Gardiner ME 04345

Call Sign: K1UH
Down East Maine Radi
Association
1117 High St
West Gardiner ME 04345

Call Sign: KB1QIV
John P Mclaughlin
1286 High St
West Gardiner ME 04345

Call Sign: W1GQU
Benjamin S Doe Jr
1335 High St
West Gardiner ME
043453535

Call Sign: N1QKL
Donald D Nealley
1117 High St.
West Gardiner ME 04345

Call Sign: KB1TNO
Daniel W Guilmette
12 Kaplan Lane
West Gardiner ME 04345

Call Sign: KB1HOX
Gary L Morissette
31 Lewiston Rd
West Gardiner ME 04345

Call Sign: K1MOH
Glenn C Bowman
810 Lewiston Road
West Gardiner ME
043453322

Call Sign: N1OYU
Michael H Mc Caslin
540 Pond Road
West Gardiner ME
043453121

Call Sign: N1GIA
Kevin A St Thomas
31 Spears Corner Road
West Gardiner ME 04345

Call Sign: N1ZB
Michael W Butler
211 Spears Corner Road
West Gardiner ME 04345

Call Sign: N1QFY
Richard F Sieberg
106 West Ridge Road
West Gardiner ME 04345

Call Sign: KB1RAI
Late Night Amateur Radio
Club
106 West Ridge Rd
West Gardiner ME 04345

FCC Amateur Radio Licenses in West Kennebunk

Call Sign: KA1TWM
Arthur A Bristol
Old Falls Rd
West Kennebunk ME 04094

Call Sign: KA1ZXG
Richard N Burgess
West Kennebunk ME 04094

FCC Amateur Radio Licenses in West Lebanon

Call Sign: WA1KTM
Richard G Cox
W Lebanon Rd
West Lebanon ME
040271047

FCC Amateur Radio Licenses in West Newfield

Call Sign: KA1YPY
Gary A Prokey
Hc 81 Box 3069

West Newfield ME 04095

Call Sign: KB1GTT
Jared A Harvey
31 Coolidge St
West Newfield ME 04095

Call Sign: KB1MRF
Laura L Harvey
31 Coolidge St
West Newfield ME 04095

Call Sign: WB1RDS
Laura L Harvey
31 Coolidge St
West Newfield ME 04095

Call Sign: KB1NZJ
Maureen M Stone
281 Garland Rd
West Newfield ME 04095

Call Sign: K1PHF
Maureen M Stone
281 Garland Rd
West Newfield ME 04095

Call Sign: KB1LCA
James L Gledhill
460 Garland Rd
West Newfield ME 04095

Call Sign: K1GCD
James L Gledhill
460 Garland Rd
West Newfield ME 04095

Call Sign: N1KMA
Robert L Stone
281 Garland Road
West Newfield ME 04095

Call Sign: KA9ORL
John F Cahill
880 Maplewood Rd

West Newfield ME 04095

Call Sign: KB1GVK
J William Chase
1027 Maplewood Rd
West Newfield ME 04095

Call Sign: N1ROM
Clement J Schaffer
14 Maplewood Rd Hc81
West Newfield ME 04096

Call Sign: KB1CFZ
Peter W Davila
45 Onamor Drive
West Newfield ME 04095

FCC Amateur Radio
Licenses in West Paris

Call Sign: KB1PKY
Donna K Moreno
22 Allen Rd
West Paris ME 04289

Call Sign: KA1FTS
Milton E Inman
Rr1 Box 420
West Paris ME 04289

Call Sign: N1DBU
Richard J Copithorne
25 Main St
West Paris ME 04289

Call Sign: KR1G
Richard J Copithorne
25 Main St
West Paris ME 04289

Call Sign: KA4JXI
Michael B Sowell
107 Tuelltown Rd
West Paris ME 042895520

Call Sign: KA1FWA
Vernon W Inman
West Paris ME 04289

Call Sign: N1JTE
Peggy A Theofrastou
West Paris ME 04289

Call Sign: WA1PCU
Robert R Corriveau
West Paris ME 04289

Call Sign: WB1GFF
Wayne C Theofrastou
West Paris ME 04289

FCC Amateur Radio
Licenses in West Port
Island

Call Sign: N1EGH
John B Swanton
171 East Shore Rd
West Port Island ME
045783517

FCC Amateur Radio
Licenses in West Rockport

Call Sign: K1UUF
Charles G Perry
West Rockport ME 04865

Call Sign: KA1HJQ
Gordon L Jameson
West Rockport ME 04865

FCC Amateur Radio
Licenses in West
Scarborough

Call Sign: KA1CPS
Richard A Buckley
West Scarbrough ME 04070

FCC Amateur Radio Licenses in West Southport

Call Sign: KA1SAI
Heather N Kent
Box 276
West Southport ME 04576

Call Sign: K4LC
Fred E Coates Jr
C/O F K Damrell
West Southport ME 04576

Call Sign: ND1M
Robert F Foster
West Southport ME 04576

FCC Amateur Radio Licenses in Westbrook

Call Sign: KA1DPX
Gary F Luke
35 Berkeley Street
Westbrook ME 04092

Call Sign: KA1LES
James M Holland
375 Bridgton Rd #45
Westbrook ME 04092

Call Sign: KA1GHW
George D Palmer
540 Brook St
Westbrook ME 040923612

Call Sign: KA1IJI
William R Landry Jr
9 Declaration Drive
Westbrook ME 04092

Call Sign: KB1IDX
William R Landry Jr
9 Declaration Drive
Westbrook ME 04092

Call Sign: K1EVU
Richard A Duntley
470 Duck Pond Rd
Westbrook ME 04092

Call Sign: K1SDT
Frederick J Mayo
138 E Bridge St
Westbrook ME 04092

Call Sign: N1EYR
Kearney G Guy
15 Everett Ct
Westbrook ME 04092

Call Sign: KB1ASN
Charles L Marsters Sr
118 Forest St
Westbrook ME 04092

Call Sign: N1EJV
Dennis P Savage
30 Giles St
Westbrook ME 04092

Call Sign: KB1RFM
Charles P Shepard
25 Graham Rd
Westbrook ME 04092

Call Sign: W1CPS
Charles P Shepard
25 Graham Rd
Westbrook ME 04092

Call Sign: KB1SDG
Cindy J Shepard
25 Graham Rd
Westbrook ME 04092

Call Sign: W1CJS
Cindy J Shepard
25 Graham Rd
Westbrook ME 04092

Call Sign: KA1ZBX
Linda P Merrill
228 Hardy Rd
Westbrook ME 04092

Call Sign: KA1ZFJ
Thomas R Merrill
228 Hardy Rd
Westbrook ME 04092

Call Sign: KA1PK
Dana A Luke
22 Highland St
Westbrook ME 04092

Call Sign: W1ROM
Dana A Luke
22 Highland St
Westbrook ME 04092

Call Sign: KB1TZW
Julita B Luke
22 Highland St
Westbrook ME 04092

Call Sign: K1JBL
Julita B Luke
22 Highland St
Westbrook ME 04092

Call Sign: N1VCL
Kendall W Woods
101 Larrabee Woods
Westbook ME 04092

Call Sign: N1HOX
Robert D Tetrault
51 Lawrance St
Westbrook ME 04092

Call Sign: N1BAJ
Janet L Cargill
35 Longfellow Dr
Westbrook ME 04092

Call Sign: KB1DUH
Frederick R Mc Lellan
75 Longfellow St
Westbrook ME 04092

Call Sign: N1JYB
Robert J Hammond Jr
133 Longfellow St
Westbrook ME 04092

Call Sign: N1MRX
Bradley C Gray
50 Lowell St
Westbrook ME 04092

Call Sign: N1MIP
Christopher J Drew
26 Madison St
Westbrook ME 04092

Call Sign: N1GRO
Michael M Kilmartin
43 Marilyn Ave
Westbrook ME 04092

Call Sign: W1MBR
Oscar A Fick Jr
77 Oakland Ave
Westbrook ME 04092

Call Sign: N1WVA
Ann E Castle
76 Oriole St
Westbrook ME 04092

Call Sign: K1EFZ
Robert N Harnois
56 Pennell St
Westbrook ME 040923352

Call Sign: K1SOW
Thomas A Valente Jr
1 Plymouth Rd
Westbrook ME 04092

Call Sign: W1NE
John A Donahue Jr
8 Puritan Drive
Westbrook ME 040924526

Call Sign: KB1ESB
Dianna D Dipaolo
3 Quaker Road
Westbrook ME 04092

Call Sign: N1KIF
Owen F Gallagher
93 Rochester
Westbrook ME 04092

Call Sign: KB1ATF
John S Washington Ii
40 Rosewood Drive
Westbrook ME 04092

Call Sign: KD1TL
Ronald L Strout
166s Saco St
Westbrook ME 04092

Call Sign: N1MDT
Gary R Jamieson
234 Saco Street
Westbrook ME 04092

Call Sign: N1LWE
Raymond M Morrill
48 Seavey St
Westbrook ME 04092

Call Sign: N1SDD
Mary S Morrill
48 Seavey St
Westbrook ME 04092

Call Sign: KB1UXA
Daniel J Boucher
147 Spring St
Westbrook ME 04092

Call Sign: KB1CPA
Terri S Peasley
9 State St
Westbrook ME 04092

Call Sign: KB1UOR
Ryan M Mcgowan
90 Stroudwater St
Westbrook ME 04092

Call Sign: KA1DXS
Lyman A Chisholm
202 The Hamlet
Westbrook ME 04092

Call Sign: KB1JWR
Michael Esty
22 Union St
Westbrook ME 04092

Call Sign: N1ICO
David S Reynolds
21 W Pleasant St
Westbrook ME 04092

Call Sign: KB1GE
Ronald J Dubois Sr
150 West Pleasant St
Westbrook ME 04092

Call Sign: K1GSF
Margaret L Harnois
Westbrook ME 04092

Call Sign: K2ISH
Lawrence M Feldman
Westbrook ME 040981153

Call Sign: N1OAG
Ronald H Carrier
Westbrook ME 04098

Call Sign: NX1A
Barnie L Reynolds

Westbrook ME 04098

Call Sign: KB1UDB
Anthony J Bessey
Westbrook ME 04098

Call Sign: N1AJB
Anthony J Bessey
Westbrook ME 04098

FCC Amateur Radio Licenses in Weston

Call Sign: KB1NDN
Dana Morrison
7 Cropley Rd
Weston ME 04424

FCC Amateur Radio Licenses in Westport

Call Sign: KB1HBC
Walter B Mc Carty
914 Main Rd
Westport ME 04578

FCC Amateur Radio Licenses in Westport Island

Call Sign: AC1O
Daryl L Grant
12 Palmer Rd
Westport Island ME 04578

Call Sign: KB1FYA
Jerry I Partelow
21 Weatherstone Drive
Westport Island ME 04578

FCC Amateur Radio Licenses in Whitefield

Call Sign: N1WPW

Darrell W Hartman
Rr 1 Box 178
Whitefield ME 04353

Call Sign: KB1HSL
Craig A Hutchinson
42 Branch Ln
Whitefield ME 04353

Call Sign: KD1XO
Donald W Morang
106 East River Road
Whitefield ME 043530254

Call Sign: N1HPJ
Kenneth S Chapman
93 Heath Road
Whitefield ME 04353

Call Sign: KB1CWH
Mark A Theriault
176 Hilton Rd
Whitefield ME 04353

Call Sign: N1REX
Richard R Beausoleil
292 Howe Road
Whitefield ME 04353

Call Sign: KB1JCA
Thomas M Feeney
81 Hunts Meadow Road
Whitefield ME 04353

Call Sign: KB1CON
C Thomas Sweet
65 Jefferson Rd
Whitefield ME 04353

Call Sign: K1FCS
Frederick C Souza
114 N Hunts Medow Rd
Whitefield ME 04353

Call Sign: KB1FNC

Michael G Sullivan
222 Pittston Rd
Whitefield ME 04353

Call Sign: W1QEE
Michael G Sullivan
222 Pittston Rd
Whitefield ME 04353

Call Sign: KB1GOW
Marlene A Sullivan
222 Pittston Rd
Whitefield ME 04353

Call Sign: N1AUY
Donald G Sprague
420 Wiscasset Road
Whitefield ME 04353

FCC Amateur Radio Licenses in Whiting

Call Sign: WA2WHU
Robert L Mallar Jr
Us Rt 1 73
Whiting ME 04691

Call Sign: WT1G
Earl L Myers
Box 43
Whiting ME 04691

Call Sign: WA1JQW
Earl L Myers
Box 43
Whiting ME 04691

Call Sign: K1ZXM
Ellis E Small
Hc 74 Box 84
Whiting ME 04691

Call Sign: KB1ONS
Walter R Grochmal Jr
254 Dodge Road

Whiting ME 04691

Call Sign: KB1VKM
Kathy A Jones
117 Lubec Rd
Whiting ME 04691

Call Sign: N1MLF
Jon T Watts
117 Lubec Rd.
Whiting ME 04691

Call Sign: KA1LYG
Wendell M Mc Laughlin
Whiting ME 04691

Call Sign: N1MCO
Anthony M Jans
Whiting ME 04691

Call Sign: N1MCR
Craig L Smith
Whiting ME 04691

Call Sign: N1SCW
Cathy J Dent
Whiting ME 04691

Call Sign: N1SCX
David L Dent
Whiting ME 04628

Call Sign: WB1EKT
Charlene M Myers
Whiting ME 04691

Call Sign: AB1JZ
Kenneth G Dwelley
Whiting ME 04691

FCC Amateur Radio Licenses in Whitneyville

Call Sign: N1QM
Wayne C Ackley

137 S Main St
Whitneyville ME 04654

FCC Amateur Radio Licenses in Wilton

Call Sign: KB1QMW
Julie A Dudevoir-Badger
81 Fenderson Hill
Wilton ME 04294

Call Sign: KB1SKX
Kirk D Badger
81 Fenderson Hill Rd
Wilton ME 04294

Call Sign: KA1IXA
Mark G Badger
81 Fenderson Hill Road
Wilton ME 04294

Call Sign: W1QB
Mark G Badger
81 Fenderson Hill Road
Wilton ME 04294

Call Sign: N1RCT
Richard C Stevens
21 Fuller St.
Wilton ME 04294

Call Sign: KB1GVW
Thomas M Cahn
60 Fuller Str
Wilton ME 04294

Call Sign: K4UNM
Jeremy R Shepard
George Shepard
Wilton ME 04294

Call Sign: KE1BN
Harold B Stone Jr
434 Munson Rd
Wilton ME 04294

Call Sign: KB1SQM
Kelley L Dyke
8 N Stockford Ave
Wilton ME 04294

Call Sign: WA1PFM
A Clifford Trend
857 Orchard Dr
Wilton ME 04294

Call Sign: N7PQK
Michael T Rowland
239 Temple Rd
Wilton ME 04294

Call Sign: KB1GPR
Michael T Rowland
239 Temple Rd
Wilton ME 04294

Call Sign: KA1TE
Robert L Welles
352 Temple Rd
Wilton ME 04294

Call Sign: N1VHI
John D Zadakis Iii
682 Us Rte 2 W
Wilton ME 04295

Call Sign: W1FKD
Harry D Thomason Jr
69 Voter Hill Rd
Wilton ME 042944044

Call Sign: KY1C
Paul E Gooch Jr
Wilton ME 04294

Call Sign: N1NHX
Steven P Gooch
Wilton ME 04294

Call Sign: N1FCU
John C Wright
131 Brand Rd
Windham ME 04062

Call Sign: AC1R
Andre L Cote
50 Brown Cove Road
Windham ME 04062

Call Sign: N1FJM
Mitchell O Finger
7 Carol Drive
Windham ME 040623325

Call Sign: N1VTR
Matthew R Stover
71 Chute Road
Windham ME 04062

Call Sign: KA1YCW
Sharon S Shardlow
37 Easter Ave
Windham ME 04062

Call Sign: K1OT
Richard A Fickett
7 Fall Ridge Rd
Windham ME 04062

Call Sign: W1BKT
Everett W Doughty
53 Falmouth Rd
Windham ME 04062

Call Sign: KB1DIH
Eric K Murch
286 Falmouth Rd
Windham ME 040624815

Call Sign: N1DIH
Eric K Murch

286 Falmouth Rd
Windham ME 040624815

Call Sign: WB1DLB
Gilbert S Marks
539 Falmouth Rd Unit 2
Windham ME 040625186

Call Sign: KC1VV
Warren P Swetz
127 Forbes Ln
Windham ME 04062

Call Sign: AC1Q
George R Fecteau
11 Goshen Road
Windham ME 04062

Call Sign: N1WIG
Samuel D Webber
241 Gray Rd
Windham ME 040624245

Call Sign: KB1GOQ
Mark J Gregg
96 Haven Rd
Windham ME 04062

Call Sign: W1CAY
Mark J Gregg
96 Haven Rd
Windham ME 04062

Call Sign: KA1VPJ
Aratus F Ames
Highland Lake Park Lot 1
Windham ME 04862

Call Sign: KB1BIH
Michael K Mack
3 Highland Rd
Windham ME 04062

Call Sign: KT1O
Thomas A O Brion

5 Kelli Lane
Windham ME 04062

Call Sign: KA1VXD
Frederick E Stacey
49 Lakeview Rd
Windham ME 04862

Call Sign: N1FRJ
Dale M Darling Ii
9 Memory Ln
Windham ME 04062

Call Sign: N1EFN
Kent M Chaney
12 Mill Pond Ln
Windham ME 04062

Call Sign: KA1MRS
Ellen V Wescott
2 Mineral Spring Rd
Windham ME 04062

Call Sign: K1CXW
Lawrence J Wescott Jr
85 Mineral Spring Rd
Windham ME 04062

Call Sign: KA1NVA
David W Joy
23 Misty Dr
Windham ME 040624145

Call Sign: W4KSR
Mark A Carlson
8 Moores Dr
Windham ME 04062

Call Sign: W1MTW
Mark A Carlson
8 Moores Dr
Windham ME 04062

Call Sign: N1BCT
Douglas R Trottier

30 Neal Rd
Windham ME 04062

Call Sign: KB1OYA
Robert F Midura Sr
41 New Hall Rd
Windham ME 04062

Call Sign: K1RPS
Robert H Muir
59 Northwood Dr
Windham ME 04062

Call Sign: N1SHL
Angela G Perry
39 Old County Rd
Windham ME 04062

Call Sign: N1SHN
James Perry
39 Old County Rd
Windham ME 04062

Call Sign: KB1CCQ
Robert E Mognet
58 Overlook Rd
Windham ME 04062

Call Sign: KB1UVZ
James I Biskup
240 Pope Rd
Windham ME 04062

Call Sign: N1RXJ
David R Young
400 Pope Road
Windham ME 04062

Call Sign: KB1IJL
Shirley J Dudley
12 Presumpscot Rd
Windham ME 040624733

Call Sign: KB1IJM
Robert F Dudley Jr

12 Presumpscot Rd
Windham ME 040624733

Call Sign: W1GEM
George E Maynard
1011 River Rd
Windham ME 040625305

Call Sign: KB1DUG
George E Maynard
1011 River Rd
Windham ME 040625305

Call Sign: KO4WR
James F Sheehan
690 Rivewr Road
Windam ME 04062

Call Sign: N1KAC
Richard M Sukeforth
25 Rolfe Rd
Windham ME 04062

Call Sign: N1RNL
Richard O Peasley
42 Roosevelt Trl
Windham ME 04062

Call Sign: N1ULO
Travis M Sparks
7 Rousseau Rd
Windham ME 04062

Call Sign: KA1WJL
Laurel T Parker
66 Running Brook Rd
Windham ME 04062

Call Sign: W1SQV
Walter M Parker
66 Running Brook Rd
Windham ME 04062

Call Sign: N1WJ
William W Johnson Sr

23 Sabatus Lane
Windham ME 040624739

Call Sign: W1BLT
William W Johnson Sr
23 Sabatus Lane
Windham ME 040624739

Call Sign: WB2BQD
Douglas N Edwards
125 Sabbady Point Rd
Windham ME 04062

Call Sign: K4SMG
Shawn M Glover
180 Tandberg Trail
Windham ME 040625102

Call Sign: K4GRG
Gene R Glover
180 Tandberg Trail
Windham ME 040625102

Call Sign: N1YF
Shawn M Glover
180 Tandberg Trail
Windham ME 040625102

Call Sign: N1YE
Gene R Glover
180 Tandberg Trail
Windham ME 040625102

Call Sign: KD4TCW
Steven M Lewis
9 Underwood Way
Windham ME 04062

Call Sign: KB1UVY
Andrew M Rogers
17 Underwood Way
Windham ME 04062

Call Sign: K1ROG
Andrew M Rogers

17 Underwood Way
Windham ME 04062

Call Sign: KB1WCR
Jason T Burke
3 Victoria Ln
Windham ME 04062

Call Sign: W1JSH
Morton L Grant
25 Walter Partridge Rd
Windham ME 040624860

Call Sign: KB1QHQ
James R Linscott
16 Webb Road
Windham ME 04062

Call Sign: KC1IV
Robert L Maurais
48 William Knight Rd
Windham ME 04062

Call Sign: KA1TXG
Stephen W Locke
262 Windham Ctr Rd
Windham ME 04062

Call Sign: AL0A
Gregory R Breeden
Windham ME 04062

Call Sign: KB1DLJ
Jeffrey S Sanborn
Windham ME 04062

Call Sign: N1FVJ
Roy A Clark
Windham ME 04062

Call Sign: KB1PHL
Zach P Breeden
Windham ME 04062

Call Sign: KB1QHU

Vincent J Micale
Windham ME 04062

FCC Amateur Radio Licenses in Windsor

Call Sign: KB1FWE
Dean E Shorty
506 Augusta Rockland Rd
Windsor ME 04363

Call Sign: K1DES
Dean E Shorty
506 Augusta Rockland Rd
Windsor ME 04363

Call Sign: KB1TAD
Andrew T Campbell
16 Bean Rd
Windsor ME 04363

Call Sign: KA1NKY
Sheridan C Mayo
Rt 17 Box 1010
Windsor ME 04363

Call Sign: KB1IVS
Audrey L Brann
Rr 1 Box 1454
Windsor ME 04363

Call Sign: N1DTJ
Donald J Lizotte
Rr 1 Box 3343
Windsor ME 04363

Call Sign: N1EHE
Vicki L Lizotte
Rr1 Box 3343
Windsor ME 04363

Call Sign: W1KTW
Ernest O Newton
25 Crosby Rd
Windsor ME 04363

Call Sign: KB1GVS
Shirley J Michaud
505 S Belfast Rd
Windsor ME 04363

Call Sign: KA1KHM
Richard E Michaud
505 So Belfast Rd
Windsor ME 04363

Call Sign: AB1FZ
Richard E Michaud
505 So Belfast Rd
Windsor ME 04363

Call Sign: WZ1Z
Richard E Michaud
505 So Belfast Rd
Windsor ME 04363

Call Sign: K1XI
Randall A Lewis
Windsor ME 04363

Call Sign: N1HBY
Gretchen L Lewis
Windsor ME 04363

Call Sign: KB1MRP
Todd L Vigue
Windsor ME 04363

FCC Amateur Radio Licenses in Winslow

Call Sign: N1HNY
Robert O Mower
788 Abbott Rd
Winslow ME 049010020

Call Sign: N1XZL
Martin R Macgown
1358 Albion Road
Winslow ME 04901

Call Sign: N1NPJ
Ronald J Manson
R 3 Augusta Rd Box 45
Winslow ME 04901

Call Sign: KB1JBM
James E Byther
Rr 3 Box 6500
Winslow ME 04901

Call Sign: KB1OLK
Paul J Doucette
18 Fuller Dr
Winslow ME 04901

Call Sign: N1UGQ
Matt L Hussey
21 Bald Eagle Ln
Winslow ME 04901

Call Sign: KB1AWS
Michael J Maliga
Rfd 3 Box 6781
Winslow ME 04901

Call Sign: KB1RVQ
James K Allen
4 Lucille Ave
Winslow ME 04901

Call Sign: KA1PXJ
Carmen L Coro
154 Bassett Road
Winslow ME 04901

Call Sign: WA1NDC
Blaine H Bailey Jr
Rr 3 Box 7125
Winslow ME 04901

Call Sign: W1JKA
James K Allen
4 Lucille Ave
Winslow ME 04901

Call Sign: W1EWW
Guy E Coro
154 Bassett Road
Winslow ME 04901

Call Sign: WA2ZYX
David V Bourque
1 Cardinal Way
Winslow ME 04901

Call Sign: W1SSF
Ronald J Manson
5 Matheson Ave
Winslow ME 04901

Call Sign: KB1CAI
Winslow Elementary School
55 Benton Ave
Winslow ME 04901

Call Sign: KB1OLQ
Harold J Rayborn
1 Charles Ave
Winslow ME 04901

Call Sign: W1SK
Joseph M Grace
13 North Garand St. Apt 4
Winslow ME 04901

Call Sign: N1NSV
Paul S Shorette Ii
Rr 2 Box 2245
Winslow ME 04902

Call Sign: KB1DLE
James N Veilleux
55 China Rd
Winslow ME 04901

Call Sign: N1VVN
Janet L Maliga
62 North Reynolds Road
Winslow ME 04901

Call Sign: N1PIK
Donald L Rowe
Rfd 3 Box 3700
Winslow ME 04901

Call Sign: K1OGY
James E Byther
870 China Road
Winslow ME 04901

Call Sign: KD1MM
Michael J Maliga
62 North Reynolds Road
Winslow ME 04901

Call Sign: N1FVH
James L Gorman
Rfd 2 Box 420
Winslow ME 04901

Call Sign: KA1CIT
William C Taylor
24 Frankwood Dr
Winslow ME 04902

Call Sign: N1UGR
Peter G Hussey
58 Patterson Ave
Winslow ME 04901

Call Sign: KA1GHL
James E Byther
Rr 3 Box 6500
Winslow ME 04901

Call Sign: N1KFM
Christopher W Taylor
24 Frankwood Dr
Winslow ME 04901

Call Sign: KA1PXI
Pamela M Hewes
106 Roderick Rd
Winslow ME 04901

Call Sign: W1RBT
Real B Trepanier
14 Sam St
Winslow ME 04901

Call Sign: K4SFB
Stephen F Bernier
44 Taylor Road
Winslow ME 04901

Call Sign: WB1GEE
Michael E Palumbo
6 Whisperwood Dr
Winslow ME 04901

Call Sign: KA1RUH
Robert B Pomerleau
Winslow ME 04901

FCC Amateur Radio Licenses in Winter Harbor

Call Sign: WI1A
Wesley E Reed
102 Birch Harbor Road
Winter Harbor ME
046930523

Call Sign: W1UVJ
Lawrence K Sprague
20 Hillcrest Drive Apt 14
Winter Harbor ME 04693

Call Sign: W1BTB
Helen M Torrey
Star Rt Box 22 Main St
Winter Harbor ME 04693

Call Sign: W1GBS
Bruce E Lanning
496 Newman St
Winter Harbor ME 04693

Call Sign: W1BSR

Larry A Torrey
Star Rt Box 36 Newman St
Winter Harbor ME 04693

Call Sign: N1LXL
Russell K Holt
Box 6578 Nsga
Winter Harbor ME 04693

Call Sign: N1MYW
Gina G Holt
Nsga
Winter Harbor ME 04693

Call Sign: KA1YTF
Thomas L Hilson
Nsga Box 6657
Winter Harbor ME 04693

Call Sign: K1NAN
Nsga Naval Security Group
Activity
Winter Harbor ME 04693

Call Sign: KA1ZYI
Neil T Buffett
Winter Harbor ME
046930267

FCC Amateur Radio Licenses in Winterport

Call Sign: KB1DRR
Carole Ann S Glueck
78 Back Winterport Rd
Winterport ME 04496

Call Sign: N1MDZ
Richard D Glueck
78 Back Winterport Rd
Winterport ME 04496

Call Sign: N1UHI
Tristan F Glueck
78 Bockwinterport Rd

Winterport ME 04496

Call Sign: N1JZW
Virginia Detmer Matyas
Rr 1 Box 1835
Winterport ME 04497

Call Sign: KC1FM
Berenice S Clark
Rfd 1 Box 500
Winterport ME 04496

Call Sign: N1IAX
Henry Beeuwkes
Rr 1 Box 613
Winterport ME 04496

Call Sign: KB1VZV
Eric Keppel
19 Keppel Point Rd
Winterport ME 04496

Call Sign: KB1WOS
Jami L Keppel
19 Keppel Point Rd
Winterport ME 04496

Call Sign: K1AGP
Bruce K Scott
1628 N Main
Winterport ME 04496

Call Sign: W1FLV
Ronald L Cook
866 N Main St
Winterport ME 044963402

Call Sign: KB1FJH
Bob W Gause
205 North Road
Winterport ME 04496

Call Sign: KD1YW
John E Howard
280 Stream Rd

Winterport ME 04496

Call Sign: W1FZL
Ernest W Hauger
443 Stream Rd
Winterport ME 04496

Call Sign: N1OJL
Timothy L Hathaway
Box 2018 Stream Rd
Winterport ME 04496

Call Sign: N1JZX
Elizabeth D Hauger
443 Stream Road
Winterport ME 04496

Call Sign: KC1IT
Peter B Caron
Winterport ME 04496

Call Sign: N1SXH
June Glidden
Winterport ME 04494

Call Sign: WB1FOT
Michael W Mc Dade
Winterport ME 04496

Call Sign: KB1FJD
William I Smith
Winterport ME 04496

Call Sign: KB1OHA
Michael W Roy
Winterport ME 04496

FCC Amateur Radio Licenses in Winthrop

Call Sign: KB1QVJ
Patrick J Saucier
573 B Stanley Rd
Winthrop ME 04364

Call Sign: N1MCW
Owen D Buck
Rr 1 Box 1602
Winthrop ME 04364

Call Sign: N1GHG
Millard C Hayden
R 1 Box 2100
Winthrop ME 04364

Call Sign: KB1QN
Lawrence R Sedgeley
Rt 3 Box 4460
Winthrop ME 04364

Call Sign: KA1ORG
Stephen E Johnson
Rt 133 Box 451
Winthrop ME 04364

Call Sign: N1KMT
George D Fuller
Rr 2 Box 4805
Winthrop ME 04364

Call Sign: W1QAE
Arthur G Clark
Rfd 3 Box 60
Winthrop ME 04364

Call Sign: KA1FML
Nancy E Strubbe
Rfd 2 Box 6609
Winthrop ME 04364

Call Sign: KA1HLY
Robert E Strubbe
Rfd 2 Box 6609
Winthrop ME 04364

Call Sign: KA1HLW
Roland E Veilleux
Rt 2 Box 7755
Winthrop ME 04364

Call Sign: N1FCT
Brian R Boudreau
43 Charles Street
Winthrop ME 04364

Call Sign: KB1OGP
Donald A Patterson Jr
89 Dexter Pond Rd
Winthrop ME 04364

Call Sign: WA1DAP
Donald A Patterson Jr
89 Dexter Pond Rd
Winthrop ME 04364

Call Sign: AA1ME
Donald A Patterson Jr
89 Dexter Pond Rd
Winthrop ME 04364

Call Sign: N1CQS
Richard L Godfrey
8 Forest Ave
Winthrop ME 04364

Call Sign: N1UOI
Michael S Miller
28 Friar Tuck Dr
Winthrop ME 04364

Call Sign: KB1EML
Angela M Miller
28 Friar Tuck Dr
Winthrop ME 04364

Call Sign: K1KRB
Virginia E La Vallee
7 Greenwood Terrace
Winthrop ME 04364

Call Sign: W1RLK
Chester L La Vallee
45 Greenwood Terrace
Winthrop ME 04364

Call Sign: WA1IBM
Leonard S Prout
28 Hanson St
Winthrop ME 04364

Call Sign: W1KFY
John R Osborne Jr
5 High St
Winthrop ME 04364

Call Sign: KA1HMB
Stacy C Morang
59 Highland Heights
Winthrop ME 04364

Call Sign: KA1SHU
Douglass W Gordon
25 Holmes Road
Winthrop ME 04364

Call Sign: K1GDI
George R Szadis
55 Lakeshore Drive
Winthrop ME 04364

Call Sign: N1ERZ
Linda M Szadis
55 Lakeshore Drive
Winthrop ME 04364

Call Sign: W1GDI
Linda M Szadis
55 Lakeshore Drive
Winthrop ME 04364

Call Sign: N1BRU
Ambrose A Maxim
9 Lambert St
Winthrop ME 04364

Call Sign: WA2WQC
Rita Moran
121 Main St
Winthrop ME 04364

Call Sign: N2JKU
John M Kaiser
30 Maranacook Station
Lane
Winthrop ME 04364

Call Sign: W2MSR
John M Kaiser
30 Maranacook Station
Lane
Winthrop ME 04364

Call Sign: N1SUL
Gerald A Nadeau Jr
239 Memorial Drv
Winthrop ME 04364

Call Sign: N2EXY
Alison A Chu
274 Metcalf Road
Winthrop ME 04364

Call Sign: N1AZH
Donald A Hanson
402 Metcalf Road
Winthrop ME 04364

Call Sign: N1CIQ
Trudy M Hanson
402 Metcalf Road
Winthrop ME 04364

Call Sign: W1LEE
William A Akins
26 Olivia Lane
Winthrop ME 04364

Call Sign: NT1N
William A Akins
26 Olivia Lane
Winthrop ME 04364

Call Sign: KB1MHH
Cathy A Hinds
26 Olivia Ln

Winthrop ME 04364

Call Sign: KB1SAW
Christopher N Perrin
117 Pamela Dr
Winthrop ME 04364

Call Sign: K1BRT
Eben B Thomas
12 Spruce St
Winthrop ME 04364

Call Sign: KW1F
Scott L Adams
380 Stanley Rd.
Winthrop ME 04364

Call Sign: K2YLM
Earl B Smith
432 Winthrop Ctr Rd
Winthrop ME 04364

Call Sign: KB1DFA
Pamela D Ashcroft
1 Winthrop Heights Apt 1h
Winthrop ME 04364

Call Sign: W2NYU
Arnold H Rand
46 York Lane
Winthrop ME 043643643

Call Sign: K1MES
Donald H Turner
Winthrop ME 04364

Call Sign: KA1CS
Leon W Weston
Winthrop ME 04364

Call Sign: KA2JLC
Charles W Schramm Jr
Winthrop ME 04364

Call Sign: W1PSI

Roland A La Vallee
Winthrop ME 04364

Call Sign: KB1MPJ
Joseph N Roy
Winthrop ME 04364

Call Sign: KB1RBJ
Mark R Allen
Winthrop ME 04364

FCC Amateur Radio Licenses in Wiscasset

Call Sign: KB1CGM
James M Edwards Jr
13 Birch Pt Rd
Wiscasset ME 04578

Call Sign: KB1ACV
Schuyler A Wentworth
Rr 4 Box 116
Wiscasset ME 04579

Call Sign: WA1HVF
Alton I Ames
Rr 1 Box 221
Wiscasset ME 04580

Call Sign: W1WZA
Donald N Adler
Rfd 2 Box 252
Wiscasset ME 04579

Call Sign: KA1KXY
Norman E Chancellor
Rr 3 Box 337
Wiscasset ME 04578

Call Sign: WA1ZBB
Shirley M Chancellor
Rr 3 Box 337
Wiscasset ME 04578

Call Sign: N1EGI

Gail L Swanton
Rr 2 Box 670
Wiscasset ME 04578

Call Sign: KA1YIW
Shaun A Blomquist
Rfd 1 Box 984
Wiscasset ME 04578

Call Sign: KA1FMI
Craig Winters
113 Federal Street
Wiscasset ME 045784006

Call Sign: KA1QIZ
Karen L Travers
2 Hammond St
Wiscasset ME 04578

Call Sign: W1ETT
Drew W Travers
2 Hammond St
Wiscasset ME 04578

Call Sign: KB1ACT
Leslie O Wentworth
Hodge St
Wiscasset ME 04578

Call Sign: K1CGZ
Paul J Cereste
5 Oak Ridge West
Wiscasset ME 04578

Call Sign: W1UJR
Bruce J Howes
10 Ox Horn Road
Wiscasset ME 04578

Call Sign: K1TGS
Daryl L Grant
12 Palmer Rd
Wiscasset ME 04578

Call Sign: N5EMR

Donna E Grant
12 Palmer Rd
Wiscasset ME 04578

Call Sign: KB1JYB
Michael P Flanagan
22 Shady Ln Box 2
Wiscasset ME 04578

Call Sign: KB1BEK
Kelsey A Sprague
Wiscasset ME 04578

Call Sign: N1RIS
Matthew J Mc Cready
Wiscasset ME 04578

Call Sign: N1UMA
Gordon D Farrin
Wiscasset ME 04578

FCC Amateur Radio Licenses in Witon

Call Sign: KB1FRJ
Joseph H Ross
Witon ME 04294

FCC Amateur Radio Licenses in Woodland

Call Sign: K1ZIL
Douglas H Manza
Box 541 Calais Rd
Woodland ME 04694

Call Sign: N1QWV
Jonathan A Susee
406 Colby Siding Rd
Woodland ME 04736

Call Sign: N5ESS
Donald W Payne
2296 S. Princeton Rd.
Woodland ME 04694

Call Sign: N1UBX
John T Leighton
Woodland ME 04694

FCC Amateur Radio Licenses in Woolwich

Call Sign: K1ABN
Henry A Seeger Sr
Rr 1 Box 1655
Woolwich ME 04579

Call Sign: K1LCD
Kenneth F Morse Sr
81 East Hedge Road
Woolwich ME 04579

Call Sign: NW1I
Thomas S Johnson
16 Goose Cove Lane
Woolwich ME 04579

Call Sign: KA0FVT
Eric S Peterson
41 John Walker Farm Road
Woolwich ME 04579

Call Sign: K1GUN
John E Doyle Jr
224 Mountain Rd
Woolwich ME 045794734

Call Sign: KB1OAQ
Amplitude Modulation
Society Of Buffalo
312 Murphys Corner Rd
Woolwich ME 04579

Call Sign: W2UJR
Amplitude Modulation
Society Of Buffalo
312 Murphys Corner Rd
Woolwich ME 04579

Call Sign: KB1RNO
Robert B Montgomery
6 Old Stage Rd
Woolwich ME 04579

Call Sign: KB1OLM
Robert R Ayer
1160 Old Stage Rd
Woolwich ME 04579

Call Sign: N1OHX
Steven D Stimpson
1238 Old Stage Rd
Woolwich ME 04578

Call Sign: K1KNJ
Reginald O Tremblay Jr
209 River Rd
Woolwich ME 04579

Call Sign: KB1VVG
Ryan C Tremblay
209 River Rd
Woolwich ME 04579

Call Sign: WA1ZGN
Robert A Meade
Tallman Rd
Woolwich ME 04579

Call Sign: KM1E
Kenneth W Wiseman
Woolwich ME 04579

FCC Amateur Radio Licenses in Yarmouth

Call Sign: KF1H
Ronald D Thompson
22 Anderson Ave
Yarmouth ME 040968300

Call Sign: KB1SYO
Janine M Hodel
35 Anderson Ave

Yarmouth ME 04096

Call Sign: KB1DUF
David S Hincks Sr
150 Bayview St
Yarmouth ME 04096

Call Sign: K1DSH
David S Hincks Sr
150 Bayview St
Yarmouth ME 04096

Call Sign: KB1PCQ
Jonathon E Hinson
329 Bayview St
Yarmouth ME 04096

Call Sign: N1PON
George W Ford Iii
371 Bayview St
Yarmouth ME 04096

Call Sign: N1NBS
Curtis A Stauffer
389 Bayview St
Yarmouth ME 04096

Call Sign: W1RGT
Robert G Thoits
29 Bennett Road
Yarmouth ME 040966911

Call Sign: AC1G
John A Christiansen
52 Birdhwood Ave
Yarmouth ME 04096

Call Sign: KB1GEV
Ross C Babcock
35 Blueberry Cove
Yarmouth ME 04096

Call Sign: W1RCB
Ross C Babcock
35 Blueberry Cove

Yarmouth ME 04096

Call Sign: KA1YGW
James H Ostis
Rr 1 Box 100
Yarmouth ME 04096

Call Sign: N1LVZ
Bruce M Tompkins
Rr 1 Box 143b
Yarmouth ME 04096

Call Sign: KB1ACC
Benjamin P Soule
Box 27a Princes Pt Rd
Yarmouth ME 04096

Call Sign: KA1UWO
Robyn J Pickering
Rr 1 Box 282
Yarmouth ME 04096

Call Sign: WA1TAX
John H Wibby Jr
Rr 1 Box 291
Yarmouth ME 04096

Call Sign: N1OYT
Robert A Bradley
Rr 1 Box 314
Yarmouth ME 04096

Call Sign: KA1RFO
Mark T Flaherty
Rr 2 Box 355b Bayview St
Yarmouth ME 04096

Call Sign: N1NFE
James T Hoag
Rr 2 Box 360
Yarmouth ME 04096

Call Sign: N1OSW
John E Barry Jr
Rfd 2 Box 362a

Yarmouth ME 04096

Call Sign: KA1UWQ
Steve S Roscoe
Box 43a Prinnces Point Rd
Yarmouth ME 04096

Call Sign: KA1DMJ
David W Ericson
Rr 2 Box 604
Yarmouth ME 04097

Call Sign: KA1RGE
Martin A Svahn
16 Bridge St
Yarmouth ME 04096

Call Sign: N1ICE
Charles G Wing
52 Bridge St
Yarmouth ME 04096

Call Sign: N1LCF
Thomas R Downing
71 Browns Point Rd
Yarmouth ME 04096

Call Sign: W3EZ
William R Jackson Jr
55 Burbank Lane
Yarmouth ME 04096

Call Sign: K3HHF
Anne O Jackson
55 Burbank Ln
Yarmouth ME 04096

Call Sign: KB1LBL
Fred C Richards Ii
49b Collins Rd
Yarmouth ME 04096

Call Sign: W1HHT
Gary D King
219 Cousins St

Yarmouth ME 04096

Call Sign: KA1YGU
David J King
219 Cousins Street
Yarmouth ME 04096

Call Sign: W1MVD
Norman L Ring
16 Cumberland St
Yarmouth ME 04096

Call Sign: KA1UWP
Russell C Sawyer
3 Deacon Rd
Yarmouth ME 04096

Call Sign: KA1YGV
Jessica L Soule
47 E Main St
Yarmouth ME 04096

Call Sign: W1CUI
David S Wheaton Sr
265L East Elm
Yarmouth ME 04096

Call Sign: N1IZU
Roy T Cogswell
81 East Elm St
Yarmouth ME 04096

Call Sign: KB1SLE
Peter C Van Alstine
87 Eben Hill Rd
Yarmouth ME 04096

Call Sign: K1PVA
Peter C Van Alstine
87 Eben Hill Rd
Yarmouth ME 04096

Call Sign: KA1YGX
Bryce A Hickey
319 Eben Hill Rd

Yarmouth ME 04096

Call Sign: N1CDF
James J Boutin
61 Fairwind Lane
Yarmouth ME 04096

Call Sign: KA1SWC
Greg F Berry
30 Farnell Dr
Yarmouth ME 04096

Call Sign: N1LCG
Paul S Best
12 Foxglove Ct
Yarmouth ME 04096

Call Sign: W1HZE
Charles R Brown
120 Gilman Rd
Yarmouth ME 04096

Call Sign: KA1UWM
Wayne S Curit
449 Granite St
Yarmouth ME 04096

Call Sign: KA1REY
Darren A Spehr
2 Grist Mill Ln
Yarmouth ME 04096

Call Sign: WA1LPY
David B Hempstead
367 Harborview Dr
Yarmouth ME 04096

Call Sign: W1ADK
Fred C Richards Ii
15b Indian Ridge Rd
Yarmouth ME 04096

Call Sign: KB1UVW
Paul F Martin
72 John Howland Dr

Yarmouth ME 04096

Call Sign: KB1BMF
Wolfgang F K Wendler
40 Kelly Drive
Yarmouth ME 04096

Call Sign: KA1IMA
Kenneth W Clarke
44 Lafayette St
Yarmouth ME 04096

Call Sign: KA1IOD
Michael D Leonard
68 Ledgewood Drive
Yarmouth ME 04096

Call Sign: KB1FTY
Adam Golonka
132 Littlejohn Rd.
Yarmouth ME 04096

Call Sign: KA1FI
Ronald W Levere
2 Lupine Ct
Yarmouth ME 04096

Call Sign: WA1RL
Ronald W Levere
2 Lupine Ct
Yarmouth ME 04096

Call Sign: KA1OGF
Michael B Whipple
333 Main Street
Yarmouth ME 04096

Call Sign: KA1VUP
Shawn J Mc Donough
7 Mast Ln
Yarmouth ME 04096

Call Sign: KA1ZBS
Justin D Davis
13 Meadow Rue Ct

Yarmouth ME 04096

Call Sign: KA1TCC
Aaron J Bernier
19 Melissa Dr
Yarmouth ME 04096

Call Sign: KA1ETX
Marcia W Macisso
32 Melissa Dr
Yarmouth ME 04096

Call Sign: KA1SWA
Shannon A Schmidt
12 Newell Rd
Yarmouth ME 04096

Call Sign: KA1UXA
Joseph E Robson
34 Newell Rd
Yarmouth ME 04096

Call Sign: KB1LSM
Richard J Dugas
66 Northwood Rd
Yarmouth ME 04096

Call Sign: KB1GRU
Karen E Barnett
23 Oakland Ave
Yarmouth ME 04096

Call Sign: KA1YSY
Candace J Reynolds
59 Oakwood Dr
Yarmouth ME 04096

Call Sign: N1IYU
Jurgen Kok
59 Oakwood Dr
Yarmouth ME 04096

Call Sign: N1ZQX
Glenn C Bridgman
230 Oakwood Dr

Yarmouth ME 04096

Call Sign: KB1MBJ
John M Sutton
5 Penny Royal Ct
Yarmouth ME 04096

Call Sign: KA1TXC
Craig S Ford
8 Penny Royal Ct
Yarmouth ME 04096

Call Sign: N1GDN
Richard M Plourde
87 Pinewood Rd
Yarmouth ME 04096

Call Sign: KA1REW
Michael R Edgecomb
47 Pleasant St
Yarmouth ME 04096

Call Sign: KB1ACB
Matt A Kirby
74 Pleasant St
Yarmouth ME 04096

Call Sign: K1PRR
Robert L Robinson
445 Portland St
Yarmouth ME 04096

Call Sign: KA1HNN
Richard A Epstein
863 Princes Point Rd
Yarmouth ME 04096

Call Sign: K1RAE
Richard A Epstein
863 Princes Point Rd
Yarmouth ME 04096

Call Sign: KD1IF
Edgar A Curtis Iii
624 Princes Point Road

Yarmouth ME 04096

Call Sign: KB1GGU
Jeffrey D Lloyd
6 Rainbow Farm Rd
Yarmouth ME 04096

Call Sign: W1JIQ
Charles P Carter
18 Rand Rd
Yarmouth ME 04096

Call Sign: KA1RIU
Jeff A Desjardins
21 Rand Rd
Yarmouth ME 04096

Call Sign: KA1UWS
Jamie S Desjardins
21 Rand Rd
Yarmouth ME 04096

Call Sign: KB1KBP
Mark W Rockwood
28 Rebecca Ln
Yarmouth ME 04096

Call Sign: K1RGB
Mark W Rockwood
28 Rebecca Ln
Yarmouth ME 04096

Call Sign: KA1TXB
Leigh H Rose
52 River Bend
Yarmouth ME 04096

Call Sign: KA1UWL
Shawn M Armstrong
20 Riverbend Dr
Yarmouth ME 04096

Call Sign: KB1HOQ
Owen J Garfield
114 Royall Point Rd

Yarmouth ME 04096

Call Sign: AA1ZN
Owen J Garfield
114 Royall Point Rd
Yarmouth ME 04096

Call Sign: KA1UWN
Daniel K Jones
Box 50 Rr 1
Yarmouth ME 04096

Call Sign: K1IWN
David E Haggett
26 Ryder Rd
Yarmouth ME 04096

Call Sign: N1LLC
Roy C Prussner
52 Sandy Point Road
Yarmouth ME 04096

Call Sign: NT1R
William R Legge
6 Sarah Goud Rd
Yarmouth ME 04096

Call Sign: WA2LUX
Edward B Simmons Jr
252 Sea Meadows Lane
Yarmouth ME 04096

Call Sign: KA1ZBR
Jacob C Goldsmith
417L Sisquisic Tr
Yarmouth ME 04096

Call Sign: KA1REZ
Eric P Gosselin
Box 419 Sisquisic Tr
Yarmouth ME 04096

Call Sign: KA1VUQ
Glen C Pierce
Sisquisic Trail Box 420

Yarmouth ME 04096

Call Sign: KA1YGY
Travis M Roy
1 South St
Yarmouth ME 04096

Call Sign: KA1TXD
Brian C Martinez
19 Summer St
Yarmouth ME 04096

Call Sign: KA1VUN
Joel B Bucci
8 Tannery Ln
Yarmouth ME 04096

Call Sign: KB1ACA
David J Lewis
9 Titcomb Rd
Yarmouth ME 04096

Call Sign: KA1REV
Derek E Tebbetts
15 W Main St Apt 2
Yarmouth ME 04096

Call Sign: KA1VUO
Brian W Hanson
9 Woodbury St
Yarmouth ME 04096

Call Sign: KA1UWJ
Michael R Hodyman
15 Woods Circle Rd
Yarmouth ME 04096

Call Sign: K1JW
Jeffrey I Weinstein
Yarmouth ME 04096

Call Sign: KA1TXE
Alan E Moore
Yarmouth ME 04096

Call Sign: KA1UWK
Brian L White
Yarmouth ME 04096

Call Sign: KA1ZBQ
Roger M Moore
Yarmouth ME 04096

Call Sign: N1KNJ
Mary P Weinstein
Yarmouth ME 04096

Call Sign: N1MSA
Charles E Pierce Ii
Yarmouth ME 04096

Call Sign: N1ZHG
David M Weinstein
Yarmouth ME 04096

Call Sign: KB1PCO
Gregory J Payson
Yarmouth ME 04096

Call Sign: KB1PEF
Yarmouth Radio Club Inc
Yarmouth ME 04096

Call Sign: W1YAR
Yarmouth Radio Club Inc
Yarmouth ME 04096

FCC Amateur Radio Licenses in York

Call Sign: KB1GLZ
Port City Amateur Radio
Club
205 Birch Hill Rd
York ME 03909

Call Sign: N1EDL
Clarence E Allen
244 Birch Hill Rd
York ME 03909

Call Sign: KB1VZA
Michelle L Lanier
1 Brixham Rd
York ME 03909

Call Sign: KB1DLK
William A K Emerson
41 Brixham Rd
York ME 039095333

Call Sign: KB1IBY
Andrew W Emerson
41 Brixham Rd
York ME 03909

Call Sign: N1YVT
Richard E Young
5 Brook Ln
York ME 03909

Call Sign: KB1NZE
Jesse P Ware Iii
17 Carrie Lynn Lane
York ME 03909

Call Sign: KF2KI
Philip A Parent
537 Cider Hill Rd.
York ME 03909

Call Sign: N1IRH
Gregory H Beal
29 David Dr
York ME 03909

Call Sign: WB1ALL
Diane R Matthews
43 David Dr
York ME 039095340

Call Sign: KT5RL
Christopher Rutledge
20 Deer Run
York ME 03909

Call Sign: KA1YLC
Dennis J Okeeffe
1 Eureka Ave
York ME 03909

Call Sign: KB1IBR
Robert G Sellin
4 Hickory Ln
York ME 03909

Call Sign: KB1IBS
Natalie E West
C/O Cowenhoven 4 Hickory
Ln
York ME 03909

Call Sign: KA1PZE
Kenneth W Hirsch Jr
14 Highland Ave
York ME 03909

Call Sign: W1LEC
Laurence E Clark Jr
4 Hogans Court
York ME 03909

Call Sign: N1XPN
Thomas A Simoneau
32 Lindsay Rd
York ME 03909

Call Sign: KC1DD
Hervey B Carpenter
64 Lindsay Rd
York ME 03909

Call Sign: N1MML
Daniel J Graves
35 Lobster Cove Rd
York ME 03909

Call Sign: KB1HUT
Arthur F Graves
35 Lobster Cove Road

York ME 03909

Call Sign: W1LHY
Norman J Cartmill
117 Long Sands Rd D301
York ME 03909

Call Sign: KB1KCF
Brian P Mycko
128 Norwood Farms Rd
York ME 03909

Call Sign: K1YK
Robert J Reed
154 Nubble Rd
York ME 03909

Call Sign: N1DNW
Charles J Mead
7 Perkins Dr
York ME 03909

Call Sign: KA1CLI
Christopher F Knight
68 Raydon Rd Ext
York ME 03909

Call Sign: KA1JHH
Thomas G Page
5 Scotland Bridge Road
York ME 03909

Call Sign: KB1QMU
Robert R Packard
10 Southside Road
York ME 03909

Call Sign: KB1PDU
Todd L Crawford
10 Woodcock Lane
York ME 039091373

Call Sign: AB1HM
Todd L Crawford
10 Woodcock Lane

York ME 039091373

Call Sign: WA1ZEC
John W Treat Jr
159 Woodside Meadow Rd
York ME 03909

Call Sign: W4NBC
Earl B Smith Jr
25 York St
York ME 03909

Call Sign: N1CFJ
David M Dodge
119 York St
York ME 03909

Call Sign: N1ZWV
Gregory R Larson
York ME 03909

FCC Amateur Radio Licenses in York Beach

Call Sign: WB1FWU
Thomas W Hodgin
63 Long Beach Ave
York Beach ME 03910

Call Sign: W1BDV
James P Saunders
69 Long Beach Ave
York Beach ME 03910

Call Sign: KB1OAJ
Albert B Kleeberg Jr
68 Nubble Road
York Beach ME 03910

Call Sign: W1AGK
Albert B Kleeberg Jr
68 Nubble Road
York Beach ME 03910

Call Sign: W1WBL

Wayne B Lindgren
45 Ocran Avenue
York Beach ME 03910

Call Sign: KA1MXM
Wayne T Murray
York Beach ME 039101747

Call Sign: KB1FZO
Wayne B Lindgren
York Beach ME 03910

Call Sign: KB1PKF
Scott A Comeau
York Beach ME 03910

FCC Amateur Radio Licenses in York Harbor

Call Sign: N1FPP
Virginia Pummer
11 Lobster Cove Rd Ext
York Harbor ME 03911

Call Sign: KC1MJ
John S Blowney
York Harbor ME 03911

Call Sign: W1RG
John H Beedle
York Harbor ME 03911

Call Sign: KB1JZZ
Jorge Sierra
York Harbor ME
039110675